The Angry West

The Angry West

A Vulnerable Land and Its Future

Richard D. Lamm
and Michael McCarthy

Boston

HOUGHTON MIFFLIN COMPANY

1982

Dedicated with love
to Beth, Brooke and Helen,
and to
Dottie, Scott and Heather

Library of Congress Cataloging in Publication Data

Lamm, Richard D.
The angry West.

Includes bibliographical references and index.
1. Environmental policy—West (U.S.)
2. Environmental protection—West (U.S.)
I. McCarthy, Michael. II. Title.
HC107.A17L35   333.1′0978   82–2902
ISBN 0–395–32066–6   AACR2

Printed in the United States of America

V 10 9 8 7 6 5 4 3 2 1

ACKNOWLEDGMENTS

WE ARE DEEPLY INDEBTED to the many people who helped make *The Angry West* a reality.

We are grateful to Richard Kahlenberg, our agent, who shared our sense of the West and helped give us direction on the project. We also owe thanks to Maxine Benson, Barbara Sudler, and Sue O'Brien, who read early drafts of the book; to the staffs of the Colorado State Library and the Western History Department of the Denver Public Library for research help; to DeWitt Johns, Monte Pascoe, and Chips Barry, who helped check the book's facts and figures; to Shirley Feller, who did a marvelous job of typing the manuscript; and to Bob Hall, Joel Phillips, and Kevin Roth, who provided graphics.

Most of all, we thank Jim Monaghan, Colleen Murphy, and Gail Brodie, who spent literally weeks of their time reviewing the manuscript for errors. More than anyone else, especially on the energy chapters, they gave us both the factual material and the outside perspective we so badly needed.

Without our colleagues, we could not have written the book. To all of them, our thanks.

Contents

Good-Bye to the West

ON SUMMER EVENINGS the sun falls slowly from the Idaho sky, bathing the land in brilliant light. In the valley of the Big Wood, where the mountains touch the desert, Hailey lies quietly in the shadow of the Sawtooths and waits for dusk. Along the highway, pickup trucks with rifle racks sit in front of cinder-block homes. Sunflowers dance in the August wind. And the vacancy sign is lighted at the Hitchrack Motel.

The valley is narrow and shimmering hot. To the west lie the Sawtooths, spiny and snowcapped against the cloudless sky. To the east, waves of foothills flow down from high mountains, catching shadows in their folds, shutting out the sun. And the river, glassy and shallow, ripples softly through willow groves and cottonwood. The fields are deep and green, waiting for harvest, laced with sprinkler rigs that bring them life. Where balers have gone, where threshers have cut their graceful contours across the land, the fields lie flat and smooth, their shaven symmetry broken only by blocky stacks of fresh hay. Cattle stand quietly, waiting for darkness, in pastures, in marshes, in the patches of sage that swirl and bristle across the prairie. To the south the road is empty. Piles of truck skeletons rust in the sun. Beehives perch in the corner of an old corral. And by the broken door of a run-down farmhouse an old man sits alone.

West of Bellevue and Picabo the desert rushes out of the south. The sky fills with reefs and banks of copper-colored clouds. Below them mountains wash away into the distance — wave after wave of ever-lighter blue, then gray, then nothing. The land seems lifeless. Moonstone is gone, with its café, reclaimed by the desert. At Fairfield a clapboard church stands empty, shedding its splintered skin in the afternoon light. Grain elevators, like towering tombstones, loom over homes of families long gone. A sign hangs limply from its arm, flapping against a gate, and tumbleweeds lie caked and shattered against its fence. Roads still lead to Rocky Bar. And Featherville. But the desert owns the rest. Out of distant canyons summer winds race across the empty space. But they are its only sound.

At sunset, for a moment, the land is washed in light. Then dusk. Green fields turn to black, orange-brown to bronze, and telephone lines crisscross like silvery webs above them all. East of Hill City a tractor cuts a final furrow in the ground and gulls dive through its dust for grasshoppers and moths. A cattle skull sits impaled on a rotted post. A rooster struts in barnyard shadows. And as the wind becomes a whisper, a lonely windmill spins left, then right, then not at all.

This is our West.

And it is dying.

It has changed dramatically in the last thirty years. It sees a decade of change each year. One West is dying and a new one is being born. Life is change. No civilization is static. Yet there is a nostalgia for the dying West.

There was something special about the West in the 1950s and 1960s. It was a unique and wondrous place for those who loved the outdoors, who cared about the land.

Its air had an unbelievable quality. It literally sparkled. In the mornings the mountains and desert and farmland stood out in crystalline clarity. And the sun shone with a special brilliance, a counterpoint to the coolness of the mountain air.

In those days a drive through the western countryside provided some of the most spectacular scenery in the nation. The West had the most beautiful interurban roads in America — green fields, and horses and cattle grazing against backdrops of snow-covered mountains. Soon they will be gone. Civilization always creeps up on human consciousness, and few westerners fully understand, even now, that land-use decisions have already been made that will fill up the remaining open space between the West's cities. We will soon see back yards where green fields once lay. We have citified, already, much of our landed heritage.

It was the outdoor life that brought many of us to the West. The skiing. The mountain climbing. The white-water trips. Hunting and fishing. Not many years ago, you still could catch a native trout, gallop a horse for miles without running into fence, track a mountain lion. Float a lonesome river. You could escape the regimentation and restrictions of a civilized world.

You could be free.

We thought it would last forever. We took it for granted.

We took for granted drinking from a running brook on a mountain hillside, leaning down and looking into a mosaic of pebbles and moss and ferns. Holding cold water in your mouth to warm it a few degrees before swallowing.

We took for granted being able to camp at random, safely and in privacy. Driving to the mountains on Friday afternoons, walking through the forests, throwing down a sleeping bag wherever sleep overtook us. Campfire breakfasts. Morning climbs. The chill feeling of space, infinity, at a mountain dawn.

There were so few people in the mountains then. It was like having your own magnificent kingdom. We would seldom meet other people, and when we did, the camaraderie of shared purpose made instant friendships. The mountains were a refuge from the noise and stench of the city. No airplanes, no litter. No sound. Only an occasional jeep trail. Only occasional civilization. It was not possible to live life in pastoral wilderness, not as our parents could fifty years before. But one could spend a weekend in the backcountry with little likelihood of seeing anyone else.

The mountains in winter were even more special: deadly, dangerous, but with a captivating beauty that cannot be described. The magnificent stillness of the winter mountain. We would ski all day, filled with an incredible sense of well-being. We would watch storms swirl around the peaks and the wind plumes shooting from them.

In those days you could come across whole deserted towns in the backcountry that looked as if people who lived half a century before had just closed the door and left. Stoves, tables, chairs, bedsprings. In time they disappeared. The stoves and tables and chairs. The towns. The stove doors went first, until it was difficult to find a stove with a door. Then the stoves themselves. Then "collectors" took the weathered wood for their game rooms and bars. The 1960s saw more destruction to ghost towns than all the winter storms and summer heat of seventy years.

Spinoza wrote of hiding sugar cookies in his papers for the unexpected joy of coming across them late at night. That was the joy of finding an undiscovered cabin high on a wooded ridge. A dividend, a link with a generation long past. A spiritual connection with the pioneers. Thomas Jefferson believed that a density of ten persons per square mile was the limit of human endurance. "Whenever we reach that," he said, "the inhabitants become uneasy as too much compressed, and go off in great numbers to search for vacant country." So, also, did another generation selfishly love space and solitude.

It still does.

We saw the West change before our eyes, but the images, the memories, linger still. Glen Canyon. The Virgin River. Kayaking down the Rio Grande and the Dolores and the Yampa — and seeing no one else. Sunflower fields, country towns, the smell of summer rain. Meadowlarks and mourning doves. Cedar smoke on a winter night. The Super Chief, like a silver snake, on the Arizona desert. The misty arc of an August rainbow.

This is our West.

And it is dying.

A new Manifest Destiny has overtaken America. The economic imperative has forever changed the spiritual refuge that was the West. Some of us have made a truce with change. Others have refused. They — we — are the new Indians. And they — we — will not be herded to the new reservations.

Nor will we be silent in what we think and feel. Or in what we write.

Our story is not a polemic. It is personal. It is not objective. It is not meant to be. It is a subjective and personal look at the West as we see it, as we feel it, a look at the way things were and the way things are and the way we would like them to be. It is written not in negativism, but in sadness. It is bittersweet, not pessimistic. It is protest, lament, anger — at the desecration of the land and air and water, at the shattering of ways of life. At the killing of dreams. It is written not to justify anger, but to explain it.

We are selfish, yes. Because we know the West will never be the same again. A new iteration will take place tomorrow, then another.

We understand the need for synfuels and coal and uranium and molybdenum and the MX.

We understand.

But still we anguish. For the West we loved and lost.

CHAPTER ONE

Roots of Anger

Fur traders, miners, timber operators, land speculators — they cleaned up and
went back East . . . While the West was chasing the mirage of a still greater
bonanza over the horizon, Eastern capital moved in and occupied. It made for
bitterness . . . [in] the West, the plundered province . . .

BERNARD DE VOTO

A RECURRING NIGHTMARE haunts the West.

On January 1, 1984, Russian warships blockade the Persian Gulf.
Overnight, American access to Mideastern oil is blocked.

The federal government takes immediate action, mandating massive energy exploration and recovery in the American West. State
and local laws are overridden as energy projects proliferate across the
land. The western states are not consulted. They are ignored. Their
rights are abrogated, their sovereignty destroyed.

Energy combines, unleashed by the government, invade the West.
Seeking profit, unconcerned with local fears, they ignore social, political, and economic considerations in the process of building. Huge
profits accrue to them and flow out. Little is left to the people and
their communities.

Boomtowns mushroom across the West's rural face, disfiguring
the land. Cedar breaks crumble to strip miners, water fills with toxic
waste, mountain valleys fall to tractor roads, and evening sunsets
blaze through polluted air.

Ways of life change forever. Values, attitudes, customs — the core
of western life — shatter. New cities, plagued by crime and violence
and nonexistent social and economic services, cannot deal with the
change.

In time, the energy rush dies. The boomers disappear. Left behind is a wasteland, its skeletal boomtowns and cratered-out landscape a graphic reminder of days past. Western people, pawns in an ugly and endless war, regroup and rebuild.

And their cyclical history begins again.

The West's doomsday nightmare is not extreme. If it is true that the past is prologue, the scenario is a real and terrifying possibility. Even without crisis in the Gulf, the invasion of the West already is reality. It began a century ago. And, given the nature of its past, the West has ample reason to fear its future.

The history of the West, in many respects, is a history of exploitation. From its very beginning, the life of the West never has been its own. Westerners settled the land, lived on it, died on it. But they seldom owned it. Small prospectors found its gold and silver, but it was eastern corporations with capital and technology that seized the field — and fortune — from them. Sodbusters nested on the prairies and built a civilization out of dust. But it was cattle kings and eastern syndicates that dominated their land, and eastern banks that bled them of their profits. Throughout its history, the West was filled with little men with big dreams. They blazed the trails, dammed the rivers, built the cities. But it was eastern power — mining combines, cattle cartels, railroads, banks, smelters, and political coalitions — that ruled.

The West was born this way, and for generations this was the way it lived.

*   *   *

In the fall of 1859, at the eastern base of the Sierra Nevada, the discovery of gold launched the most significant frontier in modern American history. In 1858, the Carson River Valley was an isolated outpost on the far western edge of the Utah Territory; two years later, from Virginia City to the California border, it was a wild and brawling mining empire. In later years, silver was found in a narrow strip east of the valley, and in time billions of dollars worth of ore were taken out of Nevada ground.

To the east, across the Great Basin where the Rockies slice through the West, a second frontier developed at almost the same time. In early 1859, in the mountains west of Denver City and Auraria, gold was found again, and in one frantic year a hundred thousand pioneers poured across the plains to the Pikes Peak country. Other strikes followed. In 1862, gold was found in the rugged

Missouri River country of Montana, spawning Helena and a second
Virginia City, and from Arizona to Idaho tiny pockets of civilization
formed around similar strikes. The frontiering came to an end in the
last two decades of the century; the discovery of silver at Leadville
and gold at Cripple Creek led to one final civilizing upheaval. The
gold and silver rushes then ended, leaving in their wake an empire
from Canada to the Mexican Gulf.

Almost from its beginning, the mining frontier was controlled by
eastern men and eastern capital. In the gold regions in particular, the
takeover was swift and complete. In the first several years of the
mining regions, independent prospectors quickly took the surface
gold. When it was gone from the streams and culverts, however, the
miners stalled. Most of them — store clerks and plowboys from
midwestern villages — lacked both the skill and capital to extract
gold that lay deep beneath the surface of the earth, locked in veins
of quartz. At the same time, eastern financiers, attracted by the
investment opportunities of the New West, and possessing both the
capital and technology to carry them out, began their invasion of the
field. In time they took it over. In time it was their machines, mills,
and smelters that built the western mining industry. But it also was
eastern men who shouldered the western mining class aside in their
rise to power. It was nameless men who lived on the cutting edge of
this world when it was born. It was they who dug the placers and
nailed together the shantytowns. It was they who died at twenty. But
it was the Guggenheims and Rockefellers who reaped the harvest of
their work.

Cattlemen, too, pioneered the West. And, except for the cattle
kings, they inherited little. In the early 1860s, moving northward out
of Texas, cattlemen scattered across the plains from Kansas to Utah
and north to Canada. In the process they became legend. No figures
in American history became more romantic than the small ranchers
and their cowboy workers; for a hundred years, from dime novels to
modern film, they have been celebrated for their courage and
strength and the imagined beauty of their lives. Today they are part
of America's folklore, and with them the land they tamed.

In reality, the cattle kingdom — like the mining frontier — was a
western extension of eastern (and European) colonial power. In
Colorado 157 corporations, all based in the East, ran cattle on the
range in 1885. The Prairie Land and Cattle Company, based in Scot-
land, owned a strip fifty miles wide from the Arkansas River to New

Mexico. It also dominated much of Montana's vast range, profiting enough to declare a 42 percent dividend on its stock in 1882. In Wyoming, the prototypical cowboy state, 23 eastern corporations, funded at more than $12 million, were formed in 1883 alone. The massive Swan Land and Cattle Company, utilizing $2,750,000 raised in eastern stock sales, controlled one strip of Wyoming that ran for a hundred miles. In board rooms in Boston and Edinburgh, decisions were made for decades that helped shape the course of western history. Contrary though it may be to America's image of the Old West, eastern power was a fact of western life.

The last of the great western frontiers was that of the farmers. In an explosive span of twenty years, between 1870 and 1890, armies of sodbusters swept westward through Kansas and Nebraska, engulfed the Dakota grasslands, and penetrated the furthest reaches of Wyoming, Montana, Colorado, and New Mexico. When the 1870s began, the westernmost line of agrarian advance was the 100th meridian, a ragged line stretching from Minneapolis to Fort Smith, stopping on the very fringes of the Great American Desert. Twenty years later, large pockets of settlement stretched as far west as Bozeman, Cheyenne, Denver, and Santa Fe.

Like miners and cattlemen before them, the farmers broke the earth and civilized the land. They also paid the price. Trapped, many of them, on some of the most hostile land in the West, beset by freezing winters and scorching summers, and always plagued by drought, they died literally by the hundreds. Crops shriveled in the summer sun, and sod houses reverted to dust, and all over the High Plains run-down graveyards attested to the savagery of frontier life. In the end, incredibly, the farmers survived. Fargo, Yankton, Pierre, Burlington — their towns became monuments to the pioneer spirit.

But farmers, too, were dependent upon eastern capital. They bought machines built in the East and sold in the West. The money they borrowed was eastern money funneled through western banks. The railroads, their sole connection with the outside world, were eastern-based, and the canals that threaded their way from the rivers through the drylands were funded by eastern corporations. Money policies, tariff rates, methods of taxation — all were dictated by the East. Farmers were the foot soldiers in the agrarian march west. But its generals were easterners.

In the early stages of the westward movement the American East was a constructive force in western economic affairs. The smelter, the plow, the liberal disbursement of capital were major weapons in the conquest of the land. But the other side of eastern benevolence was exploitation. Every coil of barbed wire, every piece of machinery, every loaned dollar carried a price.

No group better understood exploitation than the cattlemen. When depression hit the cattle industry in the mid-1880s and the cattle frontier disintegrated, one major cause of it was the overavailability of eastern capital, which led to the overstocking and glutting of the range. The giants fell first. The Swan Land and Cattle Company died in 1887, followed by the rest. Eastern money, eastern land monopoly, and absentee ownership all were major factors in the death of the cattle frontier.

Eastern exploitation was much clearer in the case of the western mining industry.

The suffocating presence of the corporations was a problem in itself. In state after mining state, they simply destroyed small enterprise by outbuying, outselling, and outproducing small operators and individual prospectors. Colorado was a case in point. In 1880, there were 126 gold and silver mining corporations in the state, most of them with eastern ties. In 1902, the number stood at 822, and 64 of those companies produced 80 percent of the state's gold and silver. What was true in Colorado was true elsewhere, perhaps even more so in Nevada. Absentee ownership of western mining resources eventually became a pattern that made local private mining enterprise obsolete.

As the prospector class became the labor class, its workers channeled by the thousands into mines all over the West, the destructive effects of colonialism became more apparent. From the beginning — as was true all over industrial America in the late nineteenth century — workers were exploited by low wages and miserable working conditions. Ten-hour days in mine shafts choked with dust and gas and filled with freezing water produced three dollars a day in wages for mine workers, but indebtedness to company stores and rent owed for company housing siphoned off most of the income before it was made. Working conditions were unspeakable. Death resulting from mutilation, disease, alcoholism, and insanity was common. But disability was a worse fate. Disabled miners, living in an era of almost obsessive individualism, were provided for by no one. They were turned away to live their lives — or lose them — as best they could.

Across the West, from South Dakota's Homestake to the Comstock Lode in Nevada, to the mines of Leadville and Aspen, corporate officers took the wealth generated by the work of other men. For the most part, mining profits flowed east. Occasionally they remained in the West, but rarely in the mining camps themselves. Nob Hill's mining kings lived off Comstock money while Virginia City remained a filthy, teeming network of earthen caves and tarpaper shacks. While silver barons turned Denver's Capitol Hill into one of the richest enclaves in the West, Leadville remained one of the ugliest, most violent towns in the world. Such was the new legacy of the corporations. The blessings they brought to the West were undeniable, but so were their continuing patterns of exploitation.

In all the West no single group was more exploited by outside forces than the farmers. True, eastern corporations did not take their land or directly monopolize their industry. But no group in the West was more manipulated than farmers were by eastern institutions and financial practices. From the Great Basin to the High Plains, most farmers became pawns of eastern business. Had they prospered, the relationship would have mattered little. But they did not. Between 1870 and 1890, agricultural prices plummeted: wheat that sold for $1.06 a bushel in 1870 sold for 70¢ twenty years later, and corn that sold for 43¢ fell to 29¢. For all their suffering, western farmers reaped little profit from their land. And for much of their plight they blamed the East.

Eastern banks and mortgage companies were partly responsible for agrarian problems, just as they were partly responsible for the limited successes. As eastern money flooded western farm districts, farmers eagerly borrowed it. Men who had borrowed in the East to get to the West now borrowed more to stay, paying from 8 to 20 percent interest in the process. Then, spurred by visions of wealth, they mortgaged their homesteads to buy machinery, mortgaged the machinery to obtain money until harvesting, mortgaged the first harvest to survive the next year. Lured by easy money, they buried themselves in debt. By 1887, per capita debt on the plains was the highest in the United States.

As land values skyrocketed, fueled by eastern capital, farm towns also borrowed heavily for capital improvements. Again, borrowed money came from eastern institutions taking advantage of western growth potential. As farm prices fell, the towns — overcapitalized and overmortgaged — defaulted and fell with them.

No less opportunistic than the bankers, in the minds of the farmers, were the eastern-based railroads. Originally, the plains railroads — the Union Pacific, Burlington, Rock Island, and others — were welcomed as benefactors. In time, however, this changed. The railroads profited immensely from land grants given them by Congress and sold off, at high prices, to incoming settlers. They also profited from monopolistic shipping practices and high shipping charges. Those who balked at the freight rates and chose not to ship their perishable crops were left with few options. Some attempted to store their grain in local elevators. The eastern-owned elevator companies, however, charged the farmers more to store their grain than to transport it. The farmers, like other westerners, felt victimized by a system they did not understand, run from distant corporate board rooms. They tried desperately to minimize the impact of eastern policies, but in the end they failed.

The exploitation of the West was successful partly because of the attitude and actions of the federal government. From the very beginning of the westward movement, the government supported, encouraged, and subsidized the domination of the West and its resources by private eastern enterprise. The federal attitude was that the West existed not as an entity in itself, but as a supplier for the needs of the nation in general. Believing this, it never wavered in its support of big business in the West, nor did it hesitate to exert its own power over the region. Its attitude, in turn, generated an antagonism in the West that grew and endures to this day.

Federal administrations, for example, consistently aided the mining corporations. Because most of the western mining country belonged to Indians, the government worked diligently to clear Indian title to the land. To that end, from the Black Hills to the White River, it carried out a policy of Indian removal that became one of the darkest chapters in the history of the West. At the same time, in 1866 and again in 1872, Congress passed mineral-land laws favorable to large operations, while the United States Geological Survey worked tirelessly to locate mineral belts for them.

On the other hand, western farmers received no federal support. Despite the government's apparent intention to open up the plains to small farmers, federal land laws generally worked counter to them. The landmark Homestead, Desert Land, and Timber and Stone acts were cases in point. Passed by well-intentioned easterners ignorant of western conditions, and signed under intense pressure from special-interest lobbies, these and other land laws invited cor-

ruption and mismanagement. Rather than help farmers, they filled
the West with land speculators and other spoilsmen who bled them.
Worse, Congress would not, or could not, establish workable alternatives. The impact of the federal laws was not difficult for westerners
to assess: by the 1890s, seven eighths of their farmland were owned
by nonfarmers.

Congress also supported the railroads in their exploitation of farmers. Railroad land grants, for example, crippled western settlement.
Congressional grants ran up to 120 miles wide and extended the
length of the roads. The companies then sold the land to farmers at
exorbitant prices, further deepening their debt. The government also
refused to regulate extortionate railroad shipping rates. What little
rate reform the farmers forced in the 1870s and 1880s was through
state action, not federal. Not until 1905 was any meaningful rate
reform achieved — and by then thousands of farmers had been destroyed.

Federal tariff policies further compounded problems in western
farming and mining regions. Throughout the last quarter of the
nineteenth century, the tariff remained consistently high, buttressing
American business by minimizing foreign competition. For westerners, however, the tariff only meant high consumer prices. Further,
retaliatory foreign tariffs struck hard at American grain exports,
wiping out some of the most lucrative markets western farmers had
ever had. As they protested, they were ignored. And as they were,
the tariff grew ever higher.

Worst of all, to western farmers and miners alike, was the federal
government's rigid monetary policy. In an era when westerners
clamored for bimetallism to ease their indebtedness, the federal government stood firm on the gold standard. The result in the West was
catastrophic: money was both physically scarce and rarely available
when and where it was needed. Further, the government's stubborn
refusal to coin substantial amounts of silver drove silver prices consistently down in a region where silver mining underpinned the entire
economy. The western battle cry for "free silver" in the mid-1890s
was significant. It graphically reflected the result of decades of economic frustration.

So it was in the West.

By the end of the nineteenth century, the West was living precariously at the colonial end of a new American mercantile system.
Every aspect of its industry was controlled and exploited by eastern-

ers and eastern institutions, leaving little profit for those who lived on the land itself. Every aspect of its life was controlled by a federal government that viewed westerners as wards of Washington and their land as a colonial empire. Sporadically, an increasingly angry West fought back — but the labor strikes and the Populist convulsion of the 1890s achieved little. As the century ended, only one thing was certain. Westerners had settled the land, dug it, planted it, and died on it.

But they had not owned it.

*　　*　　*

For the West, the new century brought little positive change. Colonialism remained. Federal supremacy grew. Cities were born and a generation died, but the western empire, changelessly, remained the property of others.

For the first four decades of the century, the West remained the primary source of raw material for eastern industry. And just as the East remained reliant on it for its natural wealth, so did the West remain reliant on the East for finished products. For the West the marriage was a poor one. In bad times — such as the depression years — the West fell when the East did. Even in flush times westerners prospered relatively little. Throughout the years the eastern political-industrial class worked relentlessly to keep the West dependent. Not until after World War II was the pattern broken. Only then, at the earliest, did the West begin to develop some small measure of economic self-sufficiency.

No area of western life was immune from eastern domination. Corporate farming — agribusiness — came of age in Colorado, Utah, New Mexico, Arizona, and the Dakotas, with many of the corporations anchored in the East. Eastern newspapers crusaded against western reclamation projects and the remonetization of silver, while eastern banks dominated western financial affairs through the 1940s. Railroad rates remained high and discriminatory, increasing the marketing cost of everything from sheep to steel.

From Colorado's Keystone Resort (owned by Ralston Purina) to Big Sky of Montana (founded by Chrysler, Continental Oil, and the Burlington Northern), eastern money poured into western tourism, changing recreational patterns and altering the face of the wilderness. And the railroads, still dominated by eastern financiers, continued to control much of the land and its resources. In Montana the

Northern Pacific owned 30 percent of the state's timberland by 1900, leading to massive destruction in the region for years. And what held true for Montana held true for most of the West.

Throughout most of the century, huge politico-economic combines — many with eastern ties — dominated the critical western water-power industry. By 1914, some twenty-eight corporations owned 90 percent of the water power developed on western public lands — and six corporations owned 56 percent of that. The Utah Securities Corporation, dominated by outsiders, owned 30 percent in Colorado, 70 percent in Utah, and 20 percent in Idaho. Montana Power owned 97 percent of the power development in that state, and as late as 1970, Montanans held only 36 percent of the company's stock.

Nothing, however, matched the stranglehold eastern corporations had on the West's mining industry. Arizona copper was monopolized by Phelps Dodge. Utah's copper industry was dominated by the Kennecott Copper Company. Through its ownership of the massive Bingham Mine near Salt Lake City — one of the most important mines in the world — Kennecott became one of the most exploitative companies in the West. It also dominated much of New Mexico's copper industry through operation of mines at Santa Rita and Tyrone (where Kennecott built its own town and then abandoned it when copper prices fell).

No state in the West, however, furnished a better example of eastern imperialism than Montana, where the Anaconda Mining Company dominated every aspect of the state's life throughout most of this century. Through Anaconda, the Guggenheim family and its Wall Street allies shaped Montana's economic, political, and social patterns more than any company in the West. From its Colorado smelters and Utah mines to the tunneled-out copper fields at Butte, the Guggenheims established the classic western dynasty. By 1940, Kennecott, Phelps Dodge, and Anaconda controlled 80 percent of the West's copper output, and only a fraction of their profits remained in the region.

Similarly, other major western mining and industrial ventures were eastern-based. United States Potash ruled its field. Steel was dominated by Utah's Geneva Steels Works and the Guggenheim-Rockefeller Colorado Fuel and Iron Corporation in southern Colorado. The New York–born Climax Molybdenum Corporation of Colorado monopolized its field from 1917 on. And as late as the

1970s the Alaskan oil industry was cartelized by America's petroleum giants, while all over the West oil lobbies became some of the most powerful forces in existence.

Throughout the century, the steady entrenchment of eastern power in the West was supported by the policies of the federal government. The high credit policies of the Federal Reserve Board, coupled with the government's steadfast antisilverism, badly damaged the western mining industry (especially in Montana) in the first three decades of this century. Farmers, victimized by prohibitive railroad rates that remained largely undisturbed by the Interstate Commerce Commission, also argued that high tariff rates and the government's refusal to establish farm subsidies undermined their prosperity.

In this century, however, no issue outraged westerners as much as the question of federal landownership and federal land policies on the western public domain.

In the years between 1891 and 1910, as the conservation movement swept across the West, the federal government withdrew from entry millions of acres of land on the western public domain — ruled out its future settlement or public use under existing land laws — and placed it under tight federal control for the first time in history. Right or wrong, westerners were bewildered and angered. Once the land had been "theirs." Farmers had tilled the grasslands, the cattlemen's herds had grazed the valleys, prospectors had mined the hills. And once the government had shared its domain with them. But in the last years of the nineteenth century, this changed. Convinced that the time had come for the government to preserve the West's vanishing natural wealth and parcel it out carefully for the benefit of "future generations," federal officials embarked on a massive land-withdrawal campaign that shook the West to its foundations. By 1910, it had blanketed the western states with multiple forms of reservations — coal lands, water-power sites, national parks, and national forests. In the space of two decades, patterns of western life changed forever.

The withdrawals themselves triggered the bitterest sectional crisis in half a century. While the government invoked its "higher right" doctrine to deal with the public domain — and the West — as it wished, the West countered with the angriest defense of States' rights since the Civil War. Westerners insisted that the massive withdrawal of lands in their midst stunted regional economic development, reduced the tax base, and crippled the delivery of social services. Always, though, at the core of their anger lay the fear of perpetual colonialism.

In time, the West accepted the withdrawals as a fait accompli. But for a generation — and to this day — it complained about federal policies *on* the lands. Favoritism, elitism, landlordism were charges heard for years. And they created attitudes that have poisoned federal-state relations ever since.

Favoritism was a fact. The government *did* favor large operators over small, and in the process monopoly often destroyed free enterprise on the public domain. In its desire to stabilize the public domain, to institute long-needed programs of resource management, to free western resources from the often destructive impact of small cattlemen, prospectors, and homesteaders, the government made every effort to minimize — or at least control — their operations on federal property. At the same time, to promote scientific range management and efficiency and "wise use" in other resource areas, the government consistently turned the land over to big units. The federal feeling was that monopoly at least was efficient, that cattle kings, mining corporations, water-power combines, and lumber cartels, operating out of self-interest, would use resources more efficiently and scientifically than small "cut-and-run" operators.

It was this philosophy, coupled with the deliverance of the public domain into the hands of big business, that galled westerners.

Coal was a case in point. Attempting to minimize fraud on the public domain, the government withdrew 140 million acres of suspected coal lands from entry for reclassification between 1906 and World War I. Because coal combines alone could afford to lease the lands, and because the government issued permits primarily to large companies, monopoly became prevalent in the coal regions and small independent operators were shut out.

Another major issue was water. In 1913, the government began withdrawing choice water-power sites from entry all across the West — an action finally consummated in the Federal Water Power Act of 1920. While the purpose of the action was to minimize private water-power monopoly, westerners argued, again, that it restricted growth and denied sovereign states the power to control their most priceless resource. As late as 1954, the argument continued with the Hells Canyon Dam controversy in Idaho. Even federal irrigation policies came under fire. The Corps of Engineers was accused, often with reason, of initiating only projects that benefited selected private contractors. Often, too, the government was less than active in supporting western irrigation projects. The West insisted that, as the largest landowner in the West, the federal government had a moral obligation to encourage maximum irrigation development on its property.

The fiercest federal-state fights of all were over federal policies on the national forests that sprawled across the West. Partly at issue were the reserves themselves; many westerners never recognized their legitimacy. More at issue, however, was the nature of federal stewardship of the reserves. The West argued — and much of it continues to argue to this day — that federal rules, regulations, permits, fees, and management practices benefited large economic operators on or near the reserves and made it virtually impossible for marginal operators to survive. Timber-cutting laws, for example, generally favored large lumber companies and placed local settlers in the position of having to steal what they needed for fuel, fencing, and building materials. Myriad mining regulations obstructed the activities of the few independent prospectors who remained. Rigid homesteading requirements — on reservations that often incorporated the best farmland in the region — made farming almost impossible.

The single most affected group was the cattlemen. In 1897 the government inaugurated hundreds of rules and regulations to restrict and control their operations on the mountain ranges, and in 1906 it imposed grazing fees on them to support the development of scientific range-management techniques. At the same time, it launched a thirty-year campaign to establish leasing on the nonforested public domain, an action capped by the Taylor Grazing Act of 1934. Many cattlemen did not survive the changes. Permits and fees drove many small operators from the range entirely, leaving behind large operations favored by the government for their efficiency. To a great degree, grazing conditions were improved in the West, but for many westerners the price for it was their own destruction. In the end, the war touched off between cattlemen and the federal government was one of the most violent the West has ever seen. And it has not ended to this day.

So it is in the West.

For a hundred years colonialism has been a way of life. It has brought good. It has created and built. But it also has destroyed. Its developmental thrust has scarred the West, exploited its resources, littered its landscape with ghost towns, and turned its wilderness to desolation. Its arrogance has demeaned westerners, filling them with bewilderment. Its cavalier approach to western law and western custom, its suffocating paternalism, have created a deep and abiding sense of fear and anger.

It is the past, then, that haunts the West. It is the past that makes the doomsday nightmare reality. In the West no reason exists to think that yesterday will not become tomorrow and that, again, it will not bear witness to its own destruction.

As this book went to press, Exxon USA announced the closing of its partially completed, multi-billion-dollar Colony Shale Oil project on Colorado's Western Slope. The move was a surprise to most people in the oil industry and the press, and, obviously, it affects some of the observations in the following chapter.

Exxon President Randall Meyer blamed escalating costs and the reduced world oil prices for the decision. In Washington, Victor A. Schroeder, president of the Synthetic Fuels Corporation, said that the suspension of the Colony project represents a "glitch" in the federal synfuels program but that the program will survive. The Union Oil Company of California, at this writing, continues its own oil shale project at a location about two miles away from the Colony site. It is the only remaining project of its kind in the country.

The new town of Battlement Mesa, with homes for 1700 families, will be heavily hit; an additional 2500 jobs in the area are likely to disappear.

While this news affects the situation discussed in the next chapter, it does not affect the authors' major conclusions—it simply underscores the moral that boom-and-bust is a recurring Western tragedy.

—Editor

CHAPTER TWO

The Rock That Burns

The western states view synthetic fuels development with no illusions. We are ready and willing to make our contribution, but we will not tolerate terms of trade that are thrust upon us in the name of the national interest.

GOVERNOR SCOTT MATHESON, *Utah*

ON A SUMMER DAY the Colorado badlands seem to flow forever. Sweeping away from the White River Plateau, they roll westward to Utah, an endless expanse of mauve and green broken only by mesas rising gently to the sky. The land shimmers in the summer sun and the dusty sweet smell of cedar hangs in the air. Arroyos — few of them carrying water — slice down hillsides through groves of juniper and wild oak, angling across the land on the way to the Colorado. The land is dry and barren, but it is not dead. It is alive with color — canyon walls maroon-bronze in the sunlight, cedar breaks of dirty green, water the color of glass. On a summer day the badlands are a thing of enormous and stunning beauty.

For more than a century, people have lived in this brooding country, clinging to its watercourses, enduring winter blizzards and summer drought, surviving in one of the most physically violent parts of the American West. In early years, as now, the upper badlands belonged to the cattlemen. Butch Cassidy rode here, Tom Horn died here, and it was here the cattlemen built one of the fiercest and wildest civilizations in the Old West. Sunbeam, Powder Wash, Maybell, Craig — their towns had little color, gained no fame. But block by block, lot by lot, they were built under some of the most brutal conditions in Colorado's history. The lower tier of the badlands, the Roan Plateau, was pioneered by homesteaders who destroyed the Utes in the 1870s and filled the valleys with farmland. Here, too, the land was harsh. But nothing matched the land — or the life — to the north. Its legacy still remains. As men molded the land, so did it mold them, shaping attitudes and values, forming institutions, establishing ways of life that endure to this day.

For seventy years, homesteaders and cattlemen were scattered across the northwest quadrant of Colorado, but as late as the 1970s the region still remained largely uninhabited. The stark, limitless aridity of the earth itself was partly responsible. But so was the federal government, whose national forests and Bureau of Land Management lands blanketed most of the productive parts of the area, leaving little else for settlement. Except for the lush Yampa River Valley — running on an axis from Steamboat Springs west to Dinosaur — the region was almost totally undeveloped. Not until the 1970s did this change — with the beginning of the West's first serious oil shale experimentation.

The region's first shale oil boom was during and after World War I, but modern experimentation dates from 1948, when the Federal Bureau of Mines began probing the dusty, desolate backcountry of northwest Colorado for production sites. It was not taken seriously, however, for a quarter century; a government, and a nation, awash in cheap foreign oil was little interested in the production of expensive synthetics. Not until the Arab oil embargo of the early 1970s did the national attitude begin to change.

In 1974, in the wake of the embargo, attempting to spur development of alternative energy forms that might reduce American dependence on foreign oil, the federal government began the leasing of selected public oil shale tracts in the West to private oil companies. The primary target was the richest oil shale region in the world — the Green River Formation beneath the convergence of southwestern Wyoming, northwestern Colorado, and northeastern Utah. On its vast, sweeping surface the 25,000-square-mile triangle from Rock Springs to Rifle to the western tip of the Roan Plateau was wasteland, a world of deep, empty skies and serrated canyons and sun. But beneath its surface lay an estimated 90 percent of America's known oil shale deposits — 2 trillion barrels of recoverable oil. Wyoming, with 460,000 acres of shale land, held 5 percent (30 billion barrels) of the region's high-grade recoverable deposits. Utah held another 15 percent — 90 billion barrels — chiefly along the Uinta River Basin from the Uinta Mountains to the Green River. But the bulk of it lay deep in Colorado's Piceance (pronounced PEE-ahnce) Basin on the

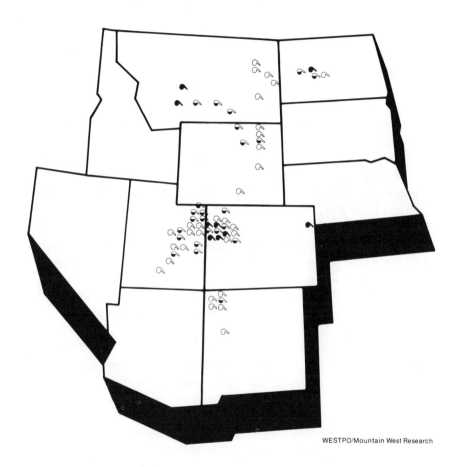

WESTPO/Mountain West Research

SYNTHETIC FUELS ACTIVITY

- Active Projects
- Planned Projects
- Speculative Projects

northeastern slopes of the Roan. In a single 30-mile-long, 25-mile-wide shale seam — 1500 feet deep at its deepest — lay 480 billion barrels, 80 percent of the world's known oil shale deposits (2 quadrillion barrels), and 60 percent of America's known high-grade deposits. Although the three states together contain 2 trillion barrels of crude — six times the proven oil reserves on earth — Colorado alone became the primary target.

In 1974, few people — including westerners — knew what shale oil was.

More than 50 million years ago, when the West was covered by ocean, its vast seabeds teemed with animal and plant life. Over eons, as it died — decaying slowly in oxygen-poor, stagnant water — organic matter became trapped in dirt and volcanic ash sifting down through the water from the earth above. In time, still rich in decaying organisms, the matter settled at the bottom of the prehistoric lakes as mud. Then, over more time, the mud hardened into endless layers of gray-brown marlstone (or "shale"), a composite of calcium carbonate and clay. Within it the organic matter slowly deteriorated into kerogens, bituminous solids convertible under proper circumstances into gasoline, jet fuel, and heating and fuel oil. To the Utes who roamed the Colorado Plateau in earlier times, oil shale was the "rock that burns." To energy planners in the 1970s it was gold.

The primary problem with shale oil is its recovery process. Because no technology had been commercially demonstrated to release kerogen from shale, the very purpose of the government's prototype leasing plan was to encourage development companies to establish and evaluate a number of techniques. Because western shales contain large amounts of minerals degradable by acid-producing bacteria, some scientists have advocated the bacterial injection of shale to break out its kerogen. But testing has shown, clearly, that the surest way to draw "oil" from marlstone is to heat it. Accordingly, from the start, most experimental technologies involved that concept.

Surface heating, or retorting, is one approach to shale oil recovery. Shale is mined either below or above ground, fed into surface furnaces, and heated; at 900 degrees Fahrenheit its organic elements escape as gas, thickening into a brackish ooze the consistency of regular crude. More complex is modified "in situ" (in place) retorting, in which massive underground chambers, or retorts, are created by blasting or "rubblizing" shale to the size of gravel, removing part of the debris, then burning the rest in place in the newly created space. While some of the rubblized shale is removed to the earth's surface and retorted there, between 60 and 70 percent is usually left. The pile, reduced to easily burnable flakes and chunks, is ignited from the top; as flammable liquid (usually piped-in natural gas and air) spreads through the debris, as air draws the burn downward, the shale is "cooked" at temperatures ranging from 900 to 1600 degrees Fahrenheit. At 900 degrees, kerogen vaporizes. Finally, pushed to the bottom of the retort by downward-moving fire, the kerogen condenses, cools, and collects in the bottom of the retort in the form of thick, heavy crude. In the final stage of the firing process the crude is pumped to the surface, upgraded to remove its impurities, and stored or pumped through pipelines to conventional refineries.

In 1974 the federal government launched its prototype leasing program by offering six potential tracts for bid in Colorado, Utah, and Wyoming. Private sector bids were received on the Colorado and Utah sites, but no acceptable bids were received for those in Wyoming. On Yellow Creek, twenty-five miles south of Rangely, the Rio Blanco Oil Shale Project was begun on tract C-a. Gulf Oil and Standard of Indiana bought twenty-year lease rights to it for $210 million; experimenting with a modified in situ process on a tract containing anywhere from 1.3 billion to 5.2 billion barrels of recoverable oil, they aimed at the building of five retorts and the production of 50,000 barrels of oil a day by 1987. Tract C-b was leased in 1974 to The Oil Shale Company (TOSCO) and Atlantic Richfield (ARCO) for a bonus payment of $117,788,000. The consortium (which briefly included Shell Oil and Ashland), hoping to implement a modified in situ process previously developed on a private site near De Beque, aimed at the commercial production of 57,000 barrels of oil a day by 1982 and 94,000 by 1990. In Utah, site U-a was leased by Sun Oil and Phillips Petroleum Company, and U-b by Sun, Phillips, and Standard of Ohio.

At the same time, in the early 1970s, oil companies also consolidated their holdings on private lands on the Green River Formation. In 1979 fourteen companies held more than 200,000 acres in the Piceance Basin alone. The region's largest effort, the Colony Project, straddled Parachute Creek north of Parachute, on the Colorado, to the Roan Plateau. Its original partners — Atlantic Richfield, Shell,

Ashland, Cleveland Cliffs Iron, and TOSCO — calculated that 160
billion barrels of high-quality shale oil lay within their lease alone.
Experimenting with surface retorting and "room and pillar" mining
techniques borrowed from coal, the Colony mined and processed a
million tons of shale — up to 800 barrels a day — as early as 1972.
In 1974, Colony officials established the production of 47,000 to
50,000 barrels a day as their goal by 1995. Meanwhile, the Paraho
Development Company (a consortium of seventeen companies) established a test site on the United States Naval Oil Shale Reserve at
Anvil Points, west of Rifle. Paraho, too, experimented primarily with
surface retorting, spending $16 million by 1978 on a model retort just
over ten feet in diameter. On the basis of its use, Paraho claimed to
have the only successful above-ground retorting technology in the
region by the late 1970s.

In its early years the industry met few of its own expectations. The
federal program, in particular, was of questionable success — full of
promise, yet plagued by incoherence and confusion. The Colorado
projects were plagued by a variety of difficulties, and the Utah projects stalled in a welter of legal problems. Two questions — one
involving land title disputes between the state of Utah and the federal
government, the other involving the status of unpatented pre-1920
mining claims — were not resolved until Supreme Court action in
1980. A third issue — Ute Indian claims to U-a and U-b — has not
been resolved yet.

To date, not a single project — on federal land or off — has produced shale oil on a commercial level.

As the shale oil industry slowly came into focus in the West, so
did its problems. At first, they were hard to see or understand; tucked
away in the remote fissures of the badlands' hills, the struggling
young facilities yielded little concrete information to the outside
world. Nonetheless, however slowly, problems began to appear. People began to sense what the infant projects would bring to their towns
and lives. Air pollution. Water pollution and water loss, particularly
in and from the vital Colorado. Pit mines. Spent shale. People.
Hordes of people in search of new jobs and big money, swamping
small towns, overloading their schools and hospitals and water systems, raising their indebtedness, disrupting customs and folkways
that had rooted with the pioneers. The Colony Project *alone* involved a 4100-acre underground shale mine, a 50,000-barrels-a-day
retort plant, an 800-acre disposal site, two water-storage reservoirs,

a 194-mile pipeline, two power lines, a 15-mile service corridor from the mine to Parachute (connecting to terminal and storage facilities there), the diversion of 9050 acre feet of the Colorado River, 1500 construction workers, and a population increase of at least 7500 people.

In its experimental stage, to the spring of 1979, the shale oil industry did no great damage to Colorado, to its people or to its towns. But, increasingly, it generated a sense of unease — not over specific problems, because they were not yet in clear relief — but over the very *magnitude* of the industry itself. More and more, by the late 1970s, people were becoming aware of its massiveness, of its power to alter and shape, of the potential it had to reform patterns of life as old as the West. As they watched the long shadow of the industry grow over their empty country, those with a sense of the western past must have looked to the future with a sharp sense of apprehension.

Then, for northwest Colorado, the future came on a July day in 1979.

Almost overnight the economics of shale oil changed, but the cause was not technological breakthrough, nor the inflation of the price of foreign petroleum on the world market to the point that shale oil suddenly became commercially profitable. The cause was federal government — its removal of shale oil production from the private marketplace, its decision that the risks and costs of production should be borne by the American public.

On July 15, 1979, President Jimmy Carter announced sweeping new American initiatives to lessen the nation's continuing dependence on imported oil. The $142 billion program — announced in a televised address to the nation — called for federal solar tax credits, support for mass transit, and increased spending for conservation. But the heart of the Carter plan was a proposal for the crash development of synthetic fuels — the spending of $88 billion on oil shale, coal gas and liquids, tar sands, and other technologies. Two new federal offices were projected to direct the development. One, the Energy Security Corporation (ESC), was to oversee investments, to ensure that a domestic synfuels production level of 2.5 million barrels of oil a day was reached by 1990. The second, the Energy Mobilization Board (EMB), was to have the power to "expedite" the development of "key energy facilities."

As projected by Carter, financing for the entire program was to come from imposition of a "windfall profits" tax on new oil revenue

— a tax designed to generate between \$142 billion and \$270 billion in federal revenue within a decade.

It took one year for any of the president's plan to materialize; not until June 1980 did Congress act on it, finally passing the Energy Security Act of 1980. As requested by Carter, substantial funding was provided for the development of gasohol distilleries, the production of biomass energy from municipal waste, and for the development of solar energy and energy conservation programs. But by the summer of that year the centerpiece of the plan was a \$19 billion, five-year program of financial incentives to encourage private industry to build synfuels plants. If the initial incentives proved successful, Congress indicated an intent to provide \$68 million more. It also mandated that projected new plants would produce 500,000 barrels of oil a day by 1987 — about 8 percent of America's then current rate of oil imports and about 3 percent of the nation's 1979 daily oil consumption — and it set the 1992 production goal at 1 million barrels a day. Administration of the financial awards was to be made by the ESC (renamed the Synthetic Fuels Corporation).

To the West, especially the oil shale West, the most significant part of the Carter package was the synfuels proposal. No part of the new program had the importance it did, and none threatened to affect the West the way it did.

Westerners, like other Americans, generally recognized the obvious need for national energy independence. In 1979, the United States produced 70 percent of its overall energy needs — but only about 57 percent of its own *oil* needs. At the time of the Carter announcement, the United States was on its way to consuming 18.5 million barrels per day (BPD) of oil. Of that, it imported 6.5 million BPD at a cost of \$134 million a day — adding up to \$50 billion a year, more than half the combined yearly net assets of IBM, General Electric, General Motors, and Ford. Between 1970 and 1979 alone, the cost of oil imported by the United States increased by 175 percent. As forecasters projected a national daily consumption rate of 30 million BPD by 2010, Americans increasingly came to understand that they could not continue to import indefinitely. Part of the reason was cost. Part of it was the chronic instability of the Mideast, the growing unreliability of Mideastern suppliers. In a word, the United States simply could no longer afford to sustain old patterns of energy dependency; it could not afford to tolerate its growing vulnerability to crisis in the Islamic world or anywhere else. It was time, said Carter, to develop

American alternatives to foreign crude. It was time for synfuels.

The West understood this. But it also understood that it would bear the brunt of synfuels development. Westerners knew even then that the price of energy independence might be the conversion of their world into a national sacrifice area. Accordingly, as the Carter plan slowly made its way through Congress, the West warily watched it. Some of the plan's elements were supported by westerners; others — primarily the EMB — were not. But at all times their fears were evident. "The scope of this project is greater than the sum total of the interstate highway system, the Marshall Plan, and the space program all combined," said Carter in 1980, and it was precisely this that worried the West. The stunning massiveness of the plan, its hugeness, the implementation of the biggest economic enterprise in American history on one of the most socially and ecologically fragile landscapes in the nation — this was what worried the West. Outsiders, perhaps, could not understand it, but those who loved the beauty of the land and the grace of its life feared the ruin of both. They had seen it happen before. Now, with an uneasy sense of déjà vu, they saw it happening again.

In the days after the Carter announcement, western leaders gave widespread support to the principle of the president's synfuels plan. Most readily agreed that, under any circumstances, the United States could no longer afford to live in the shadow of perpetual Mideastern crisis. In a situation as disruptive as depression and often as dangerous as war, they concurred with Carter that the establishment of energy independence was an immediate and critical American priority.

One day after the president's speech, governors of the then Western Governors' Policy Office (WESTPO) states — Alaska, Arizona, Colorado, Montana, Nebraska, New Mexico, Utah, Wyoming, and North and South Dakota — took the lead in supporting much of the federal position. Resolutions were adopted affirming that they were "prepared to take whatever action is necessary, appropriate, consistent with the interest of this region and our concern for the environment to assist the president in implementing this energy program." Thomas Judge of Montana spoke for many when he said that Mideastern dislocation and the oil stoppages it caused were "the most serious crisis that has ever affected this country." It was vital, they all agreed, at least in principle, that the West unite with the president.

On the question of synfuels, however, support was in principle only. If the West supported the general thrust of the Carter synfuels plan — energy independence — it also opposed the arrogant mentality that surrounded it.

The primary issue was the Energy Mobilization Board. At first glance the board looked innocent enough. As proposed by the president, its function in the synfuels program was to streamline the process of creating and starting up key energy projects. But as it first took shape in legislation written by John Dingell of Michigan, it appeared to have the power to substantially skirt state environmental law in the process. While Dingell seemed to savor his role as western antagonist, ignoring complaints that the basic tenets of federalism were being uprooted, his bill raised a storm of protest.

Rocky Mountain state governors immediately rejected the EMB, and for the next year westerners doggedly fought it in Congress. Operating on the basis of a hundred years' experience with federal imperialism, they held that an unleashed EMB would steamroll state agencies, ride roughshod over regional water rights, and destroy environmental laws — strip mining, water quality, air pollution, historical preservation — that had taken a quarter century to construct. Nonwesterners such as Senator J. Bennett Johnston, Jr., of Louisiana supported the idea of a "small, elite group" with "real powers to cut red tape." But angry westerners saw only the arrogant nullification of two hundred years of constitutional history. As a Wyoming newspaper said, the concept itself was a "radical theft of States' rights" that "made the Constitution tremble."

The attitude of the Carter administration throughout the controversy provided a classic example of why the president was never able to build a strong relationship with the West. With western governors publicly supporting the administration's synfuels program, yet arguing at the same time against its potential to circumvent state law, Carter publicly assured the West that he would not support such a concept. But when confronted with two different versions of the so-called fast-track legislation — pending before a House-Senate conference committee — White House staff supported the Dingell bill, the harsher of the two. Agreements between the administration and Dingell apparently superseded the president's pledge to ten western governors. It was a portent of things to come.

Given Carter's stance, the West refused to compromise. It fought the bill. Governors testified in Washington. Congressmen lobbied in the halls of Congress. Alliances were formed with eastern-based environmentalist organizations. When the synfuels part of the Carter plan passed Congress, the administration was confident enough of EMB approval that it scheduled an elaborate and symbolic signing ceremony for *both* bills on July 4, 1979. But the celebration was never held. On June 28, by a vote of 232 to 131, the House rejected the conference committee bill to establish the EMB. For the moment, at least, the board was dead, and while White House lobbyists sat stunned outside the great House chamber, the West exulted.

With or without the EMB, the Energy Security Act was a milestone in American energy history. Providing billions of dollars to both the Department of Energy and the newly created Synthetic Fuels Corporation (SFC) to grant to synfuels projects, it clearly signaled the beginning of modern-day shale oil development in the nation. Long-planned projects took on life; struggling old projects, sensing that public assistance would make shale development a reality, took on new life. Over the opposition of Colorado congressman Hank Brown, who argued that he did not think the United States could justify "federal support for major energy companies," and Senator Harrison Schmitt of New Mexico, who decried federal interference in the private capital market, TOSCO sought and received a 75 percent loan guarantee to cover its fiduciary responsibilities on the $1.3 billion Colony Project (coventured with Exxon). Likewise, Union Oil, which began building a demonstration plant on Parachute Creek in 1980, was extended a $400 million purchase commitment. On tract C-a the Rio Blanco Oil Shale Project announced its interest in loan guarantees, and Occidental and Tenneco (who formed the Cathedral Bluffs project near Rifle) actively pursued the same kinds of guarantees.

By the fall of 1981, several dozen subsidy applications lay before the SFC alone. At the same time, other new and relatively new ventures were begun, some of them interested in and reliant on federal aid, others not. In Colorado, Chevron USA launched its ambitious Clear Creek Project forty miles north of Grand Junction, planning the production of 100,000 barrels a day by 1994. Superior plotted a 12,000-barrels-a-day operation in Rio Blanco County, and Mobil planned another 100,000-barrels-a-day project on 10,000 acres ten miles west of Rifle and four miles north of Parachute. In Utah, Chevron began construction of a $120 million processing plant near Farmington in July 1981, TOSCO announced plans for the projected 48,000-barrels-a-day Sand Wash Project in northeast Utah, and in

September 1981 Paraho announced that it would start construction of its Paraho-Ute Project near Vernal in 1982.

But the plans of all of them combined paled beside those of Exxon.

Feeling the press of competition — stimulated by the increasing availability of subsidies — Exxon aggressively entered the field. First, it bought out ARCO's interest in the Colony Project. Then, in June 1980, it announced a challenge to the entire oil industry to produce 8 million barrels of oil a day from the shale beds of northwest Colorado. The plan defied belief, even among oil companies (who responded to it in shock and surprise). The $500 billion, 8-million-barrel figures far surpassed the figures of any previous scenario. Even without subsidies — which it did not seek — Exxon projected the collective building of eighty $5 billion plants in Garfield and Rio Blanco counties, Colorado, by 2010, a figure far greater than any before it. More than any other plan of the 1970s or 1980s, the Exxon "challenge" typified the new "crash" approach to energy development. Because of this, perhaps, the plan was greeted with much doubt — even hostility — in those parts of the West where it was to unfold.

But it made little difference. The crash concept still prevails. It has not changed.

Now, as the commercial production of shale oil moves closer and closer to reality, the West has begun to take more careful notice of it. Though the West has countless concerns about the impact of oil shale on the land and its people, one of its biggest fears is of environmental degradation. The argument is made, of course, that no beauty exists in oil shale country, but it is an argument made mainly by outsiders who do not know it. In an earlier time, before the cattlemen, grass stretched from horizon to horizon. The Utes called it *piceance* — "tall grass." Now the grass is mostly gone, and with it whatever softness the land ever had. Now it is a rutted, barren canvas of geological scars and furrows, and all that stretches between the horizons is emptiness. And yet the land has a beauty, a wild, surreal majesty that almost transcends description. Parachute Canyon on a spring morning. Scrub oak, scarlet-orange on an autumn day. The Anvil Points dusted with winter snow. The Colorado. Those who have seen understand. Those who have not, cannot.

Already the beauty has been marred. Tall concrete towers pierce the sky at Cathedral Bluffs and a factory butts up against the wrinkled walls of Anvil Points. A huge, skeletal retorting furnace sits at the edge of Parachute Creek, its thick steel beams an ugly lattice set against the canyon. And all across the region, pipelines cut under the earth and small pit mines mar its surface.

The worst of it, perhaps, is the pit mines. They are part of the future. In the hunt for oil, the land will be slit open, probed, mined, burned, and then, supposedly, revegetated and returned to nature. But the scars the process will leave — like the still-visible wagon tracks of the Oregon Trail — will remain evident forever.

If shale is commercialized, pit mining is likely to take place on a large scale. At some projects severe geological overburden makes stripping impossible. At others, however, shale lies so close to the surface that pit mining is the most economical and effective way to recover it. Such is the case, for example, on tract C-a, where the Rio Blanco Project has proposed to dig an open pit one and a half miles long by one mile wide by up to 1600 feet deep on a tract of 457 acres. Chevron, too, is considering open pits. And the original Exxon plan identified six 15,000-acre tracts suitable for surface mining. Exxon projected that in a "typical" operation, a surface mine would be over 3.5 miles long, one and three quarters miles wide, and half a mile deep — slightly larger than the great Bingham Pit copper mine near Salt Lake City. In a formal presentation made to Colorado state officials in June 1980, Exxon noted that the center of the Piceance Basin alone could accommodate fourteen such surface-mining facilities.

The concept — its incredible dimensions — is frightening. It may be that geological realities — the depth of overburden — will preclude widespread strip mining in fact. But if they do not, if the idea of stripping takes root, if the concept becomes the norm, the consequences to the land will be harmful and extensive.

A major allied problem — and another with great aesthetic implications — is that of spent shale, the waste left over after mining and retorting. Studies indicate that 600,000 tons of shale must be mined to yield 400,000 barrels of oil a day (an estimate of production for Colorado by 1990 under the Carter plan). Eighty percent of each ton of shale is spoil, or rubble, and 20 percent is oil; 600,000 tons of mined shale would produce 480,000 tons of spoil a day, 175.2 million tons a year, and 5.26 billion tons over thirty years. A 50,000 BPD facility such as the Colony Project could fill Dillon Reservoir, west of Denver, with several hundred feet of spoil during its lifetime. Over thirty years, a 400,000 BPD industry could create a pile of spent shale covering an area the size of Denver — 117 square miles — and reach more than seven stories in height.

Ironically, open-pit mining generates less waste than modified in situ. Through the so-called popcorn effect, tailings expand to 120 percent of their original volume after surface retorting; after oil is processed from shale, more waste is left to dispose of than existed in the *first* place. An underground mine using modified in situ to process 57,000 barrels a day with a surface retort would require 900 acres for spent-shale disposal over the thirty-year life of the facility. On the other hand, a facility using the TOSCO II process to produce roughly the same amount over the same time would require 1500 acres. What scars the land leaves relatively little waste behind; what damages the land little leaves much behind. This is but another dilemma the West will have to learn to live with.

Oil companies maintain that shale residue can safely and conveniently be disposed of. The Colony's plan, for example, has been to dump spent shale in the canyon of East Middle Fork Creek, a tributary of Piceance Creek. Over twenty years, according to the plan, the canyon will be filled, watered, compacted, covered with a layer of overburden (loose rock), and blanketed with topsoil. Native salt shrubs, piñon, greasewood, juniper, sage, big basin wild rye, and other grasses will be planted. Theoretically, the land will return to the way it was, but the problem is that no actual proof exists that it will work. Although it is the law, and despite the fact that the industry has made efforts to conform to it, the process of revegetation is costly and only experimental. And so far it has been plagued by problems. Both geography and climate have worked against it. Shale's darkness absorbs the sun's heat, frying seeds embedded in it, and its alkaline nature makes it not ideal for growing to begin with. It dries quickly and solidly, even when watered. It tends to become unstable under compaction and erode. Revegetation might work for the moment, in small, carefully nurtured company plots. But the future is another matter, when the companies leave the plots to nature. To date, the Colorado Mined Land Reclamation Division has compiled a list of forty-two problem areas where it cannot guarantee the success of reclamation. And no one knows how many might exist beyond them.

Again, the scale of it all, the uncertainty of it all, is frightening, and to Coloradans it suggests that changes to the land will come not peacefully, but violently. And they will last forever.

Coloradans affected by shale oil also fear that environmental dislocation will bear heavily — and probably negatively — on human life and health. Most concerns involve the future of the waterways. The badlands have few streams, but those it has are as critical to life around them as any in the West. The Colorado, awesome as it flows west to Utah, is the most important water supply in the American West. The wild Yampa provides water — the only water — for the entire upper badlands; without it there would be little human life, if any at all, for several hundred miles between Steamboat Springs and Vernal, Utah. The beautiful White, a winding silver ribbon as it rolls off its great plateau through the desert, is the lifeline of every farm and ranch from Meeker to Rangely and into northeastern Utah. Douglas Creek, Yellow Creek, Roan Creek, Piceance, the Uinta and Green — in an area an Englishman once described as "worthless waste, an accursed country," these streams have meant human survival for a hundred years.

One of the great uncertainties of full-scale shale oil development is the impact it will have on these waterways. Both surface waters and the aquifers in which they originate are vulnerable to waste from shale processing and to whatever contaminants the waste might contain. Almost certainly, pollution will occur. The only question is how much, how complete, and how widespread the damage will be.

In the Green River and Piceance basins the implication of this is particularly clear: polluted aquifers and secondary surface streams eventually find their way to crops, livestock, and people. The Colorado alone serves communities all the way to the Pacific. Oil companies maintain that spent-shale disposal procedures are safe enough to prevent water degradation, that the compacted embankment of spent shale is impermeable to water. But tests indicate otherwise — that leachates from shale, containing high levels of boron, arsenic, fluorine, mercury, molybdenum, and a host of organic chemicals, may consistently find their way into local waters through snowmelt and precipitation. Large quantities of dissolved solids, which contribute to water salinity, also have been found in local waters; in some shale samples, salinity concentrations have reached as high as 55,000 milligrams per liter (versus 35,000 in sea water). Salinity is a major problem in the Colorado already, causing its users millions of dollars a year in damages.

The known implications of toxic and carcinogenic elements in water are difficult enough to deal with, but doubly difficult is dealing

with the unknown. Shale companies today claim zero discharge on
their sites, and they minimize the problem of salinity. But what
worries Coloradans, again, is tomorrow, when massive population
growth and increasing environmental problems will change everything.

Westerners also worry about their air. In the future, air pollution
in oil shale country probably is more certain than the fouling of its
water.

A decade ago the idea that air pollution would reach to the mountains would have been ludicrous. But today it does. In some of the
most primitive wilderness areas in the Rockies the air is hazier by
the year. If full-scale shale oil production goes ahead, the possibility
exists that it will become considerably worse. In 1979 the EPA
hypothesized that a 50,000 BPD facility using the TOSCO II process
would spew more than 1000 pounds of hydrocarbons an hour into the
air, along with nearly 2000 pounds of nitrogen oxides and more than
800 pounds of particulates — all of this even using required emissions controls. At best the degradation of the air will ruin some of
the most beautiful vistas left in the West. But at worst it will exceed
national air-quality standards and endanger the health of the region's
people.

To the West, an ominous pattern is emerging. Publicly, some oil
companies have taken a stand against air pollution, promising to
comply with existing standards. In January 1972 an ARCO spokes-
man stated flatly that ARCO "will meet these [air-pollution] standards or we won't build. That's all there is to it." On the other hand,
other companies have worked either to have their operations transferred from stringent to less stringent air-pollution categories or to
have the air-pollution laws themselves changed. Occidental, for example, has already requested the elimination of Colorado's strict
sulfur-emission standard, hoping that the state might replace it with
a more flexible technology determination. And other oil companies
are actively lobbying for changes in the landmark Clean Air Act of
1970 (with its strengthening amendments of 1977), which mandates
that air quality in national forests and wilderness areas surrounding
shale oil sites cannot deteriorate below the so-called Class I standard
that prohibits any significant amount of new pollution. The American Petroleum Institute, arguing that "controls on visibility should
not be set," has proposed relaxation of clean-air rules in some of
Colorado's most pristine regions.

As Colorado moves toward the future, certain facts must be considered. It is a fact, for example, that pollution will affect scenic vistas — and that relaxation of clean-air standards probably will accelerate the process.

It is a fact, too, that large amounts of particulates and gases — sulfur dioxide, nitrogen oxide, and hydrocarbons — escape into the air from mining and retorting operations, and that as recently as December 1980, the EPA defined them as both toxic and carcinogenic. Noting, for example, that a shale oil worker may be more vulnerable to skin cancer than a crude oil driller, the EPA said that if not controlled, synfuels plants could present "potentially very serious health and environmental problems" to those who man them. Although the National Commission on Air Quality states that 940,-000 barrels of oil a day could be produced in the Colorado-Utah corner without exceeding federal Class I air-quality standards (690,-000 barrels in the Piceance Basin alone), other studies indicate that only 200,000 can be tolerated. By the year 2010, when Colorado oil companies anticipate the production of 600,000 barrels a day, they may be dangerously beyond the limit.

In light of this, any assault on clean-air standards is a danger to the West. Western governors have concurred that although they support a balance between energy and clean air, the latter is "an attribute of the West which must not be unduly compromised." This attitude, this wariness, is not pointless. It is based on the realization that, again, the West is dealing with the unknown, and dealing with it from a position of weakness at that. In effect, the West and the oil companies are playing Russian roulette with the West as the only possible loser. A century ago, America knew nothing of black lung, so it heedlessly mined its coal. And men died. Three decades ago, it knew little about leukemia, but nuclear testing was carried out in Utah and Nevada. And more people died. Fifteen years ago, the public knew nothing of Agent Orange. Twenty years from now, if people die of cancer caused by shale oil processing, no one can say the lessons of the past were not there. Development has begun; it cannot be stopped. So all the West can do is set standards and monitor problems — and hope that its fears today are unfounded.

In dealing with the effects of oil shale production in the West, westerners can ill afford to ignore its economic dimensions either. Although recent studies show that outsiders profit more than "locals" in a boom economy — with skilled and professional jobs going to in-migrants, and capital flowing from and to outside banks and holding companies — many still believe that the industry will be a blessing, providing jobs and generating income. But under any circumstances it has the power to dominate the region's economic life as nothing the West has seen before. If the shale oil industry is not harnessed, it has the ability to destroy every other economic element around it.

Tourism is one. The Green River–Colorado Plateau country is not tourist country — it never has been. And yet it is but a few air miles distant from some of the most important tourist attractions in the region. Rocky Mountain National Park lies just to the east, Colorado National Monument to the south, and Dinosaur National Monument to the northwest. In time all three areas may be affected by air pollution from the Piceance. The same holds true for every other attraction from Glenwood Springs to Salt Lake — North Park, Flaming Gorge, Grand Mesa, Canyonlands. Most vulnerable, though, is the ski industry. From Steamboat Springs to Aspen, resort owners already complain of polluted air drifting south and east out of the badlands. As the mayor of Aspen has said, "One of the treasures of coming to Aspen is the clean air. If we don't have clean air, it will destroy us."

Another endangered economy — by far the most important in the region — is agriculture. In earlier days in Colorado, some of the richest farmland in America lay along the Colorado River as it wound out of the high Rockies to Utah. Today the land is still rich — but its agricultural future is not. As oil companies move into the northwest they threaten to urbanize the land, trigger a migration of workers out of the farm labor force and into synfuels, create high production costs for farmers, and change social, cultural, and economic institutions that have lasted a century. Most immediately, though, they threaten the farmers' water.

On the western rim of the Great American Desert, water scarcity has been a fact of life for a hundred years. In times past farmers clustered their homesteads along the White and Yampa and built towns along the Colorado on the southern shoulders of the Roan Plateau. In time, Meeker, Rifle, Parachute, De Beque, and Grand Junction developed a substantial agriculture, even with a water supply that was barely adequate. Today, it is still barely adequate. Even *without* shale oil development, Colorado Basin streams — particularly the White — are dangerously overappropriated. *With* shale oil development — and the need for water in surface retorting, wetting and compacting spent shale, revegetation, and domestic use — the situation becomes potentially dangerous.

At the moment, shale oil demands have put little pressure on local water supplies. Although a 100,000 BPD commercial plant using the TOSCO II process will use from 13,000 to 19,000 feet of water each year, and a 100,000 BPD modified in situ plant will use nearly 8000, the Colorado Department of Natural Resources has concluded that an industry of 500,000 to 700,000 barrels a day could be sustained with water from the Colorado River system without jeopardizing current agricultural users.

But it is the future, not the present, that worries Coloradans. If enough water exists today, and even for the near future, it will not exist indefinitely. When and if Lower Basin states begin further utilizing surplus water flowing out of Colorado, and when Upper Basin states like Colorado fail to build more storage projects — which seems likely — water one day will become the scarcest and most precious commodity in the badlands. When the day comes, the oil companies will challenge other potential users for the surplus. Exxon already, for example, has begun negotiations with the Bureau of Reclamation for the delivery of 6000 acre feet a year of Frying Pan River water to the Colony Project, an action that local people fear will drain Ruedi Reservoir, east of Basalt, in drought years. Today the region's farmers are in a relatively good position. Many of them, in fact, have made money by selling water rights at inflated prices (up to $2300 an acre foot) and often leasing it back at less. But tomorrow promises to be different. It is then, says Colorado legislator Fred Anderson, that "there's going to be a modern-day showdown at the water hole." It is then that the war for water will begin, and in a war where water goes to the highest bidder, the farmers will win nothing.

In the end, probably no business in all of northwest Colorado and northeast Utah will be immune from the growing influence of shale oil. Tourism, recreation, farming, and stock raising all will be damaged by the shrinkage of water supplies, and even general mining may be hamstrung by the collection of labor in shale towns.

The most dangerous effect, though, may be the impact on the region's many small businesses — the core of economic life in northwest Colorado for a hundred years. Here, small businesses — groceries, bars and cafés, drugstores, service stations, even light industry

— have been a way of life since the first general store. Their diversity has consistently created a climate of economic health, and in more than one community, small business has been the very linchpin of small-town life. With the coming of shale oil this may change. Already plagued by increasing regulatory requirements, lack of affordable capital, and spiraling costs that cannot easily be passed on to consumers, small business simply may not survive the energy hunt.

The gravest danger is that the energy invasion will destroy the strong and diversified economic base of the region, pulling its people away from old, traditional, stable economies — farming, stock raising, even tourism — and into new, less stable streams such as construction and energy production. In a region where people have "done business" in certain ways for so long, such a wrenching shift from old to new is bound to cause serious long-term economic dislocation. Westerners expect disruption. They can only hope that it will pass.

They also expect boomtowns.

This part of the West — shale oil country — has changed but slowly over time. Only 160 years ago the Utes ran wild and free across the land, writing their violent history on its face. By the 1880s they were gone, replaced by cattlemen — with Two Bars and Four Jays and Pothooks — who took their land and branded it and ruled it as their own. Homesteaders came to the prairie later, shredding the grasslands with plows, strangling the cattlemen with barbed wire, building an empire of their own. Over the course of time, the two worlds met, the two cultures fused, and the badlands became a curious amalgam of both. The area's ragged towns — Meeker, Rifle, Rangely — took on farmer strength and respectability that lingers to this day, but the people's ferocious independence is the legacy of the cattlemen.

Rifle sits on the north bank of the Colorado, a hundred years old in 1982. A century ago, cattle kings ran their herds in the high grass along Government Creek and the Colorado. Small armies of rustlers, marauding out of Brown's Hole, supplied stolen beef to Mormon farmers in central Utah, and sodbusters "scratched gravel" on the region's tiny homesteads. When the railroad came down the valley, Rifle became the main shipping point for Garfield County. In later years, vanadium was mined there, and for a moment, in the 1930s and 1940s, Rifle was a Union Carbide town. Uranium, finally, came and went — and throughout it all the town changed little. Its 1940 population of 1287 grew to only 2170 by 1970. In its frontier days Rifle was raw, primitive, and boisterous; but by as late as the 1950s it was pastoral and quiet. Only on Saturday nights, when cowboys drifted in from the valley, did it come alive again.

To the west, Parachute also perches on the banks of the Colorado and waits for change. Here, too, it has been a long time coming. Parachute was born in 1886, named after the massive shroudlike mesas that stand behind it. The Cassidy gang robbed a Denver and Rio Grande train here seventy years ago, but the rest of its history has been that of farmers. At Parachute, the Grand Valley flares to a twenty-mile width as it bends to the southwest, and it is here that the Western Slope's peach empire begins. For thirty years, every August, pickers have flooded the Parachute Valley, filling rooming houses at Parachute and elsewhere, pitching tents in box-elder groves, followed by small carnivals and tent shows. There always has been a comfortable touch of the Midwest here, a nostalgic dash of Mark Twain on a summer night, but even in 1970 only 270 people lived here to enjoy it. To the east of Rifle, Silt looks back on the same kind of history. Founded in 1908, Silt was a farm town from the beginning — potatoes, alfalfa, small irrigated cash crops — surrounded by cattle. It has changed little over the years. In 1940 its population was 264, and by 1970 it had grown by less than 200.

To the north, Meeker sits on the upper edge of the shale fields, also awaiting the impact of the industry. From Oak Ridge, looking down, it is a small, distant square, a rectangular patch of brown on a canvas of green, its neat street grid punctured by clumps of elder and cottonwood. As an army post Meeker goes back a hundred years, as an incorporated town it dates from 1885, and as a town of any substance it dates from 1889, when the railroad came churning into it out of the high country. From its birth, Meeker was a farm town, ringed by cattlemen and some of the most violent outlaw enclaves in the West. On a bloody summer day eighty years ago, three cowboy bandits from Brown's Park were killed in a shoot-out on the town's main street. It was here, or from here, that the Sevens and Double O and Keystone cowboys slaughtered sheep and terrorized homesteaders and fought forest rangers attempting to maintain law on the forest reserves. And it was here that Nathan Meeker was tortured and killed by Utes in 1879, and here, at the Meeker Hotel, that Theodore Roosevelt launched his legendary White River hunting trips for nearly two decades.

Despite its colorful history, Meeker never gained great importance. As late as the 1940s only 1069 people lived there, and by 1970 the population seemed stalled at 1600. It had the largest outdoor swimming pool in northwest Colorado, a county fair, and the Range Call, Colorado's oldest rodeo. And ten dollars would buy a night at the Gentry Motor Lodge. The 1970s changed little. Today Meeker is still one of the most beautiful small towns in the Rockies — especially in autumn, when the White River National Forest becomes a shimmering ocean of gold — situated in one of the most beautiful settings in the West. And it is still quiet and pastoral. But now it, too, watches — and braces for the change that shale oil will bring.

For Rifle and Parachute and Meeker, pessimists have already written their scenario for the future. A crash synfuels plan, they say, will bring an unprecedented rush of shale oil developers into northwest Colorado and northeast Utah. New boomtowns — like Battlement Mesa — will spring up overnight in their wake, and older ones will swell to the bursting point. Everywhere tens of thousands of people will stream into remote and placid parts of the West where life has changed little over a hundred years. The new boomtowns will alter the physical and social face of the plateau country, sprawling across the landscape, suburbanizing farm and forest lands, filling open space with concrete. They will drain the labor force from community businesses and channel it into energy projects. Costs and prices will rise. Economic life will change, and as it does, disrupting social behavior and regional folkways in the process, overburdened support systems and underfunded social-services delivery systems will collapse.

On earlier frontiers Western boomtowns were sprawling and lurid, too, but they had a color and a richness — and an atmosphere of hope and progress — that tempered their ugliness. But the new boomtowns are different towns in different times, and they will not have the redeeming richness of the old. The new boomtowns, stripped of excitement, devoid of romance, will become melting pots for violence, insanity, alcoholism, suicide, divorce, vice, crime, and every other form of social dislocation. Physically, socially, psychologically, they will change forever. And historical romanticism will be unable to gloss over what they are.

Perhaps, in fact, the scenario already has begun to play out. Population figures, for example, strongly suggest it.

As late as the 1950s, for example, Rifle had less than two thousand inhabitants. It took fully three decades, between 1940 and 1970, for its population to surpass two thousand. In the past decade, affected by speculation and an emerging shale industry, Rifle grew by nearly 50 percent. Then, between 1977 and 1980, it literally exploded: in a mere three years, it grew by more than 43 percent. Regional planners project a population of 23,710 by 1990; at a time when 50 to 100 percent growth over a decade is considered difficult to manage, Rifle may grow as much as 508 percent.

De Beque, barely a town at all ten years ago, grew by 80 percent between 1970 and 1980; a town of only 350 in 1981 may grow to 27,000 by 1995. Parachute, in the eye of the energy hurricane, grew from 300 to 2000 during the last six months of 1980 and early 1981 alone, and planners expect a growth rate there of 642 percent over the next ten years. The badlands are dotted with towns like these, small towns coming of age overnight. And their growth — fast and uncontrolled — is cause of great concern.

Today, on the eve of the shale oil boom, the population of northwest Colorado is slightly more than 100,000. What it will be tomorrow, no one can know for sure, but best estimates are that a 50,000-barrels-per-day mining and processing operation will require a peak construction force of 2400 workers and an additional operating force of 2000. Assuming also that every construction worker requires .5 people in support, and that each operational worker requires one person in support (clerks, police, sanitation workers), and adding in families who accompany workers, then each new 50,000-BPD oil shale operation would bring approximately 9000 new people into western Colorado.

Based on this assumption, and if the region reaches a 400,000-barrels-a-day production level, the population in Colorado's shale country could reach nearly a million in ten years.

Already the migration has begun.

Day after day people come to Parachute and Rifle, from all over America, pulling trailers behind pickup trucks or broken-down vans, looking for work on the oil shale projects. But for most of them there is none. There is work in the *towns,* but wages are low and the work goes begging. The migration is to the projects, not to the towns. Oil shale, in fact, has pulled many workers out of the small labor pools of the towns themselves — a Rifle secretary leaves a $900-a-month job for a $2000-a-month job with an oil company, a Grand Junction clerk working for $850 a month joins another oil company to drive heavy equipment for $1800 a month. So city work goes begging. No one wants city jobs at $4 or $5 or $6 an hour. They want oil shale jobs — drawn to them the way fruit pickers were drawn to California orchards during the Great Depression — and not enough exist.

So they live on food stamps. In time, if they fail, they drift on. Those who succeed stay. They center their lives around the bars and churches. They send their children to crowded schools. And they try to find homes.

Again, there are few. And in some towns there are none. The unprecedented influx of people, coupled with spiraling interest rates, has stunted construction and left virtually every community in the shale region short of homes. Rental units often are nonexistent. Motels and campgrounds are full. Parking spaces in trailer courts get scarcer by the day. And costs and charges have skyrocketed. The combined payment for a trailer loan and parking space is prohibitive in itself. And even when they are built, homes are more expensive — to buy or rent — than in Denver. The average list price for a home in Grand Junction in the fall of 1981 was $76,000 at 17 percent interest, and a three-bedroom home built in the past three years cost just under $100,000. And Grand Junction lies on the *edge* of the shale empire, not *in* it.

So the new emigrants endure — survive — the best they can.

Near Rifle, squatters live on the back lots of Larry Lundgren's cattle ranch. "If I kick them off," he says, "where will they go?" A waitress shares a single room in a crumbling old hotel, for $320 a month, and when the hotel closes she moves to the river. Near Silt a Michigan man lives with his family in a nearby campground. They have been there for six months, and they have no hope of leaving soon. Near Parachute, says a lawman, they are "camping along every river and up every creek. We can chase them from bush to creek to river, but they're going to stick around until they find out if they can get a job." The stalls are full at the KOA campground. NO TRES-PASSING signs hang on every old shack and shanty in the region, but even the shacks and shanties are occupied. If a man has a camper and a pad for it, says a Colorado state trooper, it is "worth a for-tune." So three hundred families camp in summer campgrounds, waiting for the winter that will drive them off. And they fill the long, broad gully called Hole in the Wall on a nearby sheep ranch. They do laundry, if at all, in coin-operated machines in town. They bathe, if at all, in showers in rented motel rooms. And they try to find homes.

If life is poor for newcomers, it is not much better for those who lived here before them. They, in particular, have become dislocated in their own communities. Watching their towns become inundated by outsiders, watching traffic choke their once-quiet streets and raucous young men their public places, confronting the dust clouds and the endless noise and the steady proliferation of back-alley brawling, their lives have changed radically already. So they fight with the intruders. And with each other. Parachute has tried to recall its mayor, charging — as one critic has said — that he "is looking out for the people who will be here in the future, not the people who live here now" by "selling out" to developers. But others bitterly disagree, and they support him. As *Denver Post* writer Robert Tweedell has said, the people of Parachute are "discouraged and confused." They are being "pulled apart" by the forces at their door. They are a classic case of the destructive effects of crash development.

From all this, for newcomers and locals alike, it is but a short step to general social upheaval. It is a short step, in other words, to fulfillment of the scenario.

In the midst of upheaval, the towns themselves find it increasingly difficult to provide and build what they need for their people. The first social problems have been isolated and largely manageable. But these problems have clearly shown local officials how little immediate control they have over their own affairs. City and county officials — people like Garfield County's able and creative commissioners — have worked gallantly to prepare for growth and they have been positive and optimistic and forceful. But facing unprecedented demands in public works, public services, and housing, there is a limit to what even they can do.

The towns, obviously, have little money — and little access to money. Communities that once measured yearly budgets in the low thousands or even hundreds of dollars now measure them in the high thousands. If a crash shale oil program takes hold in northwestern Colorado, local residents will lose not only from the perspective of environment and social values but from an economic perspective as well. They will pay increased taxes for decreased services, and even then revenues may never outstrip front-end expenditures.

Part of the problem is a kind of economic Catch-22. Though their facilities need to be in place *before* the arrival of their population, the towns receive no revenue for building or expanding until *afterward*. Not until new populations swell local tax rolls can cities generate the revenue they need. So until that point they have little choice but to go into debt to pay for services and facilities. The time lag can be devastating to towns operating on marginal revenues. While two years may pass before the communities receive funds for services already delivered (a normal situation in northwestern Colorado), they remain chronically behind, unable to build, unable to deliver services, unable to struggle free of debt. They live with uncertainty, afraid of the future, of "bust" times that could easily leave them financially destroyed. Assuming impact from three shale oil plants, a peak construction work force of 2350, and a population impact peaking at 22,000 people, and assuming debt financing of 70 percent of expenditures and a 5 percent discount rate, a recent study by the John F. Kennedy School of Government at Harvard has determined that a hypothetical local government will find itself with a twenty- to thirty-year deficit and the inability — in some cases — to ever catch up.

Added to all this is the fact, as *Denver Post* editorialist Carol Green has described it, that the region's long-standing "old boy network" of local government is dying. From the beginning of the century ranchers and small businessmen — like Parachute's grocer-mayor Floyd McDaniels — have formed the region's governing hierarchy. Now, however, the old power structure is slowly dissolving; the "old-timers" are being replaced by oil executives and white-collar supervisors from the outside world. In time, at least, the result is likely to be a growing insensitivity to local needs. When the "homogeneity gets blown apart," writes Green, when natives lose grip on their own governing mechanisms, the results can easily be negative. "Where's the help for me?" says a Parachute woman. Unfortunately, for the most part, it is not from the localities.

When crash development begins the shale towns will desperately need help — from the state, from federal government, and from the incoming businesses. Funding does exist from all three sources, but under current circumstances it is not enough, or its distribution is too flawed, to be effective. State government, for example, can offer only limited assistance. To date, state expenditures to prepare north- west Colorado for shale development have been derived from the federal lease bonuses from tracts C-a and C-b, as well as from reve- nue from coal leasing and severance tax payments. But even those expenditures have been inadequate. In 1979, only $6 million of state funds were made available from the coal severance tax, yet the state faced requests for aid up to forty times that amount. Colorado will have a maximum of $25 million to $30 million available for assistance in 1982 when the towns' needs are expected to be in excess of $600 million.

Colorado's dilemma is that it does not have an effective mechanism to tap into shale oil revenue. Its severance tax is a case in point. By state law, no oil company is required to pay a severance tax until its plant has reached an average daily production of "50 percent of its design capacity." Then the tax is 4 percent on gross proceeds, due within ninety days. But even then, assuming that a plant reaches 50 percent, gross proceeds are figured by subtracting total costs from the oil's sale price. Finally, the oil companies are required to pay no tax at all for the first 15,000 tons of shale mined each day, or 10,000 barrels of oil processed, whichever is greater. In time, if development is successful, severance tax revenues will be substantial. What emerges now, though, is no front-end revenue at all.

Response by the federal government has been disappointing. A government that has leased public tracts of land for private development, has provided financial incentives to oil companies for it, and has attempted to override state and local laws in the process still has sometimes been slow to help the communities that will bear the brunt of it. It has often been slow to acknowledge the unique situation of oil shale boomtowns — that they face almost insurmountable problems in competing for funds distributed by criteria and formulas designed for other purposes. When Rifle city officials seek categorical assistance to prepare for the coming boom, they are largely unsuccessful because they cannot demonstrate an adequate level of poverty or unemployment for their town. Federal grant and loan programs simply are not structured to deal with prospective problems.

Attempts to gain congressional approval of comprehensive energy-impact legislation so far have failed. Senator Gary Hart of Colorado has introduced such a measure four successive times without success. Two Hart bills are currently under consideration, one calling for tax incentives for companies providing funds for community facilities and services, the other providing for planning grants for prospective boomtowns. There is little else they can fall back on. The single energy-impact program passed by Congress in 1977 provided limited assistance to coal towns and none to shale towns.

Oil companies, too, occasionally have been slow to respond to community requests for assistance. Sometimes, only the local control of special-use permits has forced needed help.

Not long ago, oil companies were routinely issued special-use permits in northwest Colorado's shale oil counties. But this is changing; automatic approvals, based on the notion that "development is good for business," have vanished. Local commissioners now have become more deliberate. Increasingly, they have asked the oil companies to make community commitments in the process of developing their projects, and occasionally they have tied the granting of permits to the making of such commitments. The charge of blackmail has been made more than once, but local people adamantly insist that nothing wrong exists in forcing the private sector to internalize community costs into project costs. The belief is, and it is a growing belief, that the price of developing shale oil *must* include private assistance to the public sector.

People in Parachute remember the 1950s, when the industry said it had come to stay. They remember when the retort was torn down and taken off the tax rolls. They remember when school board members were forced to sign personal notes to secure loans to pay for the schools. And they are determined that it will not happen again.

*   *   *

For years the people of northwest Colorado have watched the industry come. They have watched headframes push through the Piceance sky, watched retorts blossom on Parachute Creek, watched earthmovers rake the land at Rio Blanco. For a long time they could not assess the movement and motion around them. Intellectually, they knew that shale oil was reality — the dust and clatter and chaos in the hills told them so. But still it was hard to comprehend. Now it no longer is. It is as if one night the plateau country went to sleep with shale oil an idea, a blueprint, a cluster of makeshift projects scattered across the land, and years of rhetoric behind them, and awoke the next day to reality. Today is the next day. Shale oil has exploded on the badlands. And it will change its ways of life forever.

As Colorado stands on the threshold, it asks these questions: In a decade, in two, will the land be habitable? Will the streams be dry? Will the space be gone? Will the people survive? Some years ago, an old cattleman looked back over the passage of time and how it had changed life in the badlands. "I like to talk about the good old days," he said. "I never hear a horse bell or see a bunch of cattle going down the land but that I want to follow."

Little did he know that change had only begun.

The question now is how well northwest Colorado can tolerate it. It can, for example, if the crash philosophy is abandoned, because it will not, cannot, work. Synfuels development is so immense, so vastly unknown, so filled with destructive potential, that it may be beyond the capacity of any state, any people to absorb. Shale oil and other synthetic fuels need underpinning by caution and direction and careful phasing, not carelessness and panic.

In the rush to expoit western oil shale, advocates of a crash program have forgotten — or ignored — one central fact: synfuels technology still is imperfect. Recent studies by the Pentagon, by the Department of Energy, by the Harvard Business School have shown that synfuels in general may not be developable by the end of the century, let alone reach a production capacity of 1 million to 2 million barrels a day by the end of the decade. Technologies tested — those in Colorado, for example — have been tested only on a limited, experimental basis, producing anywhere from fifty to a thousand barrels a day at most. And all of the projects have been beset by problems even operating on a limited basis.

After two costly test burns in 1980 and 1981, which actually produced thousands of barrels of oil, the Rio Blanco Project still encountered enough problems that it announced an 80 percent reduction in its work force and finally virtually shut down until they could be corrected. On the C-a tract, where the mahogany seam lies eight hundred feet below the sagebrush surface, trapped between two giant aquifers, Rio Blanco has concluded that it is not an acceptable site for establishing the modified in situ process. The situation is further compounded by the fact that cost profiles for Rio Blanco's surface retort have doubled since originally estimated. Finally, even if cost problems could be overcome, the company would not be able to simply convert its plans to an open-pit mine with an above-ground retort. The lease of 5120 acres is set by law and is too small to allow mining, retorting, and the disposal of waste in the same space. An act of Congress would be needed to allow the company to expand the site and obtain an adequate disposal area. Until Congress acts, and until further cost and technical problems can be solved, little will happen on tract C-a.

The story is the same elsewhere. At Cathedral Bluffs, after drilling through a thousand feet of overburden to reach its shale seams, Occidental and Tenneco have bottomed out the three shafts of what will be one of the largest underground mines in the world. The service shaft, thirty-four feet in diameter, already is the largest shaft in North America and only six inches short of being the widest mine shaft on earth. Costs already have been enormous. But the Oxy process that now will be established here — modified in situ mining and surface retorting — has already been widely questioned by critics. And in December 1981, announcing that its operation was "not deemed feasible at current construction costs, oil prices, and interest rates," Occidental and Tenneco halted development work on the Cathedral Bluffs Project.

The point is that the whole industry is still plagued by mammoth uncertainties. A single, commercial-sized retorting plant would be between ten and fifty times larger than any of the experimental facilities; to commit to this, to the full-scale commercialization of shale on the basis of such tenuous technology and limitless uncertainties, is almost incredibly illogical. To expose a state, a people, to its consequences is almost incredibly irresponsible.

Colorado can survive, too, only if it receives guarantees — from oil companies and federal government alike — that they will make commitments to the state, that they will maintain them, once made, and that they will not "cut and run" as exploiters have done so often in the past.

The oil companies must become accountable. Ironically, while many companies have demanded massive federal subsidies (through the SFC) before they commit themselves to further shale development, at the same time they have largely refused to make the same kind of advance commitment to the communities they will affect. This must change. The people of the West should not be forced to bear risks and costs that the companies refuse to bear themselves.

The role and purpose of the federal government in shale oil development also must be clarified. In Colorado, one of the greatest fears of all is that the government might one day withdraw its support of projects already begun. If this were to happen, projects in place would be terminated, plants would close, companies would pull out — and badlands towns that never invited the industry in the first place would be left with its shattered remains. Overbuilt, overindebted, overpopulated, and underfunded, they would be left to recover the best they could. Under current development plans, no one in the West is as vulnerable to ruin as the shale oil towns. Literally, they live at the mercy of the developers who have overrun them and the federal government that supports them. They cannot live this way, and they cannot be expected to.

It is difficult to know what direction government will take. But it seems clear, so far, that it intends to support the industry. Caught in a massive crossfire between opponents and supporters of federally subsidized shale oil development, the Reagan administration seemingly has cast its lot with shale oil. Despite rhetoric to the contrary and a massive intracabinet dispute, President Reagan personally authorized the first three federal assistance packages made available through the Carter synfuels proposal. Two of the three awards were targeted in Colorado. In July 1981 Union received its long-sought purchase commitment, and the next month TOSCO literally was kept alive by a loan guarantee.

Despite this, however, the future of shale oil in Colorado remains clouded. The SFC has yet to dedicate more than $12 billion in federal assistance funds it controls. SFC officials have indicated their belief that oil shale is the most sensible investment of public resources, but political considerations might dictate investment in coal-based synthetics or tar sands, not in shale. Projects in Colorado could receive the bulk of the $12 billion, or they could receive nothing. Again, this scale of uncertainty, this range of impact — from none to overwhelming — makes prudent planning by state and local officials nearly impossible. In Rifle and Parachute tomorrow could bring several manageable projects, or it could bring a complete overload, and there is no way to prepare for either.

The future of shale is further clouded by what might occur when federal subsidies are ended. President Reagan, in reluctantly initiating the Carter program, has indicated that the additional $68 billion in aid, referenced in the Energy Security Act, will not be allocated. Whether the companies will be willing to risk their own capital after public assistance has vanished will ultimately determine the size and nature of the shale industry in Colorado and Utah. While others talk of slower growth, Exxon and Chevron predict massive shale development even in the absence of federal assistance. But this is not to say the federal government will neither control nor ensure development. With 80 percent of shale resources under federal ownership, bureaucratic decisions in Washington will continue to frame the future of the West.

Nothing will work, finally, until the government respects the states and their people enough to work side by side with them. The key to the future, with shale oil or any energy, is partnership. No one knows the land and its capacity better than westerners; in the case of oil shale, no people knows their country better than Coloradans. For that reason, if none other, the state, its government, and its people must become part of the siting, pacing, and phasing processes. They must be offered the front-end financial assistance their boomtowns need. They must be consulted — and respected — in decision making. In the past, the government has not thought through the synfuels program, nor has it attempted to establish a consultative relationship with affected states. Its colonial attitude has consistently prevailed. But this, now, must change.

Above all, whatever relationship is established, whatever the future may bring, the most important factor remains — for Colorado, for the rest of the West — the preservation of its land, air, and water. The environment is the most priceless resource of all. No westerner, whether he lives on the Piceance or not, is willing to see it destroyed — ripped up, polluted, filled with waste — for no reason. And for most Coloradans the destruction of the rivers and prairies of northwest Colorado for fuel for other parts of the nation is not reason enough. Colorado is not willing, today or ever, to become a sacrifice area. It will not be left a moonscape.

If a partnership is formed, if development is phased and gradual, if the social, economic, and environmental integrity of the people is not violated, Colorado will survive shale oil. If the imperial spirit prevails, it will not. In any case, it cannot hesitate to act in its own interests. It must be bold and aggressive in defense of its rights.

The future is coming at Colorado faster than it knows. When it arrives it must be ready.

*   *   *

On a summer day, wind whips across the Piceance Basin, filling the sky with a dusty mist, and wildflowers dance on the prairie floor. A farmhouse sits against a mesa wall, its skin peeling in the sun, framed by cottonwoods that rooted here before man. Alfalfa fields ripple for miles, purple-green and lush, and the fragrance of new-mown hay hangs in the air like a rare perfume. The land, the sky, the streams are life, are home.

And beneath them all lies the rock that burns.

CHAPTER THREE

Thunder in the Earth

What do you mean disturbance of the land? . . . What difference does it make
if there are piles of dirt? Geologically speaking, it's insignificant. Nature itself
is disrupting more land with earthquakes, volcanoes and floods.
                    PRESIDENT, KEMMERER COAL COMPANY
                    Kemmerer, Wyoming

THE WYOMING PRAIRIE is stark and flat north of Gillette, its
level symmetry broken only by cactus-covered hills that swell softly
around it. In the early spring the land is cold and nearly still. Mag-
pies chatter and dance in willow thickets and jack rabbits skitter
through piñon groves, but the earth itself is frozen, soundless and
motionless, waiting for the sun. To the west, the distant Big Horns
poke against the blueness of the sky, and to the north, east, and south
the horizons fill with harsh, relentless brown. The land is empty,
bleak, silent, but it is changing. It is energy country.

*   *   *

Coal is as old as the West. It was found in Nevada in 1860, near
Tuscarora and Argenta, in El Dorado Canyon, and along the lines
of the Nevada and Oregon and Oregon Central railroads. Wagon
mines were part of Utah's economy as early as the 1880s, and by the
1890s a long string of coal towns stretched from Scofield, near Salt
Lake, all the way to the Green River. In Wyoming it first was found
near Evanston in the summer of 1868, and by the late 1880s more than
a thousand men mined it, mostly for the Union Pacific along the
state's long southern edge. Northwest of Evanston, in the rugged
Bear Lake country of Idaho, coal mines dated from the 1870s. Dig-
gings on the Rocky Fork and Timberline rivers in Park County,

Montana, produced a thousand tons a day by the 1880s, and a decade later, Park, Chouteau, Beaverhead, and Gallatin counties — all of them in Montana's sweeping southwest quadrant — were producing 118,000 tons of coal a year. Colorado's first mines were dug in 1864, only a few years after the great gold rush, and within twenty years high-yield mines lay scattered all over the state. The best were dug on the southern plains, in Huerfano and Las Animas counties, around Trinidad. Others were scooped out of Jefferson, Weld, and Boulder counties, near Denver, and still more in the state's hilly midsection. As early as 1884, Colorado's coal mines covered 1500 square miles of land, and by 1890, they were producing 3 million tons of fuel a year.

For years coal prospered in America, and the West's coal empire prospered with it. Not until the 1920s did it end. Oil, cheap and clean-burning, became America's new glamour fuel. King coal died. For the next fifty years, all over the West, coal towns slipped into oblivion. For a moment, looking across the Colorado plains, or the windswept wastes of eastern Utah, or Wyoming's southern tier, it was almost as though the empire had never been at all.

But now this is changing. Coal is returning to prominence again.

The Arab oil embargo of the 1970s may have been a major turning point in coal's history. Before the embargo, the world ran on Arab oil. But after it, for the first time in half a century, much of the world began to move toward coal. Now, as the world approaches the 1990s, as oil becomes costlier (except during times of glut) and as its producing states become more volatile, coal, not oil, could become the international fuel of the future. Its cost is relatively low, and with the exception of China and Poland, it is produced in world regions with histories of relative political and economic stability. Because of this, it has become inevitable that many world nations will begin to divorce themselves from Middle Eastern oil; countries that relied on Middle Eastern crude yesterday will rely on coal from the western world tomorrow. Japan is a case in point. In the past, it imported massive amounts of Arab oil to fuel one of the most high-powered economies in the world. But now, increasingly motivated by unrest in the Islamic crescent, it has begun to explore alternatives — one of them western coal. In the future, Japan will shift its energy emphasis, and when it does it will set an international pattern that other nations certainly will follow.

As one of the world's major coal producers, the United States will be a major beneficiary of the new thrust. In 1979 the nation exported 65 million short tons of coal, a figure that could double or triple in the immediate future. In the spring of 1981 it was already supplying approximately 25 percent of the world's energy needs, mining 830 million tons of coal in 1980 alone, 90 million of them for export — a 39 percent increase over 1979. By the end of the century it could be producing more than 2 billion tons of coal a year, as much as 255 million tons of it for export (some 40 percent of the world demand). A 1980 MIT study concluded that American coal will have to supply between one half and two thirds of the world's energy materials during the next two decades.

Internal forces, too, will create massive demands for coal. Three of them — the continued construction of coal-fired electrical generating plants, the conversion of industrial plants to coal from oil, and the development of coal synfuels — may create demands, in fact, that no one today can fully comprehend.

If coal is reborn, then, what of the West?

Because of coal's abundance, the impact of its mining on western America will be deep and lasting. The West is as coal-rich as any region on earth. In 1979 alone the West produced 26 percent of America's coal. By 1990, increasing its 1979 production by 150 percent, it could be the leading coal-producing region in the nation. Forty-four percent of America's recoverable coal reserves underlie the West, including 54 percent of its bituminous reserves, 87 percent of its lignite reserves, and 100 percent of its subbituminous reserves. Fourteen mammoth coal basins stretch across the West from central North Dakota to northeastern Arizona. Most of the Dakotas, eastern Montana, and northeastern Wyoming lie in the massive Powder River and Fort Union basins; the coal fields of western Montana, Colorado, Utah, New Mexico, Arizona, and western and southeastern Wyoming lie in the Green River, Uinta, San Juan, Wind River, Bighorn, Yellowstone, Southeastern Utah, and Hams Fork basins. Coal deposits range from the almost limitless in Montana to the negligible in Idaho.

Through the years the northern Great Plains have been among the most vital coal regions in the world. According to 1979 Department of Energy calculations, Montana alone contains more than 120 billion tons of demonstrated coal reserves. Except for a small sliver at the southeastern tip of the state, eastern Montana is blanketed by coal fields from Wyoming to Canada, arching as far west as the

Bighorn River, and connecting to the fields of western North and South Dakota in the east. To the east, nearly 10 billion tons of demonstrated coal reserves underlie western North Dakota.

The Rocky Mountain Province, a six-state corridor running down the spine of the Rockies from Alberta to the Four Corners convergence of Utah, Arizona, Colorado, and New Mexico, contains most of the coal in the West. Western Montana forms its northern tier, a huge arc from Great Falls to the Canadian border, and the southern tier spreads from the rich San Juan Basin of New Mexico westward to the Navajo country of northeastern Arizona.

Historically, the heart of the West's coal empire has been Routt and Moffat counties in Colorado, and Carbon, Lincoln, and Sweetwater counties in Wyoming. Today the heart is Campbell County, Wyoming, where most coal can be surface mined more cost-efficiently than in underground mines elsewhere. Wyoming's Campbell County fields in the northeast, its Bighorn reserves near Buffalo, its Wind River and Yellowstone reserves in the northwest, and the Green River–Hams Fork basins in the southwest contain an estimated 23 billion tons of recoverable coal from a demonstrated reserve of 70 billion. To the southwest, Utah's rich Uinta-Southeastern basins hold 6.5 billion tons in demonstrated reserves. In Colorado nearly 16.3 billion tons of coal underlie 28 percent of the state's land, from Moffat County in the north to Las Animas County on the New Mexico border.

The net figures are staggering. The West contains over 200 billion tons of the nation's demonstrated reserves. Little wonder, then, that it stands to become a hunting ground.

Abundance is not the only factor that will affect the West's coal industry. Part of the importance of western coal lies in its content. The West's almost limitless reserves of low-sulfur coal become more attractive by the year to eastern industries prevented by environmental laws from using high-sulfur eastern coal. A second factor is the proximity of coal to emerging synfuels projects and electric power combines in the West itself. In the past, most of the West's coal has been exported to other states for the fueling of their industries. As late as 1979, for example, Colorado exported nearly 7 million tons of coal to thirteen states — as far distant as California and Mississippi — for use in industries, steel mills, and power-generating complexes. Increasingly, however, coal is being dug and burned at home. In Colorado today, the giant Colorado-Ute Electric Association has built huge coal-fired power-generating plants up and down the Western Slope. Its Hayden plant (units one and two) consumed more than 1.4 million tons of coal in 1980. Its Craig complex (units one and two) consumed more than 1.7 million tons during the same year. In Colorado, Utah, Wyoming, and Montana, a score of similar projects are planned for the future. Together, through the years, they could consume billions of tons.

In assessing the future of coal, the biggest variable is synfuels. The amount of synthetic fuels development carried out in the West will at least partly determine the amount of pressure placed on its coal supplies. According to one scenario, for example, 23 million tons of coal could be needed to produce the projected requirement of 4500 megawatts of electricity for shale oil production in northwestern Colorado by the year 2005. The concurrent development of shale oil and coal synfuels could boost the tonnage to a stunning 43 million for the projected requirement of 4800 megawatts.

The development of synthetic fuels from coal itself is more uncertain, but if — or whenever — development finally occurs, huge amounts of coal will be consumed in the process. Consensus is that a single coal synfuels plant will devour 14 million tons of coal a year (when the largest coal mine in America today, the Belle Ayr near Gillette, Wyoming, produces only 18 million tons a year) and that, in time, the new industry will eat up 600 square miles of coal lands, mostly in the West. Exxon has estimated that, in time, 400 billion barrels of oil can be extracted from western coal, as much as 3 million barrels a day from the Powder River Basin of Montana and Wyoming and 1.1 million more from the coalfields of western Montana, the Dakotas, and the southern Rockies. The development of coal fuels is not imminent, but prototype plants are being blueprinted in Colorado, Montana, Utah, Wyoming, and the Dakotas. When and if their day comes, they will place perhaps an unbearable pressure on western coal.

The coal hunt will bring benefits to the West, but it also rekindles old fears of colonialism. No industry in the West has a more violent and exploitative history than coal, and no reason exists to think that what has happened before will not happen again.

The West's first coal barons were railroad kings. In the early years of the industry their railroads straddled the West from southern Colorado to eastern Montana, and everywhere they ran they dominated. The Union Pacific virtually owned Wyoming, holding long stretches of prime coal land all along its southern tier and dominating the region's cities and people for three generations. Its history was riddled with land fraud, labor wars, and economic profit; through land fraud it gained much of its empire and through the exploitation of labor it wrung a profit from it. No other company, not even the state itself, ever successfully challenged UP power. For as long as Wyoming has had a government, the Union Pacific has influenced it, restricting railroad legislation, blunting labor probes, skirting environmental challenges. As one critic has written, Wyoming's legislators for years wore the "brass collar" of the UP. In fact the entire state did. Aside from Anaconda's Montana fiefdom, the Union Pacific's vast southern empire — the blistering desolation of Uinta, Carbon, and Sweetwater counties — is as good an example of economic imperialism as ever existed in the West.

Railroads also run through Montana's colonial history: what the Union Pacific was to Wyoming the Northern Pacific was to Montana. In the 1920s, the Northern Pacific burrowed into the vast, coal-rich Colstrip fields in the rolling hill country near Billings. Within thirty years, the 25-foot-thick Rosebud Seam became one of the most prolific coal beds in the world. In 1959, leasing rights were transferred to Montana Power, after Anaconda the most powerful combine in Montana's history. For years Colstrip coal poured into Montana Power's Billings generating complex, and during the same years, from the same area, Kennecott's Peabody Coal supplied utilities as far away as Minnesota. Today, with 120 billion tons of mineable coal left, Montana remains an inviting colonial target.

Colorado coal, too, belonged to railroads and their subsidiaries — the Union Pacific, Santa Fe, Burlington, and dozens of others. But primarily, it belonged to the Rockefellers. John D. Rockefeller, Jr.'s massive Colorado Coal and Iron Corporation (later the Colorado Fuel and Iron Company) was a legend in western economic history even in its own time. Its exploitative relationship with the coal camps and coal miners of southern Colorado is classic colonial history, and one of the bloody events surrounding it remains one of the most memorable in the West's long and violent life.

On a cold April day in 1914, eighteen people died at Ludlow, a gritty coal camp north of Trinidad. Some were coal miners striking against Colorado Coal and Iron. Others were women and children. Protesting low wages and brutal living conditions, the corporation's miners walked out of its southern Colorado mines in the fall of 1913.

The Rockefellers met the challenge, absorbing the Colorado state militia sent to keep peace, locking strikers out, and importing scabs to work through the winter. On the morning of April 20, 1914, as the sun broke over the low hilltops around Ludlow, militia machine-gunners opened fire on the sleeping camp, triggering a running gunfight that raged for fourteen hours. By nightfall the battle was over. Five strikers lay dead; the rest fled to the hills with their families while Ludlow burned to the ground. The next morning, probing the smoking rubble, miners found two women and eleven children suffocated in tunnels that honeycombed the Ludlow ground. They had sought warmth from winter cold, but instead they had found death.

Coal strikes rocked the West almost yearly in the period before and after the turn of the century, but there was only one Ludlow. Its "massacre" became — and remains — one of the darkest chapters in the colonial history of the West. Colorado has not forgotten:

> *John D., he was a Christian,*
> *John D., the psalms he sung;*
> *But he'd no mercy in his heart,*
> *He shot down old and young.*
> *One night when all were sleeping,*
> *All wrapped up in their dreams,*
> *We heard a loud explosion,*
> *We heard most terrible screams.*
> *'Oh save us from the burning flames,'*
> *We heard our children cry;*
> *But John D. laughed and shot them down*
> *Right before our eyes.*

In a variety of ways, colonialism has left an ugly legacy in the West. For one thing, from Anaconda to the Union Pacific, absentee ownership has consistently ignored the integrity of western land. Wherever it has existed, the colonial presence has left the landscape in chaos. Coal is a case in point. Of all the extractive industries, none has annihilated the earth like coal mining.

From an environmental viewpoint, one of the great tragedies of the West is the fact that most of its coal is strippable. Only two states — Colorado and Utah — have substantial underground operations. The rest is surface. In Montana, Wyoming, and North Dakota, surface mining has been carried out for fifty years, and in Colorado, New Mexico, and South Dakota for nearly that long.

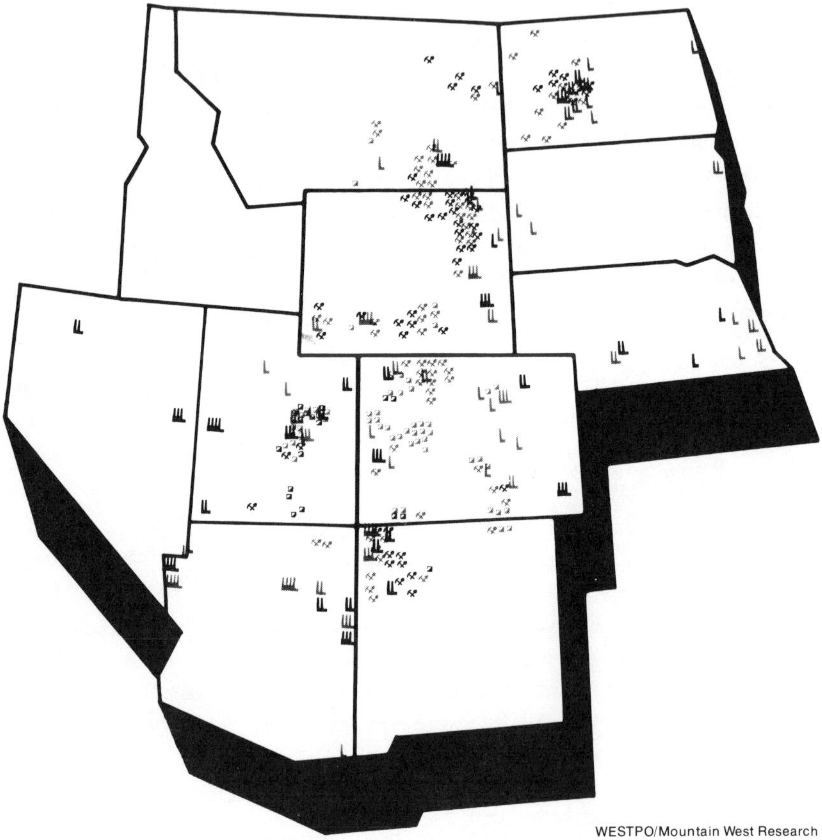

WESTPO/Mountain West Research

COAL ACTIVITY

EXISTING		PROPOSED
	Surface Mines	
	Underground Mines	
	Coal-Fired Power Plants	
	0-399MW	
	400-799MW	
	800-1499MW	
	1500MW and above	

The destruction of the land in the process of stripping almost defies description. At Hayden, on the lip of the Colorado badlands, the state's biggest dragline snakes across the prairie, dragging in scoops of earth the size of four automobiles. Near Gillette, huge electric diggers operate on staggered circular levels of land, gutting the earth around them. On Sarpy Creek, Rosebud County, Montana, a digger the size of a two-story building sits on the rim of a broad, mud-filled crater. For days, months, its huge dragline rips earth out of the crater and dumps it in towering heaps that spill into pine groves. Over the years the crater grows, spreads slowly over the low pine-studded flatlands, circles the wheat fields, eats up pasture. Finally, from afar, it sits like a large tannish scar on the earth's surface, destroying the beauty of everything around it. This is Montana, but it could be Colorado, Wyoming, anywhere in the West.

The stripping of the West may be the wave of the future. In 1980, the region produced 187.6 million tons of coal, about 89 percent of it from surface mines. And four huge mines, each producing more than 10 million tons, accounted for 30 percent of that. By 1985, if recent trends hold, it is projected that the West will have the capacity to produce nearly 380 million tons of coal a year, 86 percent of which could come from surface mines. And 32 percent of that surface mine production is expected to come from a bare handful of high-capacity mines in the heart of the West's coal country.

Sadly, stripping will only continue to put pressure on the environment. There is a great and wild beauty here in the sun-cracked earth, in the oceans of sage, in the rolling grasslands, a beauty that outsiders find difficult to see. But in time, unless the West requires the industry to follow strict reclamation and revegetation practices, stripping will destroy it. And under *any* circumstances, it will never be again, tomorrow, what it was yesterday.

The air, the western sky, is also in danger.

Standing on a hillock by the Snake, walking through a pine grove in Yellowstone, it is difficult to describe the feeling of mountain air. Even on the desert, even on a summer day, it is fresh and light, filled with the scent of sage. In 1858, William Gilpin, Colorado's first territorial governor, wrote lyrically of the "ethereal canopy, intensely blue, effulgent with the unclouded sun by day and stars by night" that blanketed the Great West from mountain range to mountain range. As long as there has been a West, the purity and clarity of its air, its skies, has been part of its life. But now Gilpin's "canopy," like the land beneath it, is under assault. If shale oil is a menace to the Big Sky, coal is a bigger danger by far.

The danger, specifically, is the massive power complexes that have sprouted all over the West in recent years. Because they burn coal, and because coal burns "dirty," filling the atmosphere with sulfur dioxides, nitrogen oxides, particulate matter, and other pollutants, they have polluted the skies with filth for hundreds of miles around them. Some plants have made an effort to adapt to federal clean-air standards, but others have not. In any case, in recent years the power combines have collided with those standards all over the West, and the future suggests the struggle will go on.

The western air wars first were touched off in the mid-1970s by the proposed Kaiparowits power project on the desert of south-central Utah. Between Kanab and Escalante, in the center of the rambling Kaiparowits Plateau, a consortium of power companies planned a 3000-megawatt coal-fired power plant that would have been the biggest in the West. Hoping to utilize the efficiency of mine-mouth technology — digging on one lot, burning on the next — they proposed a single giant complex, mine side by side with power plant. Although many local people favored the project, mainly because of the region's chronically depressed economy, environmentalists fought and helped kill it. Their reason was significant both then and now; their main fear, even beyond the disruption of the land itself, was the fouling of the air over some of the most majestic desert scenery in the world. Even so, it may be that the war has just begun. Since the death of Kaiparowits, a second plan has surfaced calling for the mining of up to 100 million tons of coal from the same region (the largest single undeveloped deposit in the United States). And, at the same time, Utah Resources International has proposed a $2 billion coal-liquefaction plant in the same area, a project that would fill the skies with more poison than the power complex would have.

Southwestern Utah has become a battleground between coal developers and power combines on one hand and environmentalists on the other. Much is at stake for both. Perhaps nowhere in the West does so much developable coal land sit adjacent to such exquisite natural beauty. An area bristling with both in-place and proposed power projects also contains wide expanses of some of the rawest, most fragile desert wilderness in the world. Within a 250-mile radius of Kaiparowits lie eight national parks, twenty-six national monuments, three national recreation areas, two historical sites, and one national memorial. And although most are protected by Class I status under the Clean Air Act amendments of 1977, all of them still are under siege.

The Kaiparowits plant directly threatened Bryce Canyon and Zion national parks and Cedar Breaks and Rainbow Bridge national monuments. But no sooner was Kaiparowits scrapped than the same area became threatened by a new development — the projected Allen-Warner Energy System, anchored in the southwest corner of Utah. As originally planned, the project included two coal-fired power plants, a 2000-megawatt unit near Las Vegas, and a 500-megawatt complex at Saint George, Utah. Both were to be fueled by 11 million tons of coal a year strip-mined from a 30-year, 25-mile, 8300-acre swatch in the nearby Alton Hills. Enraged environmentalists charged that the strip mine, which would lie 4 miles from Yovimpa Point in Bryce Canyon, would be in full view of 400,000 tourists a year. But their primary point was that the proposed Allen-Warner Valley power plant, 17 miles from the great coral walls of Zion, would discharge 3000 tons of sulfur dioxide and over 500 tons of particulates into the park's pristine air shed each year. For the moment, however, the project is dead. The Environmental Protection Agency has refused to issue it a permit. In December 1980 the Department of the Interior also denied a mining permit on grounds — as Secretary of the Interior Cecil Andrus said — that air-quality degradation in the desert country would be "unconscionable." In September 1981 Andrus's successor, James Watt, announced that he would seek to review the decision. Perhaps the project will be reborn. Perhaps not. But whatever happens to it, it vividly illustrates not only the plight of Bryce and Zion, but of all the other natural treasures in the region as well.

In the future, however, nothing will affect southern Utah as much as the mammoth 3000-megawatt Intermountain Power Project near Delta. The $8 billion project, now launched, is the largest coal-fired plant in the United States, consuming the equivalent of Utah's entire coal production each year. To date, environmentalists have not attacked it. But this does not mean they accept it. And it does not mean they do not fear for the future.

To the south, in Arizona and New Mexico, most of the region's natural wonders are also confronted by power projects. The Grand Canyon is bracketed on the south by the Mojave complex near Kingman and on the north by the Navajo. The beautiful Rainbow

Bridge and Navajo national monuments are pinched between the
Navajo project to the west and the enormous San Juan and Four
Corners plants to the east in northern New Mexico. Nearby, Chaco
Canyon National Monument, with Indian ruins unsurpassed in
America, slowly is being strangled by coal and uranium develop-
ments that have encircled it.

In the Four Corners area of Utah and Colorado the situation is
worse (although the National Commission on Air Quality recently
said that electrical generating capacity here can triple before existing
air-quality standards are violated). The San Juan and Four Corners
plants daily spew pollutants into the air that drift as far west as the
Natural Bridges National Monument in Utah, as far north as
Colorado's Mesa Verde National Park, and as far east as the Great
Sand Dunes. No plant in the West has been more potentially destructive than the 2200-megawatt Four Corners complex. Burning thousands of tons of coal a day from the nearby Navajo strip mine, at one
time the biggest producing mine in the United States, and operating
without even minimum pollution-control equipment, the Four Corners plant sends a smoky plume spiraling high enough into the
atmosphere to have been visible to the Gemini astronauts orbiting
the Earth.

East-central Utah and northwest Colorado face the same problems, and since the region also embraces shale oil country the problems are likely to become compounded in the future. Central and
southwest Utah are blanketed by more current and proposed power
projects than any area in the West, and in terms of air quality, the
Wasatch Valley already is the thirteenth worst metropolitan area in
America. Partly responsible for the condition is U.S. Steel's Geneva
Works at Provo. And partly at fault is Utah Power and Light's
Hunter plant that fouls the air as far west and south as Capitol Reef,
the Arches, and Canyonlands national parks. Time has changed
much. Centuries ago the Anasazi walked this land. Utes camped by
the thundering Green and Mormons and outlaws sparred for power
from Moab to Vernal. Today haze hangs lightly over the purple
gorges of Canyonlands, over the mauve expanse of the Colorado
Plateau, over a thousand years of history.

Twenty years ago no cleaner air existed anywhere in the West than
across the jagged expanse of Rocky Mountain National Park in
northern Colorado. Twenty years ago, from the trail heads at Bear
Lake — from the lacy, serrated slopes of Thatchtop to the glassy

walls of Pagoda and Longs Peak — every crack, every angle, every shadow stood out in clear relief. One of the most photographed scenes in America was Hallett's Peak as it loomed over the lake, with snowfields in its folds and blue sky at its back. Today air quality is deficient in fifteen western national parks — more than seventy-five major scenic vistas have become partly or completely obscured by periodic haze — and few of them have been more greatly affected than Rocky Mountain. Yesterday the air was pure at Glacier Gorge. Today, when atmospheric conditions are right, a pall hangs over the valley, over one of the most beautiful glacial basins in the world. Tourists still photograph Hallett's, but the steely blue has turned to brown-gray.

Probably never again will the parks and forests be immune from the incursions of coal. It is progress, perhaps, but it also is tragedy. In 1979 western photographer Ansel Adams recalled his early years in Yellowstone and the Tetons and the badlands of Utah. Once, he said, the air was "amazingly clear." Returning years later, however, he found changes. "I was simply appalled at the terrific volume of smoke coming out of the stacks of power plants," he said. "The sky was not as blue as I remember it. The haze was there. The clear vistas were no longer clear."

Decreasing visibility in western skies is only part of the pollution problem. Far more serious is the effect that coal-burned pollutants might have on human health. The conversion of coal into synthetic fuel, for example, releases a wide variety of virulent contaminants into the air. The National Commission on Air Quality has determined that more than 2 trillion cubic feet of gasified coal or 600,000 barrels of synthetic liquid can be produced each day without violating federal clean-air standards, but virtually every scientific study conducted so far on coal synfuels has indicated the presence of carcinogens in its emissions (partly because few legal or technical controls exist on carcinogenic emissions). It may be, in fact, as Colorado Senator William Armstrong has said, that coal synfuels produce chemical waste "nearly as dangerous as nuclear waste," and that much of it finds its way into the atmosphere.

Another menace is acid rain deposition. Although its formative process is not completely understood, acid rain appears to be created by the mingling of gaseous sulfur and nitrogen oxides with atmospheric water. Pollutants transformed into weak solutions of sulfuric and nitric acid then return to earth — perhaps far from the original point of pollution — as poison dust or snow or "acid rain." Wherever it falls, its effect is negative. Timber yield can be stunted, agricultural productivity decreased, lakes sterilized, their fish and plant life destroyed in acidic, vinegarlike water. Significantly, traces of acid rain have even been found in the Rockies. In Colorado, for example, it was first reported in 1979, in the Indian Peaks area west of Boulder, and since that time evidence of it has appeared at monitoring stations along the Front Range and in parts of the Western Slope. Today it presents no threat to the region; no conclusive proof exists that it poses a threat to human life at all. But there is always tomorrow.

Uncertainties still exist about acid rain, what it is, and how it can be controlled. But scientists do know that the oxides are combustion by-products produced primarily by auto emissions, smelters, and coal-fired power plants. In this light, the future is not promising. The level of auto emissions seems destined to stay relatively high in Denver, Albuquerque, Salt Lake City, and other growing urban areas. The West's fourteen smelters seem destined to maintain operation at current levels. And without doubt coal will continue to be burned in western power plants. "Acid rain sounds like a science-fiction nightmare," says Colorado Senator Gary Hart, but the worst may lie ahead.

As long ago as 1978 primary clean-air standards were exceeded in many areas across the upper Rockies and Great Plains — most of them, according to the EPA, heavy coal suppliers or burners, or both. Given western power production projections, little reason exists to think the situation will soon improve. According to a 1981 study prepared by and for a group of Colorado and Utah power companies, the generation of electricity in western Colorado alone will increase by 2500 megawatts by 1992, and by 5700 megawatts in Utah. Much of Colorado's new generation will come from Colorado-Ute's Craig Station (where unit number three, now under construction, will add 400 megawatts to the plant's existing capacity) and from a new 400-megawatt facility planned near Delta or Mack. In Utah, where the state has projected the building of eight new power plants between 1975 and 1985, and the mining of 35 million tons of coal a year to fire them, the Deseret Generation and Transmission Cooperative, Utah Power and Light Company, and the Intermountain Power Project expect to be generating an additional 4720 megawatts by 1992.

Most other western states have made similar projections. If even part of them come to be, pollution will continue to be a fact — a negative fact — of western life.

Despite this, the coal industry has consistently criticized the Federal Clean Air Act. In March 1981 Ralph E. Bailey, chairman of Conoco, said that it is "all but certain that the present act will have a substantial adverse impact" on energy projects — primarily coal — over the next two decades. It has been heard before, and it will be again. In the meantime, westerners can only hope the sentiment expressed by Conoco will not become pervasive. Ninety years ago historian Hubert Howe Bancroft, standing on the rim of a Utah canyon, wrote of its air, "exceedingly pure and transparent" along the blue walls of the Wasatch. In Colorado he spoke of the "tonic properties of the atmosphere" and the "healthful and bracing exhilaration" of the air. "In the blue dome of the sky," he said, "there is not cloud to stain its purity."

Now the dome is not so blue. And the purity is gone forever.

As it is with oil shale, another pressure point with the coal industry is water. It is a harsh fact that western coal country also is arid country — overall, perhaps, the driest region in the Rocky Mountain West. For that reason, any part of the coal industry that involves water — chiefly power production and synfuels — is potentially dangerous. Power plants, again, are significant. Depending upon its type, a typical coal-fired plant uses from 24,000 to 30,000 acre feet of water a year for every 3000 megawatts of power generated. And the commercial production of synthetic fuels from coal will require perhaps even more. Experts calculate that every ton of coal converted to gas or liquid will require several gallons of water in the process. The daily production of 250,000 cubic feet of gas from coal could require from 5000 to 9000 acre feet a year in processing and cooking; liquefaction could consume up to 12,000 acre feet a year for a 100,000-barrel-per-day plant. According to the Department of Energy, a small, indirect coal-liquefaction plant producing 50,000 barrels of oil a day would need 11,000 to 12,000 acre feet of water each year to operate — nearly 4 billion gallons. A larger, high Btu coal-gasification plant would need 20,000 acre feet a year. Opponents of Hampshire Energy Company's proposed synfuels plant near Gillette, Wyoming, claim — using the state engineer's figures — that the plant would use up to 5.5 million gallons a day, or twice as much as the city of Gillette itself.

Today, again, the large-scale commercial development of coal synfuels is not imminent. It lies largely in the future. Yet, as with oil shale, the future may not be far distant, and when it arrives, when development does take place, the question of water and coal synfuels will be a major one. The hottest spots in the West may be the western Dakotas and along Wyoming's Powder River, where water is scarce — and overappropriated — and where farmers and ranchers have a long tradition of militance.

Already, in fact, the militants are in the field. The issue, however, is not synfuels. It is coal slurry.

In recent years one of the biggest problems of western coal producers has been how to ship huge amounts of raw coal to distant power plants while holding down its cost. For as long as the West has mined coal, its transportation out has been by rail. Increasingly, however, consumer states have charged that high shipping rates are passed through to consumers in the form of high power rates. Seeking an alternative to railroads, they have come to advocate coal slurry as a method of transportation. The process itself is fairly uncomplicated: coal is granulated to the consistency of sugar at the mine mouth and mixed with equal parts water (by weight), and pumped through pipelines to its destination. What are not uncomplicated, however, are the economic implications of the process. Two problems exist. One, the question of eminent domain, is real. The other — water — is perhaps more perceived than real. In any case, many westerners see the coal slurry idea as yet another raid by outsiders on both their resources and their rights.

In Wyoming, South Dakota, and Nebraska the key issue is water. In 1979 San Francisco–based Energy Transportation Systems, Incorporated (ETSI), proposed a 1378-mile slurry pipeline from the Powder River Basin fields near Gillette, Wyoming, to power plants in Oklahoma, Arkansas, and Louisiana. Water — 20,000 acre feet a year — was to come from the Madison Aquifer, which underlies the entire upper plains. The proposal touched off a storm of protest. Environmentalists charged that the land would be damaged. Railroads charged that their industry would be ruined. But the biggest and most emotional protest was from the region's farmers and ranchers, and the issue was water. Powder River country is near-desert. The land is plate flat, disturbed only by lumpy sand hills to the northeast and southeast. Only one river, the placid Belle Fourche, flows through. Further east, where Devils Tower sits and the Black Hills wash across the Wyoming line, there is more water, but not much. With little rainfall and little more snowmelt, the country around Gillette has never had much water for itself. Other than the Madison. Little wonder that the ETSI proposal drew such anger.

From the beginning, the pipeline's opponents charged that Wyoming, South Dakota, and Nebraska could not afford the loss of water. A draft BLM environmental impact statement concluded that the Madison eventually might be drawn down 100 feet over a 3400–square mile area in the three states. Another draft environmental evaluation concluded that the drawdown might range to 250 feet over the fifty-year life of the pipeline, and other estimates ranged from 400 feet, by a Lusk civil engineer, to 1000 feet by a University of Wyoming geologist. To those who lived in the region, the implications were enormous.

Armed with a wide variety of figures, none of them necessarily reliable, but all of them alarming, pipeline opponents attacked ETSI throughout late 1980 and virtually all of 1981. From Belle Fourche to Newcastle, Citizens Against Slurry Export (CASE) marched with placards that read, "Without Water My Children Have No Future." The powerful Wyoming County Commissioners Association adopted unanimous resolutions against slurry. Save Wyoming Water gathered signatures in contemplation of court action against it. The Wyoming In-Stream Flow Committee attempted to have an initiative placed on the 1982 ballot forcing coal companies using Wyoming water to recharge target aquifers with new water from outside the state. Reacting to the hypothesis that deep pumping through northeast Wyoming well fields might reduce stream flow from the Black Hills, South Dakota threatened to file suit against the project. And in Nebraska, landowners adamantly refused to sell some 275 miles of right of way, ultimately forcing ETSI away from its projected South Dakota–Nebraska–Kansas path into Colorado (if rights of way can be obtained there). Throughout, the sentiment from the plains country was simple, eloquent, and adamant. As one Nebraska rancher said, "People in this area should not be asked to sacrifice their livelihood so people in the Southeast can save a few cents on their electricity bill." But their greatest fear, wrote *Denver Post* columnist Red Fenwick in June 1981, was that loss of water primarily would lead to social disruption and "create another Appalachia with all the accompanying poverty, degradation, bankruptcy, and unconquerable despair."

Much of the problem became academic on December 23, 1981,

when South Dakota and ETSI signed a contract for the sale of Missouri River water to the pipeline company. The agreement — giving ETSI up to 16.3 billion gallons a year (50,000 acre feet), approximately 6.3 billion for slurry and 10 billion for other uses — took immediate pressure off the Madison (though ETSI retained rights to its use in times of "emergency") and promised South Dakota up to $1.4 billion over fifty years in the process (which would be used by the state to finance water development). Today, even though ETSI opponents still fear for the Madison, believing that the company can define "emergency" any way it chooses, the crisis seems to have passed. The primary worry now is that of states downstream from South Dakota on the Missouri that South Dakota has set a precedent that one day may lead to the depletion of the river's water.

What tomorrow will bring is uncertain, but the slurry wars seem likely to continue. As of late 1981, only one coal pipeline was operating in the West — the 273-mile Black Mesa pipeline from Arizona to southern Nevada — but, along with ETSI, several others were projected from Utah to Nevada and southern California, and from the Powder River Basin to Texas, Oregon, and the western shore of Lake Michigan. With all of them, controversy seems likely to continue and the major issue is likely to remain water.

In *broad* terms, perhaps it should not be. A 1981 study conducted by the University of Oklahoma Public Policy Program theorized that, because coal slurry is not "particularly water intensive," because it can utilize low-quality water (such as ground water) unfit for other purposes, the West could export 200 million tons of coal a year with only 120,000 acre feet of water. In that light, the study concluded, "there is no substantial basis for the general opposition throughout the West to slurry pipelines on the basis of water use."

On the other hand, perhaps broad generalizations and general conclusions do not apply to the issue. Coal slurry may not be water intensive in *general* and it may be able to utilize low-quality water in *general,* but in the Powder River Basin, where the war so far has centered, and where it is most likely to continue, neither is necessarily true. Here, for example, much of the water is *not* low quality; here it is usable for agricultural, industrial, and drinking purposes. And here, where the *cumulative* impact of water use is — or one day will be — great, whether or not slurry is water intensive in itself is unimportant. If slurry was water's only energy-related use in the region, it would put little pressure on local supplies. But, combined with the area's projected coal-liquefaction industry (where an average facility could consume between 9200 and 11,000 acre feet of water a year), its projected coal-gasification industry (where each plant will take from 4800 to 8700 acre feet), with whatever coal-fired power plants (if any) it might develop, and with the escalating water needs of the region's booming energy towns, slurry *does* present a threat. Nor can shale oil be forgotten: the water that Exxon has proposed to import to Colorado also will come from the Missouri.

In the future, whether slurry is a real threat is not likely to matter to High Plains ranchers and farmers. So long as even the *perception* of water loss exists — this is the West's old, unchangeable conditioning — they will fight.

Arguments against coal slurry, however, go beyond ranchers and farmers and far beyond the Madison. A larger question, and one that also figured in western opposition to the Energy Mobilization Board, is that of pre-emption of state authority by the federal government.

Right-of-way legislation for coal slurry pipelines was introduced in Congress several times during the late 1970s, and each time it came to nothing. The Coal Pipeline Act of 1979, for example, sought to give the secretary of the interior the power to grant rights of way over federal and private land in target states, but it stalled in committee and failed to reach the floor of Congress. In 1981 Representative Morris Udall of Arizona introduced a similar bill, currently pending.

The West has approached all of the right-of-way legislation with caution. Initially, what irritated it was the undercurrent of haste that sometimes surrounded the legislation, its apparent focus on the fast-track solution, its stress on the legal rather than the logical, its occasional disregard of deep and significant western concerns, its cavalier treatment of water issues. In a country conditioned by still-bitter memories of colonialism, the coal slurry thrust sometimes smacked of the EMB.

But the main worry, again, was — and remains — water. Opponents of coal slurry argue that once water is appropriated to pipelines, it is lost forever — that "locking in" water today precludes its future use for other, more necessary purposes. They also believe that states will come under increasing pressure to appropriate water whether they choose to or not, and that refusals will result in limit-less — and losing — litigation. As Wyoming Governor Ed Herschler has said, if coal slurry becomes reality, court actions will become reality with it: no state will have the power to "stem the tide" of "adverse court decisions." The loss of authority, the loss of jurisdiction over local water is one of the most terrifying thoughts in the West. And no one can say for certain that Herschler, and others like him, are not right.

The West fears, specifically, that if the federal government obtains the power of eminent domain over western land, western water rights will fall next. Although the government traditionally has administered federal law in a way that preserves state control over water distribution, and despite the fact that current legislation seems to protect western water rights, many westerners still feel that no guarantees exist for the future. As the University of Oklahoma Public Policy Program study has concluded, the issue in the West "is not just where the slurry water will come from, but who will make the decisions about the allocation of the water."

Again, what the future holds no one knows, but the problem of coal slurry is far from resolved. All that is certain is the attitude of the coal states. As Ed Herschler has said, his state is willing to "do its part" in the energy hunt, but "the people of Wyoming do not desire to be exploited nor to have their most precious resource taken from them." His state, says Herschler, will not become an "energy province." Nor, willingly, will any other.

In a way, though, it is already too late.

In the summer of 1953, on a trip through Nebraska and Wyoming, historian Bernard De Voto wrote a magazine article on the "western town." As he traveled across the plains, from Scottsbluff to Cheyenne to Boise, he was impressed by what he saw. "The western town is an attractive place," he wrote, "clean and new — too new to have slums — glistening in its high, tingling air."

He was right. It was an attractive place. Boise, sitting neatly in the cup of the Sawtooths. Cheyenne, on its windswept plains. Santa Fe, in the long, cool shadow of the Sangre de Cristos. But there was more to the West than De Voto saw, or recorded. And it was not attractive. It was coal towns.

Like Rock Springs.

The bleak Red Desert country of southwest Wyoming is some of the most foreboding land in America. The 108 miles from Rawlins west to Rock Springs is one of the longest, loneliest, and most beautiful drives in the desert Rockies — on a winter day an endless ocean of white over vast, rolling patches of red earth, on a summer afternoon a blinding copper sea under the setting sun. It is near the western edge of this desolation that Rock Springs sits, a Union Pacific coal town born a century ago. Maybe geography shaped Rock Springs, or maybe it was the "hell-on-wheels" mentality of the coal miners and railroad gangs that gave the city birth. From the start it was ugly, brawling, and mean — and it grew up exactly the way it was born. In the early 1960s, even after a hundred years of life, Rock Springs remained what it had always been — Appalachia in the desert, its grimy, run-down business block pierced by a string of shabby motels, its small frame homes sitting stolidly in the shadow of Pilot Butte, slowly wilting in the desert heat.

Then, in the 1970s, Rock Springs exploded, catalyzed by the mammoth Jim Bridger Power Plant that brought hordes of people into a city totally unequipped to handle them. In the older part of Rock Springs, shacks multiplied on rutted streets and on the outskirts gleaming waves of mobile homes sprawled back toward the hills. Schools became overcrowded. Divorce, alcoholism, abandonment, suicide, child abuse increased — and at the same time services to deal with them virtually ceased to exist. Vice flourished; out of the gaudy bars, out of the littered back alleys, off the grimy main street, prostitution and drug abuse became Sweetwater County institutions. Crime became a way of life, sustained by political corruption and governmental inertia. It is better now. A reform mayor and no-nonsense police chief have made it so. But in many ways it still has not changed at all over the past years, not the gray faces of run-down buildings, not the filth that scatters through the city on desert winds, not the hell-on-wheels mentality of the people. In many ways it still remains what it has always been, a community that is not a community — 26,000 people, many of them transients living there only until they can leave.

Rock Springs is a classic case of what happens to a western community caught in the wash of a mineral boom. In the 1960s, at least, the town had a kind of seedy charm in its Saturday night raucousness, its dingy diners, the spartan rooms at the White Mountain Lodge. Now the charm is gone, often replaced by meanness. And that, precisely, is the tragedy.

To the southeast, across 200 miles of buttes and desert in northwest Colorado, there is a touch of Rock Springs in Hayden and Craig. Both lie in the valley of the Yampa where Fortification Creek and other streams slice out of the Elkhead Mountains to meet it.

Except for the rich Yampa Valley, the country is bleached and arid, miles of flatlands running east and west, flanked by low, sage-covered hills on the north and the White River Plateau to the south. Once this was cattle country, outlaw country. Now it belongs to coal. Unlike Sweetwater to the north, Routt and Moffat counties actually are "boom counties." Hayden and Craig simply happen to be their locus.

In 1975, Routt, Moffat, and nearby Rio Blanco counties projected the mining of 33 million tons of coal by 1990. At the time of the projection an environmental impact statement predicted what would happen with it: increased population (from 26,000 to 61,500), more power plants, pollution, and coal trains, further sedimentation of the Colorado River, the stripping of 23,000 acres of land to the "complete destruction" of its vitality, significant alteration of the "existing landscape and its inherent aesthetic values," and a substantially negative social effect on local communities. It has not yet come to pass, but the symptoms, the signs, are there.

Hayden lies on the banks of the Yampa at the heart of coal-rich Routt County. Jim Bridger roamed through this country in 1861, blazing a path along the river, and cattlemen engulfed its grasslands with their 7Ls and Rabbit Ears in the 1870s. The town itself began as a trading post in 1874, anchored by the Hayden Mercantile Company and built by homesteaders, cattle kings, and small bands of embattled sheepmen. Nothing distinguished Hayden. Its monotonous, dusty flatness was typical of badlands towns all the way to Utah. Its main street, built north and south to catch the morning sun, was lined by the same neat false-front stores that covered main streets throughout the rest of the West. To the north lay Elkhead and Wolf mountains, and a thousand tiny streams that rushed to the Yampa. To the south lay Pagoda Peak and the Williams River. Everything else was space. Hayden was prairie and farmers and gunfighters and cattlemen; it was Reverend Cain, on a February night, who launched a crusade against dancing. And even a hundred years later it had changed little. In 1970 it still had but a single grocery, only one school — a cinder-block square from World War II — and no theater. Its single town clerk did paperwork in the mornings and hooked up water taps in the afternoons. In 1970 its population was 763 and stable.

By 1980 Hayden had grown to 2000. Saturday night square dancing and old-time fiddling were gone. Coal had come, and Hayden was a boomtown.

Mainly responsible was the Hayden Power Plant, part of Colorado-Ute's Salt River Project, which brought a deluge of miners and construction workers into the town a decade ago and probably destroyed its tranquility forever. In five years the price of a water-tap permit rose from $150 to $1200. The school population grew from 373 to 500 and classes spilled over into school-building bathrooms. Even with the highest mill levy in Routt County, Hayden went deeply into debt; even with a $230,000 grant for a new water system and a $450,000 grant toward a new elementary school, it still borrowed $670,000 on the water system and floated a huge $1,350,000 bond issue for other needs. To a great extent, in fact, it *overbuilt,* illustrating again the difficulties of advance planning in energy-impacted communities. Today, at best, Hayden remains a financially unstable town, and as long as coal is dug here, such instability will be a fact of life. To the southeast, Peabody Coal digs hundreds of thousands of tons to fuel the massive Hayden Power Plant. Pittsburgh Midway's Edna Mine loads sixty-five 100-ton coal cars daily. And the Energy Fuels Company's strip mine — Colorado's largest — aims at the production of 4 million tons a year from its rich plot near Oak Creek. Coal production, like shale oil, means people, and people generate income, but until towns like Hayden can absorb people, adapt to them, coal will be as much a curse as a blessing.

Routt County in general reflects the problems confronting Hayden. In 1970 its coal production was a million tons, its population was 6500, and its budget was $1 million a year. Seven years later its coal output was 7 million tons, an increase of 600 percent, its population 10,500, an increase of 60 percent, and its budget $3 million, an increase of 200 percent.

For most of its life Craig has been a cattle town, perhaps the only real one in Colorado's history. In the hot summer of 1875, settlers first built here, attracted by the Yampa and the green lushness of its valley. Its first school was a run-down cabin, not far from a saloon and general store. In time, the land was virtually swallowed by cattlemen, and from Baggs to Steamboat to Meeker to the gorges of the mighty Green they turned this quadrangle into one of the most violent enclaves in America. Craig was its brawling, windswept hub, and for years after the cattle frontier had receded on other parts of the western frontier, it remained so. Not until well into this century did it begin to die.

But die it did. By the 1960s Craig was still a cattle town, but it was no longer a hub. By day it was peaceful, sitting lazily on the land, belying its chaotic past. By night, with cool prairie winds in the air, cowboys still filled the gritty bars, drank their beer, and danced to the juke-box music of Patsy Cline. In 1970 only 4000 people lived in Craig, and only 200 more in 1975. Life was routine and simple. Until coal.

As with Rock Springs and Hayden, the catalyst for change was a power plant — Colorado-Ute's Yampa Project three and a half miles south of town on the road to the Williams Fork River. When the giant was born, coal mines immediately were dug to feed it, most notably Utah International's yawning two-mile-long hole near Axial. As early as 1974, more than 23 billion tons of high-quality coal were being mapped, dug, and shipped in the region. And the people who did it, who fired the plant and dug the coal, deluged Craig. Part of the change they brought was good, especially economic change. But problems — boomtown problems — also came. And stayed. As the town has grown — by 60 percent between 1970 and 1977, with an additional increase of 220 percent projected by 1985 — unemployment has risen as high as 9 percent, schools have become overcrowded, medical services have been diminished, and child abuse has increased. Clapboard homes that sold for $30,000 in 1974 now sell for double that; select home lots alone range to $10,000. Often housing at any price is not available — and because of it, a small and growing sea of mobile homes now sweeps across the flats below Black Mountain. Worse, perhaps, a town with typically strong Old West moral standards has seen a stunning rise in crime and vice. During Craig's boom years crime has increased by an average of 561 percent; crime against property has risen 222 percent and against persons 900 percent. Craig's sheriff answers three times the calls his office did even two years ago. "A lot of hopes and dreams never materialize" in Craig, says a priest. "All of the fast-moving frenzy, people living crowded in their neighbors' lives, is more than some can bear."

In the desert country of the Great Basin a handful of Utah and Nevada power plants have affected similar communities in similar ways for miles around. In southern Nevada the White Pine and Harry Allen plants have attracted hundreds of workers into the area between Las Vegas and Ely, most of them into the same small towns.

To the east, in Utah, the massive Intermountain Power Project already has transformed life in nearby Lynndyl and Delta. In September 1981 Delta's mayor described his city as "a mile by a mile with an arid climate and a population of about 2000." He estimated that in the past month alone "200 people have moved in." In a small town with a surging population, life has been disrupted at all levels, straining facilities, overburdening social services, threatening Mormon lifestyle formed in the days of Brigham Young. Signs of boom appear more vividly by the day. Some of them are negative. Perhaps most, in fact, are. But the major impact — from more coal development, along with oil drilling and the possible deployment of the MX missile — is yet to come.

In a decade one of the most sparsely settled areas in the West will never be the same again.

Montana also has its coal towns, and some say that one of them — Colstrip — is the West's worst.

Few places in the Rockies sit on richer historical ground. In the hot summer of 1876, only a few miles to the southwest of Colstrip, George A. Custer and the United States' Seventh Cavalry were slaughtered at the Little Bighorn in one of the most famous events in American history. Indian traditions still survive there, and local place names — Rosebud, Lodge Grass, Lame Deer, Custer — still ring of the old frontier. But the bare hills and low buttes of Rosebud County belong to coal, not history. And Colstrip is a classic child of coal.

South of the Yellowstone, near Sarpy Creek, Colstrip sprang up around coal mines supplying Montana Power's Billings generating plant a hundred miles away. Fifteen years ago only 300 people lived here. Today it is a town of 4000, a sprawling mosaic of mobile homes, motorcycles, muddy streets, overcrowded schools, and social problems, all of it symbolically overlain by waves of smoke drifting across the once-blue sky. Life in Colstrip is completely dominated by the tall twin spires of its plant, by the deep black strips in its soft earth. Completely dominated for 300 megawatts of power.

Reads a sign on the outskirts of Colstrip: YOU HAVE SEEN THE FUTURE AND IT DOESN'T WORK.

South of Colstrip, across the Powder River Basin, Gillette anchors a small semicircle of Wyoming coal towns. Aside from the Craig-Hayden area, the long right angle from Sheridan to Buffalo to Gillette forms one of the most heavily impacted coal areas anywhere.

Sheridan, approaching its hundredth anniversary, has not yet been spoiled; despite the growth of the coal empire to the east, it still sits quietly at the base of the magnificent Big Horns, touched but not yet altered. To the south, though, beyond the site of the Fetterman massacre, beyond Fort Phil Kearney, Buffalo is more immediately threatened. In May 1980 Mobil announced plans to build a plant nearby to convert 30,000 tons of coal into 40,000 gallons of synthetic fuels daily; this and increased coal mining activity in general eventually will completely change Buffalo from what it once was. In the past this has been tough, brawling cattle country. From the base of Cloud Peak, eastward to the Powder River, south to Crazy Woman Creek, the bloody Johnson County War was fought here, and beyond it, through the years, more range wars flared across the land than anyone could ever count. In the midst of this chaos, Buffalo was born and raised, and from the day of its birth in 1879 it was one of the most boisterous cow towns west of Dodge City, Kansas. This, now, will change. The synfuels plants — and the coal mining that sustains them — promise an influx of 5000 to 12,000 construction workers alone, followed by support workers numbering in the several thousands. Buffalo may continue to be boisterous, but the romance will be gone from it for good.

Once Gillette was like Buffalo. A quarter century ago not 4000 people lived here. Ranches and farms dominated the spare landscape. Only the Burlington, sliding by the town's northern edge, connected it with the outside world, and highways 14 and 16 to Rozet and Moorcroft and Reno Junction. And Buffalo. Oil first tempered its calm existence, then coal. And at some point, buried in growth, Gillette lost its innocence forever.

Like most Wyoming towns, Gillette sits in the midst of desolate beauty. Broad plains swell to the northwest, beneath Spotted Horse and Recluse, Rockypoint and Lightning Flat, all the way to the Yellowstone River. To the northeast the Thunder Basin National Grasslands ripple toward Devils Tower and the Black Hills. To the south is space — and coal.

The coal was first dug in the late 1970s, and the digging was frenetic. As workers poured into the region, Gillette swelled and literally burst. Every conceivable boomtown evil befell it — alcoholism, violence, crime, child abuse, what Joel Garreau, in *The Nine Nations of North America,* has called "a bouquet of modern urban pathologies." And all the while, the city had no way, no preparation, to help. Gillette became a legend. All over the West the "Gillette syndrome" came to symbolize the cancerous destructiveness of un- planned, unprepared, unregulated boomtowns on human life.

Gillette became a lesson never to be forgotten.

Today coal camps dot the prairie where cattle used to range, where the long drive once swept north to Montana. Fifty miles southeast of Gillette Kerr-McGee's Jacobs Ranch mine sprawls across the land. Storage silos blot out the late afternoon sun and antelope graze on coal-dusted grass. And coal trains snake away to Oklahoma, Arkansas, and Louisiana. More than 300 million tons of coal still lie beneath the red earth at Jacobs Ranch, and in the early 1980s alone, Kerr-McGee expects to ship 16 million tons of it. Carter Mining Company's Rawhide mine, twelve miles south, ships coal as far distant as Michigan and Indiana. Atlantic Richfield's Black Thunder Mine produced 40,000 tons of coal in its first year, 1977. By December 1980 its long black seams had yielded 11 million tons more, and ARCO has projected the mining of 20 million tons a year by 1986. Other mines — Cordero, Wyodak, the sprawling Belle Ayr — keep pace.

All of them have affected Gillette. It has become the nucleus of one of the most mining-intensive areas in the American West. As a result, it has never fully recovered from its own syndrome. Poor housing and high living costs, as in Craig and Rock Springs, have created a city of trailers. As its population of 14,000 continues to grow, crime and social problems continue to grow with it. Billboards, ramshackle storefronts, shopping centers mark the face of a town still in painful transition. And in the bars, where cowboys and coal miners mingle over cans of beer and talk of football and Willie Nelson, there is little sense of the future.

It is impossible to envision the future from the coal frontier of today. Too many uncertainties exist on it. Most ominous is a growing "softness" in the western coal market itself. Because of increasing environmental restrictions on coal-burning power plants (restric- tions currently under examination in the Clean Air Act debate), the West's important eastern coal market has recently begun to slip. Added to this is the fact that oil deregulation has led to increased oil and natural gas exploration and discovery, further undercutting coal's domestic market. In other words, the optimistic projections of the early 1980s may never materialize. And if they do not, if the coal market ever loses its current vibrance, the ultimate impact will shake coal towns all over the West.

As unlikely as it may be, the West could still give birth to yet another generation of coal ghost towns.

*   *   *

Oil — like coal — has been part of western life for nearly a century. Settlers moving westward across the Wyoming plains found crude oozing from the prairie in the 1830s. The West's first wells were dug at Lander in 1883 and north of Casper in 1894, but not until World War I was enough demand created to support widespread development. In the 1920s Wyoming exploded with drilling activity. Overnight its fabulous Salt Creek field became the petroleum capital of the Rockies — and Teapot Dome became an American watchword.

As it did on other mineral frontiers, colonialism quickly intruded on this one. Standard Oil of Indiana took control of the Salt Creek field in the 1920s, while Ohio Oil spread across the Bighorn Basin fields to the northwest. As early as 1921 the two controlled up to 97 percent of Wyoming's production — the greatest concentration of oil production power in the United States. As oil camps crystallized into towns, they all fell under the long shadow of the oil companies. And all of them went through painful boom cycles. From Casper and Midwest, northwest to Greybull, northeast to Gillette, bleak little towns sprouted all over the prairie — tent camps, shacks, brothels, and bars — living always at the whim of the companies. Exploitation was blatant. The oil towns were dirty, depressed, and mean, filled with sullen, bored workers living in semipoverty; and while they did, the oil giants battled all attempts to force improvements.

For years, north-central Wyoming was the hub of Rocky Mountain oil activity. From Flat Top in Converse County to Sandbar and Remington in Crook, its great fields crisscrossed the entire Powder River Basin. To the northwest they underlay the Bighorn Basin from Black Mountain in the south to Silvertip and Sagecreek on the Montana line. By the early 1970s oil (and natural gas) production accounted for 95 percent of Wyoming's mineral production, and today, with a reserve of 827,000 barrels, Wyoming still contains 2.7 percent of America's recoverable crude. So it remains, then, a target state — in terms of oil, in fact, probably the most targeted state in the West. If its future is no different from its past, Wyoming will see greater boomtown problems rather than fewer, and probably a resurgence of powerful outside economic influence with it.

Oil also runs through the history of Colorado. Its first fields were discovered in 1862 and a century later crude petroleum was the state's most important mineral fuel product. Oil fields lie everywhere. Some of the biggest concentrations on the plains lie north of Denver, ranging east and north through Morgan, Washington, Weld, and Logan counties to the Kansas and Nebraska lines. But the biggest bonanzas lie to the northwest in the vast, deep fields near Rangely. In 1980 the Colorado Energy Research Institute reported that the state held a proven reserve of approximately 259 million barrels of crude (and a reserve of nearly 2 trillion cubic feet of natural gas with it).

Other oil states include New Mexico, with fully 1.7 percent of America's crude reserves, Utah (with virtually oceans of oil underlying Duchesne and Uintah counties), and Montana.

Everything, however, perhaps all the great single fields combined, is eclipsed by the potential of two other major fields that span most of the oil-producing West. It is these two fields, and what happens in them, that will shape much of the West's energy future. One, the huge oval-shaped Williston Basin, dominates the upper Great Plains from central North Dakota west to the shores of Montana's Fort Peck Reservoir, and north and south from the brown flatlands of upper South Dakota to the lower tier of Canada. Its fields, first seriously explored in 1951, still lie virtually untapped. The other field, the broad, winding Overthrust Belt, is one of the most significant energy zones in the world.

The Overthrust Belt is almost as old as the earth itself, formed millions of years ago when two continental plates crushed together along a several-thousand-mile path from upper Canada to Mexico. Sweeping out of Alberta into Montana, angling under Glacier National Park, it flows along the Mission Range to Helena, then Butte. From there it curls across the Idaho toe, along the gentle Snake, and into Wyoming south of the Grand Tetons. Bowing east to the crest of the Absaroka Range, the belt runs south along the Idaho border, curving west at the Uinta Mountains into Utah. On its way out of the Rockies, finally, it cuts diagonally through Utah, northeast to southwest, flowing almost under Salt Lake City, then the barren Sevier Desert, before rolling into Nevada above Lake Mead. As it snakes through the Rockies, the Overthrust Belt underlies some of the most breathtaking geography in the world. But the majesty of the Bitteroots or the Snake, or the Utah desert, is far overshadowed by the oil and gas trapped deep in the guts of the belt. The Overthrust is forty miles wide, thousands of miles long, and in 1981 the United States Geological Survey estimated its recoverable oil reserves at 3.2 billion barrels and its undiscovered reserves at 6.7 billion (along with 16.5 trillion cubic feet of recoverable natural gas and 58.4 trillion cubic feet undiscovered) in Wyoming, Utah, and Idaho alone. Wyoming's Governor Ed Herschler has estimated that all of Overthrust contains 15 billion barrels of oil and 100 trillion cubic feet of natural gas, but the belt is so rich that its deposits may never be precisely calculated.

The Canadian Overthrust was first penetrated in the 1920s, with major strikes coming at Alberta in the 1930s. The United States, however, was slow to move on the American Overthrust. The belt's complex geology discouraged exploration. So did the availability of cheap Middle Eastern crude that made domestic drilling futile. But again, the oil embargo of 1973 began to change the nation's attitude; in the mid-1970s, America took a second look at the Overthrust.

In December 1974 American Quasar of Fort Worth found oil near Coalville, Utah, triggering the closest thing to an oil "rush" the West has ever had. By early 1975, the so-called Pineview field in Summit County, Utah, was one of the most active drilling areas in America, and during the next five years it became one of the most lucrative drilling areas in the world. To the northeast, in Wyoming, the rich Yellow and Ryckman Creek fields followed in 1976, opening up the northern part of Uinta County. In 1977, four more were drilled, including Whitney Canyon with a 4500-foot pay zone containing 4.5 to 9.6 trillion cubic feet of gas. In 1978, Chevron tapped its Carter Creek field near the Bear River in Lincoln County, and a year later Amoco broke into huge gas holes at its Kewanee-Federal number-one mine and its number-one Millis well east of Yellow Creek. By 1980, thirty major wells were scattered across the Pineview and neighboring fields. The payoff already was substantial. Nearly 8000 barrels of crude a day were shipped to nearby Salt Lake City for refining, and 10 million cubic feet of natural gas were piped to the Mountain Fuel Supply Company at the same time.

Then came change.

As recently as the early 1970s, the narrow green corridor along highway 89 from Alpine south to Evanston was peaceful and undisturbed — and it had been for generations. Hemmed in on the north by the Snake, on the south by the Uintas, and flanked on the east by the Bridger National Forest, the tiny Bear River slowly threaded its way through one of the most pastoral valleys in the Rockies. Small farms abounded, nestled up against the Bridger's Salt Range, feeding on the creeks that streamed out of its pockets. Dairies peppered the landscape, and the smell of cattle mingled with the sweetness of valley wildflowers. Small towns — Freedom, Afton, Kemmerer, where J. C. Penney clerked as a young man — sat haphazardly on the land, facing the beauty of the Salt Range to the east, the white spires of the Uintas to the south. Like a Rockwell painting, the valley was reminiscent of an earlier West of villages and white-frame country stores and brown-faced men talking over bales of harvest hay.

But in the 1970s oil came to Uinta and Lincoln counties and spilled over into Summit. Serenity disappeared in the clank of oil rigs and the roar of cats. Pastoral life vanished with the invasion of roughnecks. Overnight, ways of life changed that had endured for a century.

Along the Overthrust no town was as victimized as Evanston.

For a hundred years Evanston sat alone in the remote southwest corner of Wyoming. In the 1840s Fort Bridger to the east was the major crossroads in the region; half a century later the Union Pacific opened up the corner briefly. But Evanston had little to offer, and the twentieth century passed it by. Until oil. In the mid-1970s, nineteen new fields were found in a thirty-mile radius of the city — six of them containing 100 million barrels of oil and 600 billion cubic feet of natural gas. Between 1975 and 1980, the town exploded; at a time when a 4 percent growth rate was considered uncontrolled, Evanston grew by 29 percent. By 1980 it counted 9600 people (even excluding two subdivisions that grew up too quickly to be counted in the census), and it expects to top 15,000 by 1985 and possibly 30,000 to 35,000 by 2000.

Evanston literally has burst at the seams. Housing is virtually nonexistent. Neon No VACANCY signs shine outside motels and old hotels where rooms rent for $35 a night. Aging single-story homes sell — if at all — for $80,000 and more. In two 600-person trailer courts near the city, all the spaces are filled. One man lives in a tepee near town, another leases a chicken coop for more than $200 a month. In scenes reminiscent of Parachute, others pull into the shallow sage breaks and live in tents, campers, their own cars. Recently two elderly people died of carbon monoxide poisoning, trapped in a trailer they had sealed tightly against the winter wind. After living in two hotels for seventeen nights without paying, one family was found living in a pickup truck. "At least I know they ate," said the father, watching his children being placed in foster homes while he went to jail. "I wish I had never come here."

City officials also cite the need for $300,000 in sewer improvements and $100,000 more for wells and water storage. As it is, raw sewage has been dumped into the Bear River because sewage plants are so critically overburdened. Because Evanston is substantially under the state average for per capita health care, it also urgently needs more doctors — and $8 million for a new hospital to house them.

And, as it has at Gillette and Rock Springs and Craig, the energy boom has torn the old social fabric to shreds.

Along with Rock Springs, Evanston has the highest crime rate per 10,000 people in Wyoming. Bar brawls have become part of life; in a single two-month period of 1980 the city's small police force received fifty-three calls for assistance, a major departure from the past. More ominously, serious crime rose 114 percent in the first six months of 1980 alone. Eight rapes were recorded in a town where doors once were rarely locked, and the number of burglaries doubled from 1979. As the malaise has grown, it also has begun to spill over into nearby Utah. Alcoholism, theft, and drug problems have increased by a third in Summit County in the past two years, and theft and livestock killing (which particularly outrages rural people) have dramatically increased in Uinta County. Oil companies are defensive about the trend. As one oilman has said, "I'm certain some oil workers have done these things, but a lot of times the townspeople automatically blame anything that happens on the newest person in town."

To argue this way, though, the companies forget the obvious: that, because of oil, Evanston is awash in rootless, restless, thousand-dollar-a-week roughnecks with no community ties. That, for them, as one has said, "there's virtually nothing to do here except drink." And that social disruption caused by them is the logical end product of this kind of chemistry. "This is the most carousing community I've ever seen," an Evanston social worker has said. And the result has been obvious.

More insidious, perhaps, has been the disintegration of family units. Family disturbances — and killings — are no longer uncommon in Evanston. Child neglect and child abuse cases rose from forty in January 1980 to eighty-three in September, and their companion, domestic disturbances, rose 136 percent. In a single 1980 week four suicides were attempted. One succeeded.

At the root of it all lies the deep, brooding kind of depression that boom camps seem to spawn wherever they are. "I stay in the house a lot," says the wife of a young roughneck.

> I get real moody. I try not to take it out on the kids, but there are times. There are no neighbors. Nobody wants to get together. I'm not sure why. I have no close friends, nobody to talk to and to talk back . . . Here I just have cleaning, cooking, and the kids. That's it, and that's not enough. . . My biggest fear is my own depression. . . This is the worst thing that's happened to me in my life. There is nothing here, you're in this trailer all day, and there is no place to go, no family . . . It feels like you're in prison, serving your time, waiting for your time to be up.

This is Evanston. A banker says that "this whole thing is simply fantastic. The town has everything going for it." And an oilman interviewed by Joel Garreau adds that "this is the most exciting place in North America."

But behind the exuberance, Evanston's shadows conceal sadness and fear. Its mayor speaks eloquently of the "disappearance" of community, of the communal sense of belonging. Not far from the Pineview fields, wells pump oil from under Main Street and dozens more bore into the low buttes nearby. And, amidst the clatter of helicopters and trucks, community development director Fred Landy muses that "when the energy is gone in thirty to fifty years, that will leave us with nothing."

Good with bad: this is the paradox of oil.

In Evanston and other oil towns, people approach the future with caution. On the one hand, the boom shows no sign of diminishing. But on the other, it does. Oil's market, like coal's, is not necessarily very stable.

Recent years have produced nothing but success for bullish western drillers. In 1979 the Rocky Mountain region produced about 900 million barrels of oil and 2 trillion cubic feet of natural gas — 29 percent of America's total oil production and 10 percent of its natural gas production. Then, in addition to continued steady production from standing fields, tentative figures in November 1981 showed that the year was the most active drilling year in the history of the Rockies. For the fourth time in four years a new well completion record was set: 6604 were drilled, up from 4839 in 1980, 62 percent of them successful. New records were set in Nevada, northern New Mexico, and, anchored by the Williston, in North Dakota. And Colorado (with 1522 new wells) overtook Wyoming as the Rockies' most productive oil state. In September I. C. Kerridge, vice president and chief economist for the Hughes Tool and Die Company of Houston, predicted that by the end of the year western oil companies would have generated $31 billion in income, just under the total gross national product of Greece.

As for the Overthrust, figures confirm that its growth shows no sign of tailing off. In the summer of 1980 geologists predicted that 1.06 billion barrels of oil and 9.7 trillion cubic feet of natural gas still lay trapped in the Overthrust's caverns and holes (though, again, estimates have ranged as high as 15 billion and 100 trillion respectively). The Montana-Idaho-Utah-Wyoming link alone holds enough oil to supply the entire United States for one and a half to two and a half years and gas for two and a half. Wyoming alone could supply 530 million to 3 billion barrels of oil and 4 to 6 trillion cubic feet of natural gas. Those facts alone guarantee Overthrust's continued exploitation.

In other words, the immediate future, like the immediate past, looks good along the Overthrust. And across the rest of the West.

And yet, danger signs persist.

In early December 1981 the Independent Petroleum Association of America reported that for the week ending November 20, American oil imports totaled 3,825,000 barrels a day — 830,000 fewer than during the same period the previous year, a drop of 17.8 percent. During October, crude imports were down 18.5 percent from *September,* and the total demand for petroleum products during October was 6.5 percent less than in October 1980.

Clearly, the trend is healthy. As America lessens its dependence on foreign oil, it increases its own energy self-sufficiency. But, for the oil West, the trend also is worrisome. If demand continues to decrease, driving prices down, foreign exporters in time almost certainly will flood the world with cheaper and cheaper crude; this, in turn, will drive prices down on the American market. Assuming the worst, in time it conceivably could shut down the American oil industry itself. In the West, exploration might stop entirely, along with production. Unemployment would rise. Oil towns would die. Evanston would die.

And boom again would become bust.

For the moment, though, the oil boom thunders up and down the Overthrust and echoes across the West from New Mexico to North Dakota.

And change continues. Writing of Wyoming in *Rocky Mountain* magazine, author Tom Clark has vividly described the world north of Douglas:

> Energy development has driven a mile-wide wedge of metal junk 20 miles north into empty country. Spilling out to blank horizons is a sea of truck-mounted drill rigs, bobbing grasshopper pumpers, squat oil and gas storage tanks, ragged clots of trailers whose backyards are a graveyard for wrecked cars, Harleys, snowmobiles, speedboats, even on occasional upended helicopter. It's a stretch that summons up images of the road out of Saigon after the fall.

And the people.

A father sits in a jail cell, his children gone. A young woman sits alone in a trailer and speaks of her prison. An old woman's purse is snatched from her in the middle of the day. A man beats his wife and kills himself.

The main street of Evanston is a long, grayish row of scabby doors and broken neon. On a rusted sign a cowboy pitches from the saddle of a bucking bronco. On the noisy street a tanker truck rumbles by.

This is Evanston.

And Evanston is the West.

CHAPTER FOUR

Troubled Land

But the rich strike, the big bonanza, the roaring boom is only half the story. The other half is the boom going bust — the dry well, the false color, the blue-sky promotion, the salted claim. The collapse of the boom is the very essence of the western experience.

BERNARD DE VOTO

ON AN AUGUST AFTERNOON the Colorado, slate-red and murky from the bludgeoning of summer rains, rolls swiftly out of Middle Park, by Glenwood Springs, on its way west to Utah. Flowing along a path traced centuries ago, it slides gently along the sloping sides of the White River Plateau, its soft eddies backing into the mountain creases. At New Castle, Elk Creek cuts in from the north, bisecting narrow green fields along the way. At Silt and Antlers, streams race down from the furrowed sides of Mam Peak, connecting with the Colorado in frothy pools. As it courses on through Rifle, it flattens, broadens, then drifts lazily between the long, slanting walls of Battlement Mesa on the south and the majestic chalky-white Book Cliffs to the north. Below Rifle, the steely Anvil Points front the river like an ancient temple. Then, from Rulison to Grand Valley, flanked by long green strands of willow and cottonwood, it glides through miles of fertile lowlands. Streams spurt into it at every bend. Towns roll by — Parachute, De Beque, Cameo, Palisade. Finally, curling gently beneath the white shale cliffs of Palisade, the Colorado meets the Gunnison.

Not many years ago the course of the Colorado was one of the most beautiful stretches of river and valley in the West, and in many ways it still is. On a summer afternoon, cottonwood leaves still flutter and snap in the river's breeze, and its coolness blunts the western sun. Red dirt sweeps up a thousand canyons and crevices to meet forests of evergreens descending the plateaus. Streams jump out of tiny valleys, chokecherry and fireweed splotch the grasslands with patches of color, and the songs of mountain birds still fill the air. Farmhouses, weathered and battered from too many years in the sun, lie in valley after valley, clumped near watercourses, some of them, others sitting alone and aloof against the mesa walls. Not many years ago peonies grew wild in the valley, peach and cherry orchards nestled in the sun along the river, and fields of raspberries, strawberries, currants, and celery swept for miles up against the Uncompahgre Plateau. They are still there today. But no one can say for how long.

The great valley is changing. Once it was farm country. Now it is energy country. Heavy traffic streams endlessly along Interstate 70. Exhaust fills the air, killing the sweet scent of aspen and pine. Picturesque valley towns, once empty and tranquil, now bristle with noise and activity. Shale towns — Silt, Rifle, Parachute, De Beque — grow larger and busier by the day. New Castle. Palisade. Grand Junction has exploded with growth. To the north of the Colorado, Meeker and Craig and Rangely struggle with the boom. To the south, Somerset, Paonia, Delta, Hotchkiss, Cedaredge do the same. All over northwest Colorado, in Garfield, Moffat, Mesa, Rio Blanco, and Delta counties, the story is the same: the Western Slope is immersed in apparently uncontrollable growth. And even with the region's current economic slowdown, uncontrollable growth still promises massive problems in the future.

Looking at life in the region today, it is not difficult to envision tomorrow.

By 1990, tens of thousands more people will live in the towns of northwest Colorado than do today. The Colorado West Council of Governments has estimated that the population of Garfield, Mesa, Rio Blanco, and Moffat counties alone will grow from an estimated 110,000 now to 212,500 by 1985. And each new resident will cost state, county, and local governments $12,000 in services. Community facilities will cost between $6500 and $7500 for each person, and public-services operating budgets for county and state roads, power lines, state institutions, and water reservoirs will increase by $500 per person. An estimated 10 million gallons of water a day will be required in sewage-treatment capacity, at a cost of $81 million, and 86

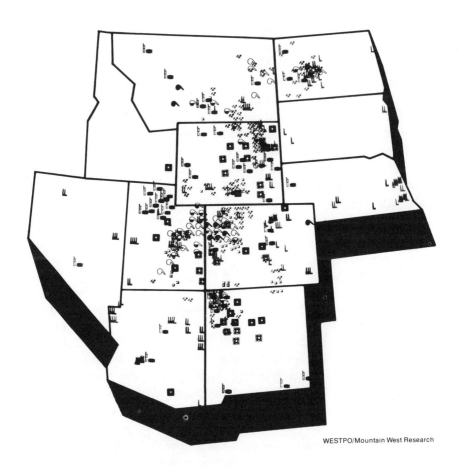

WESTPO/Mountain West Research

CUMULATIVE ENERGY ACTIVITY — 1990

EXISTING   PROPOSED

COAL

ll   Coal-Fired Power Plants   ll
✗   Surface Mines   ✗
□   Underground Mines   □

OIL AND GAS

▯•   Refineries   ▯•

URANIUM

▣   Production Centers   ▣
▟   Nuclear Power Plants   ▟

SYNTHETIC FUELS

          Active Projects   ✎
          Planned Projects   ✎
          Speculative Projects   ✎

million gallons will be needed in water-storage capacity, at an added cost of $251 million. Schools will cost the communities $156 million in just the next few years, and parks and recreation $41 million. In an area dangerously short of hospital beds and medical help, $42 million will be needed to upgrade both.

Housing, electrical power, and highways stand out as particularly pressing needs. In the immediate future northwest Colorado will need 25,000 new housing units to cope with incoming populations, and analysts see the need for up to 350,000 units on land equivalent to a corridor ten miles wide and eighty miles long in the distant future. In a region where better than 19 percent of housing is in the form of mobile homes, where lenders are wary of loaning — at *any* interest rate — to high-risk transient labor working on projects that may never jell, the cost has been estimated at between $650 million and $2 billion over approximately the next ten years. Northwest Colorado will need another $100 million by 1990 for its road and highway systems (and some estimates have ranged as high as $385 million). The cost of electrical power is almost beyond calculating. Commercial-level shale oil production alone will require staggering quantities of power; the production of even 2 million barrels will require an additional 4500 megawatts of electricity, and by the year 2005 northwest Colorado in general will need an estimated 300 megawatts more — all at a cost of $4.8 billion. The question is, who will pay for expansion? If western electrical systems subsidize shale oil, small-town users ultimately will subsidize the systems. How many of them will be forced out of the power market in the process is a further question.

A similar question is how — or whether — boomtowns will cope with the long-range impact of the energy industry on small-town economies. Wherever energy has moved into Colorado communities, it has monopolized local labor supplies, frequently damaged the local economic base — agriculture, stock raising, tourism — and created dangerous local dependency on energy extraction. It has profited outsiders — laborers, banks, efficient and well-capitalized businesses — at the expense of locals. What the energy companies have created is a "hollow" economy, healthy on the surface but unhealthy at the core. It is strong enough today, but forty years from today when the latest mineral cycle is spent and the energy companies are gone, the question is whether any of the towns they leave behind will be strong enough to stand on their own.

As for the people, their primary concern in the future must be the funding of law enforcement and social services.

Crime has risen 140 percent over the past decade in eleven Western Slope counties — more than two and a half times the statewide increase of 54 percent for the same period — and one state official has predicted a further 94 percent increase in serious crime by 1986. "This is just the beginning," he says. "Crime is not a passing thing. It's a permanent fixture of boomtown life."

There is a kind of irony in this. In its early years Colorado spawned as many thieves, confidence men, and outlaws as any region in America. The history of Leadville and Brown's Park is as much a history of crime as it is of civilization. But today is not yesterday, and the lawlessness that once ruled the Colorado frontier has long since lost its romance. Yesterday, in the streets of Meeker, Butch Cassidy was a hero, and so were his riders. Today they would be met with fear. And the larger fear — in a region that will need countless new law enforcement officers over the next decade, at a cost the region might not be able to bear — is that they would not be met at all.

Social problems have also increased. Alcoholism. Mental illness. Suicide. Divorce. In a single month in late 1980 the Garfield County Department of Social Services handled 232 cases — 94 of them involving child abuse and negligence. Men, working long hours in shale caverns, in coal fields, on oil rigs, drink, neglect their families, beat their wives. Women, living in boredom, beat their children. Children turn to delinquency and crime. And, all the while, overwhelmed social service agencies provide only minimal help. Little reason exists to believe that they will be able to provide more support for their populations in the future than they do now.

As northwest Colorado looks to the future, perhaps the most important problem it faces is the fact that most of its communities are affected by more than one boom at the same time. Colorado's energy frontier is small and compact. Its mineral regions are not separated from one another by clear-cut lines. Craig must cope with coal and oil shale, Rangely with coal, oil shale, oil, and natural gas. All at once.

The results can be devastating. They have been in the past, and they are certain to be in the future.

No better example exists than Rangely.

In 1880 a group of eastern land speculators nailed together a trading post at the junction of Douglas Creek and the White River in the far northwest corner of Colorado. In time it became Rangely. For years the Utes dominated the land around it, planting their nomadic communities on the Douglas and Stinking Water and Silvertail, harvesting game to feed their children and warring against the region's hated whites. The last chapter in the Ute wars was written here in 1887, and for decades afterward the land belonged to cattlemen and sheepmen, fanning out across the broad, undulating mesas to the south of Rangely and colliding in some of the most violent range wars in western history. Throughout it all, Rangely itself barely grew. In 1940, after sixty years of life, it had a population of only fifty-five.

Then came oil, found near the town in 1910. And natural gas. And coal. And now shale oil.

In the past twenty years, at least, oil has been at the heart of Rangely's economy. It is said, locally, that "Colorado runs on Rangely oil," and it is a fact that the Rangely and Wilson Creek fields are among the major producers in the West. In the spring of 1981 twenty rigs operated on the 19,000-acre fields abutting the town.

South, from the edge of town, the prairie teems with natural gas drilling.

Twenty-seven miles to the southeast lies the Rio Blanco Oil Shale Project.

Six miles to the north and west, Western Fuels Utah is developing the huge Deserado Mine to supply coal to the Deseret Generation and Transmission Association power plant near Bonanza, Utah.

Already, the strains are enormous.

Rangely's population of 2200 will be increased between 1500 and 1800 by coal workers alone over the next two years. Projections have been made of a tenfold increase over the next decade.

Housing is scarce. People live in campgrounds. In tents on vacant lots. "If I put up a FOR RENT sign," says a local man, "my home is rented twenty minutes later." In a city, a county, overrun by drillers and wildcatters and machinery operators, "people are desperate for a place to live."

Despite years of existence, Rangely still has few amenities. Its relative quality of life is still not high. Though things have changed somewhat since then, a 1979 study of Rangely indicated that many of its people, and perhaps most, did half or less of their shopping in the city. Only with food and medical services did they tend to shop

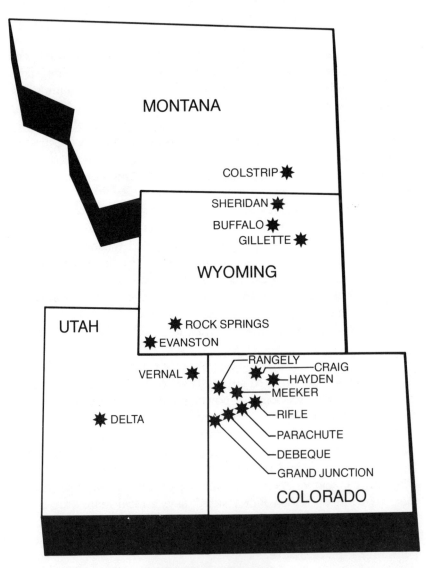

MONTANA

COLSTRIP ✴

SHERIDAN ✴
BUFFALO ✴
GILLETTE ✴

WYOMING

UTAH

✴ ROCK SPRINGS
✴ EVANSTON

VERNAL ✴

RANGELY
CRAIG
HAYDEN
MEEKER
RIFLE
PARACHUTE
DEBEQUE
GRAND JUNCTION

✴ DELTA

COLORADO

BOOMTOWNS

locally, but even then, food purchases tended to be minimal and widespread dissatisfaction existed with medical care. A chronic unavailability of adequate goods and services, a lack of selection and choice, and the great cost differential between local retail prices and those in other area cities has led to a windfall for Grand Junction, Vernal, and Craig for years.

Social problems are deeply rooted — and growing deeper.

Few cities in the region have experienced conflict between outsiders and locals as Rangely has. Older residents complain of the energy workers' rowdiness and disruption — as police chief C. W. Ivey has said, "Any place you go there will be one group, especially of young people, carousing in the bars" — and the workers complain of unfriendliness and police harassment. The result has been a kind of semipermanent state of tension, compounded, says Ivey, by a lack of housing that has placed small groups of angry people in close proximity to one another.

On a cool August night in 1981, Eric Wilfong, a twenty-year-old oil rigger, climbed atop the city post office and began firing a rifle. Two patrol cars were disabled and two deputies wounded before Wilfong was killed by Rangely police. The young man had a long history of local disturbances. And six arrests. Still, his bitter friends maintained that "the cops pick on the riggers" and that Wilfong was "harassed all the time" by them and by old-timers who "don't like the town to grow and don't like us here." Perhaps on an August night Eric Wilfong broke. An autopsy showed no presence of liquor or drugs in his body. It was something else that drove him. And killed him.

Said police chief Ivey: "It's been bound to happen."

In Rangely, as elsewhere on the Western Slope, the presence of an adequate social services system might have prevented such a tragedy. But the city has not had one to date, and the development of one in the future seems unlikely. As usual, the problem is money. Not only does Rangely face the cumulative effect of several simultaneous booms, but in the Deserado project it also faces the dilemma of absorbing impact without the money that goes with it. While Utah will derive income from the property tax, Rangely will get the growth. And the problems. Little wonder, as one local resident has said, that "we're frustrated by economic forces dictating our future."

Rangely's main street is a mile long and shabby. It seems dilapidated, almost neglected, a brick and wood mosaic of brown-gray storefronts and trash-strewn lots, with only the Bank of Rangely and the corner drugstore to break the monotony. The city is more than this, of course. It is also Colorado Northwestern Community College and fourteen churches and the *Rangely Times.* It is also people. But, whatever it is, its future is uncertain.

And so is that of every other town on Colorado's energy frontier.

The significant thing is that Colorado is not unique. Or alone. In terms of energy development, Colorado is no different from the rest of the West. What happens to it in the future will happen *everywhere.*

In 1976, a Federal Regional Council study classified 131 communities in Colorado, Utah, Montana, Wyoming, and the Dakotas as "impacted" by energy development. Fifty-three of them lay in Utah, many of them confronted by coal and oil development at the same time. Wyoming had 25, most of them oil and coal towns like Gillette and Evanston. Eighteen lay in North Dakota, 5 in South Dakota, and 6 — mostly coal towns — in Montana. A year later, in a different study, the number of western boomtowns rose to 188.

The Department of Energy has estimated that 2 million people will come West in the energy rush of the next decade. In 1980 the Congressional Budget Office projected the creation of 72,000 *direct* energy-related jobs in the United States by 1990, most of them in Colorado, Utah, Wyoming, New Mexico, and North Dakota. And, assuming that a single direct energy job translates into four to six total new people, and that each temporary construction job equates to perhaps several people more, the 72,000 can suddenly escalate to several hundred thousand. Importantly, since remote western towns have not assimilated anywhere near these numbers in the past, no reason exists to think they will in the future.

More important, it remains to be seen whether the West can carry the financial burden of boomtown growth.

A congressional study published in 1980 concluded that capital costs in energy areas would reach $400 million by 1990, and that noncapital costs of operating public services would add another $950 million. This study, however, largely ignored oil shale, oil, and gas development, and, from roads to land costs, it failed to assess several basic needs. Accounting for these oversights, the Western Governors' Policy Office has concluded that the cost of supporting energy and its workers will reach a staggering $15 billion a year by 1990. Even five years ago the Federation of Rocky Mountain States calculated that the total local public outlay for each new energy-related job was $12,400; five years from now, if inflation continues, the figure easily could increase by a third. Numbers, of course, mean little in themselves; cost itself means nothing. But cost, if not met, translates into social and economic shortfall and human misery.

And it is unlikely that the communities can cope with it.

One reason is that western communities traditionally have offered minimum services to begin with, relying instead on informal delivery through church, neighborhood, and family. Adopting new, bureaucratic — and costly — governmental systems to provide services and facilities will not be easy. Westerners have believed in self-help for too long to make changes quickly.

A second reason is that the public administration procedures of small western towns are not good. Like everything else in western life, towns and townspeople have tended to approach public administration casually and informally. Many towns have functioned literally from birth without formal governmental structures. In Parachute the town grocer is the mayor; nothing more — until now — was ever considered necessary. Now this, too, must change, but it will take time. Attitudes about governance, like the flow of western life itself, change slowly.

The final reason is financial. Not now, perhaps not ever, will boomtowns have the money they need to cope with growth. They cannot generate it in advance. Nor will they ever be able to find what they need in county, state, or federal funding. Again, Colorado is a case in point. State, federal, and trust funds will be available in the future, just as they have been in the past, but they will never be enough. By 1976, all of Colorado's impacted communities together had received only $5 million in direct federal aid, and $73 million in indirect aid. Now, because of federal budget cutbacks, Colorado's state, county, and local governments have lost an estimated $280 million in federal funds for 1982 — $200 million for state government and $80 million for cities and counties. And most of what is lost cannot ever be replaced.

So, as the energy rush escalates, a chain reaction will explode across the West in its wake.

Towns will grow, swallowing up farmlands and prairie, destroying their beauty and productivity. In time, urban sprawl will engulf some of the most beautiful land left in the West. Where meadows once stood and farmers baled their hay, trailer parks and storage sheds will sit instead.

Towns will lose their economic diversity. As economic energy is drawn away from old pursuits and channeled into new, more and more the hollow economy will develop.

Housing demand will exceed supply, and whatever housing is available will be costly.

The quality of life will decline. Prices will increase, retail outlets and services will become overcrowded, medical care will become spotty and ineffective. Public building and services will fall far behind public needs and demand.

Social problems will multiply, exacerbated — if not caused — by the nature of boomtown life (which a recent University of Wyoming study has concluded is twice as likely to create problems as life anywhere else). Dislocated outsiders will find refuge in alcoholism and violence. Townspeople, developing an angry siege mentality among themselves, will channel their resentment of newcomers into open hostility. And, at the same time, they will retreat deeply into old patterns of living, clinging to old folkways, seeking comfort and solace where they can, attempting to regain control over things suddenly lost. Towns once integrated and cohesive will become polarized — old against young, rancher against construction worker, environmentalist against developer. Native against intruder.

In the end, obviously, what the energy rush will most change is people. The changes it will bring — that it has brought already — are subtle and insidious, hard to see, hard to feel. But they are there. Mirrored in a farmer's eyes, reflected in a city street once quiet, now not, they are there. The question now becomes what the changes will do to people's lives. Environmentalists have said for a hundred years that no man can reach his human potential in a milieu of concrete and steel, that he needs space, breathing room, beauty, to enhance his life. What, then, happens to communities that lose (or never have) their open space, their parks and greenbelts? What happens when condominium clusters burst out of cow pastures and pristine valleys turn to dust? What happens when the endless silence of a mountain day disappears in the roar of earthmovers and jackhammers? What happens to the people?

Western towns are no different from any other towns in America. Along the White and the Colorado, lumped in mountain canyons, tossed on the stubbled grasslands, they have been around for years and so have their people and so has their history. They have always been isolated, provincial, tribal. As far back as societies have existed here, lives have rested on a common bedrock of trust, friendliness, intimacy, strong personal relationships, Christian morality, and the willingness to share good times and bad. For all of the frontier's vaunted individualism, towns like these, people like these, have been traditionally, stubbornly familial. But now the family is threatened as it has never been before.

Because of it, life here, in western boomtowns, will never be as good again as it once was. Where people once shared weddings and church and football games on cold autumn nights, now they will share a sense of loss. Some years ago, a Brown's Park old-timer sadly wrote that "the old days and the old ways, the free life of the white hunters and trappers who peopled this country, the Indians, the emigrants with their prairie schooners following faintly marked trails, bull whackers and prospectors and professional gunslingers, cattlemen and cowpunchers in the dusty wake of the vast steer herds on the shove up and shove down, and the homesteaders, are gone forever." He was right. They will not return again. And the West will not be the same again for it.

And then one day, perhaps, after all of the trial and all of the pain, boom will turn to bust.

Oil prices will fall. Coal will follow.

On a spring morning in 2000, perhaps, oil rigs will stand silent against the western sun. At Evanston and Rangely men will pack their trucks and drive away. Coal fields will stand idle. At Gillette and Craig families will pack their mobile homes. And drive away. Near Parachute and Rifle the retorts will come down again, as they did once before. And men and their families will pick up their lives and drive away. To another mecca.

And when they go, they will leave destruction behind them.

The West knows. It has happened before.

The whole history of western mining is a history of boom and bust. The great gold rushes of the 1860s and 1870s, for example, were followed by years of decline that wiped out towns and people. The glittering silver empire of the early 1890s crashed in ruin in 1893. In 1921 copper prices plummeted, devastating copper towns throughout the Rockies, and during the Great Depression it happened again. As late as the 1950s and the dramatic collapse of uranium, the withering cycle of boom and bust continued to plague the West.

The wind whispers through lonely pine groves today where Sts John once stood. In 1865 silver was found here, at the rocky foot of

Glacier Mountain west of Denver, and in 1866 the tiny valley was virtually colonized by the Boston Mining Company. Within two years, with its company-owned boarding houses, private cabins, and dining hall, Sts John was one of the most complete company towns in the West. For a moment the town boomed. Men thronged the streets and filled the Summit House and read Boston newspapers at the town library (because the company allowed no liquor, there were no saloons). But in time silver died, and the town died with it. The Boston Mining Company vanished as quickly as it had appeared, and almost overnight a permanent stillness settled over the willow flats where people once had lived.

Tungsten brought boom and bust to a whole region west of Boulder in the years just before and after World War I. In 1900 the Primos Chemical Company of Pennsylvania built a tungsten-concentrating mill at Sugar Loaf, an old gold camp in the Boulder foothills once owned by United States Gold. The next year it built another — the largest in the world — at nearby Lakewood, and in 1916 it alone produced $76,000 worth of tungsten for the American market. In 1904 the Wolf Tongue Mining Company, also of Pennsylvania, incorporated in Delaware, moved into the "black iron" country near Nederland and opened up the old Caribou Mine. Between 1900 and 1910, Wolf Tongue produced 80 percent of America's tungsten, earning an astonishing $4.67 a pound in 1916. The war triggered a full-scale boom in the tungsten belt, sending a flood of workers into the small towns along Boulder Creek (many of them old gold camps already once destroyed). The product came from Colorado ground, mined primarily by Colorado men, but the capital and the companies — Vanadium Corporation of America, Vanadium Alloy Steel, Black Prince Mining, Western Tungsten Mining — were all eastern.

For a single historical moment, like Sts John, Boulder County exploded. Tent cities sprouted near Caribou. Nederland, an old silver camp, mushroomed from 300 to 3000 one year later. Building lots sold for astronomical prices, hotel beds were rented in eight-hour shifts, restaurant diners were allowed twenty minutes to eat meals, and saloons added extra doors to accommodate their crowds. Stages brought a hundred men a day to Nederland, many of them rooming in barns for a dollar a night. Nearby, Tungsten was born and built from nothing in the same explosive days. During World War I it swarmed with a population of 20,000. For its moment in history it was one of the most significant towns in the West.

But the end of the war brought the end of the boom. The tungsten belt slipped into oblivion, and its boom camps with it. By 1940 Tungsten had only fifty people; today it is gone. So is Lakewood. At Sugar Loaf, where gold was so rich it could be picked off the ground, where the Primos Mill made history, patches of peas and potatoes grow in the sun. Nederland never fully grew back. Only in the summer, with tourists and artisans, does it stir again. Its tungsten days are gone. In Boulder Valley the once ghost towns are ghost towns again.

There are countless stories like these, scattered throughout the history of the West. Sts John, Tungsten, silver towns, gold towns — different times, different country, different creatures of different booms — but all of them victimized by the same things: mineral booms that died, corporate policies that changed, federal programs that stopped. Red Lodge never died, or Deadwood or Park City or Aspen. But for every Aspen, the boards and shingles of a hundred ghost towns rattle around the meadows and canyons of the West. It is littered forever with the remains of the dead.

Throughout these years, the greatest tragedy was the fact that the West's cycles of boom and bust resulted from events and forces beyond western control. Booms were triggered by outside pressures, not internal ones, and it was outside pressures that also brought them down. When the government coined silver, the industry mushroomed, and boom camps from Leadville to Virginia City prospered. But when coinage stopped, the industry fell, and the great silver camps fell with it. Even as late as the New Deal, and the Silver Purchase Act of 1934, this was true. Uranium mining skyrocketed in 1949, then crashed in 1952 when the Atomic Energy Commission decreased its purchases of it. In the Four Corners area of Colorado, New Mexico, Utah, and Arizona, it left behind a small empire of ghost towns. Western mining not affected by government policies was affected by other forces — war and war demand, international market fluctuations, and the colonial whims of big business. And, under any circumstances, the ultimate victims were the towns' people. History has treated the mineral frontiers as rich, romantic chapters in the story of America's march west. But there was nothing romantic about their instability or about the suffering of their people. Boom times were good times, heroic times. But bust times brought some of the darkest days in the West's history.

Sadly, it has not ended. Bust times are still a fact of western life. The dark days have not disappeared.

Work-force cutbacks at the Rio Blanco Oil Shale Project in Colorado in 1981 and 1982, and the halting of development work on the nearby Cathedral Bluffs Project, eventually will affect shale towns throughout the Piceance. The layoff of a few hundred men is not a crisis in itself. But the danger signs are there.

The projected 1982 closing of Idaho's great Bunker Hill and Sullivan smelter by Gulf Resources of Houston threatens to displace 2100 men and an annual payroll of $60 million at Kellogg. After the silver crash of the 1890s, it has been called the second-biggest economic disaster in the state's history. And no one can say what will happen to Kellogg.

Plummeting uranium prices have sent shock waves across the West from Wyoming to New Mexico. Eight thousand uranium miners are unemployed in the West today, and communities that have seen bust before now are seeing it again.

Mine and mill shutdowns in Colorado have virtually paralyzed Uravan, in the state's far southwest corner, and spread as far north and east as Gunnison and Canon City. Twenty-five percent of the population of Naturita and Nucla left in 1981 alone. This "is the worst I've seen things in the twenty-seven years I've been here," says Katherine Binder of Naturita.

At the beginning of 1981 more than 8500 men mined uranium in New Mexico, a number that fell to 6700 by April and further yet by the end of the year. Grants, hardest hit of New Mexico's cities, has seen unemployment rise to 10 percent in late 1981. School enrollment has fallen by 500 pupils. The once-busy Golden Horseshoe is quiet, and traffic no longer streams down Santa Fe Avenue. Signs near the city limits call Grants "the uranium capital of the world," but it is an empty distinction. Looking to the future, Grants mayor Mitchell Wells has spoken sadly of the community's "pessimistic attitude." Says another resident: "The town is dead."

Wyoming, already unsettled by uncertainties in its coal and oil markets, has been further hurt by the uranium slump. A thousand men were laid off in Wyoming in 1980 and 1660 by April 1981.

At the heart of depression sits Jeffrey City, a ragged knot of a town on Crooks Creek in Fremont County. Thirty years ago it did not even exist; tourists on the way to Yellowstone through Rawlins and Lander raced by a point on the road called Home on the Range. Not until the 1950s, and another uranium boom, did it become much of a town. Anchored by Western Nuclear Corporation's Pathfinder mine, it exploded to 4500 people, built schools and churches and fast-food drive-ins.

Now yellowcake — uranium oxide — sells for $23 a pound and Jeffrey City is dying. Eleven hundred men were laid off by Western Nuclear between January 1980 and April 1981, and 255 more in June. The town's population has sunk to 2500. Sixty percent of its 320 housing units are vacant. Its trailer parks, overflowing a year ago, are half full. Some of those who leave simply walk away, abandoning their trailers for repossession. Businesses are struggling to survive, but business is off by 30 percent at the Jeffrey City Food Farm and 60 percent at Coast to Coast Hardware, and the town's doughnut shop and furniture and clothing stores already have closed. Bank deposits have decreased by 30 percent. And the city streets, Tom Clark has written, "are as quiet as the streets in *On the Beach,* after the human race has just fallen asleep for good."

Very likely, no one will survive long in Jeffrey City. "We're not worried," says the owner of the Jeffrey City Market. "We've been here twenty-four years and seen it bust like this four or five times. It'll come back." But the town will die, says another. "There just isn't enough people to keep it going."

Meanwhile, the uranium slide, as others before it and others occurring parallel to it, takes its toll on human life. As of March 1981, ten suicides had been recorded for the year in the remote West End uranium country of Montrose, San Miguel, and Dolores counties, Colorado.

The rate was thirty times the national average.

And, finally, Anaconda.

In western Montana, not far from the Bitterroots, the town of Anaconda sits on one of the ugliest slabs of earth in the Rockies. Even on a bright day the land and sky at Anaconda are permeated with grayness. Only the undulating waves of the Flint Creek Range break the stark, grainy monotony of the landscape. Anaconda has been a company town for almost a hundred years, founded in the 1880s around one of the biggest smelters in the world. For three generations copper ore from Butte poured through the great smelter, enriching Anaconda Copper and underpinning the economic life of the town and its people. In time, however, the company's best ore fields played out, leaving it with deposits too costly and unproductive to mine and smelt at a profit. In 1980, citing its inability to comply with federal clean-air regulations, the company announced the closing of its smelter.

Aftershock still ripples through Anaconda. The town's population is 12,000, most of it dependent on the company for survival. In Jeffrey City the economy simply ceased to exist with the collapse of its boom, and here eventually it will too. Some men have worked for Anaconda all their lives, some as their fathers had before them. Now, almost certainly, this is over. Like the gypsy miners of Sts John and Tungsten, they will move on, leaving the town behind them.

So it is in the West. Forces beyond control. Bust with boom. Bad times with good. And suffering for those who live the times.

There was a time when it mattered not as much. Yesterday, at least, the mining frontiers and their roller-coaster cycles exploded on virgin land where no modern civilization pre-existed. But that is no longer true. Boom and bust now converge on places where communities already exist and people already live. Their damage now is shattering.

And it is forever.

*   *   *

The energy hunt is on. The West cannot ignore it, cannot avoid it, cannot stop it. Nor does it choose to try. It has done its part in the past; its people and its natural wealth have helped sustain the nation and its needs for a hundred years. No westerner would choose to destroy this legacy now.

But, as the hunt begins, the West sounds the caution that it will not be trampled in the process, that it will not accept the annihilation of its people for energy, that it will not accept the destruction of their rights and their lives even for the "greater good." For a hundred years the West's mineral guts have been tapped, its human resources exhausted, always for the national welfare, always for others. The West has given enough. Without something in return, it can give no more.

What, then, does it want?

First, it wants a role in the making of national energy decisions, in the formulation of national energy policy. It wants a voice in what, when, where, how fast, and how much. And it wants its role to be early, active, influential, and permanent. It has not been so before.

Too often in the past, as former governor Thomas Judge of Montana has said, decisions have been made about the West in the East, made without western advice or consent, then "rammed down the throats" of western states. For a hundred years American policy makers have created the impression, at least, that the West has value to the nation not as sovereign states but as energy colonies. If this ever was true, it no longer can be. Westerners have no desire to obstruct, to cartelize energy, to stand in the "schoolhouse door." They are not blue-eyed Arabs. What they are is angry — angry at "rape and run," angry at nonwestern paternalism, angry at their own grating, debilitating sense of impotence in the face of it all. What will help them now is a place at the table.

It is there, perhaps, that the impact of boomtown problems can be mitigated, there, in fact, that they may be prevented from happening at all.

Second, the West needs financial help for its towns and people, both from a federal government that spurs energy development in their midst and from the energy companies that reap private profit from it.

What the government can or will do in the future is uncertain, but the likelihood of ever-decreasing federal aid to the cities and states is a reality the West must recognize.

So the key to the survival of western boomtowns, perhaps, becomes the energy companies.

To a certain extent — in some cases to a great extent — they have done what they can.

The Overthrust Industrial Association, formed in early 1980 by Amoco, Chevron, Champlin, and others, has committed $2.1 million to help Evanston and other Overthrust towns meet growing local demands for public services.

In the summer of 1981 Western Fuels Utah agreed to pay $15 million to several northwest Colorado governments for what it specifically called "impact mitigation." Some funds were earmarked for Rio Blanco County. Others were for Rangely's hospital, recreation, fire, and library districts. The county also has agreed to build a $1.6 million road and bridge from Rangely to the Deserado Mine site, to help pay for expanded water and sewer facilities, and to contribute $2.5 million toward school expansion.

In northwest Colorado's oil shale towns, Union, Chevron, and

Exxon have also worked, to a greater or lesser extent, with local governments.

To minimize negative effects from its projected plant on the south edge of the Piceance, Chevron has considered either housing its workers in Grand Junction and busing them to work, or buying property near De Beque and Parachute for the development of new communities.

Union has offered to finance two additional deputies and a new police cruiser for Garfield County, to help fund a new Parachute school, and to develop several hundred housing units in the Rifle-Parachute area.

And Exxon, in the most dramatic community-oriented building venture in the energy West, has carved a whole new $60 million to $100 million town out of the long, slanting walls of Battlement Mesa near Parachute. Its conception alone is little short of incredible. While its primary purpose is to house workers on the Colony Project, twelve miles north on Parachute Creek, in a broader sense Battlement Mesa is to be an open town. Its builder, Battlement Mesa, Incorporated, a subsidiary of Exxon, projects a population of 15,000 to 25,000 in place by 1995, living in 7400 dwelling units on a sweeping 3000-acre plot. By October 1981, 1500 people had moved into Battlement's prefabricated 14-by-74-foot brown loaflike housing units. Paved two- and four-lane roads spiraled up to them, across Parachute Bridge, by golf course, school, church, and business sites, by 760 acres of planned open space.

The Battlement Mesa project, to some, is a desecration of nature. But to others it is simply an adjustment to reality. Given the options of engulfing Parachute with Colony workers or chopping town space out of a Western Slope mesa, Exxon chose the latter.

Much of this has been commendable. In a January 1981 editorial, for example, the *Denver Post* hailed the "wise, cooperative recognition on the part of the companies" that their activities pose substantial dangers to western energy towns. And yet, despite it all, an unsettling feeling of exploitation still surrounds the issue. The specter of colonialism remains.

The fact is that some corporate actions have been taken only under duress, and often they have been taken more to profit the companies involved than the affected communities.

Western Fuels' action in Rangely, as one example, was taken primarily for Western Fuels. The stabilizing of local living conditions, said vice president Kenneth Holum, would stabilize working conditions and lead to higher productivity and greater company profit.

Critics of the Overthrust Industrial Association have charged that the group formed only when threatened with placement under Wyoming's tough Industrial Siting Act. The charge itself is not accurate, but the idea that the association was formed under some duress may be. In a Sun Valley debate in the summer of 1981 a bitter Wyoming state legislator argued that while oil systematically "destroyed" life along the Overthrust Belt, oil companies did nothing they were not *forced* to to stop it. An Idaho legislator, musing over a century of oil extraction in the region without any commensurate attempts to ease its effects on local land and people, called the companies' approach "immoral and unchristian." In response, an Amoco representative countered — as energy companies traditionally have in the West — that because the company generated money that enriched Wyoming, it felt no obligation to finance social and economic improvement. "We really don't think that's our job."

Oil companies operating in northwest Colorado sometimes have also acted under pressure. In late 1980, for example, Garfield County's commissioners threatened to withhold special-use permits from Union unless it agreed to prepay water and sewer taxes and help finance a local middle school. Union agreed. In the fall of 1981, when Union requested permission to sell $35 million in tax-free bonds to finance pollution-control equipment, the commissioners held that a final decision would be based in part on the company's willingness to provide further community impact aid. It would be unfair, perhaps, to say that whatever Union does next will be done in self-interest. But the possibility, at least, is there.

It is difficult to say when, where, and to what extent energy companies will extend aid in the future. Some care. Some do not. It is a fact of life the West must live with. But without their help, whatever the motivations behind it, the West will not indefinitely survive the energy boom.

Much depends, perhaps, on the fate of the boomtown aid bills introduced in the Senate in 1981 by Gary Hart and William Armstrong of Colorado. If the laws eventually pass, if energy companies are offered tax incentives to provide direct funds for development of local services and facilities, if they are offered deductions for prepayment of taxes, they might respond more positively to local problems than they have in the past.

But perhaps not. If the colonial mentality continues to operate tomorrow as it has in the past, as too often it does now, nothing will change at all.

And if that be the case, perhaps it is time for the West to take a firmer stance on the severance tax.

The West has fought many bitter battles over the years, but none of them have been more rancorous than the fight over severance taxes. Throughout this century western states have sought to tax mineral taken out of their ground. They have treated the tax for what it is — funding for social agencies and public works, for environmental protection, a trust fund to shield future generations of westerners from the social, economic, and physical ravages of mineral extraction today. The severance tax is and has been community insurance, a vital source of funding for the present and a hedge against the future. It has been salvation for more than one energy boomtown. And it has been an everlasting source of acrimony.

When the severance tax first became an issue in the West, it set energy companies against the states. While the states treated the tax as their due, as financial security for affected communities, the oil and coal giants treated it as a direct attack on their profits. In alliance with their local advocates, the companies successfully fought its enactment for decades. Running like a thread from the 1920s through the 1960s, the tax fight became one of the most divisive in the West's history. It also was one of the most symbolic. In the short run the West won it. In Wyoming, where oil companies warred against it for half a century, a severance tax finally was enacted in 1969. As political writer Neal Peirce has said, it was a "stinging rebuke for one of the most powerful lobbies ever organized in any American state." No win came easily, though. Montana, virtually suffocated by Anaconda and Montana Power for decades, finally enacted a severance tax in the 1960s. In Colorado the battle rages still, its legislature stubbornly opposed to raising a sadly inadequate 4 percent tax.

In the 1980s the severance tax is becoming the focus of one of the angriest political battles in years. The scene has changed from regional to national, however, and the protagonists, directly at least, no longer are the energy companies. The war now, tragically, is between the West and the East, and it is waged, mainly, by nonwest-

ern politicians, utility companies, and consumer groups against ener-
gy-exporting western states.

The primary issue is coal.

In general, the battle centers on taxes levied by western energy
states on exported or "severed" minerals that add to the total price
of the product at point of consumption. Whether coal or oil or
phosphate or molybdenum, what might be mined at relatively low
cost in the West might be consumed at relatively high cost in the
nonwest. More specifically, coal that might be mined at relatively
low cost at Gillette or Hayden or Craig might be consumed at high
cost in Little Rock or Detroit.

And the apparent injustice has outraged the nonwest.

Energy-consuming states, especially in the northeast, have blasted
the coal severance tax as extortionate. Washington economist Sally
Hunt Streiter, quoted in *Time* magazine, has said that "the coal
states have the power to become our OPEC within," and New York
taxation and finance commissioner James Tully has called them "the
fuel pharoahs of the Western world." In a 1981 study of the severance
tax, the Northeast-Midwest Institute concluded that it would create
"a new kind of 'United American Emirates,' a group of 'superstates'
with unprecedented power to beggar their neighbors in the federal
system." The worst of it, according to critics, is that by "exporting"
taxes — forcing the East to pay for western needs — the West has
been able to reduce its own taxes on its own people. As an aide to
Governor James Thompson of Illinois has said, the West is spreading
its tax burdens "around the country."

In 1980, action followed rhetoric.

Legislation appeared in Congress in the summer to force western
states to cap their coal severance taxes at 12.5 percent; the inference
was that if the non-West could cap coal taxes, eventually it could
establish a ceiling on natural gas, oil, and even shale oil. Primary
targets were Montana, with a 30 percent tax — highest in the nation
— and Wyoming, with 17 percent.

For a variety of reasons the legislation died. But when it did,
severance tax opponents took another course of action.

In the fall of the year, Commonwealth Edison (Illinois), in con-
junction with ten other utilities, four mining companies, and the
Northeast-Midwest Congressional Coalition of two dozen antitax
senators and congressmen, filed suit against Montana and its coal

tax. "The case," read the Commonwealth brief, "involves an attempt by one state, having an abundant supply of vital natural resources, to extract tribute from inhabitants of its energy-poor sister states." The "excessiveness" of the tax, it continued, created an unreasonable burden on interstate commerce, violating the commerce clause of the constitution and making the tax itself unconstitutional. "What Montana seeks to do," concluded the brief, "is to force the rest of the country to pay Montana an excessive tax for the use of a vital natural resource fortuitously located within its borders."

In July 1981 the United States Supreme Court ruled for Montana, asserting that the severance tax did not block interstate commerce and was not unconstitutional. At the same time, however, the Court also clearly affirmed that Congress has the power to establish severance tax *levels* in the sovereign states. The implication is obvious: should the populous non-West now choose to organize against the West in a common antitax cause, it would have the power to reduce the severance tax in Montana or any other state to 12.5 percent — or to nothing at all. To the West, the potential for damage, in a sense, is greater now than it was before the ruling, and the fact that new antitax legislation has appeared in Congress again in 1981 makes the matter more urgent than ever before.

For certain, it is a time of crisis. The East is convinced that the severance tax is exploitation, opportunism, a mechanism — as Representative Philip Sharp of Indiana has stated it — to "stick us up." It argues unconstitutionality and self-interest. It believes that western states intend to cut their own internal taxes at eastern expense by using the severance tax, by itself, to fund their governments. And it charges, as Representative John Dingell of Michigan has, that the West already reaps large benefits from coal production, that coal producers, not the states, pay for land reclamation, and that the federal government provides substantial aid to cover state costs. Says Dingell, "These taxes seem to exceed any needs the states may have for compensation."

In a sense eastern outrage is ironic. For the first time the East has begun to see what life is like at the colonial end of the economic system. But, in a larger sense, the view is tragic. It illustrates the kind of misunderstanding that has plagued the West for years. It shows that ignorance, arrogance, and paternalism color attitudes and assumptions today just as they did at the turn of the century. It is this condition the West has fought all its life, and apparently it still must.

So it is time for the West to state its case.

First, the primary factor in rising nonwestern fuel prices is *not* the western severance tax. In the case of coal, for example, where consumer prices have increased, other factors have been far more responsible for it than the severance tax. Part of the problem, at least, lies with the utility companies that buy and burn the coal. Another is spiraling transportation rates. Senator Malcolm Wallop of Wyoming cites the prime causes of the problem as automatic fuel-adjustment clauses that allow the passing of fuel costs to consumers without regulatory hearings, and the construction work–in–progress clause that allows utilities to charge current customers for the building of future plants. Wyoming's Governor Herschler contends that the primary problem itself is federal regulatory practices — withholding taxes, federal mining royalties, the abandoned-mine reclamation fund, black lung insurance, landowner royalty payments, workmens' compensation, and health and safety laws — that drive up costs. Herschler has argued, in fact, that regulations account for fully half the cost of coal.

Wyoming's case is important. Eighteen states burn its coal; much of its income is derived from it and much of its survival depends upon it. Its coal taxes bring in one third of its general fund income. Importantly, though, it collects only 3 percent of the total price of a ton of mined coal at point of consumption. The other 97 percent goes elsewhere — to federal taxes, shipping charges, mining costs, labor, and utility charges in consuming states. One ton of 10,000 Btu coal mined in Wyoming and transported east by rail for $20 a ton generates 1900 kilowatt hours of electricity at an Illinois power plant. Wyoming loses the resource, absorbs the socioeconomic impact to its communities, and assumes environmental costs, all for $1.35 a ton; Illinois, with a 4 percent sales tax on electrical power, assumes no risks, absorbs no impact — and generates $3.04 in revenue. Wyoming coal, then, becomes Illinois income. Byron Dorgan, North Dakota's tax commissioner, has shown that a single ton of North Dakota lignite coal would produce $65 worth of electricity in Detroit; but while the state that *produced* the coal would charge only 89¢ to deliver it, the state of Michigan would levy a 4 percent utility tax on the people who *use* it. What North Dakota mines for 89¢, Michigan converts to a $2.60 profit.

Montana coal delivered to the Lower Colorado Authority at La Grange, Texas, for $32.56 a ton is subject to state severance tax of

$3.21 a ton — 9 percent of the delivered price. Governor Ted Schwinden has said that Montana's tax adds only 23¢ a month to fuel bills in Minneapolis, 6¢ in Iowa, and 10¢ in Chicago. Colorado coal, sold to Illinois Power at Havana for $37.50 a ton, delivered, extracts a severance tax of 72¢ a ton — 1.9 percent of the delivered price.

If, as Representative J. J. Pickle of Texas has complained, "General Custer was not the last one to get scalped in the Little Bighorn country," the reason is not the severance tax.

Second, the West believes that if it bleeds for the rest of the country, the rest of the country should help pay for it. Energy-induced growth is too disruptive and too expensive for western communities to carry — or to be *expected* to carry — alone. The West has paid *its* taxes for a century, on Detroit automobiles, on Pittsburgh steel, on northeastern textiles, subsidizing nonwestern economic growth, helping ease the impact of growth on nonwestern communities, on nonwestern people. It expects the same in return now.

Critics forget the fact that the West pays its dues, too, and that it has exported money east far longer than the East has shipped it west. Former governor Brendan Byrne of New Jersey has warned that eventually western energy supremacy will mean "the largest transfer of wealth in the history of the country." If this is true, it ignores the entire span of western history — when wealth was transferred *out,* not in. If this is true, no westerner can see it as unjust.

Critics also ignore the fact that thirty-three states in the Union today have severance taxes. And most of them are not in the West. Ironically, much of the antitax sentiment has come from these states. No one in Congress, for example, has fought western severance taxes more bitterly than David Durenberger of Minnesota — but for sixty years his own state partly financed its public-school system and partially built the University of Minnesota from levies on Mesabi Range iron ore. In the southwest, where Louisiana, Texas, and Oklahoma, in particular, have assaulted the coal tax, all three have severance taxes on oil and natural gas. Including Alaska, the four states earn between $3 billion and $4 billion a year. Texas alone — where Attorney General Mark White has charged that Detroit Edison customers will pay $1.3 billion by the year 2000 to a single coal mine on federal property in Montana — makes nearly $2 billion a year on the exporting of energy. Their criticism of Montana and Wyoming, the *Denver Post* has editorialized, is an "exercise in political fantasy."

The facts speak for themselves.

As for charges of extortion, charges that the western states are subsidizing current programs at the expense of nonwestern states, those who make them do not understand what would happen to many mining-impacted communities without the funds. Montana's coal tax, for example, reaped $70 million for the state in 1980 and 1981 (along with $14 million more from oil and gas). Much of the income was funneled directly into Forsyth and Colstrip and other boom-towns. Five million dollars in state coal tax grants recently went to new school construction. Millions of dollars have gone for water and sewer systems, new public buildings (such as Forsyth's new city hall), for a mental health center worker in Colstrip. Boomtown life is poor enough as it is. Children are still housed in temporary class-rooms in Colstrip. Coal trains still split Forsyth for hours at a time. But without funds to work toward solutions to the problems, life in both places would be hopeless.

As for the issue of trust funds, those who do not know the West forget another critical fact: as Vine Deloria has said, the West does not *produce* energy; it *extracts* it. And when it is extracted, it is gone forever. In other words, the mining of western energy resources reaps a one-time harvest. Then, forever, the capital asset — and the taxing opportunity that goes with it — no longer exists. Without money held in trust, future generations are left with nothing.

Montana, Wyoming, and New Mexico are building billion-dollar trust funds to prevent precisely that. "The tax is excessive," says Robert Hartwell, vice president of Cleveland-Cliffs Iron, speaking of Montana's levy. But it is not excessive to states whose taxing power will be diminished in the future by the mining that occurs today. The tax, says Governor Ted Schwinden, will help "cover the costs of today" and still "leave us something when all the coal is gone." Montana, says Schwinden, resents the inference that "we will exploit our fellow Americans. That's folderol. We will share that resource with the rest of the United States. But we will [also tax] to protect the integrity of this state . . . and give us a decent place to live fifty or sixty years from now."

Finally, the severance tax involves one of the oldest and most emotional issues in western history: States' rights. The question of East against West is serious enough, but far more serious is the question of federal power. If Congress succeeds in capping western severance taxes, it will set a dangerous precedent of interference with the taxing authority of the sovereign states. The power and ability of the state to raise revenue is as old as the Constitution. Its abridgment would have a destructive effect on the West. Nonwesterners, too, should beware. If Congress reduces the coal tax in Montana today, it can reduce oil severance taxes in Texas and Louisiana tomorrow, and wood-products taxes in Oregon, and the iron ore tax in Minnesota.

On the severance tax, then, most of the West takes the only position it can. It supports the principle now and in the future, and it promises to oppose all federal attempts to dictate its limits. It will do so in the belief that the sovereign states have the authority and the duty to provide for the health, safety, and welfare of their citizens. It will do so in the belief that the federal government does not have the power to challenge the rights of the states to write their own tax laws. And it does so out of fear that a capping precedent on the coal severance tax will adversely affect severance taxes on all other minerals. If the West stands firm it will safeguard both its own governing rights and the welfare of its people. Again, the outside world should make no mistake about western resolve. As Byron Dorgan has said, the West "is not going to be made a national sacrifice area in order to air-condition Detroit and heat Minneapolis . . . we are simply not going to allow development to proceed in a way that charges the cost of that development to a future generation."

It may be, as the Northeast-Midwest study has said, that western severance taxes will eventually trigger "dangerously divisive tax warfare" where every state in the Union taxes precious commodities "just to preserve its competetive position." It may be, as it concludes, that "we have on our hands the makings of a civil war." It may be, but for western energy states it can no longer matter. "We are descendants of a pioneer generation," says Schwinden, "relentlessly exploited by corporate greed. We are . . . determined to protect Montana for future generations." The West looks at West Virginia and Kentucky and Tennessee and it sees itself. Montana sees itself. Wyoming. New Mexico.

And it resolves that what has happened there, because no one cared, will never happen here.

*   *   *

With so much at risk, the West asks, will America's energy policies even work? If the West is to be so burdened, if its towns and its people are to be so beset, will it at least be for the national benefit?

It cannot say. But its own past could serve as a lesson for the future.

The West has always appreciated the finite. It has always had to live within limits itself. What it has learned, and how, could be a valuable lesson for all the nation.

The concept of finiteness may be more important than all of America's energy put together. Sooner or later the nation must decide if it can produce its way out of the energy crisis or if it must change some of its long-held concepts and redesign its society to use less.

The illusion of infinite resources is a deep one and it does not die easily. But, like Copernicus, Americans sooner or later must challenge such accepted beliefs: they must ask if they are correctly conceptualizing the problem. George Santayana once observed that "fanaticism consists of redoubling your efforts when you have forgotten your aim." It would be fanaticism for America to try to solve the energy crisis by merely "redoubling" its efforts.

The overriding energy question for America is whether it should attempt to feed its voracious energy habit or try to put it on a diet. It would seem, even with exploiting all the West's energy resources, that it cannot go very much further into the future before running into mathematical, physical, biological, and socioeconomic limits. Clearly, the nation cannot continue indefinitely as it does now. Today it consumes fifteen times the energy it did a hundred years ago, although its population has only tripled in that time. A 1000-year supply of an energy source at its current level of use becomes a 104-year supply at a moderate 3.5 percent annual growth rate of usage. A 10,000-year supply would last only 170 years at a 3.5 percent growth in rate of usage. President Carter stated in his energy speech on April 18, 1977, that "in each of these decades [the 1950s and 1960s] more oil was consumed than in all of man's previous history combined."

If the demand for electrical power in the United States doubles in the next ten or twelve years, as it is expected to do, the quantity of electrical energy that will be used in those ten or twelve years will be approximately equal to the total of all of the electrical energy used in the entire history of this country.

The United States cannot continue to chase such curves. It must find some way to break them.

If America cannot produce out of this crisis, it can move both toward producing more *and* using less. The West, for example, did both with its finite water. It tried to impound more water at the same time it built its institutions to use less. It moved simultaneously in both directions.

The West believes that the lesson is applicable to the nation's energy dilemma. It must produce more *and* develop a new American ethic, a conservation ethic, that will offer energy security and energy self-reliance to all, regardless of world events which daily threaten that security.

To do this, America must place the production of energy from conservation — to date, a relatively cheap, untapped source of domestic energy — at the head of its list of energy priorities. Conservation must become the nation's primary goal for the short term, to generate quick new energy, and for the long term to promote the most efficient use of the nation's finite and renewable resources. Invisible to the eye, heat, for example, flows daily from homes and businesses through unsealed doors, windows, uninsulated attics, undampered furnaces and fireplaces. It pumps unimpeded into the atmosphere like the wasted fuel from thousands of "flared" oil wells. It also pours freely through the inefficiencies in America's transportation system, creating not only the means *for* travel, but the medium of polluted air through which people must travel.

Today, Americans are discovering that in order to capture that wasted energy, they have to conserve it. In order to conserve it, they have to find ways to focus and concentrate on it at its point of use. When they do this, they not only create the energy to meet a specific need, but enable the amount *not* wasted — the untapped reserve — to be directed toward a productive use somewhere else. In fact, researchers maintain that by producing energy through conservation measures, 30 to 40 percent of the nation's total energy could be recaptured.

To underscore the pivotal place that conservation can hold in national energy strategy, studies by the Harvard Business School, Resources for the Future, Princeton University researchers, the Ford and Mellon foundations, and the American Institute of Architects all stress its untapped potential. To quote the Harvard study, "Conser-

vation may well be the cheapest, safest, most productive energy
alternative readily available in large amounts." As the Harvard study
and the others point out, energy produced by conservation is, on the
average, three times as efficient in dollars and Btus as producing
energy through conventional sources. For of all the new energy
sources — nuclear, synfuels, solar, and others — none is as techno-
logically developed as the *primary conservation strategy,* the residential retrofit, a proven conservation technique that can make any
home more energy efficient.

The production of energy through conservation measures has an
especially strong appeal to the West. As it has argued, the presence
of energy may be a burden rather than a benefit to it. Yet the nation,
not just the West, has a stake in sane conclusions to this crisis.

As the whole nation is now discovering, new energy created to
supply growing demand is far more costly than old energy. And the
higher costs associated with supplying new energy must ultimately
be passed along to western consumers through steadily rising utility
bills. Until recently, the western states have enjoyed the lowest utility
and fuel prices in the nation. But that is changing dramatically. From
the winter of 1980–81 to the winter of 1981–82 the cost of natural gas,
which heats more than 95 percent of Colorado's residential buildings, rose a staggering 40 percent. Capital costs for new plant construction have skyrocketed, too. In 1965, the first unit of a coal-fired
power plant in the Craig-Hayden area cost *$162* per kilowatt of
capacity to build. In the early part of this decade, this cost will be
more than $1000 per kilowatt for the same area of the state. And
what is true for Colorado, again, is true for the rest of the West.

To further add to the energy demand, the influx of people into the
West to run and support the new energy industry and other new
service industries is steadily increasing. Therefore, the reduction of
demand for new and more costly energy by encouraging conservation measures is the only readily available protection for the residents
of western communities against the inevitable escalation of energy
rates.

In view of these realities, it is the West's belief that it has something even more important than its resources to share with the
nation: its appreciation of the finite and its lessons in dealing with
it throughout history. America stands at a crossroads. Will it rip up
the West in an insane attempt to keep up with another energy dou-

bling, or will it learn the lesson of limits, taught by the West, and move dramatically to use less energy? It is a watershed decision for the West. And for the nation.

*   *   *

In New York board rooms, oilmen and coal men look at maps of the West — color-coded splotches of red and green strung across synthetic canvas, mazes of latitudinal lines and meridians and elevations and numbers. To many of them, *this* is the West. Many have never been west, many never will go. To them, it is an abstraction — a Peckinpah film, an O'Keeffe painting, a Yellowstone postcard. A map on a board-room wall. On a summer afternoon in Meeker, people mow their lawns and teen-agers gather at the High Country Drive-In. Pickup trucks filled with farm machinery sit stolidly at crumbling curbs, and leather-faced men talk of drought. Warm air whips off the great plateau and strands of rain hang over the distant prairie. And the Sears store advertises a sale on blouses. Across a continent, Meeker is a red spash on a map, peopleless and lifeless, a collage of angles and humps and dots. And from the maps men make decisions that shape its life. On a map the depth of overburden at tract C-a is significant; crowded schools are not. Barrels of oil drilled is significant; child abuse is not. This is the way it has always been. Copper kings saw the West this way — and they gave it Butte. So did silver barons and railroads. In the past, as now, the West never was people. It was maps.

Now, on a summer day, traffic streams along the Colorado. Tumbleweeds bound through the deserted streets of Jeffrey City. In Grants and Anaconda and Gillette and Parachute, men meet in dimly lit bars and talk softly of good times and bad.

And they long for the day when they talk only of good.

CHAPTER FIVE

The Changing Face
of the West

In general, the prognosis for the 1980s is a very dim one if you extrapolate the present situation into the future. [There could be] a war between the states in the 1980s that will far exceed anything that happened in the 1970s.

PHILIP BURGESS,
former executive director,
Western Governors' Policy Office

IN THE LIGHT OF LATE AFTERNOON, Santa Fe nestles in its valley like a swath of green cloth on a desert table. Across the Rio Grande mountains roll to the west, and on September nights the setting sun fills their canyons with gold. To the east, like snow-mantled druids, the Sangre de Cristos guard the Pecos as it flows to the south. "Kuapoga," the Indians called it, "place of the shell beads near the water." To the Spaniards it was the Royal City of the Holy Faith of St. Francis. For 360 years, by whatever name, under whatever rule, Santa Fe has been the queen of the southwest. It has always been a special place, a fusion of physical beauty and cultural grace that dazzles the mind and soothes the soul, a kind of desert Brigadoon. Its magic lies in many things, but mostly in its smallness. And that, now, is disappearing. Like sister cities across the Sunbelt, Santa Fe is caught in a whirlpool of change. Brigadoon is dead. Not for a hundred years, but forever.

In early days Santa Fe anchored the booming Southwest. Caravans filled its city center, unloading whiskey and food and bolts of cloth at La Fonda, the inn at the end of the Santa Fe Trail. On hot summer days Indians sat stolidly under sweeping cottonwoods, mingling with Fort Marcy troopers in dusty blue, and wagoneers and cattlemen filled the raucous saloons. Around them all, Mexican farmers sold peppers and corn and bought blankets for winter nights. In time life changed. The Indians were harnessed in barren reservations. Fort Marcy died. Miners and cattlemen went to the frontier and disappeared. And the railroad came to Lamy. In 1912, the year New Mexico became a state, only 6000 people lived in the city of St. Francis. What Willa Cather called "a thin, wavering adobe town" had been passed by time.

It was this timelessness that brought Cather to Santa Fe, and Mary Austin and D. H. Lawrence, this that turned the valley of the Rio de Santa Fe into one of the most important cultural enclaves in the world. Even in all the years that they wrote, the city around them grew little. In 1920 only 7000 people lived in Santa Fe, 11,000 in 1930, and 20,000 in 1940. And, again, it was the city's smallness that bred its sense of intimacy, that allowed the gentle blending of Indian, Anglo, and Spanish cultures, that gave it its beauty. Even as late as the 1960s a walk through Santa Fe was a journey into the past.

And then, slowly, the city was discovered by the outside world. As the 1960s became the 1970s, as America began its shift toward the Sunbelt, it was found. By 1980, 48,000 people lived in Santa Fe, a 19 percent increase in the decade from 1970. Almost overnight, as it had once before, life began to change. Sleepy streets became busy streets, quiet nights became busy nights, and the moon no longer shone on an empty plaza. To be sure, much of the old city's heritage remains unchanged. The Santa Fe Opera, the chamber music festival, a repertory theater, and art galleries still give life to the legacy of Georgia O'Keeffe and John Sloan and Oliver La Farge. But in time almost surely it will be altered by growth. Even now tourist shops outnumber galleries and trinkets outnumber legitimate art. Convenience stores and cheap restaurants sprout on once-vacant land. From Canyon Road to the outlying hills, homes and condominiums blossom among the piñon groves, and soaring land values price local people out of their own market. "America's Salzburg" is in danger of engulfing itself.

Change is necessary. Growth is vital. But both are painful. Sitting serenely in the long shadow of the Sangre de Cristos, Santa Fe understands. Once, wrote Elizabeth Shepley Sergeant, New Mexico had an "austere and planetary look that daunts and challenges the soul," and no town more typified it than Santa Fe, city of light. But the feeling is gone. And, sadly, it will never come again.

The West and Southwest are the fastest-growing regions in America. Together, in the decade of the 1970s, they netted nearly nine times as many new residents as the Midwest and East. The West outpaced the rest of the United States with a growth rate of 23.9 percent, placing eight of its states — most of them growing at double the national average — among the top ten growth states of the 1970s. Each day 170 people move into Colorado's Front Range, and Arizona's growth rate exceeds Colorado's. Nevada was the Union's fastest-growing state, with a population increase of 63.5 percent. Wyoming, the fourth slowest growing state in the 1960s, became the fourth fastest growing state in the 1970s. Even with the inclusion of California, it is still awesome to think that the West gained 2280 residents each day of the 1970s.

Much of the growth is urban.

America thinks of the West as rural, but beginning with World War II innumerable small western towns have grown into important regional metropolises. The West has played catch-up with a vengeance with the urbanized East, but increasingly, it is the West's urban centers that set the pace for the nation. Though it is not widely recognized, perhaps because it goes against the grain of western myth, the West is the most urbanized section of the United States. Even as early as 1970 half of the West's states were among the twenty most urbanized states in the Union. Nevada's population, for example, was 80.9 percent urban, Utah's 80.4 percent, Arizona's 79.6 percent, and Colorado's 78.5 percent. In addition, nine of thirteen of America's fastest-growing cities of 100,000 or more people are in the Southwest. While Denver and Salt Lake City anchor the middle and northern Rockies' primary growth centers, Albuquerque (up 35 percent between 1970 and 1980), Santa Fe (19 percent), Tucson (26 percent), Pima City (51 percent), Phoenix (34 percent), and Maricopa, Arizona (56%), are typical of the booming Southwest. The transformation has been startling. In 1872 a California newspaper wrote that Phoenix one day would be center of the "Garden of the Pacific Slope" and the "most important inland town" in the Southwest. Now, perhaps, its time has come, along with that of Santa Fe and the other cities of the Sunbelt.

The West has always been a magnet. Horace Greeley's "Go west,

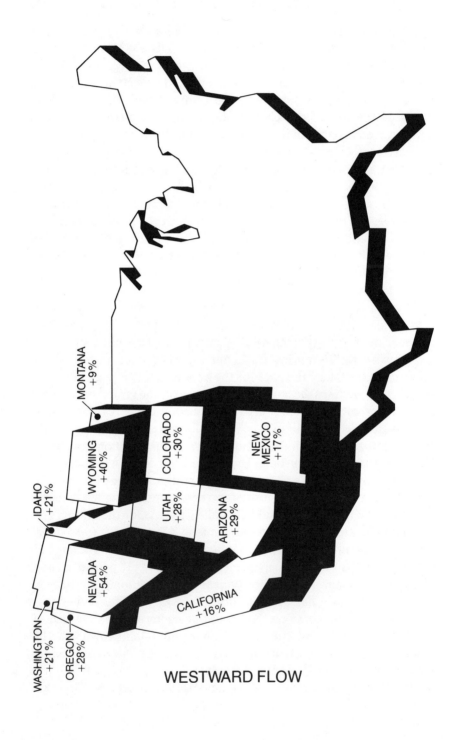

MONTANA +9%

WYOMING +40%

COLORADO +30%

NEW MEXICO +17%

IDAHO +21%

UTAH +28%

ARIZONA +29%

WASHINGTON +21%

OREGON +28%

NEVADA +54%

CALIFORNIA +16%

WESTWARD FLOW

young man, and grow up with the country" manifests both the past and present theology of the West as land of opportunity, as a geography of new starts.

It was known for its new beginnings. In Philadelphia, goes the old saw, they would ask what family a man came from, in Houston, how much money he had. But in the West the question was what kind of man he was. Ambitious people could get ahead regardless of background or wealth, and failed men could find what William Appleman Williams has called "an infinity of second chances." The premise still operates — and it vitalizes the new migration.

Now there is a gigantic economic imperative operating in the West, a new Manifest Destiny behind which thousands of people pour into the West every week. Observing it, one recalls the words of Alexis de Tocqueville:

> This gradual and continuous progress of the European race towards the Rocky Mountains has the solemnity of a providential event: it is like a deluge of men rising unabatedly, and daily driven onwards by the hand of God.

Whether it was the "hand of God" or economics that triggered the deluge, the process of settling the frontier set a whole mood for America. In a large sense it even fashioned it. "The existence of an area of free land, its continuous recession and the advance of American settlement westward, explain American development," said Frederick Jackson Turner. The West of the nineteenth century helped shape the American dream, unified the nation, and nurtured democracy.

In one important sense the West's twentieth-century boom differs from that of a century ago. On earlier frontiers a sense of adventure paralleled the quest for economic gain. Now the sense of adventure is largely gone; the new boom is primarily a search for economic gain. The West is seen mostly in economic terms — as a region where workers earn good livings. Much of the pioneering adventure is a thing of the western past. It is big dollars, not big sky, that draws most now.

Whatever the individual motivation for people coming West, it is clear that until the early 1970s, the West itself actively courted people and business in the name of growth and economic development. In Colorado, for example, John Love was elected to the governorship three times on a "bring business to Colorado" platform. Governor

Cal Rampton of Utah similarly was elected because voters thought he could bring "economic development" to the state. In Wyoming, Senator Gale McGee, gloating over Wyoming's coal, said he hoped that his state would become the "Pennsylvania of the West," and Governor Stanley Hathaway constantly campaigned for dramatic increases in industrialization and mining. Montana saw coal development as an "unmitigated good" in all its early stages.

The early 1970s, however, marked a dramatic turnaround in both public and political attitudes.

The West entered the 1970s not significantly different in some ways from the West of the 1870s — still with substantial federal and absentee ownership, still economically discriminated against by high freight rates, hidden charges, indirect taxation, and federal bureaucratic heavy-handedness. Its economy, as in the past, largely revolved around extractive industries that furnished the East with its raw materials. It was to the East what Canada was to England — a colony supplying natural resources to run the economy of the mother country. Interestingly, western historian Walter Caughey has written that westerners did not understand or mind their colonial status. "Curiously," he wrote, "westerners have shown relatively little awareness that they are cast in this subordinate role. In part, no doubt, the colonialism is not felt because it is concealed . . . and because comparatively few Westerners have much realization that the West is a region . . . the West has never been organized as a political unit, much less as an independent confederacy."

But the early 1970s brought a transformation in the western attitude. Skepticism about uncontrolled growth rooted and environmental consciousness began to spread. Slowly at first, then with a rush, "quality of life" issues gained dominance. Montana and Wyoming quickly enacted severance taxes and mined-land-reclamation legislation. Land-use planning was seriously debated for the first time, and Wyoming passed an unheard-of Industrial Siting Act and legislation to help plan, distribute, and use water. Montana's Environmental Policy Act of 1971 required environmental impact assessments, a step unthinkable at any previous time.

The West had learned its lesson. It learned that it had sold itself too well. It learned that it could never assimilate the massive inmigration that resulted from it. So yesterday's ethic of "growth at any price" changed to a mood of skepticism and caution. This is not to say that the West shut its doors. It did not. It continues to value economic development. All that has changed is attitude. As growth occurs now, and as it affects the economic, social, and environmental life of the old West, people view it with skepticism, not antagonism. They are determined to go ahead, but to go more slowly.

Even so, much has happened already that can never be reversed. Rapid urbanization, rapid population growth, and rapid industrialization have changed both the face of the West and its prevailing ethic forever.

Most important, the explosive growth of the West has created deep — and still deepening — sectional tensions.

Since the Civil War the United States has generally avoided regional conflict. Except for the Populist Revolt of the 1890s and the civil rights battles of the twentieth century, there have been no major regional conflicts in more than a hundred years. With increasing regional convergence over the years, Americans have become more and more a national people, and regional disputes have played a relatively minor role in their national policy. Their genius has permitted them to escape the parochialism and provincialism, the regional hates and jealousies of Europe. They became — as their pledge to their flag observes — "one nation, under God, indivisible."

But that now is changing. Sectional conflict suddenly has become a western way of life. Some have called the escalating tension between West and non-West the beginning of the "Second War Between the States." Others have spoken vividly of the "Balkanization of America." By whatever name it is a fearsome phenomenon — the setting of region against region, the unbecoming scramble for federal funds, the struggle to attract new industry, the concern for migrating industrial companies, jobs, and population, the talk about regional economic imbalances. The rebirth of parochialism.

The dispute centers on the controversy over the economic condition of the Sunbelt (the West and Southwest) vis-à-vis the Frostbelt (the Northeast and industrial states of the Midwest). Unlike the first War Between the States — which pitted North against South and only tangentially involved the West — the second war revolves around the West. It is under attack. "It's the West against the rest," a member of the Council of State Governments said recently. "The West has become what the South was in the 1940s and 1950s." As early as 1979 the *New York Times* said precisely the same thing — that the West had replaced the South as America's most abused and alienated area. Perhaps. Perhaps not. But one thing is certain. In the

1980s a new Mason-Dixon line is being drawn along the 100th meridian by the non-West. And its implications are severe.

Senator Orrin Hatch of Utah has said that "immigration to the West is by people who are sick and tired of being bound down by the lack of freedom in the East. It's not only that people are wanting to escape the confining attitudes and overregulated approaches of the East, but they also feel freer in the West." Hatch probably is right. But more to the point is his contention that "the West is the last great preserve of free enterprise." It is *this* that has brought the immigration, and it is this that has caused the tension. The exploding economy of the West, combined with the slumping economy of the East, has created the jealousy and fostered the misunderstanding that has fueled the new conflict.

In 1976 the *National Journal* inadvertently triggered the war when it concluded that "federal tax and spending policies were causing a massive flow of wealth from the Northeast and Midwest to the fast-growing southern and western regions of the nation . . . and eroded the tax bases of many state and local governments in the East and Midwest." An argument soon crystallized around several main assumptions. First, that a massive flow of people, jobs, and wealth from the Northeast to the South and West had begun. Second, that a heavy flow of federal revenues followed the exodus — away from states most in need to those least in need, from the needy to the greedy. Third, that states coming out ahead in the federal "balance of payments" — receiving more in federal dollars than they paid in federal taxes — were those with the most population gain, the least unemployment, and strongest gains in per capita income. And last, that states at the receiving end of federal largesse also tended to be those taxing their own citizens least for state and local government services.

This is not necessarily true. The idea that the western and High Plains states, and the states of the old Confederacy, represent a drain on the federal treasury, while the Great Lakes and northeastern states, with critical needs of their own, subsidize them, needs careful reexamination.

Shortly after publication of the *National Journal* article, the Economic Development Administration of the US Department of Commerce published a report titled "A Myth in the Making: The Southern Economic Challenge and the Northern Economic Decline," which reached substantially different conclusions. The study showed that northern states generally had a per capita income growth greater than the national average, while only three states in the South had greater-than-average increases. In other words, growth has not necessarily translated into prosperity. Contrary to what many believe, in 1979 most of the nine states with high per capita personal incomes (8 percent or more above the national average) lay in the urbanized Northeast; most of the eighteen states with low per capita incomes (at least 8 percent below the national average) lay in the Southeast and Rocky Mountain regions. Between 1978 and 1979 per capita personal income in the Rockies increased 9.1 percent, 1.9 percent less than the national average and the smallest rate of increase in any region in America. In 1979 per capita personal income in the Rockies still sat at 6 percent below the national average, second lowest among the Department of Commerce's eight regions.

In 1980 only three Rocky Mountain states — Wyoming, Colorado, and Nevada — were among America's highest per capita income states. Wyoming ranked sixth with $10,898, Nevada seventh with $10,727, and Colorado fifteenth with $10,025. And although Rocky Mountain states grew at a rate of 61.3 percent between 1974 and 1980, with an average per capita income of $8319, they still ranked second to *last* in Department of Commerce groupings. Their growth rate, great as it was, still trailed that of the Southwest (73 percent), including Arizona and New Mexico — with fairly ordinary per capita income averages of $8791 and $7841 — the Far West (67.2 percent), including Nevada, and the Great Lakes (61.6 percent). The Rockies did no better even than the Plains states, which registered an increase of 61 percent, and were only barely more impressive than New England (58.2 percent) and the Middle Atlantic group (53.8 percent). One day, perhaps, population growth *will* translate into prosperity, but the day is not yet at hand. Commerce Department reports indicate that, growth or not, the Rockies' per capita personal income will remain fully 2 percent below the national average even by the year 2000. Only Colorado and Wyoming will buck the trend.

The important "Myth in the Making" study further concluded that the "primary cause of unemployment in the North has been the death or closure of existing firms while the increases in employment in the South are due to expansion of existing firms." And it stated that "the problem of poverty is more pervasive in the South than in the North." Even eastern analysts, however, found fault with the statement. As one said, Northeast and New England policy makers will have made a fatal error if they begin to believe their own rhetoric. For although it is comforting to look outside one's region for the cause of its economic problems, one difficult truth remains: the primary cause of this region's decline can be found in decades of inaction and indifference by the region's own political and economic leaders, and not in the decisions of some distant Washington bureaucracy or western or southern political cabal. Said another, just as bluntly, "The major regional changes in the country have been determined by deep and understandable historical forces; they have only been marginally shaped by the balance of federal tax and expenditure flows."

Those who argue the existence of regional economic imbalances do so from a questionable base.

They argue, first, that the Great Lakes and northeastern states are the areas where the "needs" are. But what is their evidence? Their primary "proof" is unemployment rates — supplemented by assertions, not evidence, that the Sunbelt and Rocky Mountain states no longer need assistance once justified.

In fact, the problem of unemployment is not neatly segregated by region. While it is true that unemployment is a serious problem in some Great Lakes and northeastern states, it is no more serious in Illinois or Wisconsin than in many states of the South or West. In addition, several southern states (such as Florida) and western states (like New Mexico) have had unemployment problems that equal or exceed those in the Great Lakes and Northeast. An even more fundamental problem is that "economic distress" is defined only as a problem of "decline" in the first place. In fact, economic distress occurs when rapid economic change sets in — decline *or* growth. Given the West's growth, or the *nature* of the West's growth, economic distress *does* exist. The fact that it exists in a way undefined by the non-West is immaterial. If Cleveland hurts, so does Gillette.

Second, while making reference to the deteriorating condition of the aging infrastructure of the industrial heartland of America, critics make no references to the tremendous demands being made on the West to respond to the nation's energy needs. They say nothing of the fragile character of the western environment. They say nothing of the limited institutional and economic capacity of the West's small towns — like small towns anywhere — to absorb the new and rapid growth imposed by energy development.

So it is that energy, like slavery, is becoming a major regional issue, threatening to undermine interstate cooperation and national domestic policy. It has become a shouting match between the deaf and the dumb. Energy-rich states sport bumper stickers ("Drive Fast and Freeze a Yankee") and the East talks of the "emirates of the West" reaping vast energy profits at eastern expense. The East sees the severance tax as a symbol of rising energy costs that aggravates its economic distress, while the West sees the tax as the only way to make energy growth pay its own way.

The windfall profits tax is a similar case. In terms of distribution of proceeds, it is heavily slanted toward the Northeast and Midwest. Texans loudly complain that they will pay 55 percent of the tax but will receive only 3 percent of its profits. While the East points out that in the next ten years the four top oil-producing states — California, Alaska, Louisiana, and Texas — will receive $128 billion in royalties generated by price decontrol, the reality is that most benefits will flow to the North and East.

Looking to the future, the conventional wisdom is that growth is advantageous to an area. But, again, this is not necessarily true. It can be an advantage or not, depending upon its rate, its type, and how it meshes with existing economies. Governor Ted Schwinden of Montana says that the "problems of growth are the other side of opportunity." Without doubt the West faces extensive growth, and it faces it without several basic supports that other states have had. Unless it confronts growth with sophistication, it will never convert it to advantage.

The boom in the West, for instance, is coming at a time when federal funding has been cut back substantially. The East and Midwest, and even California, achieved their growth at times when massive federal funds were available for highways, sewers, and water systems. The federal government subsidized much of the costs of this growth (even as the non-West criticized the West for its place on the federal dole). The Rocky Mountain states will find it much more expensive to grow on their own, without this same help. As Alan Campbell, president of the National Association of Schools of Public Administration, has observed, "In the long run, and not all that long, growth in the Sunbelt will create an urban infrastructure which will lead their costs to approach those in the other regions, even though from time to time the people running those governments don't seem to think so."

Related to this is the fact that the non-West, primarily the East, built its infrastructure sixty to a hundred years ago when cheap labor (mainly from immigration) could be exploited. The West did this briefly in its own past, and it cannot and will not do it again. The result, again, is that its industrial revolution will be more expensive than those that came before it in other parts of America.

Add to this the fact that the West has always been largely devoid of its own capital. Ideally, when an "export base" industry is created, it generates not only jobs but profits as well. Those profits, deposited in local banks, become reinvested locally as mortgages and small-business loans to support housing and service sector needs created by community growth. In the West, though, much — perhaps most — economic growth is financed by eastern (and foreign) capital. The engine driving local, regional, and national growth is the private sector, and the pattern of investment by private commercial, indus-trial, and financial components drives the American economic sys-tem. In the energy area alone, the private sector will invest more than $1.2 trillion between 1980 and 1985, and in the West most of it will come — with strings attached — from outside.

This is the sad history of the West. Capital has *always* come from the outside, from the East, and western investments made by eastern-ers have always yielded more wealth to the East than to the West itself. Through 1975, for example, Bingham Canyon, "the richest hole on Earth," yielded 1,341,071 tons of copper ore, translating into 10,985,000 tons of copper. True, much outside capital vitalized the great mine and smelter, but the Utah earth provided the raw material and Utah men the labor. And they — the state and the people — received little in benefits. Bingham Canyon alone has produced nine times more in copper values than the California gold rush, the Com-stock Lode, and the Klondike together produced in precious metal values. But the profits have flowed east. The Bunker Hill and Sul-livan in Idaho, the Homestake in South Dakota, Phelps Dodge in Arizona, Climax Molybdenum in Colorado, Rockefeller interests in Colorado, Guggenheim interests everywhere — their histories are all the same.

Rarely have the interests of the outsiders been in the states produc-ing their wealth. Montana, for example, has been a classic case in point. Clark G. Spence has called it a "subject dominion, a pitilessly misused state." "From the American Fur Company to Anaconda, the Federal Reserve System and the fossil-fuel giants of the 1970s," he has written, "spokesmen deemed the region an economic, political, and cultural satrapy of other parts of the nation." Here, Montanans watched Standard Oil try to change "a land of enchantment into one of their banks." Here, wrote John Gunther in *Inside U.S.A.,* Anaconda, "a company aptly named," maintained a half-century "constrictorlike grip" that made Montana "nearest to a 'colony' of any American state" except Delaware. Here, too, William Andrew Clark came from Iowa in the 1860s, consolidated the state's copper industry, accumulated one of the world's great fortunes — upwards of $250 million — and bequeathed it all to the Los Angeles Philharmonic Orchestra, the Clark Memorial Library at UCLA, and the law school at the University of Virginia. A contemporary of his, George Hearst of California, made a similar fortune from the Anaconda Copper Mine at Butte (as well as from mines in Utah and South Dakota), and when he died in the early 1890s proceeds from his Anaconda shares were bequeathed to his son, William Randolph, to continue his career in journalism.

In 1939 historian K. Ross Toole found that the Mountain West produced $126 million dollars of copper in that year alone and that the industry made money payments of only $86 million within the region. "Even discounting overhead," he wrote, "there is here illustrated a substantial 'leak' in the regional balance of payments, too much of a discrepancy between the wealth produced and the wealth received."

In the final analysis, regional balance sheets are deceptive, their figures often elusive. Wealth flows both ways and it is difficult to accurately assess the exact nature of the flow. Nonetheless, it remains true in the history of the West that more profits have flowed out through the years, northward and eastward, than have remained. "In his whole country," Bernard De Voto once wrote, the westerner has never "been able to borrow money or make a shipment or set a price except at the discretion of a board of directors in the East." Walter Prescott Webb, in *Divided We Stand,* made the same point. Comparing bank deposits, tariffs, insurance holdings, and other economic indicators, he found the West and South lagged dramatically behind the Northeast in economic growth. The fact was — as it still is — that either the wealth of the West flowed east in the form of dividends or that people made their fortunes in the West and then moved east.

Old patterns continue today, underlying the whole Frostbelt-Sunbelt issue. Like yesterday's Montana, today's Colorado is a case in point. All oil shale companies operating or planning to operate in the state are non-Colorado companies. All of the major coal companies are as well. Colorado's major uranium production is almost exclusively by out-of-state companies. So is its molybdenum production. Even in peripheral areas vestiges of colonialism remain rooted in the state. The *Denver Post* is Los Angeles–owned, and the *Rocky Mountain News* is Cleveland-owned. Eight of ten of Colorado's major newspapers are owned from out of state. All of Denver's major commercial television stations are owned by non-Colorado companies. Nine public television stations exist in Colorado, six and a half of them owned from a distance in other states. Of Colorado's ten largest employers, only four even have corporate headquarters in the state. If size is defined in assets, only three of the ten largest corporations in Colorado are, in fact, Colorado corporations. Finally, much — and perhaps most — of the building boom in the Denver metropolitan area is fueled by out-of-state companies, and the long-term mortgage financing for Denver office space has come 99 percent from out of state.

As long as the pattern holds, in Colorado or anywhere else, it is a fact that no amount of economic movement to the West will help it. It will build. It will grow. Perhaps it will prosper. But, as in the days of the Guggenheims and the Rockefellers, it will not belong to itself. It will not control its own destiny.

Partly in light of the ownership issue, it would seem important for the nation, areas of growth and areas of decline alike, to adopt a policy that would better balance both economic and population growth. It makes little sense for some areas to grow so fast that the growth becomes counterproductive, while other areas are drained of their human and economic resources.

It is the West's strong thesis that current westward migration has a negative effect both on the states that lose population and on the states that gain it. People leave costly, long-established and fully functional school systems, sewer systems, streets, hospitals, and governmental infrastructures in the Northeast and the Midwest and move to high-growth Sunbelt areas — already strained by ballooning growth — where the systems have to be duplicated at great expense by the receiving area. In addition, the migration of professional people and skilled and semiskilled workers from the Northeast and Midwest robs those regions of important human capital and needed tax base. The whole nation becomes poorer.

The question before the nation, then, is whether public policy can and should guide growth patterns. The West submits that it not only can, but should. However, that policy should discourage migration, not encourage it.

In the world of public policy, trend is not necessarily destiny. Migration is not inevitable, and public policy does not have to blindly accept current trends. Congress, in fact, has taken halting steps toward a national growth policy. The Urban Growth and New Community Development Act of 1970 declared that the federal government "must assume responsibility for the development of a national urban growth policy" that would "help reverse trends of migration and physical growth which reinforce disparities among states, regions, and cities."

Beyond this, the Advisory Committee on Intergovernmental Relations has set forth the following initiatives as "useful approaches to the implementation of national policy regarding urban growth": First, federal financing incentives, such as taxes, loans, or direct payment arrangements for business and industrial location in certain areas. Second, placement of federal procurement contracts and construction projects to foster urban growth in certain areas. Third, federal policies and programs to influence the mobility of people, to neutralize factors producing continued excessive population concentrations and to encourage alternative locational choices. Last, federal involvement and assistance, under certain conditions (such as assurance of an adequate range of housing) for large-scale urban and new community developments.

This thrust is not new. Government policy in the past has very clearly affected locational decisions. Senator Daniel Patrick Moynihan has said, only half facetiously, that "the nation has long had a national growth policy under the more modest name of the Federal Highway Act." But certainly, along with highways, national policies in housing and mortgage loans have done much to contribute to the growth of the suburbs and the decline of the inner cities. The policies of the past have contributed to the problems of the nation's largest cities; the United States should not continue the mistake by shifting those problems to the Sunbelt region and the West.

The problem that the advisory committee addresses is not unique to America. Great Britain, France, the Netherlands, Italy, and Sweden have attempted, with varying degrees of success, to influence settlement patterns. France, in the early 1960s, was faced with a drain on its countryside and an unmanageable growth rate in Paris. The French government developed a policy of *métropoles d'equilibre* (counterweight metropolises) that set up alternative growth centers in other parts of France to serve as magnets to attract some of the growth directed toward Paris. Similarly, the Netherlands, Sweden, Great Britain, and Israel all have explored ways that national policy might affect population distribution. These policies have not only been considered successful, but have been accelerated.

Similar policies can and should be tried in the United States. Many people are moving to the Sunbelt, not necessarily because they want to, but because they have to. If there are no jobs in their hometowns, people will clearly go where they are. But the creation of economic opportunity, while primarily determined by the private sector, can clearly be affected by incentives, tax policy, procurement decisions, and other public policies.

In the 1980s the nation stands on the brink of making public-policy decisions that may rank among the most important it has ever addressed. Should it encourage, or should it even allow, a massive shift of population from one part of the country to another? Where will the East get the tax monies to cover the inevitable cost of decline? How can the nation avoid, once decline goes beyond a certain point, a downward spiral that can only end in fiscal disaster? Conversely, where will the West find water to support all of the new growth? Where will it find the tax resources to duplicate all of the municipal services for people who have just abandoned their own in another part of the country?

Public-policy makers do not have to accept as a given fact the current migration from the Northeast and the Midwest to the Sunbelt. It would appear that this particular recommendation is bankrupt and should be rejected.

In the meantime, until proven otherwise, westerners insist that charges against them are too broad, too undiscriminating, too grossly oversimplified and counterproductive to bear serious consideration. In short, the West feels that Sunbelt-Frostbelt issues are being formulated and conclusions are being drawn in ways that do injustice to western states, that undermine the basic concept of commonwealths, that tend to foster unnecessary and damaging competition among America's regions, its states, and its people. And all this is happening at a time when the nation should be trying to strengthen the capacity of its states and their elected leadership to work together to promote the public good.

*   *   *

No one knows what the future holds. But it is certain that the boom in the Sunbelt will continue — perhaps until it becomes a crisis. As long as the West continues to be seen — accurately or not — as an economic mecca, people will migrate there. The United States Bureau of Economic Analysis predicts that the total population of Colorado, Utah, Montana, Idaho, and Wyoming will rise more than twice as fast as in the rest of the United States over the next two decades. The United States Commerce Department forecasts creation of 633,000 new jobs in the West by 1983 and 3.8 million by 1990, a rise of 18 percent from 1981. By 1985 energy-related jobs alone will increase by 200,000 over 1981. The demand for engineers will jump 50 percent, managers 66 percent, draftsmen 80 percent. And Denver, Billings, Salt Lake City, Albuquerque, Tucson, Phoenix, Casper, Grand Junction, and boomtowns from Craig to Colstrip will continue to grow with the demand.

At the same time, drawn by the mountains and the desert, others will move West — as they always have — for its grace and beauty. Jackson will grow, sprawling over soft meadows and open fields. And Vail. And villages from Flagstaff and Kingman to Roswell and Ogden and Sand Point, where life has changed little in this century.

Already Santa Feans are moving to Tusuque in the foothills of the Sangre de Cristos, moving to escape the urbanization of their once-unspoiled town. On September nights the setting sun still fills the canyons with gold. But it will never be quite the same again.

CHAPTER SIX

Battle-Born: The MX

I love this lovely place. I'm so proud of our valleys. If the MX came here, it would leave scars forever on our fragile land. We stand in fear of being invaded by our own government.

SUSIE DOUGLASS,17
valedictory address
West Desert High School
near Partoun, Utah

1946.

Cold War.

America had the atomic bomb, Russia did not, and for a single fleeting historical moment it held the balance of terror in a war-torn world.

The brief advantage shifted in 1949, and again in 1956, when Russia developed its own bomb and a delivery system with it. By 1957 the balance of terror was stabilized at dead center. By 1957 America's nuclear supremacy had dissolved like snow on summer wind.

Faced with growing vulnerability to Soviet nuclear attack, the United States began construction of a massive and diversified deterrent force. At its core lay a sophisticated triad of missile-packing Trident submarines and far-ranging bombers supported by scores of deadly ICBMs buried in the quiet desolation of the American plains. In theory the triad was adequate to blunt a Soviet first strike. Military planners argued that the sheer impossibility of neutralizing three different American attack forces at one time would deter Russia from nuclear assault on the West. But doubts about the system remained, most of them focused on the apparently increasing vulnerability of America's land-based ICBMs.

At one time, perhaps, Titan and Minuteman were secure, nestled in silos deep beneath the prairie floor, pinpointed by Russian intelligence — under conditions of the SALT treaty of 1972 — but unreachable by Russian missiles. But Soviet perfection of sophisticated rocket-guidance systems in the 1970s brought a swift and stunning end to that security. America's potent "counterforce" strategy of the 1960s — operating on the assumption that the United States had enough nuclear weaponry to both blunt a Soviet first strike and then respond in kind with nuclear annihilation of its own — was destroyed overnight by the Russian development of systems precise enough to guide missiles over five thousand miles of space to within half a mile of target. The new developments specifically endangered Minuteman, the most important element in the American triad. Invulnerable, it stood as a lethal deterrent to Russian aggression; vulnerable, it literally invited it. In the 1970s Minuteman's sudden susceptibility became a major American problem. In the 1980s it is a problem still.

In America in the early 1980s two facts seem clear. First, the nation is increasingly vulnerable to a Soviet first strike. Russia aims 1398 ICBMs at America's throat — SS-17s with four nuclear warheads each, SS-18s (the so-called monster missiles) with eight to ten, and SS-19s with six. The United States counters over 5000 warheads with only 1052 ICBMs of its own — 52 single-warhead Titans, 450 single-warhead Minuteman IIs, and 550 triple-warhead Minuteman IIIs — and 2152 warheads among them. Second, because of this disparity, American ICBMs, particularly Minuteman, are in growing danger of destruction. With increasing forcefulness, American military planners argue that a Russian attack now, in the 1980s, could obliterate 90 percent of Minuteman before launch. Thirty minutes after firing, Soviet SS-18s could swoop down on Minuteman bases in Montana, Wyoming, and the Dakotas — and Titan bases in Arizona, Arkansas, and Kansas — hurling one-megaton warheads at each of the ICBM silos, incinerating missiles where they sit. The prospect is terrifying. Minuteman, in particular, is the heaviest, best-controlled, most accurate component in America's nuclear triad. Its destruction in a first wave of nuclear attack would lead to national holocaust.

Salvation — if it exists — may lie in the MX.

As early as 1974 the federal government began working toward development of a mobile, far-striking missile to replace Minuteman, or at least to implement it, an ICBM to protect the protector. The result was the "missile experimental" — MX — a 71-foot-long, 190,-000 pound white-jacketed rocket capable of carrying 3350 kilotons of destruction across 8000 miles of land and sea to Russian targets. From the day of its birth, perhaps because of its hugeness, perhaps because of the incredibility that surrounded it, MX was a lightning rod for controversy. Opponents argued, and still do, that it is a modern-day Maginot Line, easily outflanked by Soviet nuclear strategy, a system obsolete at conception. But supporters still hold that MX is sound, that in case of Soviet attack — if it is provided with mobile basing to shield it from attack — it contains more than enough firepower to destroy Russia's entire arsenal of ICBMs. In March 1980 National Security Adviser Zbigniew Brzezinski bluntly said that MX would "reduce Soviet incentives to initiate an attack" against the United States by giving it the unprecedented ability to "respond in kind." Perhaps he was right. Perhaps not. In any case, MX was only as secure as its basing mode made it, and most of the MX controversy surrounded precisely that point.

In the summer of 1980, after six years of federal work on the project, the Carter administration announced final plans for the building and deployment of MX. As outlined by Carter, the plan called for the construction of 200 missiles by 1984. Even on paper the venture was awesome. MX was to be the most expensive missile ever developed by the United States, its range of $33 billion to $100 billion in construction costs three times greater than the Alaska pipeline and its operating costs — leveling off at $440 million a year — far greater than anything in American history.

The projected building of the MX was an important matter and national debate swirled around it instantly. But a bigger matter by far was the question of the missile's *basing mode,* and here the Carter plan almost defied comprehension.

Keying on mobility and deception — precisely what Minuteman did not have — the administration proposed deployment of the MX in horizontal garages scattered through the canyons and valleys of the Nevada-Utah Great Basin. To avoid neutralization in a Soviet first strike, MX planners blueprinted 4600 shelters, 23 for each missile, located 7000 feet apart to avoid mass destruction in case of attack. On a secret, shifting timetable, the 200 missiles were to be shuffled in and out of the 4600 shelters. Unable to know, on any given day, precisely where the missiles were, and forced to bracket each garage with two missiles to guarantee destruction, the Soviet Union was placed in the position of having to fire 9200 missiles to destroy 200. The United States was willing to gamble that Russia could not afford the cost and would not afford the risk. But no one knew. The game, simply, was nuclear hide-and-seek, a colossal and outrageous shell game, a deadly dance with the fate of the world in the balance.

From the beginning, most of the Great Basin West opposed the MX. Slowly at first, then with increasing intensity, anti-MX sentiment swept through the Basin like a desert storm. But as controversial as the Carter plan was, and as bitterly fought, it was never written in stone. When Carter fell from grace in 1980, the plan fell with him. After months of debate over whether to continue it, Ronald Reagan determined that he would not. On the second day of October 1981, the president announced that the MX would not be deployed in the Great Basin.

In broad terms the Reagan defense plan projected layer upon layer of missiles, countermissiles, radar-elusive bombers, AWACS observation planes, mobile tracking stations, upgraded Trident submarines, and armed space satellites with which to counter — or deter — a Soviet first strike. At the heart of the plan lay the MX, permanently based in continuously flying bombers, in deep underground shelters, or on ABM-protected land bases — a decision to be made by 1984 — but temporarily to be housed in existing Titan and Minuteman silos scattered across the Midwest and West. Under the Reagan plan 100 missiles were to be built, not 200, the first 36 at a cost of $300 million. While their deployment pattern was not clearly defined, military analysts seemed to focus on MX replacement of Titan II in Arizona, Kansas, and Arkansas, and, later, of Minuteman III in Wyoming, Montana, and the Dakotas.

But wherever it goes, and no matter for how long, the MX will disrupt all life around it.

Sometimes the Great Plains seem never to have been touched by man. Winter snow clings to them, dazzling in the sun, turning them into an ocean of shimmering white. Summer wind roars across them, churning them to powder. The seasons bring different kinds of life to the plains — summer vibrance, winter desolation — but not even the seasons change the everlasting sameness of the land itself. Beneath winter snow or summer dust, the plains remain immutable, timeless. And the life that endures on them is the same.

There is a beauty here that transcends description. On the upper Missouri newly plowed earth flows east and west against the Montana sky. South Dakota wheat fields reach as far as the eye can see, filling space with the colors of auburn and gold. In the North Dakota sun, ragged bales of new-mown hay lie scattered across the landscape at White Earth and Wildrose, as if thrown there by the wind. Grain elevators, like prairie temples, rise from brown earth everywhere, breaking the levelness of the horizon with their peaks and spires. Country stores with faded signs. Country towns with faded pasts. Country people with faded dreams. They have all been here for generations. And they have changed little with the passage of time.

But even on a temporary basis the MX will change them forever. Manpower needs, for example, will likely drain country towns of their already small labor pools. Wildlife may be permanently dislocated. Water will be lost, especially in the making of massive amounts of cement to harden the silos, and much not lost will be polluted. The invasion of outside workers — even temporarily — will bring economic boom to towns that have never seen it, never coped with it; and those towns that overbuild and overdevelop in response to it will be left in financial ruin if MX leaves in 1984. In a sense the stakes in the plains towns are higher than in energy towns. Coal and oil, at least, have staying power, and even shale oil has some relative viability. But the MX is ephemeral, and towns building their lives around it will play a dangerous game.

On a short-term basis the West knows not what to expect from MX. It does not know, in fact, whether the MX even will be short term. If the "deep" basing mode is adopted in 1984 — the placement of MX in the south walls of western mesas and mountains — the West will be transformed in ways it cannot now possibly comprehend. The problems of small plains communities — among which, at least, the silos are already *built* — will be multiplied in high country regions already affected by energy development. Again, the possibilities — most of them negative — are limitless.

But boom and bust is insignificant beside another fact — that if MX becomes a lightning rod for Soviet fire the plains become the primary nuclear target in America.

To some extent, of course, they have always been a target. Titan and Minuteman have lain for years in the cold prairie earth. As a northern Colorado county commissioner said in the fall of 1981, "if there's gonna be a missile in there, it doesn't make much difference" which one it is. But perhaps it does. MX is a different matter from either Titan or Minuteman. The fact is — as MX critics have pointed out — that Titan and Minuteman have had so little first-strike capacity over the years that they have not generated any Russian desire to launch a pre-emptive first strike. But MX *does* have first-strike capacity, and it almost certainly will be seen by Russia as an offensive weapon. Logic suggests, then, that the MX by and of itself will greatly frighten a nation — Russia — carrying 85 percent of its nuclear warheads on land-based missiles. Because MX now will be based in fixed silos, at least momentarily, and because these silos have long been pinpointed by Russia, logic also suggests that the silos' once-in-a-lifetime vulnerability might be too big a temptation for the Soviet Union to resist. Senator Henry Jackson has said, simply, that "we have given the Soviets a bigger target to shoot at," and a more stationary target at that. This fact alone, perhaps, places the western prairie — and its people — in the eye of the nuclear hurricane.

If attack came, it would shatter the fragile world of the West. In a Soviet first strike missiles would pour out of the sky, hitting each American ICBM — MX or otherwise — with eighty times the destructive force of the atomic bomb dropped on Hiroshima. Within a two-mile radius everything living would be incinerated. Because of the relatively small population of the plains, few people would die in the initial nuclear attack. But radioactive fallout, drifting downwind from target zero, would kill everything in its path. Fifty percent of the population would die between Tucson and the New Mexico border, fifty percent across the northeastern tier of Montana, fifty percent in southeast Wyoming and northeast Colorado and the southeast corner of Kansas. Nebraska and the Dakotas would be saturated: half the population would die in the upper half of South Dakota and in most of North Dakota and Nebraska. Only Minnesota, Iowa, Missouri, Illinois, Indiana, Kentucky, and Arkansas would suffer anywhere near the same amount of destruction. "The Russians have gained on us so bad," says a northern Colorado rancher, "I figure if God wants to protect me, he'll take care of me." It is easy, perhaps, to say. But if he is wrong, he will be wrong only once. He will have no second chances.

In a September 1981 poll taken by the Behavior Research Center of Arizona shortly before announcement of the Reagan plan, 58 percent of 1150 Westerners interviewed in eight states opposed MX basing in the West. But the prairie West, so far, has reacted with caution to the Reagan plan. The National Cattlemen's Association has approved it, along with the Cheyenne City Council, and Representative Richard Cheney of Wyoming has said that if the MX comes to his state — which it will — "it would probably be in the best interests of our national defense." But Wyoming Against the MX and the Wyoming Coalition of Churches have bitterly reacted against it. More than three hundred residents of Laramie County have signed petitions against it. A Missoula minister was detained by military police after a December 1981 protest at a missile site west of Simms, Montana. Montana's two Catholic bishops have deplored it. And governors Ted Schwinden of Montana, John Evans of Idaho, Bruce King of New Mexico, and Ed Herschler of Wyoming have clearly stated that they do not want MX in their midst.

In the end, perhaps, MX will return to the Great Basin no matter what the prairie states think or do. On December 2, 1981, the Senate voted 90 to 4 to block the expenditure of $334 million for research to superharden existing silos. At the same time, Congress has appropriated $125 million to continue study of the alternate basing modes — including the desert-based multiple protective shelter plan. At a meeting of western governors at Scottsdale in November 1981, Stephen T. Bradhurst, director of the MX Project Field Office for the state of Nevada, candidly said that the "deceptive" basing mode — the desert shell game — still was very much alive as an option for permanent deployment after 1984. At this writing, in fact, it still may be the odds-on favorite.

Perhaps the Great Basin war has just begun.

*   *   *

The barren surface of the Great Basin unfurls across the intermountain West like an endless sun-bleached banner. On its western edge it rams the jagged Sierra Nevada, melting gradually into the rocky barriers of Pyramid Lake. In the east it arcs across Utah in a sterile crescent — from the dead shores of the Great Salt Lake easterly along the ramparts of the Wasatch, south across the Sevier Desert and southern Nevada to the arid wastes of Death Valley. Waves of mountain chains rib its interior, ebbing north and south across the desert, trapping empty alkali-stained canyons among them. From the snowcapped Humboldts the mountain clusters ripple eastward through Nevada and Utah like waves breaking across the landscape of an alien planet. Serrated cliffs of pink and black rise and plunge among stark mud flats. Bare hills swoop in and out of dreary expanses of rock, lava, and yellow clay. Lonely buttes stand like sentinels against the sky, their spires and terraces dropping abruptly to canyons and gorges that wind endlessly through the flatness. Stillwater, Shoshone, Monitor, Hot Creek, Diamond, Pancake — Nevada's ranges swell across the Basin like giant stepping stones. Then, across the Utah badlands, past the shimmering dry bed of Sevier Lake, the Needle, Confusion, Cricket, and Deep Creek ranges roll intermittently to the Wasatch Front.

The mountain chains rise like huge razorbacks across the endless expanse of sand. Beneath them the desert lies like a vast dead skin. Desert gives way to more desert — the Big Smoky Valley becomes Cactus Flat, Railroad Valley becomes the Escalante Desert, and to the north the Great Salt Lake Desert dwarfs them all. The desert shapes life and everything in it. Yet, like the plains, it remains timeless itself. Summer sun scorches it. Winter winds freeze it. But nothing changes it. It remains today and tomorrow what it was at the beginning of time — beautiful, impassive, and infinite.

Waterways cut through the desert like arteries, giving the land its life. The Humboldt River burrows through range after range on a 300-mile journey from southern Idaho to the Basin's western edge, where it sinks into the sand. From the Sierra Nevada, the Carson, Trukee, Owen, Walker, and Mohave pour into the region's lakes and sinks, and in the east the Bear, Jordan, Timpanogos, Spanish, and Sevier slash out of the Wasatch. The Colorado, thundering through the Colorado Plateau, forms the Basin's eastern limits on its way to Nevada. Nowhere in the world, perhaps, is water more precious. And nowhere does life cling more tenuously to it.

The Basin is filled with life. On its mountain rims and along its watersheds, forests of dwarf cedar reach across shallow hills to the desert's edge. Ribbons of elder, cottonwood, and willow wind through the valleys. In the fall oceans of red and gold blanket the far mountains, studding miles of blue-gray with patches of blazing color. In the spring flowering trees thread through the valleys, and thickets of gooseberries and currants and wildflowers grow in small meadows. On the desert floor scorpions and rattlesnakes slither through miles of bunch grass and piñon while hawks circle above them in the sky. Sage spreads like a purple-gray carpet as far as the eye can see, broken only by waves of bronze-colored greasewood and clumps of yucca and soapweed bursting from the sand. And cactus, its flame-colored blossoms brilliant in the spring, stretches lazily in the sun.

The air is sharp and crystalline, filled with the pungent scent of sage. The skies, translucent blue, fill the horizons. Empty one minute, they fill with storms the next — dust storms, rolling inland across the Sierra Nevada on warm ocean winds, thunderstorms swirling above the land in summer, snowstorms that rake it in winter, then slip quietly away. It is a land of violent extremes, and yet, as Hubert Howe Bancroft wrote a century ago, in the desert "seasons glide into one another almost imperceptibly." Only May is fickle; only May "spurts thunder and lightning between her smiles."

From the Sierra Nevada to the Salt Lake the Great Basin is a region of stunning and everlasting beauty. In the mind, its scenes are unforgettable — crags, like ancient totems, standing against a summer sunset, stars blazing through black desert nights, arroyos, like giant fingers, snaking through islands of pink sandstone, a rainbow over the Black Rock Desert, a cactus petal framed in snow. In the western mind these are the desert's images. And to those who live in the desert, they are precious images.

And now the MX.

The Great Basin is one of the most fragile ecosystems on earth; placement of the MX in its midst would be a menace to its very existence. Perhaps the vast, empty space of the desert could absorb small-scale building, but the MX is not small scale. Perhaps the Basin could absorb minimal physical destruction, but the MX would threaten physical destruction on a scale that no single part of the nation has ever seen. Its numbers alone are staggering: 46,000 shelters, 200 missiles, 30,000 workers. The very magnitude of the numbers frightens desert westerners (in the same way the shale oil industry frightens Coloradans). The incredible, almost incomprehensible hugeness of the numbers leaves them bewildered and angered. In December 1980 a draft environmental impact statement said that permanent and "rapid, large-scale changes in the character of human environment" would follow in the wake of the MX. Outsiders have no comprehension of this, but westerners do. They have seen it before.

The MX would appropriate an almost incredible amount of desert land — land that has stood empty and unspoiled for centuries. Almost certainly, its delicate ecological balance would be altered. Possibly, it would be destroyed. Air Force planners estimate that the 4600 shelters could be sited on 7000 to 9000 square miles of land, and that the project's entire "action area" — 70 percent of it in Nevada, 30 percent in Utah — would consume 30,000 to 46,000 square miles altogether. The project would spread over the region like a huge fishnet, its fenced canyon shelters fused to 7000 to 10,000 miles of roads slicing through the desert into its natural basins. Logically, desert life could not be expected to survive the disruption. More than 160,000 acres, at the least, would be cleared, scraped, and gouged for construction; as men and machines moved in they would literally pulverize the landscape. Environmentalists warn that some animal species would be wiped out. Plant life would be damaged — some of it destroyed forever. Desert people fear that land restoration would take decades to centuries to accomplish, if it could be accomplished at all, and in the meantime topsoil would loosen and blow away on summer winds, reseeding would stop, and erosion would disrupt natural drainage patterns. Parts of the desert would die. Its people, better than others, understand the limits of the Basin. And they fear the obvious: that the MX goes beyond them.

Today, on paper, the MX would incorporate a total land space as big as Pennsylvania. Tomorrow it could be more. Westerners fear that any escalation of Soviet missile building might trigger an American escalation in shelter construction; overnight, 200 missiles would become 400 missiles, 4600 shelters would become 13,500 or 23,000, and suddenly the Basin — as westerners have known it — would be gone. The Bureau of Land Management has warned that the MX would have "the greatest effect on the public land of any project ever." More bluntly, an angry Nevadan has said that it would "rip the heart out of the land."

The desert's mineral resources would be bled from it. The MX would consume 6 million tons of sand, 87 million tons of gravel, nearly a million tons of fly ash. It would take 2.7 million tons of cement — twice as much as that used in the Grand Coulee Dam — only a few years after much of the West was affected by crippling cement shortages. More important, perhaps, the MX would absorb 2.9 million tons of steel. The figures are important. The fact is that this massive concentration of resources in one project would be supremely dangerous for the region; what the MX would use, other projects could not — and southern Nevada and Utah would run the deadly risk of paralyzing other industries, other growth, in favor of the MX. This situation, again, would not be new to the West. For many years its copper and tungsten and lead and uranium have gone to others, for the enrichment and profit of others, leaving the West itself with little else but cratered-out hills and unfulfilled dreams of wealth. But now an expanding West can ill afford the loss of its mineral wealth, or its destructive concentration, unless some of the benefits — for once — fall to it.

Paradoxically, perhaps, the other side of the argument is that the MX would stifle the search for minerals *not* needed in the project. Mine owners fear that mining would be stunted or stopped by the widespread reservation and closing of desert lands to mineral exploration. The Air Force insists that MX sites would avoid known mining areas, yet much of the land already targeted is prime prospecting country. The Great Basin's broad alluvial valleys are rich in barium, beryllium, molybdenum, gold, silver, lead, potash, and uranium. Much of the Basin sits squarely astride Overthrust and its vast pockets of oil. Eight of nineteen strategic minerals — minerals *already* overimported by the United States — lie here, from manganese and aluminum to tin, potassium, mercury, zinc, and tungsten. Despite Air Force assurances that mining would not be interrupted, mining companies still fear the worst.

If the industry's fears have been exaggerated, it still would face critical problems in living with MX. It would find itself in bitter competition with the project for labor, water, construction supplies, and housing. It also remains to be seen whether modern mining methods would be compatible with the existence of MX. The federal government has said time and again, in attempting to assuage the fears of angry westerners, that the MX and the mining industry could exist side by side, but the industry is skeptical. Large-scale mining — open-pit blasting, underground caving, the massive use of heavy machinery — almost certainly would be disruptive to the sensitive strategy of the MX. Very likely they could not coexist; very likely — in time, at least — the mining industry would be forced to retrench. In a major economic address to the nation on February 18, 1981, President Reagan firmly endorsed accelerated mining activity and mineral leasing on the federal lands of the West. He said that they are "the more promising areas of the nation for undiscovered or undeveloped energy and mineral resources." If this is true, the mining industry is right. The MX would be an unwelcome, and possibly damaging, interruption.

As serious as they may be, though, alterations to the land and the curtailment of mining at least would be tolerable to the people of the Great Basin. But the loss of their water would not. Every study of the MX has underlined one horrifying fact: it would sap the region's water resources as nothing before in its history.

On the floor of the Great Basin the sage lifts its arms to skies that never rain. Desert animals wait for brooks that do not exist. Summer skies fill with pitch-colored clouds and lightning dances nightly across the mountaintops, but the storms bring little rain. Nevada is the driest state in the Union; Utah is second. The average yearly rainfall in the Great Basin is only eight inches — and uneven distribution, quick evaporation, and the porousness of the soil itself negate much of that. The streams that dash out of the hills rim only the edges of the desert — avoiding its core — and even most of those die in the sinks and flats at the desert's edge. Over the course of centuries the plants and animals of the Basin have adapted to its aridity. The Indian paintbrush stands defiantly in mountain crevices, lacing canyon slopes with strands of pink and coral. In the sun's withering heat, even without rain, the barrel cactus sprouts clumps of blossoms like papier-mâché. The kangaroo rat goes a lifetime without water; the honey ant fills itself with water from birth, drawing on it later in times of drought. Animal and plant have adapted, but man has not, cannot. This is perhaps the greatest significance of the MX. Its assault on a water supply already precariously out of balance might be the ultimate calamity to the people of the Great Basin.

The MX would consume 30,000 to 50,000 acre feet of water a year at the peak of its construction, a figure that would soar to 121 billion to 172 billion gallons over twenty years. It would be vital in every phase of construction — 900 billion gallons, for example, would be used in making cement — but most would be used in the generation of electrical power. This in itself is a controversial point among the desert's people.

Excluding power needed for heating and cooling its system and for its support bases, the MX would require 180 megawatts of electrical power for construction and operation — enough to supply a city of 180,000 people for a year — and at its peak it would need a minimum of 257 megawatts. At the same time, in an area filled with new power plants, the MX has not been included in their growth projections. If the Air Force tapped into local power loads — such as the 3000 megawatts of the Intermountain Power Project — it would swamp utilities all across the Southwest. All it could do, then, would be furnish its own water — and it is this, precisely, that local people fear.

In all of western Utah, and most of Nevada, surface water rights are committed — even overcommitted. This means that the government would have to buy land and the water rights on it. As in northwest Colorado, where oil companies have triggered a bidding war for water rights, the government would be forced to do much the same in the Great Basin. Land would be bought at inflated prices — with ranchers the primary beneficiaries — and drilled. As wells were sunk, the region's water supply would feel the shock. No table, no aquifer, would long sustain the kind of depletion the deep drilling would bring; not even the impact of coal slurry pipelines on Wyoming's Madison Aquifer would be as lethal as this. In time, inevitably, the water table would drop, wells would draw down, spring and ground water flow would slow or stop. The very sources of important waterways would be threatened. At Milford, Utah, for example, the level already is dropping. In other areas the threat so far is only imminent. At Coyote Spring Valley near Las Vegas, for another example, the source of the Muddy River Springs is endangered; its destruction, more than remotely possible, would wipe out all downstream communities dependent upon irrigation, including the Moapa River Indian Reservation northwest of Lake Mead.

In a waterless land the loss of water is loss of life, and unless western fears are overdrawn, the MX would threaten the desert's people with nothing less. It is a simple fact: the reckless appropriation and absorption of Great Basin water would damage the region's farming and ranching, impair its physical beauty, destroy much of its plant and wildlife, and reduce the quality of life for everyone who lives on the land. Desert people are unwilling to accept this, nor can they accept the continuing inability of nonwesterners to understand the problem's significance. Visiting the sere, flat desert along the Wasatch Front a century ago, Hubert Howe Bancroft wrote: "Mark the prophecy: the valleys of this whole region will one day be rich fields and gardens, supporting flourishing populations." From the first days of Brigham Young, the desert's settlers fought the desert, pushing back its sand hills and salt flats, nurturing it with water from the rivers and the rain, watching it blossom. Water gave Utah and Nevada life. They would be unwilling now to give it to the MX.

No town in the Great Basin, not even those on its periphery, would escape the impact of the MX. Many would become boomtowns; as oil has transformed Evanston, and shale oil has changed Rifle, the MX would change them. The massive appropriation and reallotment of mineral resources and water would alter economic patterns that have endured since the first Mormons. Labor demands would change work patterns in the same way. Society then would change under the other pressures. In fact, because the Basin's towns have been more untouched than most over the years, they would be altered more radically than boomtowns elsewhere.

If the MX is built in the Great Basin, during the next decade one of the most sparsely settled areas of the United States would be inundated by the builders and operators of the missile. Between now and 1990, between 100,000 and 160,000 people would flood the Basin's small communities. Federal planners estimate that the construction force alone would range from 16,000 to 60,000. The problem, though, is that estimates are uncertain; builders of the Alaska pipeline anticipated an influx of 5500 workers — but employed 22,000 at its peak. The unknown plagues western planners. Officials of Basin communities know the impact would be massive, but no way exists for them to plan for it.

In Nevada the MX would touch towns for hundreds of miles around, many of them frontier communities little changed from silver rush days. In the north, along the Humboldt, twenty-one potential MX shelter sites fan out to the south and east of Elko. More than a hundred years ago Elko County was one of the finest grazing and farming areas in Nevada. Yesterday its rich soil produced wheat and barley, cattle grazed its creek beds, and flour mills and smelters worked side by side. Tomorrow it may belong to the MX. In southern Nevada, where the desolate Mojave nudges into the Great Basin, projected shelter sites nestle in the basins of the Monitor, Hot Creek, Pancake, and Quinn Canyon ranges from Tonopah to Pioche. A century ago this was mining country. South of Tonopah silver camps in Esmeralda County produced millions of dollars in bullion by the 1890s. Pioche was the most vibrant town in Nevada in the 1870s. Overrun by outlaws, leveled four times by fire and flood, it still survived. At its peak, in the 1870s, Pioche held 6000 people. Tomorrow, surrounded by nearly fifty MX shelters, it might face two to three times that.

Most of the MX installations would jut into canyons off highway 50 as it snakes between Ely and Austin. Towns along this axis would be the most profoundly affected in Nevada. One is Ely, an old, threadbare copper camp, once a Kennecott town, lumped in a piñon-covered valley only a mountain range away from Utah. City planners — who have courted the MX because of poor local economic conditions — would expect an influx of 6500 to 9500 employees and families if the Air Force located a support base there. Today, only 10,000 people live in all of White Pine County, 6000 of them in Ely, and MX critics fear the impact of up to 25,000 new people would be overwhelming in an area where only one person now lives on every 565 acres. The same holds true to the west where Eureka sits at the edge of the Diamond Mountains as it has for 110 years. At one time Eureka was a smelting town, a stage and rail center for Salt Lake–to–San Francisco traffic; with two daily papers, two banks, and two schools, it was one of central Nevada's important cities. Eureka County, which grew up around it, was rich in mineral resources from the Tuscarora Mountains in the north to Summit Mountain on the south. Its great days now are long gone and so are most of the traces of its past. But MX planners envision the appearance of 3500 construction jobs overnight if shelter construction were to begin.

Long, blocky Lander County, split in half by the Reese River, was built on silver in the 1870s and 1880s; sustained by its rich Battle Mountain mines, it spawned numerous frontier towns. One, Austin, would be the westernmost anchor of the MX system. Hubert Howe Bancroft wrote in the 1880s that Austin was "an anomaly of modern times, a city in the midst of wilderness, grown up like a mushroom, in a night." Before it lived too long, though, Austin was dead, its 10,000 people gone. In recent years it has stabilized its population at 200, but Austin, like its neighbors, is still a ghost town. Now, ironically, it may return, "like a mushroom, in a night."

The scene is the same all across the Nevada desert. On a Sunday afternoon at Austin or Alamo or Ely, trailers lie scattered haphazardly over littered lots, and cinder-block bungalows fringe the highway as it slips through the towns. Travelers can find gas or a hamburger or rifle shells or hardware at the Texaco station or the country store. Or they can find peace.

It should be enjoyed, like a long breath of desert air on a spring morning, for tomorrow it, too, may be gone.

None of Nevada would feel the effect of the MX as deeply as the handful of Utah towns that lies at the Great Basin's edges. One reason is Mormonism. In general, though many Nevada communities sprang from the same roots, Utah's Basin towns are more extensively Mormon, more fixed in traditional beliefs, more insulated from the outside world, and historically less adaptable to social, cultural, and economic change than non-Mormon settlements. The intrusion of the MX would be a test unlike anything rural Utah has ever faced. Not only would the disruption of resource distribution patterns alter farming and ranching styles that go back generations, but the overwhelming invasion of non-Mormon outsiders — and outside ways of life — would shatter cultural and social systems that date back to the beginning of Mormonism itself. Because of this, the church itself has adopted an unyieldingly hostile attitude toward the MX.

The other reason is that, unlike Nevada, many of Utah's Great Basin communities are at least first-stage boomtowns already. In more than one dusty desert settlement oil drilling already has created a boom climate, and what oil has not done the mammoth power plants have. This, perhaps, is the greatest danger faced by southwest Utah: not singular development, but multiple — more than one large economic development in the same place at the same time, unleashing growth forces far beyond the ability of any small community to control even under the best of circumstances.

Most of Utah's MX system would be clustered in the Sevier and Black Rock desert country southwest of Salt Lake City. Several proposed shelter sites lie due west of Eureka, one of Utah's most historic mining camps, but most spin north and south off highway 50 as it sweeps southwesterly along the edge of the Great Basin. Fourteen potential sites lie in a semicircle around Delta, where the Sevier River cuts through the desert; the rest run perpendicular to the Nevada border, in and out of the valleys of the Confusion and House ranges, beneath the awesome front of Notch Peak, in some of the emptiest land in Utah.

No town here would escape the coming of the MX. At Leamington, for example, a massive new Martin-Marietta cement plant would hire 2000 workers and pump perhaps hundreds of thousands of dollars into an economy that yesterday was nonexistent. As far away as Cedar City, north of Zion, planners expect that the population of 800 would double. At Lynndyl, where most residents have descended from a single, tightly knit Mormon family, its population of only 64 would be engulfed. Even without the MX it faces a population jump of 1200 by 1987 because of the nearby Intermountain Power Project. The town is not prepared for this kind of shock, let alone the added pressures of the MX. Lynndyl has no police or fire department, no schools, no sewer system, a single grocery. Its water supply — leased from the Union Pacific — is low. It does not have the millions of dollars it would need for improvements. Predictably, social divisions already have begun to appear. Townspeople in favor of the MX (for economic reasons) have drawn the anger of those against it, and many on both sides have attacked ranchers who sold land — and its water rights — for huge personal profit. In a limited way, Lynndyl has seen this before. In the 1930s and early 1940s, it was a small railroad boomtown — with 1600 people, an automobile agency, four stores, and a pool hall. The end of the war brought the end of the boom. Now, nearly forty years later, it has come full circle. Lynndyl survived one boom, but the question remains whether it could survive another.

Delta sits on the sun-washed eastern edge of the Great Basin, staring westward at the endless expanse of the Sevier Desert. Its main street, highway 50, dropping down from Eureka, Leamington, and Lynndyl, comes from nowhere and goes on to nowhere; to the west it by-passes old Fort Deseret, skirts Notch Peak at Skull Rock Pass, and melts into the Nevada desert. For a century Delta was part of the Utah backwater — remote, isolated, unimportant to the outside world, content with its farming, its peace, and its Mormon ways. But that has ended. Two years ago the Intermountain Power Project located near Delta. And now the MX has projected fourteen missile sites to the west, across the Sevier River, and possibly a support base near the city itself. The two enterprises together would either make Delta one of the richest cities in the southwest or kill it. Local sentiment is divided on the MX. Some favor it for both economic and patriotic reasons. Others oppose it in the belief that the town could not support such massive development. The power plant is there to stay; it cannot be moved or changed. But the MX is not yet in place, and because it is not, many Deltans have declared war on it. It is a classic confrontation, the kind of conflict that development has brought to the West. On one hand stand forces of change — energy companies, federal government — and on the other stand those who prefer life the way it is, the way it always has been.

Because of the Intermountain project, life in Delta is changing. Its population is growing uncontrollably. City officials predict that it will balloon to 10,000 people in the next five years *without* the MX; with it, especially if the Air Force locates its support base here, they estimate an overwhelming 20,000 (with some predictions soaring to 50,000 by 1988). Because of this, a kind of speculative frenzy has settled over the city. Land (with water rights) sells for ten to twenty times its price of two years ago. The price of homes has skyrocketed, and Delta, like other western boomtowns, has filled with trailers.

The boomer mentality has antagonized many townspeople. But more serious to them, many of them third- and fourth-generation Mormons, have been the alien attitudes and lifestyles that came to Delta with the Intermountain and would come again with the MX. Assaults have increased, for example, and in a town where it virtually did not exist before, rape has appeared. Theoretically, the MX would make it worse. As one Mormon farmer says, "We send our girls off to the picture show and they walk home at eleven at night. That would end if the MX comes."

Because of this kind of fear, many Deltans believe their town no longer is an acceptable place to raise children. In fact, at least in their eyes, it goes far beyond this. Most of the solid old Mormon families believe that "rowdyism" has become a way of life, threatening culture, social environment, and personal safety alike. Simply stated, Mormon values are under assault — and in the end they may not prevail; peace, stability, religious values may become a thing of the past. Not long ago, one day in 1980, a middle-class Mormon businessman looked around him at the "new" Delta. As he spoke of his city's problems, the dilemma of the town and its people became clear:

The number of assaults has gone up. We've got drillers, thumper crews, construction, most of them nice people, but they get lonely, angry, and that's the result. You get a boomer society — young, unmarried men making good money. They buy all the toys they can — big, four-wheel-drive trucks with coyote lights on top, dirt bikes, boats. Then all the other guys look at them, think they're having a great time, emulate it. The divorce rate goes up. You get a lot of well-heeled young guys and single women. They go on welfare. These guys are high-living and they don't accept any responsibility. You get trailer camps, with every pad jammed with their stuff, crowded conditions, a lot of depression.

In such circumstances, said another weary father, "we're going to have to reprogram our children, teach them the ugliness of life."

There is little that Delta can do to change the course of things. It needs a new hospital and more policemen — and it cannot fund

either of them. It has declared a moratorium on trailers, but it has
no way to promote affordable housing. "In five years," the mayor has
said, "it's going to be unreal" — and no amount of preparation will
change the outcome. Utah governor Scott Matheson has put it more
ominously: "Delta is in the eye of the needle."

The entire Great Basin is in the eye of the needle, and it is fearsome
to think what the future might bring it.

In the 1980s, as sentiment crystallizes against the MX, several
themes are interwoven.

One is opposition to multiple development in the same region at
the same time. As Matheson has said, the Great Basin "cannot be
a major source of energy growth and minerals while at the same time
serving as a national sacrifice area for deployment of the MX."
Energy development and power plants by themselves have affected
resource use, water, farming, ranching, and mining. They have disrupted long-standing economic patterns and created boomtown
problems all across the Great Basin. The result is that no one has
profited — not the region, not its people, and not the energy industry
itself. It may be that the root problem is incorrectable: the power
plants are fact and the MX may be. What the area must have, then,
is federal help in planning. Only that might mitigate the impact of
the MX and reduce the incredible developmental pressure on the
Basin itself.

A second theme also runs through the region's anti-MX rhetoric:
the theme of federal government as opportunist and exploiter. Much
of the West's rage, in fact, is aimed more at federal attitudes surrounding the MX than it is at the destructive potential of the missile
itself. Whether the MX comes to the desert or not may almost be
irrelevant. The central issue in the matter is the trampling of western
rights. Throughout the controversy, westerners have experienced
nothing but condescension and paternalism from the government. So
they sense duplicity. They suspect deceit.

Controversial siting decisions have angered the desert West from
the beginning. Ostensibly, at least, the Air Force would site the MX
in the Great Basin because of its deep bedrock, its accessible water
table, and its distance from coastlines and international borders.
Given the immense uncertainties of the MX, however, its limitless
potential for social, economic, environmental, and even human destruction, westerners believe that the government acted in haste, even
carelessness, in even *tentatively* placing the project in their midst.

Some say, bitterly, that if the MX finally is situated among them, it will be because of their "expendability." The view is cynical and possibly unwarranted, but this makes it no less explosive. Nevadans do not question it, nor do their neighbors to the east.

Many believe the Air Force has taken advantage of the West's extreme sense of patriotism in the whole MX affair. As one Utahan has said, the government sees the West as a "bunch of colloquial farmers who really pay no attention to anything, but have a tremendous amount of patriotism." Says another, "People have a hard time here justifying saying no to the federal government . . . it tears them to the quick." Perhaps this is true. Nearly ninety years ago, a Colorado congressman complained that easterners saw all westerners as "rattle-brained farmers." Perhaps this has never changed. Perhaps the federal government, building on assumptions as invalid now as they were a century ago, counts on a power play to sweep the MX into the western desert. Maybe it counts on the Mormons' powerful sense of honor. If this is so, the government grossly underestimates the people of the desert. After an ambiguous start, the staunchest hawks in the American Senate — Howard Cannon, Paul Laxalt, Jake Garn, Orrin Hatch — have fought the desert siting of the MX, patriotism or not. And so have their people. Again, what rankles westerners is *attitudes.* Federal arrogance has inflamed them before, and in the MX it has again.

There is also the question of trust.

Desert westerners harbor a deep distrust of the federal government. In Utah the feeling goes back generations to years when the national government made war on Mormon polygamy; in Nevada it goes back at least to the turn of the century when the conservation warriors of Theodore Roosevelt turned the state into a federal fiefdom. In recent years the mood has intensified and deepened, ripening into the acrid "Sagebrush Rebellion." One reason is nuclear testing carried on by the government in the Utah-Nevada desert two decades ago — and the calculated deception that surrounded it. On this question the government long ago radicalized its own people, and to a great degree today's distrust is rooted in yesterday's lies.

On the black morning of May 19, 1953, nuclear death came to the Great Basin. Shortly before dawn, a billowing orange fireball climbed high into the Nevada sky, turning night into day. Shock waves rolled like thunder across the endless flats, shaking the hills, splintering the earth. For a few seconds the boiling mushroom cloud towered above the desert, purple-black in the dawn, then disintegrated in high spring winds. Below it, soldiers stared in awe from observation trenches near Camp Desert Rock. To the east, Utah farmers watched from pickup trucks parked along country roads. To the north and west, Nevada cattlemen watched from horseback, their herds milling uneasily in the chill morning air. As they stared skyward, clouds of coral-pink drifted over them, showering particles over the land, coating it with fine ash and dust. No one knew it then, but they were materials of destruction.

From 1951 through 1963, the federal government conducted more than a hundred above-ground nuclear tests in the arid desert of southern Nevada. And, from the beginning, an atmosphere of unease permeated the small towns that surrounded the site. From the beginning something seemed amiss. The explosions split the earth open and tumbled people like tenpins miles away from the site. Their brilliance penetrated the flesh of hands shielding eyes from the flash. They filled the sky and air with dust that settled on homes, cars, laundry, crops, and people. Herds of pigs and sheep fell dead within days of the first shot. Looking about them, the desert's people asked for reassurances from the government that they were safe, that their children were. And from the beginning, without hesitation, the assurances were given.

From 1951 through the 1970s, the government insisted that nuclear testing did not menace human life, not in ground zero and not beyond it. Army researchers maintained that the detonation of 32 kilotons at 2000 feet was so insignificant that humans could enter the direct impact area immediately after explosion and drink water from open tanks. It sounded incredible to country farmers whose exposed skin was burned bright pink by the fireball, who felt postexplosion droplets of rain miles away that burned like acid. But no one questioned. After its thirty-first detonation the Atomic Energy Commission officially stated that "no one inside the test site has been injured ... no one in the nearby region of potential exposure has been hurt." People believed what they were told. They trusted.

Then they began to die.

In Cedar City, St. George, Garrison, Parowan, and other southwest Utah towns the cancer rate suddenly began to rise. It also rose in Nevada — in Baker, Caliente, Alamo, and other towns on the rim of ground zero. As early as 1976, United States Public Health Service studies showed excessive leukemia deaths in the region, but the studies were never published. Nor were others like them, leading to the growing suspicion that they had been suppressed. In any event, not until the 1970s did the truth begin to surface.

St. George lies quietly at the far southwestern corner of Utah, on the low-running Virgin River, a hundred miles downwind from ground zero. Ten thousand people live in St. George, and many of them remember waking to see "the sky lit up like day." In the 1950s the town was tranquil and complacent, living off the land; the periodic fireballs to the west were curiosities, not sources of concern. But the complacency was destroyed, replaced by fear, in the summer of 1978, when a study showed that eighty-five of St. George's people had cancer and seventy-eight others had recently died of it. Medical experts began to suspect widespread nuclear contamination, and in time worst fears were realized: over the course of a few years, for a radius of 100 to 150 miles around the Nevada test site, cancer rates had soared. In time literally hundreds of cases of blood, bone, and thyroid cancer were reported, and leukemia, in particular, became the desert's deadliest disease. The inference was clear: nuclear testing had killed people. Worse, for all the desert communities knew, the dying had only begun.

From the beginning of the nuclear testing controversy several years ago, the government has taken a defensive position on charges of federal negligence. It has argued in the 1970s and 1980s what it did in the 1950s — that the tests were not lethal. It has placed primary blame on industrial pollution — in a region where there is virtually none — and on the natural carcinogenic effects of tobacco and alcohol — in a population 75 percent Mormon where few people either smoke or drink. In a region such as the Great Basin, where the cancer rate should be 22 percent below the national average, instead it is far above. And the people of the Basin finally have come to understand why.

Several facts stand out. First, the government acted recklessly and carelessly. It took few, if any, safety precautions during nuclear testing; sporadically, at best, did it warn downwind communities of impending danger. Second, in choosing test sites and dates, it selected times and places where the wind would carry radioactive debris over less populated areas such as St. George rather than more populous urban areas such as Las Vegas. Third, and worst, evidence increasingly shows that the government calculatedly covered up news of rising cancer rates in desert towns. When finally confronted with evidence that its tests were responsible, it began a long litany of denial. Over the course of twenty years, lying, deceit, and diversion became the standard federal response to the question. Faced, even now, with rising evidence against it, it simply has turned away from the issue and ignored the growing militance in desert towns. "Nothing must get in the way of these tests," AEC Commissioner Thomas Murray said in 1955. Indeed, nothing did. Not even the lives of innocent people.

All of this relates directly to the MX controversy: those towns and those people directly affected by the likely permanent basing of MX are the *same ones* affected by years of nuclear testing. No one can forget or ignore the fact that the MX, too, is a nuclear weapon. And no one can forget that it would sit on the same ground. A St. George woman owns a scrapbook with photographs of 200 people — friends — who have died of cancer in the town in recent years; 10 people in a one-block radius of her home have died and 30 more suffer from cancer now. A St. George man has lost his wife and nine members of his extended family to cancer. In Cedar City 75 people recently have died of cancer; at tiny Parowan 175 people in a population of 2000 have cancer, many of them children at the time of the desert tests. Yesterday life in the desert was destroyed by radioactive isotopes raining from the sky. Tomorrow 2000 nuclear warheads may lie buried beneath its surface, inviting destruction again. No one, least of all the government, can say that it cannot happen.

In a decade, the Great Basin may sit atop 670,000 kilotons of nuclear destruction. But, besides this, the presence of the MX would also invite nuclear destruction from the outside. Its position in the desert makes the desert itself a prime target for nuclear attack. The 4600 proposed shelter sites have been spoken of as "aim points" — in the middle of which lie dozens of towns. Military tacticians have equated the desert itself to a giant sponge, in the midst of which people live, absorbing attacking missiles. If attack came with the MX in place, if Soviet missiles raced across America to Great Basin targets, the Basin would be annihilated. Virtually all of Utah, Colorado, and Kansas would suffer 50 percent casualties, and perhaps half of Nevada the same. Nebraska alone would absorb between 15 and 50 percent. It may be that such a nightmare is too horrible for the region's people to contemplate — perhaps this is why anti-MX protest has been fairly free of doomsday rhetoric. But the awareness cannot ever be too far away. As Scott Matheson has said, "the bull's eye is a pretty big one."

Those who have watched their families die know.

As for the government, the Basin's people no longer rely on it for truth: if government lied to them about nuclear testing, they believe that it can lie to them about the MX. Many believe it already has. For two full years the government failed to notify the state of Utah that the system might be placed there; neither Utah nor Nevada initially was advised — nor have they consented. The government consistently has played down the nuclear danger of the MX, and it has continued to minimize its impact on the land. Its draft environmental impact statement was delayed for months beyond its original publication date; when it finally was published, graphically warning that the MX would transform life in every respect, the government substantially ignored it. The MX plan, it continues to insist, would be "manageable."

Whether federal deception is real or imagined, westerners are convinced that they would receive no planning help. At no time, for example, has the Air Force committed itself to designating a set number of shelters, a fact that has made it impossible for Basin towns to plan. Delta knows not whether to expect 5000 workers or 50,000. Or any at all. And at no time, so far, has the government attempted to coordinate its own parts; instead, its own branches have gone in different directions, announcing different and often conflicting policies at the same time. Westerners who do not suspect deceit suspect at least the playing out of a kind of ritual mating dance where the West is courted, disarmed, then forgotten. As one embittered Utahan has put it, the government "don't care about the environment, the wildlife, the livestock, but what the hell difference does it make what we think?" Perhaps none. That is the tragedy.

The war over the MX has just begun. Where or when it will end no one can say. But one thing is certain: until the federal government clearly addresses questions of boomtowns, environment, and human health, the war will not end at all.

On the plains or in the desert, the boomtowns will have to be helped. If not, in no uncertain terms, people would suffer for the MX. So far government seems not to understand that towns like these — Alamo, Delta, Ely, as well as Minuteman prairie towns — are filled with people who cannot possibly shield themselves from the problems that boom times bring. They are filled with elderly too old to deal with social change, with disadvantaged who live in the same wilted frame shacks their fathers did, eking out a bare living on the land even in the best of times. They are filled with people watching old ways of life disintegrate before them.

Already they have lost much. Already, in the desert, bickering and division have replaced old friendships and value systems that have been the bedrock of frontier communities since there has been frontier. People "want to keep . . . a caring community," according to a Delta woman, but ideals, like "caring," have begun to vanish. Some look at boomtowns primarily in a physical sense — Nevada governor Robert List has said the MX would leave behind "rusting old leftover rattletrap facilities, blowing in the wind" — but, far more than this, they are human. And they would need help. Desert people or not, proud and independent or not, they could not survive alone.

Nor could their wilderness environment. To many Basin people, the desert's perpetual beauty is all they have. "I've always sought out the lonely places," one Utah man has said, "the places where there's peace, quiet, tranquility, the hush of the land." Without increased federal concern, this, too, could disappear. Without more respect for the desert's ecosystem, without more concern for water, with more emphasis on proper land management and less on fast-tracking the MX through environmental safeguards, something yet could be saved. If not, the land's beauty surely would be lost.

The ultimate tragedy of the MX will be if it kills its own people. It has happened before; the 1950s witnessed it. No one can see tomorrow today; no one can predict the first strike. No one can foretell Armageddon. All the desert people can ask for is honesty — no more nuclear lies. As a child, a young Cedar City woman stood at her window on summer nights and watched pink clouds rising in the Utah sky. Her brother died of cancer at twenty-seven. Unless someone protects her, cares about her life, perhaps she will die, too.

It may be, of course, that nothing will change — that the government will remain arrogant and the desert West will remain antagonistic. In December 1980, responding to the MX environmental impact statement, Air Force Undersecretary Antonia Chayes said that "while the impacts may appear severe when viewed from the perspective of a little-developed area of the country, from a national perspective — and the MX is a national program — the impacts are not that large." This is the kind of obstacle the West faces — the contemptuous century-old attitude that it exists only for the "greater good" and that the private agonies of its people are their own. But the time is coming when the West no longer will accept this. In the desert expanse of Utah and Nevada perhaps the time has come. "Patriotism is a feeling toward their own land, toward their ranches, toward their town, toward their way of life," one man has said, explaining the growing belligerence of desert towns toward the MX. "It's a feeling they have for their mountains, their valleys, and for what little water they have." To the federal bureaucracy the Great Basin is a geographical term, a stark, empty bowl on a demographic map. But to the people who live there it is life itself. And it is menaced by the MX.

Until it is not, they will rage.

CHAPTER SEVEN

The Oasis West

What is the heart of the West? Where is the center from which the shaping force and power radiate? The answer is simple if we would only see and accept it. The heart of the West is a desert, unqualified and absolute.

WALTER PRESCOTT WEBB

THE REAL WEST is not mountains. It is desert and prairie.

Southwest of Phoenix, Sentinel lies in the middle of four hundred square miles of Arizona desert. Mountain ranges ring it, shield it — Growler to the south, Eagle Tail and Gila Bend to the north — but the town itself sits on desert. In the spring the land is soft; nights are chill, and by day oceans of yellow flowering greasewood fill the air with fragrance. But the environment is hostile, and survival is not easy at Sentinel.

Two hundred miles of scorching desert lie between Albuquerque and the Texas line. Spaniards called it the Llano Estacado — the "staked plain" — so flat and endless they drove stakes in it to mark the way to water holes. No one ever tamed it — not the Spaniards, not even the Comanche. It was "boundless as the ocean," wrote an American in 1849. "Not a tree, shrub, or any other object relieved the dreary monotony of the vast illimitable expanse of desert prairie." A hundred years ago, Billy the Kid roamed the flatlands here, Charles Goodnight blazed his cattle trails, and boot hills sprang up at the ragged edges of Endee and Montoya. It was here, they say, that Pecos Bill lassoed a tornado. The course of time has changed the country little. At Cuervo and Glenrio, small clusters of stores hug the highway and worn frame houses stand forlornly in the sun. Bunch grass sprouts from the baked earth, rippling off toward distant hills, and yucca lifts its spiky arms toward the sky. And at Santa

Rosa and Tucumcari, as they have for generations, ranchers and farmers hold off the desert.

In northwest Utah, where the Uintas arch off the desert floor, miles of sage blanket the nearby flatlands. From Duchesne to Dinosaur, alkali plains roll north toward the Uintas and south toward the Tavaputs Plateau, broken only by blunt hills clothed in salt grass, and arroyos with no water. The towns are all the same — small, weather-beaten and barren, small stores and gas stations and farmers tilling pockets of alfalfa in summer sun. At Jensen and Duchesne, the verdant mountains are far away. Reality here is not mountains. It is the desert.

What the desert does not own, the prairie does.

South of Minot, North Dakota, the wide Drift Prairie flows emptily toward the badlands, ebbing around Washburn and Hazleton and other settlements in its path. From Max and Underwood, highway 83 stretches evenly for miles, splitting fields of corn and flax, on the way to Bismarck. The Mandan owned this prairie once, living off buffalo and Missouri River water. In 1804, Lewis and Clark passed across it on their way to the Pacific, and years later Theodore Roosevelt ranched in the badlands to the west. Today it is farmland, and where the Drift lies, windmills and dry farmers hold it at bay.

In south-central Nebraska, Red Willow County farmers have fought the plains for a hundred years. Settlers first moved here in 1871, huddling along the Republican River, cutting channels from it into the drylands to farm. To the sodbusters, life was little more than existence between droughts. Crops were sporadic, bankruptcy was common, life was tenuous. In time, as one of them said, they learned that it was "injudicious to depend on crop raising alone" for survival. Those who did "have been unsuccessful." This still is true today. In a good year the wheat and corn still grow at Indianola and McCook, but the prairie still sits at the doorstep — and it still shapes life.

Most of the West is desert or near-desert, and it begins where the 100th meridian slashes through the Great Plains from Canada to the Gulf. At Minot and Bismarck, at Pierre, North Platte, Dodge, and Abilene, the plains begin their great westward sweep to the mountains and desert. The northern Great Plains cover 275,000 square miles of land, including virtually all of the Dakotas. In Wyoming, the plains are blunted by the Medicine Bows as they swell into the southeast, but north of Casper they extend as far west as the Big Horns. And eastern Montana is an endless landscape of open plains and naked foothills. Where the Pine Ridge Escarpment curves across the top of Nebraska — miles of stubby cliffs covered with juniper — the southern Great Plains begin. Splitting off the western halves of Nebraska, Kansas, Oklahoma, northwest Texas, and the dry eastern flanks of Colorado and New Mexico, they continue on to their southern limits — the Llano Estacado.

The plains stop at the Rockies, and except for western Montana and western Colorado, they do not return again. Instead, the desert begins. In Idaho, what Hubert Howe Bancroft called "sterile sand deserts" swoop across the southwest quadrant of the state. From the Sierra Nevada east, the bleak Great Basin covers most of Nevada and Utah, and the Red Desert lies across the bottom of Wyoming like a barren tapestry. The foreboding Mojave, Death Valley at its core, penetrates southern Nevada, and to the west the Sonoran Desert fills Arizona from Tucson to Lake Mead. In Union County, New Mexico, the road from Clayton to Raton winds through some of the darkest, fiercest desert country in the West, and to the south the blistering Chihuahuan Desert creeps out of Mexico. From White Sands to the Mojave, from the Painted Desert to the Sevier, the desert, like the prairie, is a fact of western life.

The land's curse is its endless, relentless aridity. Lack of water has molded the western past like no other single factor. Like a malevolent vise, aridity has constricted, controlled, and channeled, shaping settlement patterns, dictating economic systems, influencing the style and substance of life itself. Whatever the West became, whatever it is now, it is no more than aridity has allowed. Colorado writer Thomas Hornsby Ferril once wrote that "here is a land where life is written in water." It is a fact. Aridity is the central force in western life. It has been from the beginning, it is today, and it will be tomorrow.

Spring days along the Mississippi are filled with soft rain, bringing out azalea and magnolia in fountains of color. Spring brings rain to New York and Ohio, and along the Blue Ridge it paints the countryside green. Boston gets forty-three inches of rain a year and New York City and Philadelphia forty-two. Along the south Atlantic coast, it rains fifty-three inches a year at Jacksonville, fifty at Charleston, and inland, Atlanta receives forty-seven. In both rain and snow, Cincinnati gets forty inches of precipitation a year, Chicago thirty-three, and Indianapolis thirty-nine. Just to the east of the Great Plains, Des Moines receives thirty inches a year and St. Louis thirty-five. Here, where precipitation is abundant, it is taken for granted.

In the West, precipitation is not abundant — and it is not taken for granted. The West in general receives no more than twenty inches a year — most of it in the mountains. Along the 100th meridian, the Great Plains average from ten to twenty inches — Pierre gets sixteen, North Platte eighteen, Dodge City nineteen. Further West, where the plains roll to the mountains, average precipitation is fifteen to twenty inches, dropping as low as ten along the eastern edge of Wyoming, Montana, Colorado, and New Mexico. On the western side of the mountains where the deserts begin, vast parts of Idaho, southwestern Wyoming, Utah, and Arizona accumulate only five to eight inches. Phoenix records no more than eight inches a year, Winnemucca, Nevada, nine, Albuquerque eight; more fortunate are Denver with fourteen, Boise with eleven, Helena with ten, Salt Lake City with fourteen, and Cheyenne with fifteen.

On a summer day thunderheads boil over the Uintas and the Big Horns and lightning skips raggedly across open prairie. Rain begins, but rarely does it fall. Much of it blows away in atmospheric winds. Most of it evaporates as it falls to earth, disintegrated by the land's heat. If it does break through, often it comes quickly and violently, crashing on hard-packed earth that cannot absorb it. Rushing into gullies and streams, it plunges finally into desert rivers, gone for good. On a July afternoon a rainbow may arc across the South Dakota sky. But the land beneath it will be dry.

The lush vegetation of eastern and midwestern states is vastly different from that of the plains and desert. At the eastern edge of the Great Plains a narrow belt of tall grass stretches from Canada to the Texas panhandle — needlegrass, slender wheat, bluestem, all reflecting the nature of the soil and climate. To the west long grass fades to short — wire, grama, buffalo — and mixes with sage and greasewood, all the way to the walls of the Rockies. In the sun-washed deserts of the southern Rockies, the land nurtures cactus and yucca, piñon, mesquite, and endless miles of scrubby desert grass. Nothing is more beautiful than the yellow-petaled paloverde in spring, or clusters of blossom-studded saguaro, but the fact remains that the land is dry, desolate, and unproductive. The fact also remains that the desert is massive. Together with the prairie, it constitutes most of the West.

For well over a century, westerners have fought the desert and the arid prairies, damming rivers, storing snowpack, ditching, fluming,

WESTERN WATER SYSTEMS

channeling their way through wastelands from Nebraska to the California border. In a sense they have succeeded: most of the West today — most of its cities and people — sits on arid ground made habitable by the damming and diversion of water. On the other hand, because of the long and killing nature of the process, the taming of the arid West is one of the bitterest chapters in its history.

The Transmississippi West came to the United States in two stages — in 1803 when Thomas Jefferson bought Louisiana, and in 1848 and 1849 when James K. Polk conquered Oregon and the Mexican Empire west of the Rockies. From the beginning, though, the West was too forbidding for settlement. Stephen H. Long, exploring between the 98th meridian and the Platte River Valley in 1821, called the land the Great American Desert — and the name remained on it for a generation. Like a long, deadly wall, it kept a westward-moving nation at bay, and not for twenty-six years was it first breached. Mormons, trekking from Fort Laramie across the lumpy base of the Uintas, descended from the western rim of the Wasatch into the Great Basin of Utah in July of 1847, and there they established the Kingdom of Deseret. The land was stark and ominous. Ninety-five percent of it was mountains and desert — an empire of bunch grass and rattlesnakes where it rained as little as three inches a year. But it was a beginning, and it launched an invasion of the western plains and desert that continued for another half century.

In the last five decades of the nineteenth century, settlers poured into the arid West. The explosion engulfed Nebraska, which grew by 240,000 people in the 1880s alone. Two distinct "booms" brought farmers swarming across the Dakotas and by 1885, there were 550,-000 people living there, filling river bottoms first, then pushing into the plains. In the 1880s, pioneers threaded their way into the High Plains of Wyoming, homesteading along the eastern lip of the Big Horns, and in Montana nesters followed the Northern Pacific Railroad up the valley of the Yellowstone. In the late 1880s, finally, sodbusters spilled into Colorado from Kansas and Nebraska, following the Burlington to Akron and Yuma or the Rock Island to Burlington and Flagler. Where Arapaho and Cheyenne had hunted buffalo, farmers now planted corn. "Their farms have not yet assumed much beauty," said the *Denver Republican* in 1888, but "the lands for from 1 to 10 miles on each side of the road are dotted with newly-erected cottages."

Astonishingly, settlers also trickled into the desert regions of the southern Rockies. Arizona Mormons moved into the Mesa, Lehi, and Salt River districts as early as the 1860s. Boom times came to New Mexico twenty years later when farmers settled up and down the Pecos Valley and then moved to the northeastern and eastern plains. Even in Nevada, around Pioche, 150 farms were located within a hundred-mile radius in 1873; in tinder-dry Lander County, 2700 acres were put under cultivation in 1880, and 16,000 in nearby Elko. To the east, even the Utah desert blossomed under the persistent hand of the saints.

But it did not last. Thousands of settlers crossed the plains in the belief that "water followed the plow," that massive soil tilling triggered rain, that in fact a natural "rain belt" was drifting ever westward above the moving settlement line. But there was no rain belt, or if there was it evaporated in the heat of the prairie sun. Before long, when the rains did not come, settlement after settlement failed; all over the plains, crop failure after dust storm after crop failure shattered the budding empire. Only those with access to irrigation survived — and most of them for not long. Most of the surface water lay in the hands of speculators and land promoters who preceded the farmers, appropriated water, built shabby, furtive irrigation systems, and sold water "rights" at inflated prices. In the early 1890s, when the depression destroyed most of these systems, the farmers, finally, were left with nothing. By the 1890s, at the latest, they came to understand the reality of the desert: for most of them there was no water — no rainfall, no snowpack, few streams — and without it they could not survive.

In the last two decades of the century, depression and bankruptcy swept the arid West like a tidal wave. As the uprooted poured out of the region — 100,000 from western Kansas and Nebraska alone — whole towns, whole regions died. Frustrated and bewildered, farmers channeled their fury into the Populist upheaval of the mid-1890s. But that, too, failed, and in the end they achieved nothing. They had set out to transform cactus wastes and sage flats into the Garden of the World, and to spread the gospel of Jeffersonian agrarianism in the process. They had their dreams, but they did not have water, and what they built instead was an empire of dust.

Throughout the process, from beginning to tragic end, the federal government added to the problem. Because it had no arid-lands policy, because it insisted on settling the arid West like the East — when there was no similarity — the government was greatly responsible for stimulating much of the disastrous settlement in the first place. Encouraging settlement under the 1862 Homestead Act was a serious mistake, compounded by the Desert Land Act of 1877. Even the Carey Act of 1894 — aimed at attracting legitimate private capital to western irrigation projects — failed. For twenty years, living in the backwash of misguided federal land policy, devastated western states demanded changes in it. Above all, they sought federal help in irrigation and reclamation matters where the states were powerless to help themselves.

The Newlands Act of 1902 was a beginning, bringing federal money and the new Bureau of Reclamation into western affairs. In time they helped change the face of the arid West. As the nation moved into the twentieth century, the plains again were pushed back, farmers returned to abandoned sites and sank their plows in the earth again, and new farmers came in waves to the last unsettled patches of the West. At the same time, disease-resistant crop strains were developed to reduce crop failure, dry farming was pioneered, and for the first time the West's great aquifers were tapped. In time, on the Great American Desert, life improved.

Still, the arid West lives uneasily on the desert's edge. It watches the sky for rain, for snow, and waits. Walter Prescott Webb once wrote that dreamers "look the other way, towards greener country, and let themselves think that the desert has gone away. But that is myth, for the desert abides." At Sentinel they dam the hills' narrow washes to catch the rain. They, too, understand: the desert abides.

* * *

Throughout its history, the West's salvation has been its rivers. Literally, they have stood between it and extinction. Like slender threads of life in a lifeless land, the great rivers have watered plains, nurtured crops, and provided for the needs of cities for a hundred years. They are the lifeline of the West. Here, where water is blood, water is rivers.

In a land as big as the West, where rain is as elusive as a summer rainbow, the rivers have had to supply the West's most critical needs. In 1970, for example, a year of mild drought, rivers provided western power plants with 1.1 billion gallons a day, municipalities with 2.9 billion more, manufacturing with 0.9 billion, and agriculture with 57.7 billion. Even so, the West still lives close to the edge. The total stream flow in western states is only 154 billion gallons a day, com-

pared with 790 billion in the East and 136 billion in the three states
of the Northwest. The West, an arid land space of just over a million
square miles, receives only 14 percent of the nation's annual stream
flow.

The West has learned to live with reality. Tapping into its relatively small network of rivers, it has made much of little for years.
In 1968, Frank Quinn wrote in the *Geographical Review* that one of
every five people in the West is served by a water supply system
(usually rivers or river-fed reservoirs) that imports water from a
source a hundred miles or more away. In total tonnage, he added,
the amount of water moved exceeds the freight carried by all of the
region's railroads, trucks, and barges combined.

Six massive basins span the Rocky Mountain West, sending water
thousands of miles from California to the Mississippi. The Upper
Missouri, Arkansas, and Rio Grande basins drain the eastern slope
of the Rockies from Canada to Texas, and on the western slope, the
Colorado River and Upper Columbia basins bracket the desolate
Great Basin of Utah and Nevada. The Missouri, Yellowstone, and
Platte rise in the Upper Missouri region, the Arkansas and Canadian
in the Upper Arkansas, and the Rio Grande and Pecos to the south
in the Upper Rio Grande. Only the Humboldt begins in the Great
Basin, rushing headlong to nowhere. In the Upper Columbia, the
Snake winds out of the high mountains, and the Green, Gila, and
Colorado begin in the Colorado's basin.

The Missouri dominates the northern Rockies, born where the
Jefferson, Madison, and Gallatin tumble together at Three Forks,
Montana, meandering 2400 miles through Montana and the Dakotas
on its way to the Mississippi. The long, murky river — "Smoky
Water" the Indians called it — floated Lewis and Clark into history
175 years ago, and in later years it became a major avenue into the
northwest wilderness. It was, and remains, a romantic, ugly, and
capricious river, but, above all, it is a watery lifeline for some of the
driest parts of the plains West. So, too, is its neighbor, the Yellowstone. To the south, the Yellowstone sweeps out of the cracks and
canyons of the Absaroka Range in northwest Wyoming. For 670
miles, along sulfur-tinted rocks that gave it its name, through aspen-
covered bottomlands, the Yellowstone flows through some of southern Montana's flattest and driest land. East of Billings, in Treasure
County, it is swollen by the Bighorn at the end of a 330-mile journey
out of the Bridger and Owl Creek mountains of central Wyoming,

and at Miles City it intersects with the Tongue. Most impressive of all — and most important — is the narrow, yellow Powder, twisting out of Wyoming through the cut clay and sand banks of southeast Montana, to join the Yellowstone in Prairie County. The Powder is one of the most celebrated rivers in the West, river of the Sioux and cattle kings and sodbusters and a hundred dramatic years of High Plains history. In 1938, Struthers Burt vividly described it as "a buckaroo among rivers, a bowlegged, broken-nosed buckaroo, casual, insouciant, but swift and deadly in action, a small river, fierce in spring floods, coiling torpid and slow in the summer heat like a rattlesnake." Whatever its nature, however great its unpredictability, the short, murky Powder is a critical part of the Yellowstone drainage system.

The Upper Missouri Basin's southernmost river, the Platte, rises in the Colorado Rockies and flows through south-central Wyoming and northeastern Colorado before pushing across the low Nebraska plains to the Missouri. The North Platte forms in North Park, Jackson County, Colorado, winding 618 miles through Wyoming to North Platte, Nebraska. Along its reedy banks the Platte River Road brought emigrants to central Wyoming a century ago, to Casper, by Independence Rock, up the Sweetwater to South Pass. Today, it irrigates the dry southern edge of Natrona, Converse, and Niobrara counties and the entire central corridor of Nebraska. The South Platte, born above Fairplay, Colorado, in the chill remoteness of the Park Range, glides softly through South Park on its way north. In its early stages, on the green valley floor, it is one of the most deceptively beautiful rivers in the West. Later, it bisects Denver and fronts the Rockies before turning east across the plains to meet the North Platte.

Irrigation projects on the Missouri River system through the years have tamed its streams, controlled their floods, and channeled them into the arid flatlands. They have furnished a vivid example of what the arid West does to survive. In most cases, the moving force has been the federal government, operating generally under the mandate of the 1902 Newlands Act. Because of this, the projects also illustrate the West's great reliance on federal funding for survival.

The mammoth Fort Peck Dam, built in the 1930s, was the Missouri's first, holding 19 million acre feet of water for irrigation purposes. In 1944 the so-called Pick-Sloan plan, authorized by Congress, launched the building of seven more dams on the Missouri and its feeders. Yellowtail on the Bighorn, for example, was built for a capacity of 1,375,000 acre feet of water; Canyon Ferry, 2,051,000; and the Fort Randall Dam in South Dakota, 6,300,000. In 1966, Congress authorized the Garrison Diversion Project in North Dakota, designed to provide water for up to 1 million acres of nearby drylands. Planners projected the largest rolled-earth dam in the world — 2 miles long, 210 feet high from the river's bottom, 3/4 mile wide at the base, impounding 23,000,000 acre feet of water in a 200-mile-long reservoir.

To the south, the North Platte is contained in a series of dams and reservoirs dating to 1909. In Wyoming, two huge reservoirs — the Pathfinder and Seminole — store more than 2 million acre feet of precious water for the parched flatlands east of Rawlins, and the Glendo near Douglas captures 800,000 more before the Platte escapes to Nebraska. The 1941 Kingsley Dam, which backs up Lake McConaughy in Keith County, Nebraska, adds another 2 million acre feet to storage.

On the Great Plains surrounding the Missouri, penetrating its great basin, 70 percent of precipitation is lost in run-off and evaporation. This is a condition as old as the plains themselves, and throughout this century — despite severe climatic and economic risks — it has forced an unbreakable reliance on dry farming. If anything is to break this bond, it will be irrigation. Already, in fact, the blooming of the plains around existing projects illustrates what the future may be.

In Montana today, much of the land north and west of Fort Peck is irrigated, and virtually all of the Yellowstone, Bighorn, Tongue, and Powder River valleys as well. Indirectly, this irrigation supports two of the most densely populated areas in the state — the Billings region and the Miles City–Glendive–Sidney corridor to the North Dakota line. In western South Dakota, 10 percent of the land's farms are irrigated today, most of them from Fort Randall and the Oahe, and future irrigation projects are planned up and down the Belle Fourche, White, and Cheyenne rivers to the west — all of them Missouri feeders. Only North Dakota lags behind, and where one farmer told John Gunther in 1947 that "it hasn't rained here in seven years," no guarantee exists that it will not happen again. Apparently, in time, increased irrigation will minimize its effect. Given North Dakota's water project plans, the strip roughly along the 101st parallel — including the eastern end of the Garrison Reservoir and the

Oahe's northern tip — one day will be far more irrigated than it is now.

Along the Platte, both North and South, irrigation is more developed than anywhere else in the Great Plains region. In Wyoming the large dry bowl formed by the Medicine Bows on the east and the Red Desert on the west is watered by North Platte storage, and from Torrington to Kingsley Dam the land is a mass of irrigation canals. In Colorado, from Eleven Mile Reservoir in South Park to the Nebraska border, the South Platte Valley has been one of the nation's richest farming regions for a generation. Along river banks that homesteaders trudged to the Oregon Country in the 1840s, that Mormons followed to Deseret, today Nebraska farmers grow wheat, potatoes, and sugar beets. In James Michener's *Centennial* the South Platte symbolized the birth and growth of an empire — an empire rooted in a river. Today, no less than before, the arid world around the Plattes depends on them both for its existence.

The Upper Arkansas Basin to the south drains a region far more barren than the Missouri. The hot, dry southeastern Colorado plains are among the most inhospitable areas in the West, and the northeast quarter of New Mexico is worse.

The Arkansas is formed by dozens of streams cascading out of Lake County, Colorado, near Leadville. Moving south, it fronts the Collegiate Range to the west, turns east at Salida below the white-mantled Sangre de Cristo Mountains, plunges through the Royal Gorge, and flattens out as it enters the plains. From Canon City, where it splits the Wet Mountains from the southern flank of Pikes Peak, it begins a lazy, 1450-mile trip across Colorado and Kansas to the Mississippi. No river in the West is more important to its region than the Arkansas. North and south of it, on long prairies matted with squirrel grass, dry farmers at Eads, Kit Carson, and Cheyenne Wells fight for survival. On these same plains settlers waited for the rain belt a hundred years ago, and many of them died as they did. In the 1930s they huddled at the storm center of the Dust Bowl where black rollers raged a mile high and for days blotted out the sun. As late as the 1950s they still endured drought, and in the mid-1960s Lyndon Johnson declared most of the region a national disaster area. Only the Arkansas brings life to this country, and only it ever has.

The Arkansas Valley is one of the richest and most intensely cultivated areas in Colorado, maybe in the West, a lush, green ribbon as it stretches east to Kansas. At Holly and La Junta and Las

Animas, small farms cluster in cottonwood groves and grow sugar beets, alfalfa, corn, bell peppers, and onions. Rocky Ford still produces melons famous all over the world, and east of Pueblo on summer afternoons, booming outdoor vegetable markets flank US 50 for thirty miles. At the heart of it, sixty miles upstream from the Kansas line, lies the $15 million John Martin Dam, Colorado's largest when it was built in 1948. The reservoir, which controls the flow of the entire lower Arkansas, holds 645,500 acre feet of water, 367,-000 of it reserved for irrigation and supply storage. Potentially more significant, however, is the half-completed Frying Pan–Arkansas Project. In 1962 Congress approved the $180 million project (since escalated to $270 million) to divert water from the Frying Pan River north of Aspen through a tunnel under the Continental Divide to the Arkansas. It also will be among the most ambitious transmontane diversion projects ever attempted in the United States.

The sterile desert and lava country of northeast New Mexico is pierced by a single central river — the 900-mile-long Canadian. It springs from the eastern slope of the Sangre de Cristos in Colfax County, gathering force and momentum from its meeting with the Cimarron, and flowing south and east into west Texas. The Canadian is wide and crooked, choked with sandbars that make its course erratic and unpredictable. But its value is unquestioned. In 1819, Stephen H. Long scoured the land around its headwaters, and it was here, he said, that the land bore a "manifest resemblance to the deserts of Siberia." Yet today, crops grow in the desert where the Canadian runs, and two towns of size — Tucumcari and Raton — live at its edge.

The Canadian drains 16,000 square miles of land, most of it saline and sandy, overlain by a thin carpet of grass. In the northern Canadian Valley most of the land from Maxwell to Springer is irrigated. What once was wild, brawling cattle country has been heavily subdivided over the years, but numerous reservoirs remain, filled with enough acre feet of water to irrigate south for miles. Sugar beets, fruit, grains, alfalfa, and beans grow not far from old Fort Union, where Geronimo and Billy the Kid once were imprisoned. Further south, below the Mora, one of the state's biggest projects has allowed the river to work effectively as it grows larger. In 1939, the United States Corps of Engineers completed the Conchas Dam and Reservoir where the Canadian makes its big bend toward Texas. It holds 600,000 acre feet of water — 100,000 in permanent storage, 200,000 for flood control, and 300,000 for irrigation. The Conchas, ranging over twenty-five square miles, waters 60,000 acres near Tucumcari alone, allowing farmers to plant sorghums and wheat where once there was nothing. The land here is a study in contrasts. Farmhouses and windmills clash with the burnt yellow of the hills, and yucca and bunch grass grow up against young wheat fields. John Steinbeck's Joads passed this way in *The Grapes of Wrath,* traveling west along Route 66 through Tucumcari. In the 1930s the land was desolate, as Steinbeck described it, but today much of it has changed.

One other Canadian Basin project — Eagle Nest Reservoir near Red River — stores 100,000 acre feet of the Cimarron before it courses downstream to the Canadian. Built in 1913 in one of northern New Mexico's most beautiful settings, it irrigates more than 70,000 acres of drylands in Colfax County.

The last of the three great eastern drainage systems, the Upper Rio Grande, spawns the Rio Grande and the Pecos, two of the legendary rivers of the southwest.

The Pecos, which heads in the same mountain valleys as the Canadian, reaches south and east for 735 miles from Mora County, New Mexico, to Texas. On the way to the Gulf it literally splits the Llano Estacado, bringing water to its parched interior from the southern base of the Sangre de Cristos through four huge desert counties. East of Santa Fe the Pecos is a small, raucous stream, churning through fragrant pine groves below spiny cinnamon-colored cliffs. North of Santa Rosa it widens, and beyond it bare grasslands that once supported buffalo begin a long westward sweep to the Rockies. The Chavez and Eddy County plains, from Roswell to Carlsbad, are among the most heavily cultivated areas in all the southwest. Where Pecos Bill's Perpetual Motion Ranch once sat, flat farmlands now curve away from the river's edge.

As anywhere else in the desert, water diversion and storage keep the land alive. In the north, the Alamogordo Reservoir near Fort Sumner irrigates a large part of Guadalupe and De Baca counties. In the south, the Carlsbad Reclamation Project, launched by the federal government in 1902, waters nearly 100,000 acres of reclaimed desert land. Anchored by two large lakes, McMillan and Avalon, the project diverts its water through an intricate network of canals and ditches — and through the largest underground flume in existence. In addition, the whole lower Pecos region sits atop a massive artesian basin that funnels more water into the broad valley bottoms.

The muddy Rio Grande winds its way through as much history as any river in America. Centuries ago, the gentle Pueblos planted squash and corn in its marshy bottomlands, watching for enemies from the north. Instead, they came from the south. Francisco Vásquez de Coronado, stalking the Seven Cities of Gold, journeyed up the "Rio Bravo del Norte" in 1540, opening up nearly three centuries of Spanish conquest. In time the Indians were destroyed and their land filled with Spanish forts and trading posts and settlers tilling the same bottomlands.

The Rio Grande really is two rivers — the sluggish, slate-colored stream that flows out of Colorado's San Juan Mountains, along the Sangre de Cristos, to Santa Fe, and the broader, swift-running Rio Grande between Santa Fe and El Paso. The northern stretch runs through broad grassy plains as it enters New Mexico, then broken timberlands vividly colored in the fall with the yellows and reds of aspen and oak. The lower stretch parallels desert so fierce the Spaniards called it the Jornada del Muerto, "Journey of Death." The river is erratic everywhere, particularly at flood stage, but without it life would not exist in much of western New Mexico. To the Spaniards it was the Rio Bravo — bullying, savage, wild, untractable — a "benevolent despot," as one author has written, but one "bestowing largesse on the tilled fields and giving hope when the sky withholds it."

From beginning to end, from Colorado to Mexico, the Rio Grande's 1885 miles of water are vital to the land it runs through. Its long, curving path from Monte Vista, Colorado, to Taos County, New Mexico, makes the San Luis Valley one of the richest farming regions in the United States. From Taos to Los Alamos and Albuquerque it serves New Mexico's most heavily populated area, with enough water left over for peach orchards at Velarde and plots of alfalfa and wheat at Los Lunas and Belen. Near Socorro livestock and grain farms fill the valley, pushing back stubbled hills of creosote and cactus. On this strip of river, from the Colorado mountains to Socorro, one major project has been instrumental in the growth of local irrigated agriculture. The Middle Rio Grande Conservancy District, born in 1930 at a cost of $10 million, established 363 miles of canals on 120,000 acres of land. Further north, in Colorado, the Bureau of Reclamation's half-finished San Juan–Chama Project plans to divert 110,000 acre feet of the San Juan's headwaters into the

Rio Grande Basin for the irrigation of 39,000 acres of New Mexico land.

The lower New Mexican reaches of the Rio Grande run through lonely, trackless desert. Two small villages lie immediately below Socorro, then no more appear for miles. West of the river the rumpled San Mateo and Magdalena Mountains bear down on it, and to the east the Jornada del Muerto presses up to its banks. In the midst of it all lies the massive Elephant Butte Reservoir, perhaps the most important body of water in New Mexico. Elephant Butte, authorized by Congress in 1906, dates from 1914. The reservoir itself holds 2,-207,000 acre feet of water in a serpentine forty-five-mile-long bowl, most of the water used for local irrigation. From Truth or Consequences south to Las Cruces, cotton, alfalfa, corn, onions, and melons grow at the very edge of the Jornada del Muerto.

On the western side of the Great Divide three huge drainage systems carry water from the mountain crests to the desert.

In the sprawling Upper Columbia Basin, where the Continental Divide nudges into Montana, a handful of small, vigorous rivers drain the broken western flank of the Bitterroots. The Kootenai and Clark Fork–Pend Oreille circle out of the Bitterroots into Idaho, Oregon, and British Columbia, watering scattered patches of flatlands as they go. The region's biggest reservoir, the Pend Oreille in northern Idaho, catches Clark Fork water and impounds 1,542,000 acre feet of it for irrigation in the Idaho tip. To the south, in Idaho's midsection, the Clearwater, Salmon, and St. Joe flow west. They run brimful most of the year — the Kootenai and Pend Oreille alone carry 27 million acre feet of water — but because they run through regions of fairly abundant rainfall, they are not so critical as the Snake below them.

The lower half of the Columbia Basin is anchored by the Snake, one of the wildest and most beautiful rivers in America, a thousand-mile ribbon from Wyoming to Oregon carrying 40 million acre feet of water a year to the distant Columbia. The Snake begins almost tentatively, forming in the soft alpine meadows of Teton County, Wyoming, widening at the Gros Ventre Range, then rolling swiftly south through its Grand Canyon to Idaho. Here, on its run from the lower Tetons to Alpine Junction, it is at its most beautiful, swooping around bends and through open valleys with awesome power. Indeed, the flat, silvery Snake from Jackson Lake Lodge, the Tetons rising in the background, is one of the most beautiful sights in the West.

At Alpine it begins a long loop that carries it through Idaho's blistering southern desert, then north along the Oregon line into Washington. The land here — where the Snake River Plain levels off onto the Mountain Home Desert — is as menacing as anywhere in the West. From 35 miles wide, north to south, near Idaho Falls, it flattens out to 125 miles wide in southeast Idaho. As the sterile northern extension of the Great Basin, it is as flat and empty as the Llano Estacado, as sinister as the Jornada del Muerto, a vacant, gashed, ridged wasteland "so terrifying," one author has written, that "in most of it even sagebrush and greasewood grow precariously." It is through this desolation that the Snake flows, for the most part fast and clear, to the west.

In desert country where rainfall is not ten inches a year, the Snake is a lifeline. With it, southern Idaho exists; without it, it would not. It is the state's good fortune that the Snake is as deep and powerful — and as inexhaustible — as it is. Its watershed, ninth largest in America, spans 110,000 square miles, and its annual run-off is fully 30 percent of all western rivers combined. Part of the Snake's desert valley is irrigated by deep springs, by the Snake Plain Aquifer, but the bulk of its irrigation comes from harnessing the river itself.

Nowhere in the West, perhaps, have more dams been built and more reclamation and irrigation projects been launched than along the Snake. On both it and its fifty-six major tributaries over eighty reservoirs have been built through the years, with a storage capacity of more than 5,700,000 acre feet. Beyond this, ninety-six more sites have been identified for future development, with a storage capacity of 7,750,000 more acre feet. The Jackson Lake Reservoir, built in Wyoming in 1911, was the Snake's first major project, and the towering Hells Canyon Dam the most important in recent years. West of Pocatello, however, the mile-wide American Falls Dam rules the river for miles, and it has for five decades.

At the beginning of the century the narrow strip along the Snake between American Falls and Burley was typical of southern Idaho — miles of sage and bunch grass, pinched into a broad, dry plain by lava beds on the north and ragged sandhills to the south. But the twelve-mile-wide American Falls Reservoir, built in 1927, dammed 1.7 million acre feet of Snake water and poured it through canals into

600,000 acres of land. In time, the long valley blossomed into fields of corn, sugar beets, and potatoes, and it became one of the main agricultural areas in all of Idaho. Downstream, along the old Oregon Trail, Lake Walcott Reservoir waters 160,000 acres of land near Rupert with 107,000 acre feet of the Snake, and nine miles further west 121,000 acres at thriving Burley. Milner Dam, completed in 1905, irrigates 331,000 acres near Milner — the largest contiguous irrigated acreage in the United States. In an earlier time, Washington Irving wrote that this was "a land where no man permanently resides, a vast, uninhabited solitude . . . looking like the ruins of a world; vast desert tracts that must ever defy civilization and impose dreary and thirsty wilds between the habitations of man." But this was another time. Today, through irrigation, the wilds have been thrown back.

In the raw alkaline expanse of the western Great Basin, only the Humboldt challenges the desert. More than a century ago forty-niners tramped its chalky, dusty banks to California, followed by cattlemen and gold hunters and railroads. The Humboldt became one of the West's most historical rivers, battering its way through some of the harshest desert on earth and bringing pioneers to the Pacific in its wake.

The Humboldt rises in the desolate Goose Creek Range of southern Idaho and in high upland swamps of Elko County, Nevada. Fed by a handful of small foothill streams, it coils slowly out of the northeast, by Elko, gathers speed as it moves west past Winnemucca, then plunges headlong into the depths of the Humboldt Sink and dies. For all its historical importance, perhaps no major river anywhere has been more hated than the Humboldt. A hundred years ago pioneers knew it only for its acrid, stinking water. Mark Twain said drinking from the Humboldt was "like drinking lye, and not weak lye at that." Hubert Howe Bancroft charitably wrote that "among the major watercourses of the world it can lay claim neither to great beauty nor to remarkable utility," but W. Eugene Hollon, author of *The Great American Desert,* writing in 1966, more bluntly said that to early emigrants its course "bore a remarkable similarity to the bottomless pits of hell." Even so, the Humboldt is the only major river the western Great Basin has. In a wasteland almost devoid of human life, it supports two towns of some size — Elko and Winnemucca — and below Humboldt Reservoir, at the base of the Trin-

ity Range, it sends a few spidery irrigation channels shooting into the
badlands around Lovelock. Nevada, with 8.81 inches of annual rainfall, is the driest state in the Union, and the Great Basin is the driest
part of Nevada. "The Humboldt," said one early settler, "was filled
with what the Lord had left over when he made the world, and what
the devil wouldn't take to fix up Hell." But from Elko to Palisade,
to Battle Mountain, Winnemucca, and Lovelock, without the alkaline Humboldt, very likely life would not exist at all.

In the eastern Great Basin where the desert finally plays out
against the Wasatch Range, the Sevier, Jordan, and Bear — all heavily dammed — water Utah's dry and barren center.

The Sevier rises among the copper-colored crags and pinnacles of
southwestern Utah, winding north by the Sevier Plateau, then arching back almost upon itself before gliding into the dead bed of Sevier
Lake. On its way the river greens a narrow strip of desert from
Panguitch to Delta. Seven dams catch Sevier water between Richfield and Panguitch alone, and small Mormon farms checkerboard
the bottomlands between the towns. On its westward leg, where the
river bisects the Sevier Desert, it cuts through five thousand square
miles of the Pahvent Valley, allowing irrigation both north and south
of Delta.

The Jordan, linking Utah's two largest lakes, irrigates most of Salt
Lake County, and it has almost since the days of Brigham Young.
The Bear, to the north, waters much of the sterile Utah uplands from
Salt Lake to Idaho. Fur trappers once worked up and down the Bear,
fighting off marauding bands of Utes, but today sugar beets, peas,
wheat, barley, potatoes, tomatoes, oats, hay, and alfalfa grow in lush
fields along its banks. From Lewiston and Richmond south to Logan
and Ogden, irrigation canals spill the river into what has become one
of the most productive regions in Utah. Typical is the Bureau of
Reclamation's Hyrum Dam and Reservoir, built in 1935 to impound
18,000 acre feet of the Bear for the irrigation of 10,000 acres of land.
The Bear is short, flowing less than a hundred miles from its source
in the mountains of southeast Idaho. But like the Jordan and Sevier,
it waters some of the most critical population centers not only in
Utah, but in the entire Great Basin.

The Colorado is the king of western rivers, but it is only a whisper
as it slips out of the chill high country of northern Colorado on its
way west. It first forms in clear alpine springs on the Never Summer
side of Rocky Mountain National Park, then catches icy rills cascad-

ing through fields of wildflowers to Lake Granby below. It is here in the lake that the great river collects, and here that it begins its long journey to the sea.

As the Colorado wanders west, fed early by the Blue, Roaring Fork, Eagle, Fraser, and Williams Fork, it quickly gathers strength. In years of high run-off it runs deep and swift by State Bridge and Radium, then Glenwood Springs and Grand Junction, colliding with the Gunnison on its way to Utah, and the wild Dolores north of Moab, Utah. South of Moab the Green bursts through the mottled walls of Orange Cliffs Canyon, then meets the Dirty Devil and the San Juan, which courses gently along scalloped red bluffs below Mexican Hat, and Hovenweep and Natural Bridges national monuments. Much of the river is trapped and backed up into the towering crevices of Glen Canyon, but at Page, in northern Arizona, it begins again. Rumbling through Marble Canyon, swollen by the Little Colorado, the great stream twists and turns through the breathtaking halls and valleys of the Grand Canyon to Lake Mead. Then it swirls south, joins the Williams River near Havasu Lake and the fast-moving Gila at Yuma before reaching Mexico and the Gulf of California. By the time it reaches Sonora's Great Desert, the Colorado has traveled 1300 miles. From wintery patches of tundra and small grassy springs in the high meadows of the Rockies, the Colorado builds and swells and roars through much of the wildest, most terrifying, most beautiful — and most barren — land on earth.

One day in 1540, Coronado stood on the rim of the Grand Canyon and first saw the Colorado, coiling flat and silver-red through the Canyon's purple shadows. Coronado could not have known that this river one day would be the very heart of the West. The Colorado and its powerful tributaries are the central life-support system of the desert. They drain more than 240,000 square miles of land in seven arid states, including half of Utah, nearly half of Colorado, the far western edge of New Mexico, the southwest quarter of Wyoming, and all of Arizona. Whatever life this land has, the Colorado and its feeders give it. The harnessing of the Colorado system in this century has been the key — the *only* key — to much of the most critical development in the West's history.

In Colorado, for example, while the Dolores has not yet been controlled (the Dolores Project will be completed in 1985, at a cost of about $14 million), the 150-mile-long Gunnison to the north has been trapped and diverted all along its course. In the process it has turned the lower Gunnison Valley into a garden. In 1909 the Bureau of Reclamation's massive Uncompahgre Project built the Gunnison Diversion Tunnel near Montrose — a $3 million, 5.8-mile, U-shaped bore to deliver Gunnison water through deep mountain walls to the dry Uncompahgre Valley. At its peak the tunnel channels 1300 cubic feet of water a second into the valley, irrigating hay and bean fields and some of the largest peach and cherry orchards in the central Rockies. To the east, the Bureau added the Morrow Point Dam at Cimarron in 1963 and the Crystal Dam at the head of the Black Canyon. Two years later the Blue Mesa Dam was constructed, holding 940,000 acre feet of water in fourteen square miles of reservoir.

To the south, the deep blue-green San Juan curls out of northwestern New Mexico, irrigating bitterly dry desert on its way to the Colorado. From a distance — from the Gothic Mesas or the Aztec Ruins — the San Juan is a single fertile strand running east to west through the brown desolation of the Navajo Indian Reservation. Anchored by the Navajo Dam in the east, with 1,709,000 acre feet of water impounded in its reservoir, the river cuts a gentle furrow through Aztec, Farmington, and Shiprock before splitting the Utah–New Mexico line at Four Corners. In its wake it leaves rich grazing land, cornfields, berry groves, and orchards — none of which would survive on the hard land without it.

To the west, where the San Juan runs through the bleached sagebrush flats of southeast Utah, Blanding and Bluff live almost completely on irrigated farming. There was a time when the often violent Utah stretch of the river was fearsome to those who lived near it: one traveler in 1921 described it as a torrent of "ragged, splashing sand waves," walls of silt six feet high with the appearance of "red molten metal." But in a land where rain never comes, where creek beds lie dry year round, choked with sand and red dust, where rabbit bush and greasewood grow as far as the eye can see, the San Juan is a godsend. Racing from the north through the Tavaputs Plateau, the powerful Green pours into the Colorado at Orange Cliffs after a 730-mile journey from high mountains in southern Wyoming. Along the way it churns through some of the most spectacular canyons and most terrifying terrain in Utah. Exploring the Green in 1869, Major John Wesley Powell vividly wrote that

the landscape everywhere, away from the river, is of rock — cliffs of rock, tables of rock, plateaus of rock, terraces of rock, crags of rock

— ten thousand strangely carved forms. Rocks everywhere, and no vegetation, no soil, no sand . . . a whole land of naked rock, cathedral-shaped buttes, towering hundreds of thousands of feet, and cañon walls that shrink the river into insignificance, with vast, hollow domes, and tall pinnacles, and shafts set on the verge overhead, and all highly colored — buff, gray, red, brown, and chocolate.

Beyond the canyon walls, east and west, lies desert — low red hills splattered with cactus and sage, dead mud flats packed hard and baked by the sun, sandstone outcroppings of magenta and vermilion, banded by strands of black and gray, luminous against the vast blueness of the Utah sky. This is the Green's savage country, where mountain men first collected in rendezvous, where Utes fought their last bloody wars, where the pony express riders galloped their way to the Pacific.

The Green itself is alive with tributaries — most of them key irrigators and many of them studded with major projects. In Wyoming the Big Sandy Reservoir on Big Sandy Creek and the Eden Valley Reservoir on the Little Sandy have led to substantial irrigation in Sublette and Sweetwater counties. In Colorado both the White and Yampa swirl out of shale oil country to the Green, and both are tapped for irrigation along the way. Below the Uintas five dams sit on Ashley Creek and the Uinta, Lake Fork, and Strawberry rivers where they skip through the Tavaputs. One of the dams, the 1915 Strawberry, is the most important manmade storage facility in Utah, diverting irrigation water west into the heavily populated Utah Valley from American Fork to Provo. To the east the Moon Lake Project irrigates desert lands near and in the Uintah and Ouray Indian Reservation. Further south lie the Scofield and Joes Valley dams on the Price and San Rafael rivers. The Scofield, impounding 43,000 acre feet of the Price River in an eighteen-square-mile basin, is another of Utah's most critical dams. Not far away, to the south, outlaws once hid in the sandstone crevices of Robbers' Roost and Butch Cassidy haunted the streets of Castlegate, Helper, and Price. Now, through the Scofield Project, small Carbon County farms dot the open landscape. And because of the nearby Emery County Project, the same is true at Huntington, Clawson, and Castle Dale.

The Green itself has only two major projects on it — the old Fontenelle Dam near La Barge, Wyoming, and the breathtaking Flaming Gorge Reservoir on the Utah-Wyoming border. Flaming

Gorge is one of the most spectacular sights in the desert West, a stunning expanse of red-stained canyons and glassy cliffs that flare into the deep emerald waters of the Green. In 1963 the gorge was dammed at Dutch John, Utah, trapping 3,789,000 acre feet of water in it, and control of the Green here dictates life on it all the way to the Colorado.

In Arizona, the Colorado's southern tributaries spill out of the Rockies into the most intricate system of dams and reservoirs on the river.

The capricious Little Colorado, a small, glittering stream at birth, becomes a muddy torrent 300 miles later as it glides into the Colorado at the Grand Canyon. On the way, as it flows along the southern rim of the Colorado Plateau, its own tributaries water the dry borderlands between the Hopi and Navajo reservations. The Zuni and Rio Puerco also reach into northwest New Mexico where they irrigate large areas of San Juan and McKinley counties. Along the Little Colorado itself, at Holbrook and Joseph City, small patches of cultivation mingle with sage and creosote, their greenness set off vividly against the pink and purple haze of the Painted Desert beyond.

To the south, the Salt and Gila wind off the Continental Divide through cactus plains and chaparral thickets to bring water to the very heart of Arizona.

The Gila starts in narrow valleys wedged among the Black, San Francisco, and Mogollon mountains of New Mexico. Flowing off high plateaus through forests of yellow pine and cottonwood, it drains 13,500 square miles of land, 6100 square miles in New Mexico, before it enters Arizona. The narrow stream waters 8000 acres of western New Mexico near Gila, Cliff, and Redrock, then more in eastern Arizona near Duncan and Safford where the valley becomes a patchwork quilt of grain and fruit fields. From its junction with San Simon Creek, the Gila flows by Phoenix, then Gila Bend and the yellow-white waste of the Sonora to Yuma.

It is here that the Gila and its dams become most critical. Without them there would be no Phoenix. South of Globe sits the huge, bubbled Coolidge Dam, the first and largest multiple dam ever built. Constructed in 1927 for $5.5 million, it impounds 1,210,000 acre feet of the Gila in the $4.5 million, twenty-three-mile-long San Carlos Lake. Water is released for the irrigation of more than 120,000 acres of alfalfa, citrus fruit, and cotton land in the Casa Grande Valley.

To the west, the Ashurst-Hayden Dam, built in 1921, long ago turned Florence into the river's main agricultural center. The Painted Rock Dam near Sentinel, with 2,491,000 acre feet of water, and the Gillespie Dam near Arlington, regulate streamflow in the alfalfa-rich lower Gila Valley near Yuma. East of the city more than 125,000 acres are irrigated in the important Gila Project.

The Salt is the other central Arizona artery, cutting a zigzag path west from the junction of Black and White creeks near the Fort Apache Reservation and meeting the Gila at Phoenix. Its network of dams long ago made the Salt Valley an agricultural oasis in the desert wilderness. What work the Mormons began here in the nineteenth century, the great dams have finished in the twentieth.

The dams anchor and nourish Arizona's richest farming region. With the desert at its edge, the 1925 Mormon Flat Dam at Tortilla Flat holds back Canyon Lake for local farming, and Horse Mesa — fringed with high thickets of lavender-colored ironwood — holds seventeen-mile-long Apache Lake. The Stewart Mountain, built in 1930, contains Saguaro Lake, a sparkling, ten-mile-long reservoir, and Granite Reef, two miles away, implements it. The key link in the fifty-nine-mile chain of dams is the archaic Roosevelt, lying stolidly on the Gila at the base of the Sierra Ancha. In a narrow gorge at the junction of the Salt and Tonto Creek the Bureau of Reclamation built the Roosevelt in 1906, one of the first irrigation projects in America. By the next year it was pouring 1,382,000 acre feet a year through valley ditches, watering fields of sorghum, cotton, carrots, lettuce, and alfalfa, and charging the Arizona Canal as it cuts its forty-mile path through citrus orchards and date groves in Phoenix. Over the years, little has changed. The Roosevelt still dominates the river. And on the nearby Verde, dropping out of the north, the Bartlett and Horseshoe dams implement its storage and flow.

Including its feeders, the Colorado itself pours millions of acre feet of water a year through the plateaus and gorges of Colorado, Utah, and Arizona. The upper Colorado alone carries 6.3 million acre feet through the Painted and Great Basin deserts, swelling to 15 million by the time it challenges the Mojave and Sonora. In terms of American rivers, its flow — no more than that of the Hudson — is insignificant. But how much is less important than where — and from the moment it streams past Glenwood Springs, the Colorado waters land where largely there is no other water and never will be.

Dams and diversions attack the river almost from its birth. The Colorado–Big Thompson Project, one of the first and most significant transmontane diversions in the United States, funnels 310,000 acre feet of the Colorado through a maze of reservoirs, tunnels, canals, and dams into the Big Thompson River in northern Colorado. From there it flows to the arid flatlands of Colorado's northern farm counties. In 1954, in the midst of Colorado's first major drought in twenty years, the Big Thompson saved the plains from disaster. Today, drought years or not, the Colorado's water underpins grain, vegetable, corn, bean, and sugar beet production from the Big Thompson's canyon to the Nebraska line.

To the southwest the Frying Pan–Arkansas Project diverts 70,000 acre feet a year more from the Colorado — through the Frying Pan, a key Colorado tributary, to the headwaters of the Arkansas. At Grand Junction the Grand Valley Dam channels irrigation water through a six-mile tunnel into the Grand Valley Project. The Grand Valley Dam, along with the Vega on nearby Plateau Creek and the dam network up and down the Gunnison, have turned the valley into a maze of gardens and fields and peach orchards, hillsides of vivid orange and green set against the dull red of the plateau cliffs.

At Page, on the Arizona-Utah border, the stunning Glen Canyon Dam catches the Colorado and bottles it up in the jagged expanse of Glen Canyon. Lake Powell, 186 miles long, with a shoreline of 1860 miles, stores 27 million acre feet in its glittering bowl, guaranteeing riverflow to lower basin states even in times of upper basin drought. To the southwest, cutting around the Grand Wash and the pitch-colored Black Mountains, the Colorado is backed up for 115 miles in Lake Mead. Lying behind the towering slanted wall of Hoover Dam, Mead holds 30 million acre feet at capacity, nearly twice the annual flow of the Colorado itself, and delivers it to desert communities from southern California to Mexico. Eighty percent of southern California's water comes from the lake, and three quarters of a million acres, most of them in California, are watered from the same reservoir.

Downstream, Mojave and Havasu lakes sit shimmering on the desert floor. Mojave, impounding 1.8 million acre feet of the Colorado, lies above Davis Dam, ebbing back against the river for sixty-seven miles. Ninety miles south, Havasu sits wedged at the western base of the Mojave Mountains, contained by the 1938 Parker Dam. At nearby Parker its water is shunted through the 242-mile Colorado River Aqueduct to San Diego and Los Angeles. In time, too, a system of aqueducts and dams will be built from Havasu east; the Central Arizona Project, authorized by Congress in 1968, will create a 250-mile-long pipeline network to carry 1.2 million acre feet a year from Havasu to Phoenix and Tucson, primarily for irrigation of the area's rich croplands. Further south, near the old mining town of Ehrenberg, the Colorado makes a last fierce run below Black Peak before it runs into the Headgate Rock and Palo Verde dams. Here much of it is funneled into the Colorado River Indian Project, the only major irrigation project on the river between Yuma and Utah.

The Colorado is flat, silty, and sluggish as it reaches Yuma. Much of what is left of it after Palo Verde is captured by the Senator Wash Dam near Palo Verde, California, and the huge Imperial and Laguna dams north of Yuma. The 1908 Laguna irrigates more than 109,000 acres near Yuma, much of it on the lush mesa south of the city. The nearby Imperial diverts the Colorado into the All-American Canal — part of it 80 miles into California's verdant Imperial Valley, the rest 130 miles to the Coachella Valley. In twenty-five years the canal has delivered water to produce $2.5 billion worth of crops — thirty-seven times the federal investment in its building. And the dams have turned the Yuma Mesa into one of the most productive farming regions in America. Where Apache once hunted, where Spanish friars built adobe missions in the Arizona sun, farmers now grow cotton, wheat, alfalfa, and barley, and where forty-niners forded the river on the way to California gold, now it nurtures grapefruit, date, and pecan orchards. Even at the end of its incredible journey, dammed, diverted, silted, and polluted, the proud Colorado — as it always has — still gives life.

From the beginning of this century the West has been an oasis civilization, born and raised on the desert, nurtured by river waters from the shining mountains. Its lifeline is a slender one. In a region where average rainfall is not twenty inches, 12 million people live on 130 million acre feet of water a year from six fragile river basins. It is a fact that no westerner can ever forget. "The overriding influence, the force that shapes more things in the West than all else," wrote Walter Prescott Webb in 1957, is the desert. The desert "is its true unifying force. It permeates the plains, climbs to all but the highest peaks of the mountains, dwells continuously in the basins and valleys, and plunges down the Pacific slopes to argue with the sea. It is the heart of the West."

* * *

On a stunning spring day in 1977, eighty years of western history came to an end with the announcement of the Carter water-project "hit list." As part of a sweeping new "water-policy initiative" designed to improve federal water-resource management, President Jimmy Carter deleted eight major western water projects from the fiscal 1978 budget. In the West the action was shattering. Overnight the hit list became the center of a storm that is still raging.

The message from Washington was clear: the day of the federally funded water project was over. The time had come, said Carter, for the nation to shift away from reliance on water projects for survival and toward water conservation, away from dams and diversion toward more careful water-resource management. In that light, both previously authorized projects and potential new projects were to be reviewed by the Water Resources Council. Those projects that survived review would be approved only when consideration was given to conservation and reuse possibilities first, only when environmental quality was guaranteed, when the cost-benefit ratio was greater than one to one, with wide distribution of benefits, when the individual states began to share project costs (between 5 and 10 percent), and when an independent review board — the Water Resources Council — had guaranteed their integrity. Carter insisted that deemphasis of the projects would decrease waste, improve federal water planning and management, and establish better relations between the government and the states.

According to Carter, the eight western projects violated all aspects of the new policy. First, they threatened major adverse impact in their regions — destruction of forests, farmland, wildlife habitat, and several hundred miles of free-flowing rivers and streams. Second, their cost-benefit ratio was too low to warrant construction. Third, all eight conflicted in some way with other federal water-resource management policies, interfering with public scientific, cultural, and recreational benefits as well as with effective flood-control and water-purification procedures. The Carter mandate carried budget reductions of $289 million for the eight, aiming at long-term reductions of up to $5 billion.

The president's action directly affected six arid western states — Arizona, Colorado, Wyoming, Utah, and both Dakotas. But, indirectly, because of the precedent set, the new directions suggested, it affected every state west of the 100th meridian.

In Arizona the critical $1.5 billion Central Arizona Project — 20 percent completed in 1977 — was threatened. After nine years of construction, the government concluded that the 1.4 to 2.2 cost-benefit ratio was too low to warrant further funding. In addition, according to the government, massive environmental dislocation would result from it. Specifically, read the federal complaint, the eventual inundation of 18,000 acres of land and fifty miles of streams — some of them on national forest and Indian property — would damage stream fishing in the region, impair other forms of recreation, increase salinity in the rivers, and disturb the nesting grounds of the southern bald eagle.

In Utah the Bonneville Unit of the long-planned, long-disputed Central Utah Project was attacked on similar grounds. The government charged that its completion would flood 22,000 acres of land — including large wilderness tracts and 90 percent of the region's rangeland — and 200 miles of pristine streams; from Rock Creek Canyon to Utah Lake, aesthetic and recreational values would be destroyed, along with the native habitat of beaver, waterfowl, moose, and deer in the Upper Stillwater Valley. In a sense, the federal position was not surprising. For thirty years Utah sought funding for the project (designed to carry water from the Uintas through the mountains to the heavily populated Salt Lake City–Provo corridor) and it came slowly and piecemeal even in the best of times. Now the intricate Bonneville Unit, 16 percent complete and carrying 300,000 acre feet a year from the Colorado watershed to the Wasatch Valley, is threatened again. And threatened with it is Utah's ability to utilize most of its water allotment under the Colorado River compacts of 1922 and 1948.

On the 100th meridian, where the arid West begins, the Carter list proposed to wipe out the two biggest projects in the dry Dakotas.

North Dakota's massive Garrison Diversion Unit Project was 19 percent complete in 1977 when the administration suggested elimination of its funding. From its birth in 1966, the project's purpose has been to create an irrigation system for the Missouri's dry lowlands, but the government has maintained that whatever benefits it might bring would be far outweighed by the damage it would cause. Federal analysts have concluded that the project ultimately will require condemnation of 220,000 acres of productive farm and grazing land (occasionally displacing farmers who live on it) and destroy the Cheyenne Lake Wildlife Refuge and damage seven more. More important, by spreading Missouri water to the eastern part of the state, with mineral salts, fertilizer, and pesticides accumulating in it in the process, the project will degrade water quality in the James, Red, and Souris rivers.

To the south the Oahe Project faces the same criticisms — inundation of productive land, displacement of farmers, intrusion on wildlife habitat (chiefly that of the bald eagle and peregrine falcon), and destruction of water quality in the James River. The purpose of the project is to establish a shunting system for some of the 23 million acre feet of Missouri River water impounded behind Oahe Dam — second largest earth dam in the world — east to the James Valley. But arguments have raged over it for a quarter century already, and Carter's action may have sealed its fate.

Of all the hit-list states, none felt the impact as much as Colorado. Five of its projects were attacked, four of them completely in Colorado and a fifth in Colorado and Wyoming. The Savery-Pothook Project, shared with Wyoming, was designed to irrigate 28,700 acres of badlands in northwestern Colorado and southwestern Wyoming by tapping the Little Snake River near Baggs, Wyoming. The government has charged that the damming of the river would lower streamflow and increase salinity in the Yampa, Green, and Colorado, damage wildlife habitat by converting rangeland to cropland, and ruin ten miles of fishing stream. The administration stated that the adverse effects of Savery-Pothook are compounded by its low cost-benefit ratio.

The Narrows Project in northeastern Colorado, Dallas Creek Project near Ridgeway, Fruitland Mesa Project on the Gunnison, and Dolores Project near Cortez all were included on the Carter list partly because of low cost-benefit ratios and negative environmental impact on land and life around them. The administration claimed that both Fruitland Mesa and the Dolores Project, in particular, would inundate productive land and streams (particularly fifteen miles of the Dolores), reduce flow in other nearby streams and in the Colorado itself, increase salinity in the Colorado, and damage the native habitat of the area's elk and mule deer.

In the spring of 1977 again the point was clear: the day of the federally funded water project was over.

However well-intentioned it may have been, the Carter hit list was a study in federal arrogance. Its assumptions were questionable. Its conclusions were faulty. It was riddled with antiwestern prejudice and wrapped in antiwestern ignorance. It reflected no understanding of western conditions, of western people, of the nature of their lives, or of the relentless, crushing aridity that shapes their land and everything in it. What ultimately happens to the hit-list projects is important to the West. But far more important — and frightening — is the attitude that snared them in the first place.

The fact that the West was not involved in making the hit-list decision says much about the attitude. In formulating its action the government did not consult with western congressmen, Indian representatives, water-conservancy districts, affected communities, or state governments. Decisions were made, instead, somewhere deep in the recesses of federal bureaucracy, far distant from western scrutiny, far removed from western concerns. For the West it marked a bitter return to the past. Grover Cleveland conceived America's first forest reserves in secrecy. So did Theodore Roosevelt plot his. The practice is old. Only the subject has changed.

Paternalism, arrogance, secrecy — it is this attitude that galls the West, that triggers its great rage. It is the same attitude that underlies and spurs crash synfuels development. It is the same attitude that trumpets the MX. It is the same attitude that fires sectionalism. The hit list, said the *Denver Post,* was a political vendetta — "vengeful opposition" by a president to a region that repudiated him in 1976. Representative Jim Johnson of Colorado called it "ignorance, intransigence, and obduracy." What happened, though, has no label, and it matters little what it is called. Whether rooted in vengeance or ignorance, or both, the action was a graphic reflection of a hundred years of western history. Synfuels and the MX vividly illustrate the West's terrifying vulnerability to federal whim. So, too, does the hit list.

Western anger is directed beyond the executive branch. The attitude of the East and Midwest in general has been an endless source of irritation to westerners in Congress as far back as water wars have been fought. For eighty years nonwesterners have bitterly opposed western irrigation and reclamation projects in Congress, even as they have promoted their own. Through the years their position has never changed: eastern projects are vital, western are not. When the Carter water plan went to Congress in 1977 and 1978, it was a powerful eighteen-state coalition of northeasterners and midwesterners that rose to support it. Its angry charge was that while eastern cities decayed, the Sun Belt boomed; while eastern water systems rotted, the West continued to build. In 1978 Representative Silvio Conte of

Massachusetts angrily said that "big-city water and sewer spending ought to be the first priority" of Congress, and a year later a report by the Consortium of Northeastern Organizations suggested that for $25 billion Congress could amply fund urban water-system renewal — while trimming western projects at the same time. As the question of water-project funding has weaved in and out of Congress, many eastern Corps of Engineers projects have found funding — while many western projects have not.

The hit list sprang from ignorance of the West, and the assumptions that surround it sadly reflect that fact.

One critical assumption is that the damming of western water has spawned a kind of "waste ethic" among westerners, the belief that rather than conserve the water they have, they should build dams to catch what they have not. The assumption is simplistic. Nonwesterners do not understand, and never have, that their concept of conservation is invalid in the arid West; to them conservation is reduction of *use* (or what Governor Scott Matheson of Utah has called the "brick-in-the-toilet mentality"), but in the West conservation is *physical control,* or storage. In the desert, reduction of use is implausible, even harmful. In the desert water is recycled constantly as it moves downstream, recharging aquifers and flowing again. Where rain does not fall, land and people live on run-off, stored in dams, carefully diverted, recycled, rerouted, reused again and again. In the West physical control is not waste. It is not, as easterners charge, pork barrel. It is adaptation to brutal and unique natural circumstances. It is survival.

The question of control has been surrounded by controversy throughout this century. The hit list did not create a new issue. It revived an old one.

For years after the settlement of the West, western water law was rooted in the idea of "first in time, first in right." The doctrine of prior appropriation held that water belonged to whoever could catch it first, hold it first, and first put it to "beneficial use" (and beneficial use — generally meaning any economic use — became the basis, measure, and limit of right). In time, however, downstream states on the area's vital rivers challenged the doctrine, charging that unregulated upstream use left them with nothing. Challenges led to counterchallenges and the eruption of virtual war over every significant stream in the Rockies.

Even in the violent West, no issue ever triggered more savage interstate conflict than the question of water rights. And no state was uninvolved. In 1897 when Kansas attempted to claim Colorado's Arkansas River run-off, the militant *Rocky Mountain News* called it an "invasion of state and individual and community rights." Warning Kansas to back off, the *News* angrily editorialized that "any attempt to invade the irrigation system of the commonwealth must be fought to the bitter end." In 1934, to stop the flow of Colorado River water into California, Arizona's National Guard was mobilized to halt the building of Parker Dam. As late as 1979 Wyoming and Nebraska waged a bitter fight over Laramie River water near Wheatland, Wyoming. Only in time were agreements reached — and compacts written in blood.

Modifying the doctrine of prior appropriation, the compacts sliced up the West's major rivers by acre feet and allotted them proportionately among the states. Colorado River water goes to seven states and Mexico, the Platte and Rio Grande to three. At the same time, however, the compacts held that any state unable to back up its water allotment with physical containment — storage — could lose it; water passing through a state, even if allotted to it, could be used by another. And, though it has yet to be written into law, the growing fear in the West today is that if the utilizing state puts another's surplus to beneficial use, in time it will gain legal right to the surplus. Water rights once lost, then, may not be returned, and it is for that reason that western states must "dam the flood" while they can. The state that cannot faces ruin. Tomorrow, literally, is too late.

Historically, no river in the West has caused the contention the Colorado has. The 1922 Colorado River Compact split its basin in half at Lee's Ferry, Arizona, and allotted both its Upper Basin states (Wyoming, Utah, New Mexico, and Colorado) and Lower Basin states (Nevada, Arizona, and California) 7.5 million acre feet a year to divide among themselves. In addition, 1.5 million acre feet were given to Mexico. Most important, Lower Basin states were given "first rights" to the water: under any and all conditions, including drought, they were to be supplied first; Upper Basin states took what was left.

The 1922 allotments were based on projections that one day the Colorado would carry 15 million acre feet. But it never has. Today it flows at 13.5 to 14 million acre feet a year. With Lower Basin states due 7.5 million, regardless of river flow, Upper Basin states clearly face an eventual shortfall. All that prevents it now is their relatively

low storage capacity, their inability to capture and store their allotment. Today Colorado, Wyoming, New Mexico, and Utah take only
3.6 million acre feet of their 7.5 million allotment; by 1990 some 5.3
million acre feet will be available, but if storage has not increased
— and federal water policies indicate that it will not — they will lose
it as well. At the same time, under the blunt doctrine of "use it or
lose it," any downstream state that can take Upper Basin surplus and
put it to beneficial use may keep it. Owing to ever-increasing downstream demands, it is feared even now that Upper Basin states will
never receive their allotment. It is this simple and desperate fact that
has triggered opposition to the hit list.

On or off the Colorado, no western state is unaffected by the
problem of static storage capacity. The destruction of the Oahe
Project will deeply affect South Dakota, especially if water is diverted
from it for shale oil or coal slurry. If the Garrison is stopped in North
Dakota it will kill plans to irrigate an additional 96,000 (formerly
250,000) acres of Dakota prairie. Governor Allen Olson has fought
back bitterly, saying that "it is time to break the connection with the
Carter administration scheme to destroy this project," and to "follow
the obvious intent of Congress to get on with construction without
further delay." Failure, he has said, would be to leave it "dead in its
tracks," resulting in "irreparable harm to the state of North
Dakota." In the winter of 1981, Senator Mark Andrews called the
continued stalling of the Garrison a "tragedy."

Wyoming governor Ed Herschler has called the hit list "the complete strangulation of the western states." In North Dakota, at least,
he is not far from right.

Utah faces similar problems. Some say that the death of its Bonneville Unit will cripple its efforts to claim its full 23 percent allotment
from the Colorado's Upper Basin. At the same time, the projected
use of 50,000 acre feet a year from the Dirty Devil by the mammoth
Intermountain Power Project will further drain Colorado water from
the already tinder-dry southwest. Because of these things, a sense of
urgency exists in the state. In 1979 Governor Scott Matheson said
that the West "must be about the business of building [the projects]
before spiraling costs and interminable delays bring water-resource
development in this country to a complete standstill." "Considering
the government's hit-list approach to water," said another official in
1980, "we in Utah have trouble seeing any continuation of partnership with the federal government." In that light, Utah, like Wyo-

ming, has begun moving toward funding its own reclamation projects and building its own systems.

Arizona, too, will be unable to claim all of its 2.8 million acre feet allotment of Colorado River water unless the Central Arizona Project is completed. After its initial placement on the hit list, the project was revived by the Carter administration itself. Now, unless it is killed again (an unlikely possibility despite occasional sparring over it by James Watt and Morris Udall), its completion in the mid-1980s will allow diversion of more than a million acre feet a year to Phoenix and Tucson that now flows to California. California, in turn, currently importing 5 million acre feet a year, substantially over its allotment of 4.4 million, will seek legal rights to Upper Basin surplus to cover its loss — and the ultimate loser will be Colorado.

Colorado is the Rockies' greatest paradox. Four of the West's greatest rivers are spawned there, rippling out of its high country to desert and prairie. Its waterways carry nearly 16 million acre feet a year through nineteen states, watering land and supplying cities from California to the Mississippi. Ironically, however, Colorado itself gets less than half of its own water — roughly 5 million acre feet a year. The South Platte produces 2.2 million acre feet a year, 2.1 million of which go to Colorado. The Rio Grande produces 1.4 million acre feet, of which Colorado's take is 1.01 million. It also takes 1.12 of the Arkansas's 1.17. The biggest problem is Colorado's small piece of the Colorado River. Its allotment is only 34 percent of the entire river and 51.75 percent of the Upper Basin. Beyond the question of rights, however, lies the larger question of storage capacity. Colorado loses 3 million acre feet a year to other states, half of which it is entitled to keep. The loss comes primarily because it lacks the facilities to dam its allotment.

The Colorado, again, is critical. The state is entitled to between 750,000 and 1 million acre feet of the river above and beyond what it now uses (roughly 25 percent of its allotment). Its hit-list projects — along with others in the planning stage — were designed specifically to increase storage capacity in the river's basin so that it could take its share. Now, as elsewhere in the Upper Basin, the plan is in jeopardy. As Colorado watches its surplus flow south to Arizona and California, and as the two put it to "beneficial use," Colorado faces the day when its water legally may be gone forever. In the Central Rockies some believe that, in time, with water in the fields and political power in Washington, California, in particular, might destroy all further water development in the Upper Basin. When and if this happens, no state will lose more than Colorado.

In 1977, promoting "conservation" over damming, the federal government made gravely incorrect assumptions. It also failed to take into account one other critical fact — that if western states do not develop their storage and reclamation sites, and claim, impound, and use their water, the private sector will. If the West does not act in the public interest, private developers will act in theirs.

It has happened before. Water flows to money, it has been written, and during every stage of the frontier's life it did. Cattlemen dominated water holes as medieval lords dominated their manor lands, and cattle kings appropriated as much frontage on the rivers as their hired guns could hold. Ditch companies, most of them eastern, tapped the waterways and bled settlers who needed them. Irrigation companies and land speculators entrapped sodbusters, then watched them die in their own dust. During the early years of this century water-power combines swarmed over every river in the West, harnessing them to their own ends. Water in the West, like a magnet, attracts power, and too often in the past the power has been malevolent. It is the abuse of power, precisely, that the hit list invites. It is this, precisely, that westerners fear.

The biggest threat comes from energy. Energy companies have appropriated western water for years, and as the bidding price goes up — which it will — they will take more and more in the future. In Colorado, for example, existing energy facilities already use 45,000 acre feet a year, and by the year 2000 usage will approach 200,000. Shale oil companies already have amassed water rights on the rivers of northwest Colorado. In Montana the Boysen and Yellowtail Projects, built to impound irrigation water, fell to energy giants long ago; Exxon, Gulf, and Peabody Coal own 35,000 acre feet of the Boysen and 623,000 of the Yellowtail. Fully half of the Yellowtail's water has options on it, mostly by oil companies. Coal slurry threatens the Powder and Bighorn and every other stream in eastern Wyoming and the western Dakotas. Coal-fired power plants suck water from every major basin in the Rockies, and if coal synfuels become reality their plants will do the same. In Utah and Nevada the MX soon will pull water by the millions of acre feet from the most arid desert land in the world. Sadly, as energy and defense and real-estate developers have moved into the western water market, prices have skyrocketed. Twin Lakes water, near the mouth of the Arkansas, jumped from

$1100 an acre foot in 1974 to $7500 in 1980. Big Thompson water rights that sold for $2 to $7.50 an acre foot in 1947 now sell for up to $2000 and by the year 2000 the asking price will be $20,000. In central Colorado a rancher recently sold 1700 acre feet for $2.3 million, and near Delta, Utah, another rancher, selling water for $1750 an acre foot, made a profit of $3 million on his land. In time, if not now, private development may destroy much of the West. Although some are conscientious, no private developers can automatically be counted on to maintain minimum streamflows, protect wildlife, allow recreation, or fight salinity. And no developer can be counted on to work toward stabilizing the price of water. Washington has maintained that western water projects are damaging to the West, but the private projects that take their place are likely to be more so.

From the Drift Prairie to the Salt River Valley, the biggest losers will be the farmers.

In the West today farms consume 90 percent of its water, much of it bought from the region's water projects and poured over 8 million acres of arid land. In the past, cheap water from the big reservoirs has shielded farmers from escalating water prices and allowed them to compete in the western marketplace. Now, given the new direction of federal water policy, the day of the subsidy apparently is over, and with it, the farmer's protection. If the West's half-finished projects are abandoned and if Washington's "no-new-starts" mandate continues to hold, sooner or later it will cripple the farmers. No farmer can afford to pay $100 an acre foot. No farmer can bid with Exxon.

A militant new mood is emerging in Washington. Carter reflected it, the hit list implied it, and so far the Reagan administration has followed it — the idea that energy is more cost effective than farming, that it produces more for the money than farming, and that water diverted from agriculture to energy is a sane and intelligent investment in the future. This is partly true; no one can argue that farming is more cost effective than coal. But it ignores the fact that in the past, at least, western water projects have been as good a financial investment as the government has ever made.

The damming of the West was not an act of federal charity, and westerners bristle at those who say it was. The Reclamation Act of 1902 requires repayment of all construction and operating costs by those who benefit from the projects. In early years revenue collected from the sale of impounded water to local beneficiaries made up the repayment, implemented by public-lands sales and the leasing of mineral lands. In later years electrical power was produced and sold by many of the projects and its revenue channeled into the reclamation fund. The payback was sporadic and fraud was not uncommon, but in time the system improved. The approximately 80 percent payback record of western reclamation projects has surpassed almost any federal funding system ever devised.

As of September 1979, two and a half years after Carter's pointed criticism of the low cost-benefit ratio of western water projects, the federal government had spent a total of $19 billion on them. Despite charges to the contrary by angry nonwesterners, the expenditure is not a subsidization of western water. Of the $19 billion spent, only 17 percent is non-reimbursable — but because water projects meet such national goals as recreation and flood control, it is made so *by the law itself.* Of the rest, 37 percent is fully reimbursable (though without interest) and 46 percent is reimbursable with interest equal to the rate on long-term federal borrowing at the time project construction begins.

On the other hand, eastern Corps of Engineers projects generally are completely non-reimbursable.

If all federal money spent had a return equal to the return on western water projects, the United States would have no national debt.

Westerners object to groundless accusations of subsidization by the federal government. They also object to rules changed in the middle of the game. Most of the hit-list projects were formulated years ago and approved years ago, and when the process began they *were* cost effective. Now, decades later, it is destructive and senseless for the federal government to set forth new sets of numbers and ratios in the middle of construction. The value of water cannot be determined by numbers, nor can the value of the projects to the dryland areas they serve. No cost-benefit ratio yet written has taken into account the billions of dollars returnable to the projects in the form of tax revenues, the gross value of crops grown by project water (more than $4.5 billion a year), power sales ($250 million), prevention of flood damage ($100 million), recreation revenue, or the number of people (18 million a year) who draw water supplies from behind project dams.

The West senses hypocrisy in the hit-list mentality. No sense of eastern outrage surfaced over the Chrysler subsidies, or Amtrak or Penn Central. No protest was raised over the $6 million subsidy for the District of Columbia subway. To the outside world western agriculture may be less cost effective than energy, too unimportant to save from the energy kings. But to the West itself, its value remains incalculable.

The chief purpose of this century's water projects has been to preserve western agriculture, as both an economic system and a way of life. The projects of the 1970s and 1980s have the same purpose — to support farmers and farm communities through the economic turbulence of the next decades. Now, with the killing of some projects and the stalling of others, no one can know what the future may hold. In 1958 farmers generated 10 percent of the West's economy, but today they produce only 3 percent. Tomorrow it will be less, and the hit list and the antiwestern mentality behind it can only accelerate the fall. Each day the West fails to act, or cannot act, the amount of water available for agriculture decreases. How long it can survive the trend only time will tell. In 1892 Hamlin Garland wrote sadly of High Plains farmers, "helpless, like flies in a pool of tar."

Perhaps time has changed nothing. They are helpless still.

In the early 1980s expanding western drought conditions and deteriorating aquifers have created a particular sense of urgency around the issue of agriculture, rivers, and water-storage projects.

Drought is nothing new to the West. Memories of the Dust Bowl linger everywhere, memories of hot summer days in the 1930s when whirlwinds spun across dead wheat fields and dry water holes, enveloping the land in dusty fog, choking cattle, killing people, ripping apart the earth and all the life in it. In a sense the whirlwind never fully lifted; drought, like the plague, has dogged the West for fifty years, always near, always menacing. Dust Bowl days have not yet returned, but they may not be far away: all across the West the winter of 1980 was the driest in memory. Luckily the spring of 1981 was wet, but a dry summer and a second drought winter still will always bring the West to the edge of disaster. For the West, the day may be at hand when every drop of impounded water will be the most precious thing on earth.

In every corner of the Rockies, winter snowpack was frighteningly low. In March 1981, New Mexico's snowpack was at a record low, Montana's 33 to 66 percent of normal, and Utah's 25 to 50 percent. Wyoming's, at 62 percent of normal in April, was fully 10 percent below its previous record low, and Colorado's, at 28 percent, was the lowest in forty-five years. In a region where snowpack provides 75 percent of the total water supply, the implications were terrifying.

In March 1981, streamflow was particularly poor in Arizona, Montana, and Utah. In southern Idaho the Snake flowed so low that power production dropped radically and the state was forced to buy supplementary power elsewhere. In Nevada it was recorded at 40 to 55 percent of normal, at 33 to 50 percent in New Mexico, and in Wyoming low flow and spot shortages nearly everywhere led to strict spring conservation measures. In Colorado the situation was acute: a state that relies almost totally on snowpack — which runs off in sixty to ninety days in the spring — found itself with a run-off 35 to 55 percent of normal in March. As early as May, snow depth readings in some parts of the state registered at zero — meaning the snow had melted and run off *already.* In an area where snowpack generally *increases* anywhere from 10,000 to 11,000 feet between April 1 and May 1, snowpack actually *decreased;* its skimpy run-off, which usually flows into area streams, simply seeped into the ground. In the spring of 1981, looking to a summer of the lowest streamflows ever recorded in Colorado, state officials predicted that the Arkansas would run 25 percent of normal, affecting irrigation all the way to Kansas; between April and September, usually months of high run-off, the South Platte was projected to run 28 percent of normal, the Big Thompson 51 percent, the Upper Colorado 58 percent, the White 44 percent, and the Rio Grande 50 percent. In May officials also warned that late spring and summer run-off would be unprecedentedly low — one third to one half of normal in New Mexico, 50 to 65 percent in Nevada, and the same in Wyoming, where the North Platte was to run at its lowest level in history.

As it turned out, greater than usual spring rains created good carryover storage. But this did not change the fact that Colorado and the West still cannot survive dry winters and springs indefinitely. All that saves them from disaster now is their storage. Drought or not, western reservoirs have stockpiled enough water to see the West through one bad year, maybe two. Without them, the drought of 1980–81 already would have brought consequences to the West that most people have never imagined.

Drought creates a powerful argument against the hit list and the idea of water "conservation." Westerners know, as nonwesterners do not, that drought tends to be cyclical, settling in perhaps twice in a decade, then staying and searing and suffocating everything it touches for several seasons. Though westerners know their history, know the cycles, they remain at the mercy of drought. All they can do to survive is dam, impound, and protect every acre foot when times are good and hold it until times are bad. There is no fallback. And there are few alternatives.

The aquifers of the West have been its only other life source in this century. But now they are slowly dying, putting strain on river systems to supply what they cannot, and creating another argument for damming.

All over the West, from the Artesian Basin of New Mexico to the Snake River Plain Aquifer of Idaho, vast areas of porous water-bearing rock underlie the land. Many of them gradually are being pumped dry. The Madison Aquifer, for example, under assault from coal-slurry interests, is dropping yearly even without slurry. So are aquifers in exploding Douglas County, Colorado. In Nevada the overdraft of Truckee Valley aquifers (coupled with excessive diversion from the Truckee River) have so decreased waterflow into Pyramid Lake that one day it may die. In the Gila River Basin of Arizona, where huge tracts of desert have been plowed under to raise cotton, ground-water supplies are being horribly depleted. Near the massive Paloma Ranch, where the Northwestern Mutual Life Insurance Company cultivates 20,000 acres of desert for cotton, some wells already have been driven 500 feet below the earth's surface.

One of the most vulnerable areas in the West is Tucson. With 450,000 people, it is one of the fastest-growing cities in the United States. It grew 26 percent between 1970 and 1980 alone. By 1990 its population will stand at 625,000 and by 2000 it will rise to 800,000. And most of the population in Pima County will draw its water from wells driven deep into the water table.

Tucson is the largest city in America to rely entirely on ground water for survival. With its stunning growth, it already has overdrafted the water fields around it by 185,000 acre feet a year. The overdraft in the Santa Cruz Basin, in fact, is as severe as anywhere in the United States. In the lower Santa Cruz 552,000 acre feet of water are used each year, primarily for agriculture; by 2020 it will exceed half a million feet. In the upper Santa Cruz depletion is even worse. Geologists believe that its water table will be exhausted completely within a century. The situation is similar in the nearby Avra Valley; its aquifers, too, at present rates of usage, will be dry within a hundred years.

Tucson waits for the Central Arizona Project — and deliverance. In the meantime it consumes itself. Wells in the region have dropped 110 feet in the past ten years as the city pumps out five times the water that goes back in. To sustain itself until CAP — which may or may not ever reach Tucson, and then may or may not be able to deliver allocations from the shrunken Colorado — Tucson has bought and retired 12,000 acres of farmland. Mining companies, also active in the region, have bought up and retired 8000 more. By 1985 the city alone will have bought 36,000 acres. The city will live. But farming will be dead.

The most seriously endangered aquifer in the West lies far to the north and east of Tucson, roughly along and under the western edge of the 100th meridian, beneath southern South Dakota, central Nebraska, eastern Colorado and New Mexico, the Texas and Oklahoma panhandles, western Kansas, and the southeastern corner of Wyoming. The mammoth Ogallala is the largest freshwater reserve in the world, 2 billion acre feet trapped in prehistoric sand and silt beds beneath the High Plains. For forty years the great aquifer has been the wellspring of 225,000 square miles of life above it. Between 1949 and the mid-1970s, irrigated acreage on the plains increased from 2.6 million to 9.6 million, an area twice the size of New Jersey. Furrowed cornfields and wheat fields blossomed, even in drought times, underpinning the growth of hundreds of dryland cities. Feedlots multiplied and grain production tripled. In 1981 Ogallala water irrigated 16 million acres of drylands. High Plains states produce 386 million bushels of feed grain a year on it and provide the nation with 40 percent of its fed beef. In eastern Colorado agricultural sales quadrupled from $218 million in 1959 to $932 million in the mid-1970s, as irrigated acreage soared from zero to 500,000 acres. Nebraska corn, the state's leading crop, valued at $1.5 billion in 1978, is watered by the aquifer that lies under virtually the whole state; so are fat Nebraska cattle that brought the state $1.6 billion in 1977. Above all, perhaps, the Ogallala supplies drinking water for 2 million people. From Dakota to New Mexico the story is the same: the Ogallala provides what the rivers cannot, brings life to land that rivers cannot reach.

But today the aquifer is dying. Over the years the deep wells that penetrate the Ogallala have taken their toll. Every year farmers take more water from the aquifer than the entire flow of the Colorado. At the same time, little water returns — partly because rainfall itself is scarce on the plains and partly because the aquifer's rock cap blunts the moisture that does seep down through the earth. The result has been disastrous. In 1930 the region was saturated by water fifty-eight feet deep. Now it is eight feet and falling. In recent years the water table has dropped between six inches and three feet a year across the prairie. Deeper declines have appeared in Nebraska and Kansas, and in Colorado, where the Ogallala has lost 50 percent of its volume in thirty years, the water table fell forty feet between 1964 and 1976 alone. Already, irrigated acreage is falling in five of six states drawing on the aquifer.

By the year 2000, in parts of the plains, the Ogallala will have been depleted by 40 percent. By 2020, for many, the aquifer will have ceased to exist entirely. By then 6 million acres will have reverted to dry farming in eastern Colorado and New Mexico, western Kansas, west-central Nebraska, and the Oklahoma panhandle. Those acres still under cultivation will change radically: water-intensive sugar beets and pinto beans will disappear, corn will fail; only alfalfa and wheat and sorghum and cotton will remain — and they perhaps not for long. Across the plains, optimists say the Ogallala has forty years of life left, but in some regions it has less than fifteen, and in other regions its life virtually is over now.

In time the Ogallala will die, and when it does High Plains farms will not survive in their present condition without new water. Already farmers have begun to look to the rivers for deliverance — to the already overtaxed and understored Arkansas and Missouri. One plan, formulated in 1980, would divert the Missouri at Fort Randall, South Dakota, and channel it through Nebraska to eastern Colorado. Downstream it would be diverted again at St. Joseph, Missouri, and funneled into western Kansas. A third plan would catch the Arkansas as it flows into Arkansas and run millions of acre feet into west Texas. Perhaps such massive diversion is not actually possible; at the minimum it would cost $29 billion in 1980 dollars, along with another billion dollars a year for energy to lift the water out of the riverbeds and push it across the plains. On the other hand, no one can say for certain what is possible and what is not. Only one real certainty exists: if the rivers one day are overtapped by users, and if storage has not increased in the meantime, the drain on them will be incredible and fatal.

Without dams, without reservoirs, without the ability to "store the flood," the West will not survive.

In the future life of the West, nothing — not energy, not the MX — will be as critical as the nature and direction of federal water policy. What ultimately happens to hit-list projects and those still-born under the no-new-starts mandate is vitally important. But as the West journeys through the 1980s, a vastly larger concern is the future of federal water policy in general. Old policy is dead. It has been since 1977. The West, then, must determine what options — if any — exist.

Federal policy has unfolded slowly in the Reagan administration. The Reagan program, in fact, is no different from Carter's. Hit-list projects remain stalled. No new starts have been initiated. And the disliked Water Resources Council — under a different name — nears revival.

Reagan's winning of the West in 1980 was based in no small part on his stated support for western water projects. But his drive to balance the federal budget has stymied water-project action the same way Carter's drive to eliminate pork-barreling blunted his. The emerging Republican position — identical in effect to Carter's — is that the federal government cannot and will not bear the brunt of further water development in western states, that it particularly cannot afford the cost of projects with limited beneficiaries, and that it particularly cannot afford their staggering front-end costs. Accordingly, the Reagan administration has begun to press for joint federal-state financing and the creation of a small, powerful superbureau that would plan, implement, and monitor selected projects.

The question of federal-state financing goes back at least to Carter. As early as 1977 the Carter administration proposed that projects with vendible products would contribute 10 percent of their building costs, and that projects without products would contribute 5 percent. Of projects already begun, those that shared costs would be approved over those that did not, and under any circumstances, no new projects would be started without the agreement.

The controversial Domenici-Moynihan bill (after senators Peter Domenici of New Mexico and Daniel Patrick Moynihan of New York) of 1981 has borrowed and modified the Carter concept. Hoping to pare the twenty-six-year span from project planning to project implementation to between three and four years, the bill provides for annual federal block grants to the states based on 1980 population and land area, and contributions of 25 percent by the states to the projects — all of it paid at the front end, where costs are highest, instead of later through users' fees. The states then would make their own project decisions and recoup their investments through users' fees.

However reluctantly, the West has moved slowly through the years toward acceptance of cost sharing. Even in 1977 westerners in the National Governors' Association supported the idea in principle. On the other hand, both then and now, the West also has had serious reservations about it. And so far they have been serious enough to prevent its full acceptance.

The West fears, for example, that the new federal thrust might abrogate existing agreements governing the building and maintenance of future projects. Of major concern is the apparent Domenici-Moynihan disregard of existing federal-state agreements on Colorado River Basin projects. The 1956 Colorado River Storage Project Act decrees that power revenue from hydroelectric dams be set aside to help fund further projects, but Colorado's Senator William Armstrong has charged that the future of such agreements is unclear as written in the new bill. Loss of revenue — were it to happen — would cost the West hundreds of millions of dollars a year. At the same time, any change in agreements might imperil those projects now under construction. Whether they would be completed under old arrangements — or subject to new — also is unclear.

A second fear is that if existing agreements are nullified, if states are forced to share costs, it will happen with a suddenness that state financial systems cannot tolerate. To saddle the West with costs never anticipated and never agreed upon is a serious enough matter; to do it *immediately,* as New Mexico's state engineer has understated it, "would be most inequitable." A sudden shift to 25 percent front-end state financing would mean, simply, no projects — at least for the foreseeable future.

Finally, westerners are convinced that the Domenici-Moynihan allocation system fails to consider need in making block grants. Their concern is that lightly populated western states with little rainfall might fare no better than heavily populated nonwestern states with ample rainfall. Given the likely nonwestern tilt of the granting body, the concern is a real one.

Very likely the Domenici-Moynihan bill will not pass in its present form, especially in a House fearful of giving too much power to state legislatures. On the other hand, cost sharing is an idea whose time clearly has come. Assessing western opinion, the Washington-based National Water Resources Association has found its "rather universal acceptance" in western states. If the West's primary concerns are addressed, if the exact status of current projects is defined and agreements governing their building and maintenance are honored in order to guarantee the survival of the states in meeting payments, the idea will continue to be accepted. The West is — has always been — pragmatic.

Several states already have begun moving toward a more self-reliant relationship with federal government. Utah and Wyoming are at work on plans for state-funded projects. In 1981 Colorado appropriated substantial seed money for project studies, preparing for the day — if it comes — that it can begin to pay its own way. As one legislator has said, with or without federal money, Colorado "must take responsibility for its own destiny."

Also of grave concern to the West is the emerging water super-bureau of Secretary of the Interior James G. Watt.

In the spring of 1981 Watt moved to consolidate federal water policy under himself in the Department of the Interior. He abolished the Water Resources Council (WRC) and the Office of Water Research (OWR), both in Interior and both instrumental in the past formation and coordination of national policy. The West has mixed feelings about the shift. The region has had little objection to the OWR, which mainly passed out study funds. But it has had a long-standing hostility to the WRC — composed of the secretaries of Interior, Agriculture, Army, Commerce, and Housing and Urban Development, as well as the administrator of the Environmental Protection Agency — as ineffective and unknowledgeable about western water needs. On the other hand, Watt's proposed alternative — an Office of Water Policy run by a cabinet-level Council on Natural Resources and Environment — has caused virtually as much worry.

Watt's objective is clear. He hopes to create a small, compact, fast-tracking office with total power over water affairs. The Office of Water Policy, with a staff of twenty-five, would develop policy, handle liaison with the states, and take charge of planning water projects. The core Council on Natural Resources and Environment — Watt, Vice President George Bush, Secretary of Agriculture John Block, Energy Secretary James Edwards, and Attorney General William French Smith — would make ultimate decisions. Westerners generally approve of Watt's prowater, pro-West, prodevelopment position. But they also fear the vesting of such critical power in the Watt group, partly because, like the old WRC, it has relatively little knowledge of the West, and partly because Watt himself has shown little inclination to discuss his plans with state and local agencies.

The West also fears Watt's dogmatism. One of his own aides has said that Interior will take a "hard line" on water development, and that no project will be approved that cannot pay for itself through user fees. Watt also has stated that he will look first at projects with multiple usefulness and not at ones geared exclusively (or even primarily) to agriculture. The West may support both intentions in principle, but in the arid West principle often collides with necessity. If a hard line impedes the development of western projects, the region will be hurt. And if projects with agricultural focus are scrapped, it will be hurt more. As one nervous westerner has said, "Carter's proposals weren't a good approach" to water policy, but "we may look back in a few years and wish we had as good a deal."

To date, Watt's only challenge has come from Congress. Democrats opposed to his policies in general and Republicans irritated by his independence — or arrogance — have combined in both House and Senate to block formation of the Council on Natural Resources and Environment. In the House Texas Democrat Abraham Kazen, Jr., has proposed creation of an *independent* National Board on Water Resources to establish principles, standards, and procedures for the development of further federal projects without the influence of Watt. In the Senate, Republican James Abdnor of South Dakota has proposed essentially the same thing — a board composed of the secretaries of Interior, Agriculture, and Army, and the EPA administrator, with an independent chairman.

While water policy is made, the West waits. In the end, whether it will or will not accept the Reagan program, in particular, no one can say. So far a mood of tentative acceptance — or resignation — exists. If yesterday's rage has softened, however, it is at least partly in response to the Reagan style — the *way* Reagan and Watt have approached the West's water crisis. Carter chided and demeaned the

West in gutting its water programs. Reagan has not. If Carter took the right actions, the West still would argue that it was for the wrong reasons. It also would argue that what triggered the avalanche of western anger was as much the shrill, unreasonable, and unwarranted Carter attack on the West as it was the hit list itself. The tragedy may be, in fact, that in his zeal to smash the pork barrel Carter destroyed the credibility of his own arguments as well.

Reagan has changed nothing except attitude. While maintaining the Carter policies, he has replaced criticism and condemnation with a cautious hopefulness. The West, so far, has responded in kind with uncharacteristic grace. In any event, paralysis continues. Most hit-list projects remain stalled and projects stillborn under the no-new-starts mandate remain stillborn. How long the West will tolerate stalemate is questionable. Even now, given the Reagan style, hostility is not far from the surface. A Colorado congressman has complained that Reagan "gave the impression that he understood about the need for water in the West," but that so far he has delivered no more than Carter. The complaint is not isolated, and it would take little for it to build and grow.

As takers converge on western water, and federal government paralyzes storage projects, the West approaches flash point. Looking to the future, it is left with one choice: with all of the force it can muster, it must fight for its water. It must stand aggressively against federal "reforms" in water law that goes back to the beginning of the West, against federal encroachment on the right of the states to establish their own water policies and allocate their own water resources. It must remain wary of the Council on Natural Resources and Environment or any other federal bureau with massive water power. It must continue to challenge the hit list and the ill-informed mentality behind it, and it must demand its due for the energy pulled out of its earth and the MX harbored in it. Above all, it must work to destroy the myth of the pork barrel. If it does these things, it may stave off doomsday. If not, just as it once sprang from dust, so will the West return to it.

*   *   *

Hamlin Garland had a vision of the West, of hot August afternoons and prairie wheat fields "deep as the breast of man, wide as a sea, heavy-headed, supple-stalked, a meeting place of winds and magic." "Stand before it at eve," he wrote, "when the setting sun floods the world with crimson and the bearded heads lazily swirl under the low, warm wind, and the mousing hawk dips into the green deeps like the seagull into the ocean, and your eyes will ache with the light and color of it." This is the poet's West, the rich, green, grain-fat West of yeoman farmers and amber waves and hayfields in the sunset. But it is not reality. John Steinbeck saw reality. Looking at the prairie West through the dark night of the Dust Bowl, Steinbeck, in *The Grapes of Wrath,* wrote of death:

> the sun flared down on the growing corn day after day until a line of brown spread along the edge of each green bayonet. The clouds appeared, and went away, and in awhile they did not try anymore ... The surface of the earth crusted, and as the sky became pale, so the earth became pale. In the water-cut gullies the earth dusted down in dry little streams . . . then it was June and the sun shone more fiercely. Rainheads dropped a little spattering and hurried on to some other country. The rain crust broke and dust lifted up out of the fields and drove gray plumes into the air like sluggish smoke . . . and the corn fought the wind with its weakened leaves until the roots were freed by the preying wind and then each stalk settled wearily sideways toward the earth and pointed the direction of the wind . . . Men stood by their fences and looked at the ruined corn, drying fast now, only a little green showing through the film of dust . . . Then the women asked, What'll we do? And the men replied, I don't know.

At Sentinel and Duchesne, in Red Willow County, along the Llano Estacado and the Drift Prairie men again one day may look at brown fields of ruined corn while their cities sit desolate beside them.

The women will ask what they will do. And the men will reply that they do not know.

CHAPTER EIGHT

Lords of the West

We *must* have freedom. We *must* have our colossal land and waters. We *must* have room for many millions, and the room must not be closed up and bricked up by National Policy. The genius of growth must not be buried alive, in a wall, by the federal government . . . We are not a colony or a dependency or a reserve territory; we are a sovereign state, and we want to people our lands and use our waters and open our mineral fields *now.*

DENVER POST
June 19, 1907

SUMMER COMES SLOWLY to central Wyoming, crawling across the cold earth like a warm mist. Along the Powder, near Kaycee and Sussex, the wilted grasslands come to life, feeding on melted snow rushing in rivulets from the cracks and corners of the crimson mesas. To the west the ragged Big Horns spear the late spring sky, shredding its clouds to tatters. To the east, across Pumpkin Buttes, cattle stand in silent clusters against the rising sun while sleepy-eyed men on horseback hunch against the wind. Coal miners dig the earth nearby, and to the south oil pumps sit against the pink horizon like giant insects, the clank-clank of their rocker arms echoing across the shallow valleys. Everywhere the land is alive, and everywhere the sharp, sweet smell of new clover hangs in the air.

This is ranching country along the Powder. It is also coal and oil country, energy country. But above all, it is the government's country.

In the swollen, broken, cratered-out wasteland of southwest Idaho, Owyhee County sweeps across some of the most terrifying land in North America. South of Mountain Home and Silver City, where the Bruneau thrashes through the deepest river canyon on earth, the land is a black-brown mosaic of gashes and tears, of spiraling tar-colored cliffs and bony plateaus and silver-gray sage plains that run forever. In early summer stonecrop and mountain lily poke from twisted scraps of earth and the badger hunts its prey. At dusk the plains glow softly from the fire of distant sunsets. Owyhee is a sandscape, blank, desolate, and surreal, 7600 square miles of empty space. It is good for cattle and little else. And it, too, belongs to the government.

Some years summer never comes at all to the convulsed, sky-covered expanse of the southern Colorado Rockies. In early June the Rio Grande and Los Piños and the Gunnison's Lake Fork thread out of Hinsdale County, dancing through silent valleys, by Uncompahgre, Wetterhorn, Redcloud, and Sunshine peaks. In the summer sun the mountains' white mantle blazes like whitecaps on a choppy sea; but when there is no sun, when thunderheads roll across the Divide, the mountains turn black. The San Juan country is high and dark and frightening, rocky corridors filled with mist, granite gorges riddled with streams, cold, breezy meadows of wild rose and fireweed and Queen Anne's lace. Once Hinsdale was silver country. At Lake City relentless men burrowed into the Hidden Treasure and the Golden Fleece, and above them, on Cannibal Plateau, Alferd Packer became a legend. The land still is rich. Mineral veins lie beneath it. Sheep and cattle graze above it. And Hinsdale County — 95 percent of it — belongs to the government.

* * *

Today, in the 1980s, a storm is building over these lands. From the Great Plains to the Pacific Rim an anger is rumbling across the public domain that the nation has not seen in decades. At issue is federal control of the American West. The intensity is new, but the issue is not. It is an old and acrid controversy, rooted deeply in the past, in the whole turbulent history of the public domain.

In the early winter of 1777, as the American Revolution raged across the bare valleys of New York, America's first government was born nearby in Philadelphia: the Articles of Confederation created thirteen sovereign states and a central congress to coordinate them. From the beginning, the new nation-states were mired in controversy, arguing bitterly over the disposal of western lands, between the Appalachian chain and the Mississippi, that would come to them with the defeat of England. States with no claims — six of them —

feared that land accrual in the hands of the other seven states would suffocate them, cut off their westward advance, destroy their tax base, and leave them at the mercy of others. Maryland angrily argued that western lands wrested from England by the "common blood and treasure of the thirteen states" should belong to them all in common — and it refused to ratify the Articles until the big states acceded. Reluctantly, they did. New York led the way, giving up her claims to western lands in 1770; Virginia followed in 1784, and the other five by 1802. The public domain was born in strife. Little wonder that for generations it remained immersed in it.

In the nineteenth century, under the banner of Manifest Destiny, America moved relentlessly to the Pacific. And the public lands grew as it did. In 1803 the Louisiana Purchase brought most of the High Plains under the American flag — Nebraska, South Dakota, eastern Montana and Colorado, the southwest quarter of North Dakota, and northern and eastern Wyoming. In 1845 Texas ceded eastern New Mexico and an L-shaped sliver of Colorado from Wyoming to Arizona to the Kansas border. The Anglo-American Treaty of 1846 delivered Idaho and western Montana, as well as Oregon and Washington. In the wake of the Mexican War of 1848 the United States annexed California, Nevada, Utah, virtually all of Arizona, southwest Wyoming, the westernmost part of Colorado, and western New Mexico. The Gadsden Purchase of 1853 added the dry southern tier of Arizona, and the purchase of Alaska in 1867 added nearly 80 percent of the nation's total land area to it. Then it rested.

In the early years of the republic, American government quickly disposed of its lands. The Land Ordinance of 1785 opened up the Old West, the land between the mountains and the Mississippi; in 1803 Ohio became the nation's first public-land state, and between 1816 and 1821 it was joined by half a dozen others. More than a million acres of public lands were sold in 1814 alone, rising to 3.5 million by 1818.

As pioneers moved through the Old West, their government marched through the New West to the sea. As the frontier cleared the Mississippi Valley, the conquest of Mexico at midcentury led to a new explosion of land disposal. The Swamp Land Act of 1850 and the Graduation Act of 1854 joined a bewildering array of earlier disposal laws, and because of them all, fully 13 million acres of privately owned farmland were carved out of the public domain by 1850. In 1862 the Homestead Act accelerated the process, opening up the High Plains and sending armies of sodbusters pouring across the Great American Desert. The General Mining Law of 1872, the Timber Culture Act of the next year, the Desert Land Act of 1877, the Timber and Stone Act of 1878, and the Land Grant Act of 1887 conveyed millions more acres to private ownership. By the 1890s a century of giveaway had stripped the public domain of most of its best lands. Farmers had plowed, dug, and planted from the Mississippi to California. Cattle kings had taken the grasslands from Texas to Canada. Railroad rights of way cut long checkerboard paths across the prairies and through the mountain gaps, lumbermen leveled the forests, and miners gouged out hillsides on every tract in the Rockies.

Then, suddenly, in the 1890s, the age of disposal came to an end.

As the westward movement accelerated in the last quarter of the century, the civilizing process left massive and irreparable resource devastation in its wake. Looking at the tattered remnants of the public domain, much of America began to fear the results of its headlong cut-and-slash rush into the future. Prophets warned of resource extinction and the destruction of future generations. And slowly, agonizingly, the conservation movement was born.

The conservationists preached a gospel America had not heard before. They believed, as Frederick Jackson Turner did, that America had to preserve what was left of its vanishing frontier as a crucible in which the nation's character could continue to be formed. As Turner wrote in the 1890s, the frontier experience had shaped America from its birth, had forged the "American" and molded his civilization. Conservationists reasoned that if American values and institutions were to continue evolving, the frontier had to be maintained. They also believed that the state of nature — or those scraps of it left over from the bludgeoning of civilization — had to be preserved for the aesthetic enjoyment of man. Like Thoreau, they understood that urban man needed refuge to survive his own world, places of solitude and beauty where he could be immersed in silence, where he could feel the mountain wind and watch eagles soar in the sky. To evangelists such as John Muir, land and forest regenerated, calmed, energized, and ultimately underpinned civilized existence. In the 1890s the spirit of Walden was disappearing and the forests of the East had all but vanished. But the West was still fresh — and salvageable.

In the history of America's public lands, the conservation era began in 1891 with congressional passage of the landmark General

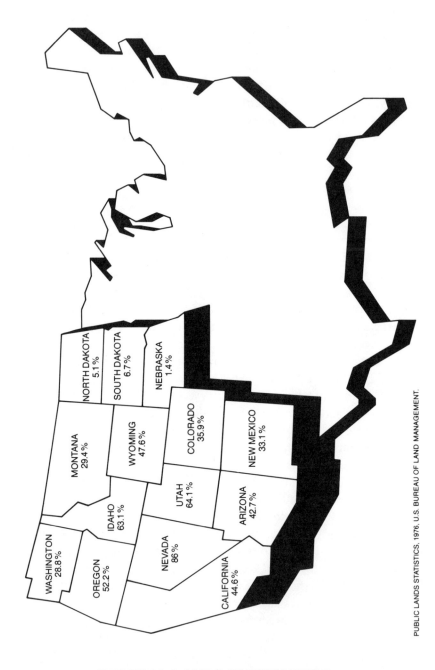

NORTH DAKOTA
5.1%

SOUTH DAKOTA
6.7%

NEBRASKA
1.4%

MONTANA
29.4%

WYOMING
47.6%

COLORADO
35.9%

NEW MEXICO
33.1%

IDAHO
63.1%

UTAH
64.1%

ARIZONA
42.7%

WASHINGTON
28.8%

OREGON
52.2%

NEVADA
86%

CALIFORNIA
44.6%

PUBLIC LANDS STATISTICS, 1976. U.S. BUREAU OF LAND MANAGEMENT.

FEDERAL LANDS IN THE WEST

Revision Act authorizing the creation of national forests in the West. In 1891 and 1892 Benjamin Harrison created six — Yellowstone in Wyoming, and Plum Creek, South Platte, Pikes Peak, White River, and Battlement Mesa in Colorado (the last two of which sit squarely in the middle of the energy controversy a century later). On a single earthshaking day in 1897, Grover Cleveland added thirteen more, spanning 21 million wilderness acres of Wyoming, Montana, Idaho, Utah, South Dakota, Washington, and California. As the decade ended, a century of public-lands history and tradition lay shattered on the floors of federal government. The age of disposal essentially was over. The age of reservation had begun.

The conservation movement struck the West like a thunderclap. For the next fifteen years the idea spread, engulfing the West in a tide of national forests, parks, wildlife refuges, and monuments. Water-power sites and reclamation sites were withdrawn, mineral lands and grasslands closed. By World War I the most productive areas of the West no longer were open to entry. But throughout the years westerners tirelessly and hopelessly fought back — and their endless war against the government became one of the most dramatic chapters in the nation's history.

The longest, deepest, bitterest controversy surrounded the national forests.

On a spring morning in 1891 westerners awoke to the new reserves. The day before, the land had been open and free and — in their minds — theirs. Now, suddenly, it was locked up, closed. The timberlands were gone, the mountain meadows, the mineral pockets. No one was untouched. Timber cutters could not harvest the rich timber stands. Homesteaders lost access to the woodlands for fuel and fencing and homes. Cattlemen lost their lush meadows. Prospectors lost their minerals. Overnight life changed, and it changed so deeply, so profoundly, that pioneers never fully understood what had happened.

Almost from the beginning of the West, tough, independent, self-righteous pioneers had lived in the great forests, running cattle in green meadows, building homestead cabins in aspen groves, digging for minerals along fast-running streams. Like pioneers anywhere, on other frontiers in other places, they sought fortune. For many of them the Rocky Mountain West was the last frontier, the last hope, the last stand, the last place to survive in an ever-urbanizing world. But like other people on other frontiers, westerners in the 1890s also believed passionately in their civilizing mission in the wilderness. Like others, they had long romanticized the West as the Garden of the World, an American Eden, where — under their productive hand — the perfect civilization ultimately would root and grow. They saw themselves, and always had, as a special breed, carriers and planters of the seeds of civilization. The morning they awoke to "conservation," to the lockup of their forest empire, was the most shattering day of their lives. Economic survival was threatened as it never had been before. Worse, their mission was over.

So began the war.

In all the years that followed, the West's bewildered and defiant people never reconciled themselves to the cataclysmic change in their lives and the frontier land they lived them on. As they began and sustained their long litany of protest, much of what they said and felt and believed was agonizingly right. It was true that they had decimated the land around them and it was true that, in time, they would have left the West a wasteland for their own children. It was true that their ranks were filled with exploiters and spoilsmen whose only goal was to strip and cut and dig — like locusts in fields of new wheat — until everything was gone. But it also was true that these people, *these* pioneers, had conquered the West — and in the process had left it littered with the gravestones of their brothers. The tragedy of conservation was that the frontiersmen were in the wrong place at the wrong time. The evangels of conservation were right; only fools could deny that they saved the West from itself. But the pioneers were right, too. And their dogged insistence that they were filled the conservation era with strife.

As protest began, the central issue was the federal imperative. For the West a number of interrelated questions stood out. What was the extent of federal authority in the land affairs of the West? Did the federal government have the right to withdraw land from entry within the boundaries of sovereign states, to isolate patches of the public domain from any form of settlement? Did it have the power to outlaw the land to local use? Did it have the right to formulate rules and regulations for it, to mandate use permits, to levy taxes? Legally — though the West refused to recognize it — many questions already had answers. Congress *did* have the right to authorize forest reserves. Presidents *did* have the right to create them. Federal agencies *did* have the right to lock up, shut down, abolish, outlaw, or regulate. The withdrawn lands were public lands, always had been public lands; they had never belonged to western states or to the people who used them. The West had no conceivable legal claim to land that never had been its own. Legally the West was wrong, but the questions it asked about its place on the public domain went far beyond legalities into shadowy areas of ethics and morality where answers did not come so easily. And in those areas western confusion and protest took on more validity.

One central issue was that of tactics — specifically those of Grover Cleveland and Theodore Roosevelt — in the creation of the national forests. Cleveland's stunning "Midnight Proclamations" were made only ten days before he left office, and they were calculatedly made without the advance knowledge of the West. Ten years later Roosevelt repeated the same process. On a single shattering day in 1907 he withdrew 17 million acres of timberland from entry in twenty-one new national forests in six western states. The action, which sent shock waves across the West, preceded by a matter of hours the enactment of a measure prohibiting creation of future forest reserves without the consent of Congress. In a legal sense both actions were proper. In both cases the executive branch had been prevented from acting on vital conservation matters by the arrogant and unremitting hostility of Congress. Yet both actions raised serious constitutional questions about the relationship between federal government and the West.

Cleveland touched off what one historian has called "the most remarkable storm in the whole history of forestry in America" partly because his action had blatantly political overtones. In the early 1890s Cleveland's gold policies had been savagely opposed by the prosilver West, and western antagonism, in part, cost him renomination in 1896. To a great extent the proclamations were an act of political revenge — "as outrageous an act of arbitrary power," said a Wyoming congressman, "as a czar or sultan ever conceived." Ten years later, with the stroke of a pen, Roosevelt increased the number of western reserves to an enormous 159 covering more than 150 million acres of land. Again, executive action was plotted in secrecy and silence without even a hint of western advice or consent. And again politics was no small part of the issue. Roosevelt's running war with the West over conservation was one of the bitterest political fights in this century, and without doubt the "Midnight Reserves" were at least partly an attack on insurgent westerners for their role in it.

Both actions gave rise to questions about the separation of powers. Both Cleveland and Roosevelt contemptuously ignored the age-old process of advise and consent with Congress, and Roosevelt arrogantly defied both the spirit and intent of the 1907 Fulton amendment designed to halt the wholesale creation of reserves by the executive branch. Dictatorial attitudes such as these poisoned relations between Washington and the West virtually forever. But federal tactics never changed. Power continued to flow from the top of government, from the executive branch, by-passing and ignoring local institutions and grassroots groups. Westerners were cultivated, used, abandoned, and left in rage. Speaking of Roosevelt and the Midnight Reserves, a Colorado newspaper editorialized that "very few of the monarchs of the world would so dare to set aside the will of the people this way." The statement had merit. A pattern had begun to form. And in the dark days of the conservation era it was a thought for the West to ponder.

To the bitter end the insurgent West never recognized the validity of the reserves themselves. It argued one central point, and it did so passionately and without reservation: that the whole *intent* of the Founding Fathers in creating the public domain had been to hold it in trust *only so long as it took to dispose of it to individual ownership*. The federal government, said the West, had been established as custodian of the public lands, not owner. Further, when western public-lands states relinquished claims to those lands within their borders as conditions of statehood, they did so partly on the assumption that this distinction would never change, that the government would always act as steward, not owner, and that the lands would always be open to settlement. Now, however, the distinction had blurred. And the West felt a sense of betrayal, what one leader bluntly called a "breach of faith." To the angry West, the reserves were a calculated, radical, illegal departure from tradition, custom, and law, the stunning end of a century of progressive, civilization-building disposal and settlement, the beginning of federal landlordism.

The West was right. In fact, it *had* been the belief of the Founding Fathers that government should act only as trustee, and even then no longer than necessary. It *had* been their intent that land disposal should take place as quickly as possible. It *had* been their goal that the public lands should be "settled and formed into distinct republican states which should become members of the union and have the rights of sovereignty and freedom and independence like the other states." But much of this spirit disintegrated in the conservation tide of the 1890s. Born in its place, said Coloradan Henry Teller, was "the most extraordinary proposition ever presented to an Anglo-Saxon, self-governing people" — a system that threatened to reduce western people to a class of "servile peons."

Part of the issue was economic. The West argued that federal withdrawals within the boundaries of sovereign states stopped settlement, restricted their tax base, damaged economic growth, and generally denied them "equal footing" with older states.

Again, there was truth in the charge. Political sovereignty — in the name of greater good or not — *was* abridged. *No* state could maintain political credibility and vitality in the family of states when much — or most — of the land within its borders was outlawed to entry by its own people and lay beyond the jurisdiction of its own government. And no state could achieve political strength without a strong, healthy, economic base. Westerners clearly understood the obvious — that unsettled land yielded nothing.

Nothing galled the West more than the fact that restrictions placed on the use of the public domain had never been placed on the non-West. Part of the equal-footing theme related directly to this. The East had utilized — or plundered — *its* frontiers, so the western argument ran; the West was entitled to the same opportunities. In 1911, for example, United States Senator Thomas Carter of Montana said that "the states of Maine and Illinois and Iowa enjoyed the full benefit of the natural resources the Great Creator placed there; but these [western] states, where nature presents the hardest conditions settlers have ever faced on this continent, must conduct their local affairs subject to the federal government." It was a theme repeated over and over again, and always it had the distant ring of truth. Said Nevada's William Stewart: "The reserves exclude the people of the West from the use of the country in which they live while it is dedicated to folly and barbarism. What do you think would happen if the people of West Virginia were saddled with reserves?"

To the West the answer was obvious.

The argument was a critical one in a region long victimized by economic colonialism. For half a century eastern corporations and their federal allies had whittled away at western land and resources, siphoning off the West's great wealth, bleeding it of its vitality, denying it any semblance of economic parity. Even given the West's

deep and abiding anti-eastern paranoia, creation of the reserves —
withdrawal of western resources from western hands and their placement in the custody of what the West saw as an "eastern" government — had a sinister look about it. Right or wrong, westerners saw
the action as simply another piece of an old and hated pattern.

One fact was indisputable: the first reserves were *not* open to local
use. In their early years the land *was* locked up. Timber cutting,
mining, and grazing *were* outlawed. In 1897 the reserves were un-
locked, but only on paper, and subject to extensive rules and regulations that made their practical local use all but impossible. Never
again, in fact, were the lands as accessible to pioneers as they had
been in the past. And for those who lived on the land, or near it, who
relied on its resources for survival and always had, the effect was
devastating.

The West cried out in anger. Emotionally, its people refused to
recognize what they intellectually understood, that their claims to
the land were empty and invalid. Instead they argued the issue on
moral grounds — that, as a Colorado newspaper wrote, "the hardy
pioneers of the forest were treated as outlaws" in their own land. Said
a Redcliff rancher, "The idea that anyone in the peaceful pursuit of
private enterprise can be prosecuted as a trespasser in his own land
is repugnant to the principles of American liberty and the spirit upon
which our institutions are trying to stand." Speaking eloquently of
"the ranchman and the small stock grower, the man who has built
up the country," a Colorado orator in 1902 thundered, "The streams
and the mountains are his. Uncle Sam has been paid a thousandfold
already for the land by the blood and bones of those people."

To some extent this was a strangely shallow fury, shot through
with hypocrisy and arrogance. No power on earth existed to keep
spoilsmen at bay — out of the backwoods, away from the rich timber
stands and deep meadows; no law, no regulation had ever been found
that could stop them from their rape of the land. But, contrary to
federal and eastern beliefs, not every westerner destroyed the public
trust. And not many could live without access to the federal lands.
For every spoilsman who dug and burned, an honest settler went
without wood for fuel and a state went without revenue from settlement — and perhaps a man died on a windswept prairie for nothing.
Granted, the land was — and should have been — saved for future
generations. But in a real and tragic sense the saving was subsidized
by the suffering of the existing one — by its "blood and bones." And

throughout, equal footing was a distant hope never realized.

Above all, perhaps, the West despised easterners who extended their "guardian angel arms" over the West and its lands. Westerners saw threads of eastern conspiracy woven all through the fabric of conservation — and this illusion, more than any other single factor, gave their anger its force and power. There was no conspiracy. Conservationists, in fact, warred more among themselves than with the West. But the illusion persisted and grew. And festered. And even defenders of the East could not dispute the reality that the western reserves were created by eastern presidents mainly on recommendations made by eastern men, not western, and that reserve rules and regulations were written by eastern men with no knowledge of the West and carried out in the field by eastern men who often did not care. The long shadow of the East constantly loomed over the West, spawning feelings of persecution and distrust that rooted and grew like summer sage.

It was a fact: easterners stood behind every major timberland withdrawal of the times. Gifford Pinchot influenced Roosevelt. Cleveland's 1897 reserves were based on the recommendations of six men — five of them easterners — who saw the West and its land problems by train. Rarely did those who made land decisions ever see the land itself or witness the lives of the pioneers who lived on it. Both Roosevelt and Pinchot had only a passing, and distorted, acquaintance with the West. The provincial Cleveland never saw it in his life. It was this kind of arrogance, one historian has written, that "set the West aflame." Little wonder that westerners raged against men who shaped western destiny from the velvet luxury of Pullman cars, "goggle-eyed, bandy-legged dudes from the East and sad-eyed, absent-minded bugologists" who invaded, patronized, slandered, demeaned, and changed the course of western life forever.

The scattershot approach of eastern conservationists to western land withdrawals and reserve rules and regulations had predictable results. Too often reserve boundaries included massive amounts of nontimbered acreage — farmlands, pasture, mineral lodes — and too often, even after resurveying, it was not restored to entry. In Wyoming Senator Clarence Clark, a bitter enemy of the national forests, complained that not enough timber existed on Wyoming's reserves to build a four-rail fence around the state. In the Black Hills, one of the richest areas on the gold frontier, some of South Dakota's best mining lands were incorporated into the reserves. The same was true in Colorado. Through the years many boundaries were modified, but the process took time. In the meantime, western settlers lived in a painful limbo, victims of eastern-mandated de facto reservations that altered every aspect of their existence.

Washington bureaus also made forest reserve rules and regulations — made them from a distance, without any knowledge of the land they made them for, made them often without compassion or concern about the people who lived on the land. For the most part, too, at least in the early years, regulations were enforced in the field by eastern adventurers and spoilsmen dumped on the West by eastern politicians.

The first reserves were criminally mismanaged. In theory, the government froze the timberlands to protect watersheds and deteriorating range, and to be sure, Washington bureaucracy flooded the Rockies with laws to do it. But the regulations were poorly conceived and written by the same distant men with the same lack of knowledge about the West and its conditions. Local application of the laws by the pathetic, graft-ridden ranger corps was haphazard, ineffective, and hostile. The result was overbearing local bureaucracy that managed little and achieved little except the alienation of the settler class. No one in the West was more hated by westerners than the Department of the Interior's General Land Office (later the Bureau of Land Management) and its "distant dictators," inept laws, and army of political parasites that rode the high country. The system could not and did not work. Under it, settlement was stunted and spoilsmen and profiteers ran wild. And honest settlers — bewildered to the end — remained mired in a web of laws they never understood, enforced by a system that never understood them.

The system improved under Roosevelt and Pinchot in the early 1900s, but improvement brought new dangers to the West. Roosevelt's men, easterners all, preached the quasi-scientific "gospel of efficiency," the belief that the public lands could best be stabilized by turning them over to large, efficient economic operators. Progressive planners such as Roosevelt and Pinchot were less interested in the question of resource ownership than the question of resource use, less concerned about the prevention of monopoly than the prevention of waste. Their belief was that traditionally most resource devastation had been caused by small operators — small farmers, lumberers, stockmen, and miners who used the land, often ruined it, and moved on. Conversely, they held that large operators, interested in stabilizing the land around them for their own long-term use and profit, were far less destructive and far more efficient. Operating on these assumptions, which had substantial basis in fact, Washington — perhaps reluctantly, perhaps not — tacitly shaped its reserve rules and regulations to help sustain big over small, monopoly over free enterprise. In time land policies did stabilize the reserves and begin to create a healthy balance between preservation and use. And the ranger corps, overhauled by Pinchot, became far more effective and less oppressive than it had been in the past. On the other hand, many a marginal operator was driven off the land in ruin in the process. Because of this, insurgent westerners reserved and nourished a special hatred for Pinchot, whom a Colorado newspaper called the "epitome of egotistical, theoretical eastern bureaucracy," and the whole doctrine of efficiency that favored the land and cattle barons and "destroyed the masses, the bone and sinew of this country."

So ran the course of conflict. But it was not the only conflict. In the chaotic years before World War I a handful of other public-lands issues rose, exploded, and faded away, leaving the West, in each case, more embittered than before.

Trumpeting the gospel of efficiency from every pulpit in government, federal officials expanded their crusade to save the West to several new fronts. In 1901 they moved to extend federal protection to the public domain's nontimbered grazing lands. In 1906 they included the West's endangered coal lands, in 1913 general mineral lands, and after 1913 water-power sites. And in all cases they proposed to bring "efficiency" to the land through the most hated process in the West: withdrawal and leasing.

In 1901 federal officials first recommended the leasing of western grazing lands. Five years later, in July of 1906, Roosevelt withdrew 50 million acres of coal lands from entry for eventual leasing, a number that rose to 140 million by 1916. In 1909, 3 million acres of oil and potash lands were withdrawn in Wyoming, Utah, and Oregon, and in 1914 another 3 million in Wyoming, Idaho, and Montana. Meanwhile the controversial Withdrawal Act of 1910 and the proposed (and failed) Ferris, Kent, and Lever bills of the Wilson years came within an eyelash of establishing the principle in national law. Withdrawal of water-power sites on the western public lands raised a storm even in states unaffected by the action. Because the states owned the water that flowed through them, and because they held regulatory power over public utilities as well, the government used the only leverage it had to stop monopoly — the withdrawal of power sites on lands that bordered the waters. The West saw this action, like federal action on the national forests, as a gross and unprecedented violation of the states' rights.

In moving against the West, the government took action long overdue. The open range was disintegrating. Cattle kings owned it and hired guns ran it. And overgrazing had turned much of it to dust. Aided and abetted by archaic land laws, spoilsmen openly raided the public domain's precious coal and mineral lands, building monopolies and fortunes on the public trust. And all over the West power combines silently engrossed water-power sites. In no case was the public good a consideration. The game, as it always had been, was rip and run. For that reason the government's action was vital and proper. And yet, in each case, the West erupted in protest.

Dissent crystallized — quickly and violently — around a handful of themes as relevant to leasing as they had been to forest reservation. One was the government's "power" to withdraw and lease; consistently westerners argued that the power did not exist, partly because it undermined the political sovereignty of the states, partly because it denied them equal economic footing with others, and partly because it ran counter to the original intention of the Founding Fathers to dispose of the land. At a meeting of the insurgent Public Domain League in Denver in 1909, Congressman John F. Shafroth of Colorado said what many had before him — that "it is certain that the national government never, until recent years, attempted to exercise such great powers over the public domain." At the time of their admission to the Union "upon equal terms with the other states," western states "never imagined that it possessed such rights." Many westerners could not imagine it still. Others never tried. Leasing, said one, was "as obnoxious and repressive as English landlordism in Ireland." The statement was extreme and inflammatory, typical of the fiery and often ludicrous rhetoric that came out of the West in the Progressive era. Excessive it was, but pointless it was not.

The East, too, remained a moving target. Again, the West argued that eastern states had "eaten their cake" and now wanted to "share with those who have scarcely had a chance to nibble theirs." No one spoke the western mind better or more bluntly than Edward Taylor of Colorado, later author of the Taylor Grazing Act. "Western resources," said Taylor, speaking to the East, "are the property of the people who go there and develop them. If you want a share of them, come out to our country and help us. You are welcome to your share. But you have no right to sit cosily in the East" and take them by force. And, again, equal footing. "How in the name of common sense," said Taylor, can any one of the western states come into this Union upon an equal footing if you take from our states one third of our territory and hold it in perpetuity? Give the pioneer settlers of the West a fair share of the [land] and let them build their roads, maintain their schools, educate their children, and build the West as you have the East."

The point was well taken. It was both proper and just for the West to hold the East accountable for its role in the leasing fight. Eastern men in Congress supported leasing just as they did forest reserves — while their own states had neither. And no one promoted leasing more persistently than the government's eastern-oriented apostles of efficiency. Their belief that scientific range management and government-held mineral land and water-power sites would stabilize the public lands was admirable in theory. But it was flawed in a way that only westerners could understand. As in the forests, "efficiency" relied primarily on placing the public domain in the hands of big operators, or at least of providing them easy access. Pioneer settlers and pioneer states had one overriding fear — that only coal and water combines, copper, phosphate, and oil giants, and cattle syndicates could afford leasing when it came. If that were true, the government might save its land — but destroy the pioneer class in the process. In central Colorado, cattlemen called federal control of the range a "death net." It was a vivid and appropriate term. On the western range, where the cattlemen's profit margin was as thin as rope, grazing fees and leasing promised extinction. And lumbermen, prospectors, perhaps even states, might follow.

In the end, of course, it mattered little. Surrounded by forest reserves, westerners knew that leasing, too, would come one day no matter what they believed or said. In the summer of 1907 a Colorado insurgent said that leasing was "a question of whether we are going to have control of our lands or the government is going to become a landlord and place them under a system of tenantry." But the question was academic. The answer, long ago, had already been given.

Throughout these years the West stubbornly made its case against conservation. And what it said — even given the emotionalism of its rhetoric — had more truth to it than most of America might have admitted. Much of the talk, of course, was demagoguery. The western theater was filled with scavengers, political hypocrites, and other ravagers who strutted across the public stage and filled the air with piety and lies. But for every lie there also was a truth.

The limitless antagonism of the East was a truth. The exploitative impulse was fact, not fancy, and paternalism, contempt, arrogance, and distrust were as commonplace as snow on a Utah mountainside. The attitude was as old as the West and East themselves. The West was suspect. It always had been suspect. The East romanticized western life and history and lionized its heroes, but only discreetly, from a distance. All the while it saw it as a remote and frightening world of political radicals, economic misfits, and other fools cast out from civilization. Perhaps the Populist convulsion deepened the gulf, sharpened the revulsion. Perhaps not. The West never knew. All it knew, all it experienced, was a scathing contempt hurled at it from the eastern shore, the unstinting conviction that westerners were plunderers and thieves and that if the public domain was to be saved, the East would have to do it. Perhaps nothing catalyzed western rage as much as these humiliations. Idaho's militant William Borah angrily decried the government's "lynx-eyed detectives" who hounded settlers "upon the presumption that they all are criminals." "Is it true," said Colorado Congressman Herschel Hogg in a fiery House address in 1906, "that all of honesty and patriotism and virtue is to be found only in the departments at Washington and that the men of the West are nothing but thieves and rogues?" Too often, to the West's everlasting bewilderment, this was precisely the pattern of eastern thought.

In a sense, the conservation conflict was a national morality play. In the eastern mind, savers held the earth; takers destroyed it. And easterners were the savers. The tragedy was that the East never understood the desperation of western life, the quiet panic that underlay the living of each day. Conservationists, disciples of Thoreau and Muir, fought for the lockup and nonuse of the wilderness without any thought of western consequences; cloaked in moralism and self-righteousness, they branded dissenters "vandals" and "destroying angels." Even moderates — Pinchot and his apostles of efficiency — understood little more. Men of science and technology, they knew nothing of the West, nothing of the fierce economic faith that drove it and its people, nothing of the relentless compulsion of little men to settle and build. And survive.

A chasm separated East and West that could not and would not be bridged. Eastern technocrats spoke of "integrated planning" and "central direction" — all of it from federal bureaus and all of it circumventing, or trampling, local people and local jurisdictions. But along the Powder, in Owyhee County, in Steamboat and Belle Fourche and Billings, the "redeemers" triggered only revulsion. Trapped between the wilderness on one side and the wilderness cult on the other, the West raged at "forest enthusiasts" and "cranks," at "college professors and landscape gardeners," "dreamers," and "mad theorists who sit in their marble halls and theorize," who held that "trees are more important than human beings." They scorned those who would "conserve the resources of the western states not for the people of those states but for the benefit of the people who have wasted their own resources." And they violently denounced the eastern belief that it had to save the West from itself. As John Shafroth tiredly said in 1897, "You may have the power, but it is not right."

For the West, perhaps, it was a fitting epitaph.

The domination of federal government also was a truth. From the 100th meridian to the Pacific Rim the federal empire sprawled across the West, dead and dormant, cutting off settlement, blunting growth, transforming the nature of life from the White River to the Gulf. Looking about them at the federal monolith, westerners feared for the very existence of the West as they had known it, feared for it in a way that no easterner ever could have understood. In the chaotic aftermath of Cleveland's proclamations one distraught westerner said that western states saw the day coming when "their very existence as commonwealths shall be disposed of by the stroke of a pen," as though they were "mere provinces and not sovereign states." The theme was repeated again and again over the years — the belief that the West literally was being conserved and governed out of existence.

The issue of federal power triggered the most venomous insurgent attacks in all the conservation era — attacks on "feudalism" and "un-Americanism," against "alien landlordism" and "intolerable tyranny." Senator Joseph Rawlins of Utah called federal land policy "as gross an outrage as was committed by William the Conqueror, who destroyed hundreds of thousands of people," a feeling that was echoed all over the Rockies for two decades. To the end, in defense of their ever-withering rights, the states stubbornly insisted that only they had the power to determine the disposition and use of the land, timber, and water within their boundaries. And they hinted darkly that failure to regain their sovereignty one day might lead to civil war.

In 1917, when world war closed the conservation era, the American West looked back in anger on a quarter century of protest. The war was a watershed: on one side of it lay the West's dreams of renewal and power; on the other side the dreams lay shattered. The national forests lay unchanged, massive mottled green splotches on maps of the West where once there had been nothing. National parks and monuments lay interspersed among withdrawals of mineral land and water-power sites. Federal law ruled, written by distant federal agencies, enforced by federal agents in every valley, on every prairie. For all its fire and fury, insurgency had achieved nothing. As protest dissolved in the roar of war, only its echoes remained.

The West's world, like that of Eliot's hollow men, had ended — not with a bang but a whimper.

For the next fifteen years, a kind of brittle peace settled over the West. Sectional antagonism, broken down by war, did not quickly form again. At the same time, the radical retreat of Harding, Coolidge, and Hoover from the militant conservation policies of the Progressive Era swept away the last remnants of anger from every corner of the Rockies. The 1920s were a lull between storms. The distant future held a resurgence of conflict, but for the moment it was quiet. The West, briefly, was at peace.

In 1920 the federal government enacted two of the most important laws since the General Revision Act of 1891. The General Leasing Act and the Federal Power Act settled the leasing question that had raged across the West for two decades. The first American wilderness area was created in New Mexico in 1924 and the Clarke-McNary Act was passed in the same year, providing for the extension of national forests on public lands. None of the new laws drew western fire. Only the 1926 Stanfield bill provoked anger, and it only among cattlemen. While it proposed the opening of national forests to grazing and the abolition of permits, the bill also called for the freezing of grazing fees at current levels and the organization of "grazing districts" whose members would control them. As they had in the past, the West's small operators again bristled at the intrusion of "efficiency" — and monopoly — on the range. "The bill that turns over these lands, under perpetual control, to the big stockmen," said one western paper, "is a noxious measure and should be killed."

It was, and for several years no other land issues surfaced. With Republican conservatives in power and the last voices of progressivism stilled, Washington largely returned to laissez-faire on the public lands. Operating on the assumption that most of the public domain still would pass into private ownership, the government radically cut back public investment on it. Regulation and management largely ceased to exist. For the West, for a fleeting moment, it was a happy return to the 1880s.

The Great Depression spawned the first critical public-lands law in a generation — the Taylor Grazing Act of 1934. Written by Edward Taylor, the law was the first in memory intended to protect the grazing lands of the unreserved public domain: 80 million acres of public grasslands were to be segregated and organized into grazing districts for controlled, permitted grazing under the Department of the Interior. In 1934, buried in Dust Bowl depression, the West more readily accepted the law than it would have a decade earlier. Even so, it was not without question.

On one level the Taylor Act simply protected western grazing lands, but on a broader level it signaled the beginning of the end of the government's active land-disposal policy in general — and the beginning of a policy of land management. The thought chilled the insurgent West. Land disposal had fueled western fortunes for two centuries, had made the West everything it was; even the most optimistic westerner understood that a shift from disposal to management meant federal stewardship in perpetuity and the final closing of the public domain. Looking to the future, a Wyoming congressman tiredly said that "it was never intended that the federal government would be an arbitrary landlord." The rhetoric was old, but so were the fears.

They soon were realized. In the spring of 1935 Franklin Roosevelt withdrew the entire 165.7 million acres of remaining public domain from entry for classification as grazing lands, national forests and parks, and water-power sites — all of it to remain under the *permanent* control of the federal government. On February 5, 1935, the public domain was closed to settlement forever. Westerners had braced for this day for a hundred years. But when it finally came, it still profoundly shocked them.

As depression and a second war receded into history, conflict again returned to the public domain. Angered by the government's new management thrust, fearful that federal power again was being massed against it, the West showered Washington with protest over formation of the Bureau of Land Management in 1946. It also launched a twenty-year war over three of its national parks and monuments. Federal efforts to expand Dinosaur National Monument in northwestern Colorado were met with savage opposition — mostly from northeastern Utah — and the dogged efforts of western congressmen to reduce the boundaries of Olympic National Park in Washington and Grand Teton National Park in Wyoming were beaten back by the government the same way. Westerners argued, as they always had, that federal reservations blocked western resource development and — said Senator Arthur Watkins of Utah — served to "perpetuate government monopoly." For the first time in years the fierce rhetoric of the early 1900s again echoed across the Rockies — from charges of Big Brotherism to the contention that the government's program "would do credit to the masters of political corruption in the Kremlin." In Utah a state official bitterly said that under federal "socialism" the "states will be stripped of all authority and the power of the federal government will be oppressively overwhelming." This, he concluded, "is what happened in Germany." What the nation needed, said an Idaho newspaper, was a "cleansing" of Interior, a sweeping out of the "fuzzy-haired boys, their aims and ideas," so that the West's "natural resources could be developed under American principles and through the cooperation of the states."

In time, protest spilled over into all areas of federal land policy. In the mid-1950s western insurgents declared war on Eisenhower's moderate secretary of the interior, Douglas McKay, in an effort, as one said, "to get the federal government's foot" off the neck of the West. They attempted to transfer jurisdiction over grazing lands to state and private owners, sought to establish the principle of state taxation of property in federal parks within the states, and bluntly challenged proconservation representatives in the congressional elections of 1952 and 1954. If gains were made, though, they were fleeting. A federal counteroffensive in the 1960s set insurgency back years. The Classification and Multiple Use Act of 1964 defined the government's policy of land retention for the first time, making explicit what had been only implicit in the Taylor Act. For the first time, too, the government spelled out its new commitment to multiple use — the responsibility of preserving, balancing, and accommodating all of the public lands' potential uses. In the same year, after nearly a decade of acrid debate, Congress also passed the Wilderness Act, eventually placing 15 million acres of pristine forest wilderness under the permanent protective custody of the federal government. Both laws were vital, to the nation and to the West itself. But in the dusty corners of the Utah desert and the high forests of Montana they still generated feelings of rage in a society that did not understand.

For the embattled West, the 1960s were years of dying dreams. Hopes for state and private landownership grew more distant by the day, and by the day, the federal imperative grew. But the 1970s brought no relief. In 1976 Congress enacted the revolutionary Federal Lands Policy and Management Act, and the next year — the hundredth birthday of the public domain — it passed the Roadless Area Review and Evaluation Act. One critical point linked the two: both mandated accelerated federal classification of the public lands, and both were firmly based on the concept of permanent federal land retention.

Following a pattern begun forty-two years earlier by the Taylor Act and reaffirmed by the Classification and Multiple Use Act of 1964, the Federal Lands Policy and Management Act (FLPMA) became the first comprehensive statement of public land-management policy in American history. It formally and finally ended the practice of land disposal that had ushered the nation through most of its life. It clearly mandated that the public domain be held in federal ownership forever, for the general good, and it sharply reaffirmed the still-untested principles of sustained yield and multiple use. At the heart of the law was its directive to the Bureau of Land Management to inventory and classify its 175 million acres of land in the lower forty-eight states. The Roadless Area Review and Evaluation Act (RARE II) had the same purpose: while BLM classified the unreserved public domain — prairie, desert, small patches of forest, and miscellaneous tracts scattered all over the West — the Forest Service was mandated to survey all undeveloped national forestlands for tracts wild and unspoiled enough to add to the new National Wilderness Preservation System. RARE I, conducted between 1971 and 1973, had been haphazard and inadequate, leaving large parcels of unspoiled forest wilderness open to destructive development. RARE II was to correct the oversight.

To most of America the two laws were rational and uncontroversial: FLPMA was the logical end of a four-decade drift from one national land philosophy to another, and RARE was simply a belated affirmation of national sanity. Both reflected rising national concern about the continuing disappearance of America's landed heritage, and both had spiritual roots deep in the Progressive Era. But much of the West did not share the concern or the vision of either. Special interests untiringly opposed the laws — chiefly cattlemen and mining groups, traditionally the heaviest users of the public domain and historically the groups most convinced the land was "theirs." But they were not alone, no more than they ever had been. The moderate West, too, was anxious.

The primary issue — as it always had been — was the loss of land in twentieth-century states that could not afford it. The classification of grazing, energy, recreational, and wildlife management lands met little resistance in the West. These lands were *accessible;* if they did not pass to private hands, at least they were open to private *use.* But wilderness was a radically different matter, and it was over wilderness that the controversy centered. Like forest lands withdrawn under the Wilderness Act, lands designated wilderness by either BLM or the Forest Service were to be withdrawn from entry and locked up from virtually all public development. Even moderate westerners saw happening again what had happened so many times before — the lockup of productive, usable land, the establishment of conflicting management policies on it, and the overriding of state and local will in creating it. Most supported — or tolerated — essential reservation, but they could not and would not support more. Most of the West had had enough.

For three years the two inventories ran side by side. BLM finished its first cut in June 1979 and the entire process in November 1980. The RARE inventory, begun in the spring of 1977, ended two years later. As both ran their course, western opposition dogged them all the way. Again and again, a century-old scenario was played out. And again, though the agitated West was condemned for what it did and said, much of what it did and said was as valid in the 1970s as it had been eighty years earlier.

BLM was a constant insurgent target, and so was the law it operated under. When westerners moved against them, they took what environmentalists called an "intimidating and dictatorial stance" in questioning both the validity of the law and the legal right of BLM to implement it. Much of the West saw FLPMA as a federal betrayal of one of the oldest mandates in American history — the charge to dispose of the public domain rather than govern it. The inventory that flowed from it, threatening to bottle up the West's only remaining developable space, was seen in the same light.

Much of the argument began and ended there, but the economic issue was never far distant. One theme stood out: that federal blocking of mineral and energy exploration in an age of growing energy dependence was national idiocy. America — the West — so the argument ran, had to dig its coal, drill its oil, and develop its shale oil; if it did not, it would remain hostage forever to the convulsive politics of the Mideast. And in an era of simmering cold war, with Russia self-sufficient in twenty-one of the earth's most critical minerals and the United States in only five, the argument held added urgency. "It is a frightening fact," said the president of the American Mining Congress in 1979, "that land areas equal in size to nearly all the states east of the Mississippi — although most of them are in the minerally rich West — have been posted with federal signs that say MINERS KEEP OUT." It was an argument heard time and again, not only from nonwestern energy interests located in the West, but from westerners themselves dependent on the interests. And although it begged the question of whether conservation was not a quicker route to energy independence than more domestic production, it still held a basic logic.

RARE, to the developing West, was particularly obnoxious. The 1964 Wilderness Act allowed mineral exploration until December 31, 1983, but not beyond, and any land added to the system through the RARE process was to be subject to the same rule. To western energy interests the stipulation was absurd: they had less than four years, if that, to explore and develop RARE lands — and no company, no matter how large, could risk exploration under such circumstances. Given the almost incredible amount of time and capital involved in stalking backcountry mineral tracts, let alone developing them once found, the companies backed away. Ironically, said the interests, even as America imported more energy and more precious minerals, it locked up more and more of its own land. In Wyoming, along Overthrust, in Colorado and Montana and Utah, this was one of the bewildering paradoxes of the 1970s.

If there was justice in expanding the wilderness system — and even given the pressures of the energy thrust there was — there was also a blatant injustice in how it was done. Under RARE, lands *considered* for wilderness designation were withdrawn from all commercial activity *during* the inventory; until final classifications were determined, these lands became *de facto* wilderness, subject to the same laws that governed *established* wilderness areas. Specifically, the RARE process froze both mining and lumbering activities on those lands; ventures already begun were allowed to continue, but nothing new was authorized. Energy and mining interests bitterly watched the clock run out on them, ticking toward 1984. Little wonder they were incensed.

Little wonder, too, that western lumber interests and lumbering communities were angry. What jarred most was the schizophrenic attitude of the federal government: on one hand the Carter administration, in 1979, called for dramatically increased American lumber production to offset the rising cost of housing, but at the same time, under RARE, it shut off millions of acres of timberlands to development. At one point Representative Richard Cheyney of Wyoming charged that some areas in his state had been studied four different times under RARE and that local lumbering was dying because of it. The same complaint was heard up and down the Northern Rockies, an area brimming with anti-RARE prejudice. More than once frustration exploded into action. In the hot summer of 1977 wilderness opponents swarmed to RARE hearings everywhere, packing, dominating, disrupting. In Bonner's Ferry, Idaho, for example, a fleet of logging trucks, motors roaring, disrupted one hearing; when the hearing was moved to a local football field, it was buzzed by lumber company helicopters until it broke up. Opposition was so fierce in southern Arizona that the Forest Service dropped half a million acres of roadless areas previously earmarked for wilderness from further consideration. Even so, the indisputable fact remained that much commercial-grade timber still lay in the de facto wildernesses and very likely would lie in official wilderness later. The fact remained, too, that lumbering communities would suffer because of it. Nearly a hundred years ago a belligerent White River homesteader told a federal ranger that "this timber belongs to us and we're going to get it. The government officials can't stop us either, even with an army." Significantly, in the late 1970s the mood, the feeling, still remained deeply entrenched in the western mind. When it came to public lands, to wilderness, to the urgencies of living and surviving on alien land, a century had changed nothing.

Slowly, surrounded to the end by controversy, the inventories drew to a close. In June 1979 BLM dropped 113 million acres from further wilderness consideration, and in November 1980 it raised the figure to 150 million. The remaining 25 million acres were subject to further study, with final recommendations due to Congress by 1991. In the meantime the land itself existed in limbo. As for RARE, in January 1979, after eighteen months of review, the Forest Service recommended transferring 15 million acres of unspoiled national forest land into the wilderness system, returning 36 million acres to multiple use within the national forests and retaining 10.8 million acres for further study.

The last recommendation set off new protest all across the West. Just as the public-lands storm seemed to be passing, it swirled up again — this time its eye was the "further study" lands. By congressional mandate these lands were to remain undeveloped — again, de facto wilderness. Timber cutting was to be allowed only in case of "national emergency" and mineral and energy resource exploration permitted only under rigid leasing. The purpose, obviously, as it had been all along, was to protect the wilderness character of any land that eventually might have passed into the wilderness network. But, again, the land remained in limbo — and its people with it. And as long as it did, the war promised to go on.

*   *   *

A storm is building on these lands. Along the Powder, near Kaycee and Sussex, men on horseback hunker against the spring wind and talk of changes in their lives. In Hinsdale County, in Reno and Phoenix and Boise, in fields and pastures, in the corridors of Congress, western men speak softly of lost liberties and altered freedoms and encroachments of federal power on their existence. Where Thomas Carter of Montana thundered against the government's "course of empire" eighty years ago, Idaho's Senator Steven Symms today speaks of the federal "monster." Where a western newspaper wrote of the "seeds of civil war" a generation ago, a Nevada assemblyman has said today that "the war in the West has just begun."

They are wrong, these westerners, unable to understand that they cannot lose what they never possessed, unable to understand their own history — that it was their own fathers who leveled the timberlands, who grazed the grass to stubble, who plowed the earth to dust, who breathed life into the Muirs and the Roosevelts and the Pinchots who came to haunt their existence. Perhaps now it makes little difference. Perhaps it never did. All they know now is that their fathers and brothers and their fathers and brothers before them earned rights to the land that transcended both logic and law, vague, undefined, powerful moral rights that passed from generation to generation to families, to communities, to states, to a region. "The mountains have ever been the preserves of human liberties," a Medicine Bow homesteader eloquently wrote in 1891. "Do not blight ours." Somehow, some shadowy, mystical way, that mood lingers nearly a century later. And it fires westerners with a passion, often misguided, that no outsider will ever understand.

A storm is building on these lands. Along the Powder, in Hinsdale County, across the shimmering badlands of Owyhee, people watch and listen. They dream of yesterday. And they await tomorrow.

CHAPTER NINE

The Gathering Storm

The real questions are: How do we get the federal government off our backs? How do we get them out of our way? We feel about the federal bureaucrats as the peasants used to feel about the baron in his palace. Now the palaces are along the Potomac, and the barons are the bureaucrats who inhabit them. The serfs are rebellious . . . We want to be free. We don't think we have to bargain for our freedom. We thought we were guaranteed that freedom. What we seek is the opportunity to live our lives and make our own decisions.
                    U.S. SENATOR JAMES MCCLURE, *Idaho*

NEVADA WAS BATTLE-BORN, a child of Washington, and it has spent its life in the federal shadow. Republicans conceived it in Civil War and silver kings gave it life. And from the beginning both bled it of its strength and power. California took its silver money and left it barren and poor. Federal government took its land. And through the years Nevada lived as it was born: an imperial appendage of both.

Federal power brought benefits. Water projects opened up the desert. Defense spending created income. Fiscal policy bolstered silver. But power also brought liabilities. It brought paternalism and control. And it brought nuclear fireballs to the Nevada sky.

Despite its history — or because of it — Nevada has always had a maverick strain. Its first settlers were southerners bearing seeds of insurrection. Its Populists bore more. A state with no forest reserves was one of the first bitter foes of conservation. Through the years, antifederalism has consistently underpinned its politics. In a nation that shunned divorce and legalized gambling, Nevada has courted both. John Gunther has called Nevada "naughty," but it is more than that. Nevada, always, has been a renegade.

For this reason, perhaps, and the fact that it has always been dominated by cattlemen, it has never lived easily as federal property. Eighty-six percent of Nevada belongs to the federal government. In all the Union, only Alaska has a higher percentage. Washington owns almost 61 million of Nevada's 70 million acres: the Forest Service controls 7.2 percent, the Fish and Wildlife Service 3.1 percent, the National Park Service 0.4 percent — and the Bureau of Land Management 68.4 percent, the largest percentage in the West. Indian lands cover another 1.6 percent of Nevada, and 8,163,000 acres are in private ownership. Nevada itself owns 614,954 acres — an invisible 0.9 percent.

There was a day when it was tolerated — when cattlemen had the run of the land. But that ended with the Federal Lands Policy and Management Act. Then the land was no longer exclusively theirs. And their anger rolled off the desert like a distant storm.

In the summer of 1979 the Sagebrush Rebellion began. On the second day of June Governor Robert List of Nevada signed a bill, authored by cattlemen, to return 49 million acres of federal land to the state. All public lands except those held by the Departments of Energy and Defense, the Bureau of Reclamation, and national forests, parks, and Indian reservations were included. Immediately, under the law, they became the property of the state of Nevada.

The law was bold, anarchic. It reflected the maverick strain. Its rationale reached back 115 years to the day Nevada was battle-born. The public lands had never been intended to be held in perpetuity by the federal government, Nevada said. It had been brought into the Union on "unequal footing." Sovereign states were meant to control their own destinies — but without land they could not do it. "We're not just a bunch of wild-eyed cowboys out to lynch some federal officials," said Attorney General Richard Bryan. "We're serious people asking for a serious look at the unfair treatment the West is receiving." Said rebel Calvin Black, it was time to end "federal colonialism."

Nevada, 1979. The revolt was born. The shot heard 'round the West.

And it echoes still.

Nevada was ground zero, but the Rebellion exploded everywhere. And everywhere it had the same trigger: a convergence of unprecedented simultaneous pressures on the public domain — more pressures at one time, in one place, than the West had ever known.

In 1974 oil was found along the Overthrust Belt. Five years later it was one of the most heavily drilled regions in America — most of it public land.

In 1976 FLPMA "locked up" BLM lands for multiple use, and a year later the RARE process threatened to do the same to much of the West's remaining wilderness.

In July 1979 the Carter energy initiative launched an invasion of western oil shale lands.

And in the sparkling wastes of the Great Basin loomed the menace of the MX.

Suddenly, in the minds of those who had used it at will for years, the land began to vanish. As the hunt for energy and national security collided with RARE and FLPMA, it simply began to disappear. Other factors intensified the problem — the Carter hit list of 1977, the coal-slurry fight of 1979, sectional conflict over the severance tax. All of them deepened the West's ageless paranoia. But land was the key.

What westerners understand that nonwesterners do not is that the West is small, not big. Its imagery is big — Big Piney, Big Horn, Big Timber, Big Sky — but its usable land area is small, like a tiny painting in a large frame. Land is scarce, precious, finite, and the endless struggle for what little there is is precisely why the West's history is so Darwinistic. The West was nursed on survival of the fittest; the battle for life in a small arid jungle is a battle that has raged forever. It is this same struggle that triggered Sagebrush. In the 1970s, looking about at their shrinking habitat, people who lived on public lands, or near them, people who derived their living from them, suddenly feared for their existence. In that fear they reacted, and out of reaction came revolt.

*　　*　　*

In 1979, and today, the heart of the issue — as it always has been — is federal ownership and regulation of the western public domain. In 1981 the federal government owned more than half of the American West, a landmass larger than western Europe. Again, Nevada is almost entirely federal property. Utah is 64 percent federal property, Idaho 63 percent. The government owns 47 percent of Wyoming's land area, 42 percent of Arizona's, and 36 percent of Colorado's. In the West, only South Dakota (6.7 percent), North Dakota (5 percent), and Nebraska (1.4 percent) have escaped the federal net. In vivid contrast, the government owns no more than 12 percent of any state east of Colorado, and the average in thirty-eight nonwestern states is only 4.3 percent. Illinois, for example, is only 2 percent federal property and New York is just 0.8 percent.

Three superbureaus own virtually as much of the West as the West owns of itself.

The National Park Service owns 25 million acres of land in the United States — 20 million of them in the West. In Wyoming, where the state owns 3,600,000 acres of land, the Park Service owns 2,-310,000. In Arizona, where 1,219,000 acres are in private ownership, the government owns 1,630,000.

The Forest Service owns 187,500,000 acres in the United States — 163,420,000 in the West. It owns 38 percent of Idaho, more than 20 million acres in a state of only 53 million. In Colorado, where only 3 million acres are owned by the state, the Forest Service owns 14 million. In Arizona it owns nearly 2 million acres more than the state itself owns.

The Bureau of Land Management owns an awesome 174 million acres of the American West — almost 37 percent of its total land space. In Nevada, heartland of the Rebellion, BLM controls a stunning 48 million acres. It owns 42 percent of Utah (22 million federal acres to 5.5 million owned by the state and 11,774,000 owned by private landholders), 28 percent of Wyoming, 22 percent of Idaho — all of them states with large numbers of Sagebrush rebels.

What the departments of Agriculture and the Interior do not rule, other agencies do. The Fish and Wildlife Service, for example, owns 6 percent of both Idaho and Montana. The Bureau of Reclamation holds 2.5 percent of Utah. The Department of Defense owns more than 5 percent of Arizona, 4.5 percent of Nevada, and 3.5 percent of Utah — just over 4.5 percent of the entire West.

In the 1980s, the West's land is managed, regulated, and overseen by seventeen federal agencies.

The West lives with the fact: like Nevada, it is Washington's child.

Problems exist in any colonial relationship. Ownership establishes dominance, and the greater the extent of ownership, the greater the dominance. It is a fact the West understands. It has suffered a sense of alienation, of physical and emotional disenfranchisement from its very beginnings, and the root cause has been the nature of the owner-renter relationship. Owned and managed across a continent, the West is controlled by outside forces as no other region in America is. Much of the control is negative: prejudiced patterns formed a century ago have never been altered, antagonistic attitudes have never changed. The West cannot remember years when federal government was totally sensitive to its needs, and it cannot remember many years when it was not treated with paternalism and disdain. For this reason the angry West long ago saw landlordism as a cancer. Critics today still argue that government fails to differentiate between its role as landlord and the sovereignty of the western states. They argue, instead, as the American Farm Bureau has said, that the West has "federal control without federal responsibility." And they war not only against specific wrongs, but against the whole negative federal mentality — what an angry Wyoming newspaper has called "boodle-passers and social welfare experts and intellectuals in the circles of the mighty who have taken charge of our thought processes as well as our assets in the name of helping the people."

In the fall of 1909 Colorado's abrasive Henry Teller raked the government's "obnoxious arbitrary landlordism" in a speech before the United States Senate. In the winter of 1980, seventy-one years later, Representative Jim Santini of Nevada said it again: "Uncle Sam in recent years has become less of a friendly uncle and more of a distant landlord. So we tenants have gotten angry and started a rebellion."

Absentee ownership, "distant landlordism," breeds ignorance, which breeds arrogance. It transcends and circumvents the rights of the states. And it raises old questions of "unequal footing" that have never been fully answered.

Ignorance and arrogance go with landlordism like golden leaves with Montana autumn. Insurgents cite a decade of federal laws and public-lands management practices as proof. And they speak of Jimmy Carter.

With regard to public lands, and issues related to public lands, the Carter administration was a western nightmare. At no time, apparently, did the president understand the needs and interests of the West. At no time did he have a western strategy. Out of uninterest or contempt, or both, Carter went to the Rocky Mountain West only four times in his term. Time and again he preached cooperation and partnership. Time and again he pledged to renew federalism. And time and again he was the first to ignore his own call.

Carter's problem was ignorance — the provincial ignorance of a southern man who never knew the West — ignorance of western concerns and western people, of the West itself. His administration was clumsy, not evil, but it was clumsy and uniformed enough that it posed a genuine menace to many western interests. When Carter announced the huge synthetic fuels program in 1979, for example, his stress was placed on scale and scope, the massiveness of the program; apparently forgotten were the people and the land in its path. "Carter has sold the West down the river to win votes in the East," said an angry Coloradan. The naive attitude was typical of ill-considered federal actions that constantly kept the West off balance and sustained its sense of mistrust.

Other public-lands actions showed a similar lack of grasp. The implementation of FLPMA and RARE II both fell to Carter, and again his uncertain knowledge of the West raised a storm of criticism. The same was true of his MX plan. In the end, victimized by its own provincialism, the Carter administration alienated the West as no administration had in years. Poor tactics, inept public relations, and arrogance reminiscent of Grover Cleveland and Theodore Roosevelt ultimately translated into what the *Denver Post* called "irresponsibility." In the fall of 1980 western columnist Red Fenwick wrote, "Bigness — of mind, spirit, dedication, conviction, and motivation — this is what the country and particularly the West must demand of its officeholders. In this regard I hold President Carter guilty of failure to be big. When he ran for office, he wrote off the West. He flies over the heartland and around it," but never to it. The West did not forget. Its shattering repudiation of Carter in 1980 spoke more eloquently than Sagebrush rebels ever could.

A second volatile theme — States' rights — also runs through the issue of "landlordism" and the West.

In the early 1980s federalism has collapsed. As Governor Ed Herschler has said, "The system is badly out of kilter. Federal encroachments on state and local governments are at an all-time high." This in itself is nothing new to the West. From the imperial days of Cleveland and Roosevelt the western states consistently have been held at bay in public-land matters. Executive action and midnight proclamations are a way of life. But never before in the West's history has that fact been so important. In March 1981 Governor Bruce Babbitt of Arizona said that "what galls westerners is not so much the fact of ownership, but rather the federal insistence that it is entitled to act not only as landowner, but also as *sovereign.*" It has been said before, many times. And in the blistering rhetoric of the Sagebrush Rebellion it is being said again.

Though they crisscross each other, two problems exist. One is the federal practice of ignoring the West in the decision-making process. The other is the growing federal tendency to override or skirt state and local laws. The MX was tentatively sited not only without western consent, but without its knowledge. The Energy Mobilization Board (EMB), in terms of States' rights as vicious a proposal as the West has seen in decades, threatened regional water rights, environmental statutes, and the very principle of local sovereignty. Carter's threat that the federal government would assert its legal right to water originating on federal property menaced the West's entire system of water law. Proposed coal-slurry legislation — giving pipeline companies the right of eminent domain in states targeted for pipeline construction — threatens western land and everything on it. Even the RARE II and BLM inventories, as productive as they were, were mandated and carried out without the significant participation of local governments, and Environmental Protection Agency actions on clean-air standards, as important as they were, often have infringed on local sovereignties. The point is that, good laws or bad, the West has been voiceless in making them. That some have been good does not alter the hard fact that the West has become legally emasculated, that it is treated with arrogance and indifference, and that it still is living with the old, archaic federal-eastern assumption that the federal government is better equipped to rule the West than the West is to rule itself.

In recent years the EMB has been the most frightening example of what federal arrogance can do to western states. But nothing — perhaps not even the EMB — has disturbed the West like the Ventura County case of 1979.

For years Ventura County, California — like other communities throughout the West — has enforced its county zoning ordinances with regard to energy development on federal lands within the county, imposing conditions that preseve the interests of county residents. In 1976 Gulf Oil, possessing a lease to drill on federal land, refused to comply with the ordinances. The county sued and lost; determination was made in federal court that the Mineral Lands Leasing Act of 1920 — one of many acts bitterly opposed by the West in the first conservation period — pre-empted state and local regulation of leasing operations on federal lands. In 1980 the United States Supreme Court upheld the decision.

For the West, the implications are frightening. The courts, in effect, have denied *any* local government the right to apply its laws, zoning ordinances, and environmental and land-use regulations to lessees of the public lands. If Ventura stands, western communities will have lost one of their oldest and most precious rights to the federal government — the right to control private activities on federal lands on or near the communities, the power to extend legislative sovereignty over the land on which they live. If Ventura stands, western communities will be powerless to regulate oil drilling, coal digging, shale oil development, or any other activity conducted under federal protection.

It is this kind of action, taken over and over again in the history of the West, that underpins the Sagebrush Rebellion. In fact, Congress had no desire to allow pre-emption when it wrote the 1920 law. Even if it had, its power to pre-empt state regulation of federal lands is severely restricted by the Constitution. But now it is academic. The West must accept Ventura. At the Denver Public Lands Convention in 1911 a bewildered western governor commented that the federal government seemed to have "lost all sense of the rights of the people of the western states," that it believed that "these states are not competent to legislate to protect themselves." EMB and the Ventura County case indicate that nothing has changed. Federalism disintegrates. States' rights erode. The West goes on living as it always has. As colonies.

Inevitably the insurgent West returns to the question of equal footing — one of the most persistent and emotional themes in Sagebrush rhetoric.

When western states entered the Union — most of them in the second half of the nineteenth century — their admission bills contained the understanding that they entered on equal footing with other states. At time of entry, however, one major factor already separated them: while older states had had full use of public lands within their boundaries, the new West did not. As a condition of admission, western states were forced to relinquish title to all public lands lying within them. Idaho's constitution, for example, clearly stated that "the people do agree and declare that we forever disclaim all right and title to the unappropriated public lands" lying within the state. Colorado's Enabling Act said that the state would "forever disclaim all right and title to the unappropriated public lands" lying within it, and that the lands would "remain at the sole and entire disposition of the United States." The condition was uniform throughout the West; no state escaped it. Each received two sections in every township for schools (four in Utah, New Mexico, and Arizona), but nothing more.

Momentarily it did not matter. Because of the federal government's liberal land-disposal policies, westerners were confident that the land would come to them anyway. But it did not. What came, instead, were conservation and forest reserves and FLPMA.

At that point protest began — and it has never stopped. Nearly eighty years ago, in the spring of 1907, the Colorado state legislature articulated the mood of the entire insurgent West. "Assuming all the rights of a private landowner," it noted in a bluntly worded resolution, "the action of the Federal Government in usurping the rights of the states and its citizens to develop and acquire title to these public lands and to utilize their resources as part of the state, we believe to be contrary to the spirit and the letter of the Act of Congress creating the state of Colorado." In 1979 the Nevada legislature placed the same argument at the heart of its new law, and since then equal footing has been a Sagebrush rallying cry. Western dissidents do not, cannot, argue that they have legal claims to the land. But they do argue, with some justification, that federal conditions for admission — land relinquishment — were discriminatory and unprecedented, and that the West gave up its lands on the explicit understanding that federal land disposal would never cease. Radical or not, there is a technical truth in what they say. Conditions imposed upon the West were unique; no other American states had been so constricted, no other American citizens had been denied the opportunity to exploit the land about them. And, in a sense, FLPMA *was* a betrayal, the smashing of an old and sacred covenant born in the first moments of the nation's life. Partly because they believe in it, partly because it is their only viable tactic, westerners often approach legal questions from a moral position. Such is the case with equal footing. Only time will tell how strong the moral claims are.

Finally, beyond questions of States' rights and equal footing, the Sagebrush Rebellion argues that federal landownership places immense economic and social burdens on the states. Nevada, in particular, maintains that with only 12.4 percent ownership of its own land space it cannot generate a large enough tax base to support public services. On the other hand, in Nevada or any other state, revenues from private property taxes are commonly used to provide public services that benefit federal employees as well as private-sector workers. To make matters worse, the Carter administration scaled back the payments-in-lieu-of-taxes program designed to correct precisely this problem, and in the fall of 1981 the Reagan administration called for allocation of $63 million less than a Senate-House conference committee wanted for the same purposes. To some extent the argument is simplistic — it ignores the many other ways that federal government funnels money into local economies. But this argument, even with its flaws, contains its own hard truth.

In the emotional context of the Sagebrush war, the question of ownership is vital. Echoing a theme from the West's past, the president of the Idaho Cattlemen's Association has complained that westerners are "serfs," that "there is no way to control our destiny while Washington controls the land." Right or wrong, the Rebellion is an attempt to take control. In the 1960s, Governor Scott Matheson has said, "when the federal government wanted to do anything, the states rolled over and played dead. As far as we're concerned, that's over." Adds Jim Santini: "It is past time for the West to begin to control its own destiny. We have been pushed around long enough."

Control is the central issue in the Sagebrush Rebellion. Federal control of western land and life. Federal control of the West's fate. Like Santini, Utah's Orrin Hatch seeks to "return control of our destiny" to Utah and the West. Governor Ted Schwinden of Montana has said precisely the same thing — that "what we don't want to do is turn over control to outsiders, and that means OPEC, Washington, and the East." The issue runs like a bitter thread not only through the Sagebrush revolt, but through the whole exploitative history of the West. And it involves infinitely more than the question of ownership itself.

What is at issue is the *quality* of ownership. The heart of the problem, and the source of control, is federal *management* of the western public lands — and often the water that flows through them.

For longer than it can remember, the West has known government by bureau. From territorial days to the 1980s, government by Interior, by Agriculture, by General Land Office and Forest Service and Reclamation, has been a way of life. The result has been mixed. Some of the West's most enlightened governance has come from these departments. But at the same time they often have blighted the West with their arrogance, ignorance, paternalism, and numbing inefficiency. The West has always hated bureaucracies and the distant placemen who run them — and at no time in its history has it not had reason. The bureaus have sown resentment whenever they have been, whatever they have done.

No agency in the West has failed to antagonize those who live there. The Bureau of Reclamation, for example, lowering the water level of the Colorado River and proposing to add turbines to Glen Canyon Dam in order to produce more hydroelectric power, has outraged both environmentalists and the river recreation trade in Utah and Arizona. River runners complain that shallow rapids have destroyed the Colorado's small craft traffic, crippled river tours, and threatened to kill a \$12 million-a-year industry. Environmentalists have attacked the plan with some of their fiercest rhetoric in years. One of them has said it will turn the river into a "hydro-power flush trench unsuitable for riparian life" and that it must be seen for what it is: "the deadening habit of grabbing at a fix, the insanity of not seeing ahead." Although the Interior Department killed the turbine proposal in September 1981, tension still remains high on the river.

The Army Corps of Engineers has been embroiled in a number of recent western arguments, most notably in Colorado. In the late 1970s, in alliance with EPA and local environmentalists, it stalled the controversial Foothills water project near Denver. In general its reasoning was sound. What angered many Coloradans was the principle involved, the appearance, at least, of federal interference in the state water-planning process. The principle, like most embedded in the Sagebrush Rebellion, has roots deep in western history. Shortly before World War I, the *Denver Post* wrote that "the menace of federal interference and control of our public streams is a danger more baleful and sinister than any other on our horizon." In an essay in the same newspaper in 1980 one state leader wrote that "we Coloradans along the Front Range . . . hardly had any say-so" in the Foothills project. "Instead, conflict is resolved by a bureaucracy which is not accountable and whose basic philosophy unfortunately is patterned after the values of the East."

In Gunnison County, Colorado, the Corps has been accused of using the Clean Water Act to limit local growth. Under the act, which prohibits private construction in areas declared federal "wetlands," the Corps has declared much — the people say virtually all — of the county's green lands wetlands. Most of the county has never welcomed federal government or any form of conservation. In

1905, when it was encircled by national forest, the virulent *Gunnison News-Champion* swore resistance to the "autocratic government." To moderates who counseled caution and cooperation, the paper raged that "the history of the world does not show a case where the tyrant has failed to appear when invited." The spirit still exists, reincarnated in Sagebrush. Arguing that the government's action stops coal, uranium, and molybdenum mining, as well as building growth, local citizens have protested the "oppressive and dictatorial" agency and its "arbitrary and capricious decisions." Colorado senator William Armstrong has introduced legislation to restrict the expansion of federal authority over nonnavigable waters. Likely, however, nothing will defuse local anger. "It is bureaucracy at its worst," one citizen has said. "We've been treated shabbily. People in the valley are fed up with government permits and regulations." The feeling remains — right or wrong — that the tyrant is still at the door.

The National Park Service, normally one of the government's most pliable western agencies, also has come under attack. Like the Bureau of Reclamation, it has been accused of impeding rafting and other river traffic on the Colorado. Ironically, claiming that the agency's "arbitrary, elitist policy" would "deprive the public of its right to use and enjoy the park," the conservative Mountain States Legal Foundation — then headed by James G. Watt — filed suit against it in the spring of 1980.

At the same time, in late 1979 and early 1980, the Service was charged with "land grabbing." Families living in Teton County, Wyoming — already 96 percent owned by the federal government — claimed that the government was encroaching on private lands in Grand Teton National Park. In collusion with the Fish and Wildlife Service and the Forest Service, according to the militant National Parks Inholders Association, the government restricted the rights of private property owners to improve their own land. In an attempt to drive them out of the park, federal officials offered them buy-outs below market value, harassed them when they refused to deal, and in some cases illegally appropriated their land. Under Watt, the Department of the Interior's projected policy of restricted land purchasing in favor of expanded park maintenance may solve Wyoming's problem. But it will not temper feelings of resentment in a state that has one of the bitterest anticonservation records in the

West. As the Inholders Association has resolved, it will continue to "resist National Park Service abuses of power" and "fight for human dignity and property rights."

In western coal states one of the West's smallest agencies, the Office of Surface Management (OSM), also has been one of its most disliked. In coal country it has typified the ageless problem of government from a distance.

At issue are the office's regulations, most of which deal with coal strip mining. Not unlike the old General Land Office, which yearly blanketed the West with inane land laws designed in Washington bureaus by easterners who had never seen the West, the OSM consistently has written ignorant, unreasonable, and unworkable regulations. Coal men argue that OSM law is geared to Appalachia, not the West, and that compliance is costly enough to drive marginal operators off the land entirely. State leaders argue that it collides with — and often overrides — state agencies charged with the same functions. There is no doubt that OSM has been zealous in doing what it sees as right. But often it has been too zealous, carrying unrealistic regulations to the point of absurdity.

Governor Ed Herschler of Wyoming, OSM's most intractable opponent, has said that its mining regulations "bear the stamp of trust in a state practice in Philadelphia," not in the West. They are a "lawyer's maze, designed to confuse and harass an adversary." No coal state is without its examples. Utah operators insist that "they've got regulations adopted against eastern abuses to handle things we don't even face out here." In the northern part of the state, they claim, OSM has mandated the covering of reclamation piles with four feet of topsoil in a region where "we can't find two inches, let alone four feet." It also has ordered installation of refuse facilities on flatlands in an area — again, northern Utah — filled with canyons and mountains. Wyoming has conducted a running war with the bureau over strip-mine reclamation standards that Herschler calls unapplicable and "overkill." He claims that mountaintop mining regulations are dictated when Wyoming *has* no mountaintop mining. And, only half humorously, he tells the story of how the federal government required the operator of a one-man mine to acquire a stretcher in case he was hurt — when no one else lived for miles around to carry it.

To much of the West these are not laughing matters. "I have been frustrated, annoyed, infuriated, exasperated, bewildered, appalled, alarmed, and disgusted," says Herschler, who at one point refused further correspondence with the bureau. Apparently he has found an ally in James Watt. Disgusted by the proenvironment tilt of Carter's OSM, Watt has proposed slashing both the functions of the office and the manpower to carry them out (a plan so far thwarted by Congress). In a statement made in the summer of 1981 he said he would "bring the regulations back to what Congress intended them to be, rather than [maintain] the excessive regulations. put into existence the last few years." Watt has called OSM one of the most abusive bureaus in government — "embodied in this one office we find every abuse of government centered in one agency, directed at one industry." Herschler adds, "Let's abolish OSM and take them to Lower Slobbovia. They're a pain in the backside." Citing the fact that most western coal states have adequate reclamation programs of their own (Wyoming and Montana in particular do, only Utah does not), Herschler says that the time has come to "redirect the OSM function away from interference" with those programs. Wyoming, for one, is ready to assert its rights. State primacy will be established, says Herschler, either by Interior — or by the courts.

The same kind of anger often has been leveled at the Environmental Protection Agency. Western interests, large and small, have warred with it for a decade. And judging from Sagebrush rhetoric, the war is not over.

In 1980 EPA was involved with the state of Colorado and the city of Denver in a particularly bitter States' rights fight.

In 1979, when the city of Denver failed to meet federal auto emissions standards, EPA threatened to withhold $300 million in federal sewage-treatment and highway funds from the state. The legislature angrily responded with a bill, which was rejected by EPA as unsatisfactory. Several times more the agency rejected state plans; not until May 1980 did it accept a legislative bill, and not until July did it lift sanctions. In the meantime it touched off angry denunciation of federal power in Colorado and raised serious questions about the legislative sovereignty of the state.

Part of the blame lay with Colorado. For years its legislature balked at passing a clean-air law strong enough to clear up one of the filthiest air masses in the Rockies. On the other hand, EPA's intrusion on Colorado's legislative process was outrageous. Speaker of the Colorado House Robert Burford (now head of BLM) said,

"The real issue is not just the imposition of sanctions . . . the real issue is the right of the people of Colorado to live under the laws they want to live under."

What stunned Colorado was EPA's incredible rejection of several state legislative proposals — a kind of federal blackmail unprecedented in the West's history. That the agency finally selected one — and one that will benefit the state — is academic. What is important is the fact that it meddled. Even Colorado moderates supported sanctions, but when EPA invaded the legislative process, as the *Rocky Mountain News* wrote, it "veered out of control." The *News* was right: EPA's job was "not to write legislation or to nitpick. For the agency to demand . . . that some broad action be taken is one thing. For it to dictate the language of the legislation . . . is something else. EPA has gone too far."

In the midst of it all, twenty-seven state legislators sued the agency, supported by the Mountain States Legal Foundation. Their counsel, again James Watt, vehemently argued that "the voices of citizens attempting to participate in the legislative process were drowned out by the more powerful voice of the federal govenrment." EPA had been "virtually a third house in the Colorado legislature," said Watt — a fact, for one brief moment, frighteningly true.

The battle over auto emissions was one of the few not fought over public lands or issues connected with public lands. The rest have been.

Energy interests — again, generally outsiders with substantial local support — have charged that EPA's air-pollution guidelines threaten their survival. In northwest Colorado, for example, EPA Class I standards, along with state standards, long have been on a collision course with shale oil development. In coal country the same kind of conflict has been generated between EPA and power companies over power plant emissions.

Few westerners deny the positive intent of the law — its attempt to mitigate air pollution and preserve the West's scenic vistas. But like many federal laws with western applications, it is flawed. One issue, originally, was the law's vagueness. As a Colorado power company protested in 1980, EPA was "dealing with an unknown subject, unknown causes, and unknown effect," charging helter-skelter toward a goal that is an absolute unknown." Without clear objectives, without even a clear definition of "visibility," EPA's law was as murky as its target. And by enforcing it, vagueness and all, EPA threatened virtually every industrialized business in the West.

Stung by threats of legal action, EPA drafted specific regulations clearly defining "integral vistas." Incredibly, the law now reads that EPA can protect vistas *outside* Class I boundaries if they are visible from *inside*. In the West, where a hundred-mile view is not unusual, anything that mars it — dust from a farmer's plow, smoke from a town lumber mill — is a potential violation. The implications are frightening.

In the growing West, in or out of the Sagebrush Rebellion, business and community survival are paramount issues. Those who remember the region's boomtown history instinctively challenge any force that threatens them. Compliance already has taken its toll: a huge Kennecott mine-smelter was dismantled in Nevada in 1979, and the great Anaconda tragedy has been attributed to the company's inability or unwillingness to meet federal air-pollution standards. Those businesses that do comply will pass on massive retrofitting costs to local consumers, blunting economic growth all over the West. The question is, then, at what point the cost of maintaining pure and healthy air becomes too prohibitive to consider. Westerners are torn, but the *Denver Post* has spoken at least for those arguing for limits. "As desirable as it may be to keep the air pristine," it said in the spring of 1981, "there are levels of protection we simply cannot finance."

For the energy interests it may be that the problem will correct itself. It well may be, in the next few years, that EPA head Anne Gorsuch and regional director Steve Durham will change EPA's entire course. So far neither has shown interest in enforcing current agency law. In the meantime, EPA's opponents — and in some cases EPA itself — have taken dead aim at the federal Clean Air Act itself. Their hope is that the law, which expired in September 1981, will not be renewed. But if it is, what sections they cannot gut they will attempt to modify.

The oil and power companies are not alone in their war. Throughout their fight large numbers of angry farmers and cattlemen have stood with them.

The issue is still air: against some of the most passionate opposition in the West, EPA often has outlawed or regulated the use of weed spray and animal poison in regions where farmers and stockmen argue they are essential to their survival.

Westward from the Great Plains, farmers have been menaced by grasshoppers since the days of Brigham Young. And the day of the gull is gone. In the 1980s farmers live and die on the effectiveness of their insecticides. EPA regulations often have played havoc with them. Among other things, they require buffer zones and consent from adjoining landowners for aerial spraying — both of which diminish the effect of pest control and both of which often are impossible to obtain. In Colorado's spring and summer of 1980, for example, when hoppers engulfed its eastern plains, EPA ordered no spraying within one mile of homes, schools, churches, recreation areas, highways, and crops, or *anywhere* when the wind blew more than ten miles an hour. In effect, the ruling meant no spraying at all, leading one enraged farmer to comment that the government treated grasshoppers as endangered species. Worse, from the viewpoint of crop growers, the bureau also has restricted the *kinds* of sprays they can use. Aldrin, dealdrin and others have been banned in favor of the far less potent malathion. In Colorado, again, and to no avail, state officials argued that malathion and carbaryl 7 spread out thinly over sprayed acreage caused no damage to humans. To the outside world these small struggles are insignificant. But in the West itself such things as the potency of a chemical spray can mean the difference between whether a farmer does or does not survive a growing season. California's stunning fruit fly war in the summer of 1981 graphically illustrated the kind of silent, deadly, debilitating struggle western farmers face every day of their lives. In the Dust Bowl days clouds of hoppers blotted out the High Plains sun, shredded wheat fields to stubble, turned corn to powder. In western Nebraska, in eastern Colorado, farmers understand: it could happen again.

Stockmen fight the same war. Only the enemy is different. The stockman's hoppers are prairie dogs and coyotes; gophers kill the land, coyotes kill the stock. Predator control is one of the most emotional issues on the western range, and it has been for years. Stockmen claim that predators are decimating their industry. In Colorado, between 1972 and 1980, the state suffered sheep losses to coyotes that ranged to $6.6 million a year. Across the West stockmen have claimed $100 million in cattle and sheep losses in 1979 alone. In 1981 both the National Cattlemen's Association and the National Woolgrowers' Association asked EPA to declare a predator-control emergency.

For stockmen, the suffering is real. What is a distant problem to the East is as real and immediate to western stockmen as dead ewes and calves lying in their pastures. At hearings in Denver in July 1981 one Montana sheepman claimed that coyotes killed between 8 and 19 percent of his lambs in the first two months of the summer alone. Another Montanan claimed that his sheep losses ranged up to 39 percent of his flock each year — enough that he was finally driven out of the industry. Dave Flitner, president of the Wyoming Farm Bureau, retired from sheep ranching in 1979 after losing $30,000 worth of stock. One Utah group claims that coyotes kill one fifth of the state's lamb stock each year, with losses mounting to $5 million a year through November of 1981. It is this way virtually everywhere. Wherever there is range, there are coyotes. And where there are coyotes, there is death.

The issue among stockmen is predator control. The issue, specifically, is the fact that EPA banned the most effective control poison — compound 1080 — in 1972. Since that time, says one frustrated rancher, "we just haven't been able to bring predator losses to a level we can live with." They make little attempt to conceal their bitterness. Compound 1080, they argue, was "canine specific" and offered little threat to noncanine species. What was "one of the most selective predicides" ever developed was banned simply through the "biased maneuvering of the environmental community." With 1080 banned (and sodium cyanide, approved in 1975, totally ineffective), stockmen have herded, fenced, trapped, and gunned down coyotes from helicopters swirling over the range. Nothing has worked. Tom Spencer, a cattleman in Pueblo County, Colorado, rarely lost a calf on his Box T Ranch before the banning of 1080. Later, when the coyotes moved in, he "tried to shoot them, but that just don't affect them when their numbers build up."

With the "situation completely out of hand," according to Flitner, stockmen have banded together to reopen the question of compound 1080. Seeking its reauthorization, they have found at least limited support from Secretary of the Interior James Watt. In October 1981 Watt — through the United States Fish and Wildlife Service — asked EPA to register a sheep collar containing 1080, and in November he planned to request an EPA permit for lethal-dose compound 1080 baits. Both marked the first step toward possible EPA approval of the reintroduction of the poison in bait situations. But even so, stockmen remain skeptical. "We're rather disappointed," says Ron Michieli of the National Cattlemen's Association. "This program falls short." Jessie Baker, executive director of the Wyoming Wool-growers' Association, has stated it more bluntly. "We have waited and waited through about four administrations," he says in anger. "We supported Secretary of the Interior James Watt. We expected some support and we don't feel we're getting it."

The fact remains, say stockmen, that they need more help, massive help, and that it must come soon. Until it does, EPA remains a threat to their industry.

In 1975 Congressman Andrew Hinshaw of California told the story of God applying to the Heavenly Environmental Protection Agency (HEPA) for a permit to create the world. When he stated his intention to finish creation in six days, HEPA informed him that it would require a minimum of one hundred eighty days to review the application and environmental impact statement. It would take twelve months more before a permit could be granted. Said God: "To hell with it."

Sagebrush rebels would agree.

The federal bureaus — all of them — have left an indelible impression on the western mind through the years. "Big brother has got his arm solidly around you," a Montana rancher has complained. "It's rules on this and rules on that. They've got us in knots." But, of all the bureaus, none have had as much of an impact on the West as the Forest Service and BLM. Of all the issues, none have touched off the sustained fury of RARE and FLPMA. OSM and EPA have done their part to widen and deepen the gulf that separates the federal government and the western states. But the Forest Service and BLM alone would be enough to ensure a Sagebrush Rebellion.

The issue of BLM management is one of the most volatile in the West.

It was not always so. In the early years of the century, BLM lands — ragged remnants of desert and timberlands left over from the age of disposal — were lands no one wanted. Forgotten by the public, ignored by the government, they were administered poorly and haphazardly, if at all. Only cattlemen saw their value. Some called it opportunism, exploitation; others called it vision — the ability to see the life that lay in the sagebrush wastes. Whatever it was, whatever it is now, the cattlemen virtually took over BLM lands. Aided by the nonchalance and ignorance of the federal government, they swarmed over public lands from the Gulf to Canada. Many carved out small empires. Many more did not. But they all shared one thing in common: reliance on the public lands for survival. The years of taking were good ones. Few people ever understood that one day what was taken would have to be given back.

FLPMA changed the old order overnight. It dictated multiple use, not single, and in the process it destroyed the cattlemen's primacy forever. Laissez faire disintegrated, gentlemen's agreements disappeared. The managers began to manage. There were other "dispossessed" — lumberers, mineral and energy producers, farmers and sheepmen — but no one felt the crippling impact of FLPMA like the cattlemen. So anger came quickly and easily — the deep, sweeping anger of men who had fought more ferociously for their place on the land than any other group in the West's history. It focused on the managers. And it seeded the Sagebrush Rebellion.

The West's oldest antigovernment themes also are its newest — landlordism, ignorance, arrogance, insensitivity to local people and local problems. Charges once hurled at the Forest Service now are directed at BLM. A consortium of Colorado county governments, for example, has charged that BLM refuses to adhere to its "memorandum of understanding" with them regarding the enforcement of county zoning regulations, building codes, and sewage-disposal regulations. It also has voiced fears that proposed federal legislation empowering BLM employees to carry firearms will weaken traditional western reliance on state and local law enforcement. More gently than most, Senator Henry Jackson of Washington has said that "managers come out here from the federal government and act like dictators." Likening them to the Sheriff of Nottingham, Utah's intemperate Orrin Hatch has charged that "the West is subject to the whim and vagaries of the politically and bureaucratically inspired."

Resentment runs canyon-deep. Militants such as Nevada rebel Dean Rhoads say, simply, "The people resent Washington coming out here with a packet of regulations and policies telling us what to do." Even moderates such as Bruce Babbitt are angered. Babbitt has deplored the fact that "land use for 70 percent of Arizona's surface area is planned on C Street in Washington" — much as Arizona's future was planned years ago by Wall Street bankers and Arizona copper kings meeting in smoke-filled rooms. In the sunburnt desert country of east-central Utah, where extremism runs high, one man perhaps has said it best: "Government agencies such as BLM are throwbacks to the age of the feudal lords, controlling huge kingdoms of public lands with an iron fist." The insurgents of 1907 could not have said it better. What disturbs is the fact that seventy-five years later it must be said again.

There is truth in what the rebels say. Part of the problem is that BLM's staff-rotation policy has destroyed consistency and continuity in the field. It has put men in the field, says one western official, who "don't know sagebrush from piñon." But it is also true that in recent years many of BLM's fieldmen have been at odds philosophically with western land users. Many BLM managers have been young, idealistic, often environmentalist, and often eastern; the people they regulate often have not been young, or idealistic, or environmentalist. A Utah man has sarcastically said that "many of the best natural resource students from the Earth Day era ended up employed at BLM." This may or may not be true — it does not matter. What matters is the fact that, in the western mind, the *perception* exists that it is. The perception exists — a holdover from the days of Pinchot and his eastern planners — that BLM's entire managerial apparatus is tilted against the West, and it is precisely this image that has driven many of its people into the Sagebrush Rebellion.

A second truth exists, too. Western bureaucrats, BLM or otherwise, have few incentives to consider the full social costs of what they do. Many BLM fieldmen — perhaps most — are westerners. But this seems to mean little. The fact remains that their inability to obtain a profit from the system they oversee often makes them uninterested in it. They may have a greater knowledge of western problems than others, but much of the West has seen no evidence that knowledge translates into interest or concern. The simple fact is that the bureaucrat, without a stake in the public interest — be it grazing regulations or wild horse control — may not act in the public interest. Instead, says a Colorado insurgent, he tends to make the public "prisoners of a state of mind that finds sanctuary in central planning and uniformity rather than freedom and diversity." This, again, is the West's perception, and as long as it is, BLM managers will remain a target for Sagebrush attacks.

The litany of abuse is endless, and it comes out of every desert, every valley in the West. In Nevada, BLM recently ordered a rancher off federal land while he was fighting a fire. In New Mexico, along the Pecos, angry sheepmen have protested BLM efforts to remove coyote-control fences so that antelope could have free run of the land. BLM's proposed Snake River Birds of Prey National Conservation Area along the Snake in southeastern Idaho has terrified farmers living on irrigated land in one of America's most desolate sections. The bureau's plan is to set aside 515,257 acres of land to protect the food source — squirrels and prairie dogs — of raptors inhabiting the adjacent Birds of Prey Natural Area. Farmers protest that the land should be used for agriculture instead of wildlife, that southeast Idaho cannot have both productive farmland and the protection of prairie pests for destructive raptors.

In the fall of 1980 BLM evicted Gerald Chaffin and his family from their home on BLM land five miles south of Midwest, Wyoming. In what the bureau called a "general cleanup," Chaffin was ordered to destroy his home and clear, drag, level, and seed the land it stood on to return it to its original condition. In one of the West's most publicized events in years, Chaffin burned his home to the ground in October 1980. The next morning newspapers all over America carried the picture of the Chaffins watching it burn. Like others before him, Chaffin felt victimized by a system with no soul. "I feel the government let us down," he said. "We worked hard to build this up." Walking away from the ashes, his wife said that "crying time is over." Like others before them, they started again.

Not even the states themselves have been immune. In 1979, for example, the state of Montana collided with BLM over the positioning of a power-line route from Colstrip to Hot Springs: when the state approved one route, BLM disapproved it in favor of another. Briefly, Montana adopted a position of States' rights; in time, however, faced with the right of the Bonneville Power Authority (a federal agency building the corridor for Montana Power) to supersede state siting laws, it backed down. The line is under construction today, creeping steadily up and down unspoiled valleys where families have lived for a hundred years.

Those threatened most by BLM are cattlemen. Once, says a Nevadan, "there was nothing but sagebrush flats between high, barren mountains under a clear blue sky. I felt free. There was a feeling you were your own man." No more. Besieged by environmentalists, skiers, strip miners, they see themselves as a class on the edge of extinction. So they lash out — chiefly at BLM. They anger at BLM restrictions on the use of sagebrush-control chemicals, at the agency's multiple-use commitment to endangered species, at the slow speed of environmental impact statements, at the literally hundreds of other rules that bind them every day. A disgusted Montana cattleman has said, "People sitting behind desks all day in Washington are just making them up. You can't turn around without colliding with another regulation." They are angry, too, at what they define as BLM arrogance and insensitivity. And they despise what they judge to be a continuing strain of environmentalism among BLM officials.

But, mostly, they are angry at anything that threatens grazing.

Nothing is more menacing than predators. As mentioned earlier, coyotes cost ranchers millions of dollars in losses each year. Part of this is due to EPA's ban on compound 1080, but part of it also is due — say cattlemen — to BLM's "softness" on the issue. What cattlemen want is a strong, responsible damage-control program in which lethal methods are not prohibited. So far, however, except in Watt's limited new initiatives, they do not have it.

Wild horses also are predators of a sort. Cattlemen charge that they kill the land: uncontrolled, they overgraze, destroying grasslands that economically pressed cattlemen cannot afford to lose. And for the better part of a decade they have been uncontrolled and unregulated by the single agency with the responsibility to do it: BLM.

Colorado, for example, has four major herds — at Sand Wash near Craig, Little Book Cliff near Grand Junction, near Norwood, and on the White River. In the four areas, virtually unchecked by BLM between 1971 and 1980, the herds grew from 200 horses to 800. Near Rock Springs the uncontrolled wild horse population grew from 2364 in 1972 to 6129 in 1979 (with an additional increase of 1100 to 3400 on nearby private lands). Range conditions have steadily deteriorated in most herd areas, and in Wyoming BLM has responded by temporarily cutting back grazing allotments — penalizing cattlemen rather than horses.

In the spirit of the Sagebrush Rebellion, cattlemen have begun to fight back. In 1979 Nevada filed suit against BLM to force it to fulfill its legal responsibility to remove wild horses from the range. Cattlemen near Rock Springs filed a similar suit, holding Secretary of the Interior Cecil Andrus *personally* responsible for their losses and asking for damages of $250,000. In March 1981 the Mountain States Legal Foundation declared that BLM director Frank Gregg also should be held *personally* responsible for range losses. "At what point," said its chief attorney, "do you put the welfare of horses above constitutional rights?"

In a similar step, one taken in frustration over the government's entire predator- and horse-control program, the American Farm Bureau Federation has gone to court to dispute a variety of federal actions — or nonactions. It has defended a plains rancher suffering stock damage by wolves protected under the Endangered Species Act, and it has supported a South Dakota rancher who charged the government — BLM — with failure to control coyotes and prairie dogs on his leased range. In all the cases the ranchers have insisted that predator destruction constitutes property damage by law-protected animals, that ranchers are entitled to the "protection of efficient federal management," and that if protection is not given, citizens are due just compensation for their losses. The central question is precisely who owns the public's animals and who is responsible for their actions and costs. Western ranchers, beset by coyotes and mustangs, insist that it is the government.

A bigger and deadlier enemy than mustangs, though, is grazing cutbacks. They happen, and always have, for what westerners consider poor reasons. In one Idaho district BLM has limited grazing — with cutbacks of up to 35 percent — while vegetation grows back. Ranchers insist that more grazing easily could be allowed, and Senator James McClure, Idaho's soft-spoken militant, has said that, because of the restrictions, "a good number of people are talking in terms of revolution." Near Picabo, in Idaho's desert country, BLM has attempted to take back 15,000 acres of grazing land from a man whose family first homesteaded nearly ninety-two years ago — for the purpose of converting it into winter deer range. In New Mexico, along the bleak Rio Puerco, BLM recently sought substantial grazing cuts, most of them involving thirty-five Mexican-American ranchers who barely survive on the land during the best of times. In southwestern Utah the Fish and Wildlife Service has set aside thirty-five square miles of range for protection of the endangered desert tortoise — 62 acres for each of 400 left. Because of the action, BLM has ordered grazing reductions in the habitat — an area where the history of some families goes back 150 years. Says one rancher bitterly, "Cattle have brought a lot more money into the county than tortoises ever have."

In 1974, over one of the longest and most vociferous cattlemen's protests in memory, a federal district court in Washington found BLM in violation of the National Environmental Policy Act for failing to prepare sufficient environmental impact statements (EISs) on public grazing lands under its care. The bureau was required to write 144 statements on 162 million acres of land. The process will be completed by 1988, but on nine EISs completed to date BLM has reduced livestock use on 44 percent of its allotments. What the rest of the statements conclude — whether a district can or cannot bear its current grazing traffic — will affect virtually every cattleman in the West. Where allotments are reduced, they will be devastated.

One important condition exists on the western range that outsiders — those who make and judge the law — do not understand. Most western ranches are not large units; the "Ponderosa" image that most nonwesterners have is more myth than reality. Most ranches are small and compact, scattered haphazardly among huge patches of public domain — private islands in a federal sea. For a century, in order to *create* large (and more productive) units, cattlemen have relied on the leasing of public lands adjacent to their own. In the past, again,the federal government did little to discourage consolidating; acting as an ally, BLM routinely granted ten-year leases at low cost. But now times have changed; the range no longer belongs to the cattlemen. Too late, perhaps, they have come to understand their overreliance on federal government. The environmental impact statements have the potential to change the whole configuration of the range, the power to break, to destroy. So the cattlemen wait out the process. Uncertain about the present, unable to plan for the future, they have learned to live in limbo.

They also live in anger. One of its sources is the government's cavalier approach to the element of time. The EIS process has been long and drawn out, something few cattlemen can afford. In Idaho's Magic Valley, for example, the government delayed for two years before writing an EIS. When it was finished — with 400 pages of text — it gave stockmen forty-five days to respond. Again and again this has happened, making a mockery of the Federal Administrative Practices Act, which requires ample time for public discussion. And people now say, "God damn it, get the federal government out of here."

Another source of anger is the fact — debated in the West since the first leasing controversy eight decades ago — that serious disagreements still exist among range managers about the scientific determination of range carrying capacity. BLM's critics argue that the bureau's formula is not accurate and that any impact statements based on it are invalid. The Colorado state legislature's Interim Agriculture Committee has spoken for many westerners, calling the

EIS process "ill-advised." But others see something more. Cattlemen born and bred in a conspiracy-minded region believe that the EISs are a legal ploy on the part of BLM to reduce grazing on the public lands forever. In any case, few cattlemen believe that grazing reductions in the name of range improvement actually will lead to improvement. Cynics among them flatly state that few grazing fees are plowed back into the range at all. East of Helena, for example, where the land lies broad and flat in the shadow of the Little Belts, and the Smith River flows unimpeded through cattle country, much of the land is BLM's, and ranchers here long have complained about its grazing policies. Here they believe that BLM inertia and deception and arrogance have blunted any hope of range improvement — even while they face cutbacks to ensure it. Montanans are not alone. Wherever they live, from Montana to Mexico, cattlemen face unprecedented new realities. "If we can't use the public lands," says an Idaho rancher, "the industry as we know it will cease to exist."

He is right. It will.

All of this might be tolerable, say stockmen, if BLM effectively managed the land it holds. But the western charge — true or not — is that it does not. According to Orrin Hatch, BLM controls eight times the land amount of Utah that the state Bureau of Land does; it has twenty-three times more employees and twenty-four times the budget. The state bureau spends one third of the money per acre that BLM does — and earns four times what it does. In Colorado supporters of the Sagebrush Rebellion maintain that BLM employs seventy-three workers for each million acres managed, spends $2.18 an acre on management, and generates $4.13 in income; the state land board employs ten, spends 20¢ per managed acre, and earns $4.39.

Numbers are relative; they say whatever their manipulators want. But again and again the rhetoric of rebellion has centered on the flawed stewardship, the idea of federal inefficiency. Most insurgents agree with State Senator Norman Glaser of Nevada, who has said, "Nobody can convince me that we couldn't be better stewards of the land than that perfidious absentee landlord who resides along the Potomac." More specifically, a Coloradan commented in 1981, "I can't understand why anyone with an intelligence level above that of a moron wants the federal government to do anything for them. When you do, you settle for a low level of mediocrity at three times the price. BLM can be eliminated."

The mood is ugly in the backwoods, across the deserts of the West.

In Montana, along the Smith. In Owyhee County. Along the Pecos. The overwhelming belief, as an angry New Mexican has said, is that "when the feds take control the ranch operator is no longer necessary. He's a federal caretaker." They are tired, as their fathers were, and their grandfathers before them, of being caretakers. In the warm, gathering dusk of a southern Idaho evening, a man says, "You have to be a rancher to feel as deeply as we do. It's now a matter of having to stand and fight."

And the biggest fight of all is over wilderness.

The wilderness conflict remains one of the oldest and most violent in the West, stretching back a hundred years to the days of John Muir and the first western insurgency. Reborn in the Wilderness Act of 1964, renewed over the RARE and BLM inventories of the late 1970s, it remains one of the deepest, most passionate, most divisive issues in western life. Closure of the two inventories in 1979 only sharpened it, with the setting aside of 36 million acres of public domain for further wilderness review and possible removal from multiple use. Frightened and angry, antiwilderness forces have massed under the banner of the Sagebrush Rebellion to salvage what they can. They have until 1991 to influence BLM recommendations to Congress on its 25 million acres, but they have fewer years than that to influence Forest Service recommendations on its 10.8 million acres of "further study" lands. In 1913 fiery William Borah of Idaho said that "so far the West has been unable to see either the beauty or the benefits of tying up 200 million acres of timberlands." Seventy years later many still do not see it.

The wilderness issues of the 1980s are the same as they have always been. The insurgent philosophy is the same. The dissenters — cattlemen, lumbermen, miners — are the same. Like a play that never stops, the actors come and go. But the story never changes.

At the heart of the drama is the philosophical collision between the insurgent West and environmentalists. It is an ageless conflict. It was born in another generation and it will end in another. In the meantime, it underpins the wilderness war in this generation.

The issue itself is not complex. A hundred years ago environmentalists gave the West national forests — and the suffocating federal power that went with them. In the 1960s they gave the West the Wilderness Act, and more federal power. Today they seek yet more — more land, more power. Those who live on the land, survive on it, long ago drew the line. They see environmentalism as a malignancy that ate its way into the national mind a century ago and never stopped. In the broadest sense their hatred is indefensible — understandable, perhaps, but indefensible. What *is* defensible, however, is the western loathing of environmental *extremism*. In the name of the "greater good," argue its critics, it has suppressed three generations of westerners. And in many ways, they say, it does still.

In the minds of many westerners, environmental extremism is a fact. It appears clearly in the wilderness concept. It is subjective, difficult to gauge and define, but it does exist. And it does affect the West.

It is most apparent, perhaps, in the environmentalists' relentless drive for land. As the *Denver Post* said in an editorial in 1980, "What we're beginning to suspect in watching the environmentalists' game is that they want to go on adding endlessly to wilderness preserves."

The insurgent West believes it has wilderness enough. In 1973, even before RARE II, more than 33 million acres were locked up in western wilderness and primitive areas (including pending and study tracts). The West, even then, held nearly 38 percent of the nation's total wilderness. Nearly 9.5 percent of both Idaho and Wyoming were covered by federal wilderness areas — 12 million acres of land — and Wyoming's massive Bridger-Teton wilderness was (and remains) the largest in the continental United States. The West's two most arid states — Nevada and Arizona — contained 6 percent wilderness apiece, Montana 5.7 percent, Colorado 4.4 percent, and New Mexico and Utah each 2.5 percent. In January 1980, upon completion of RARE, the Forest Service recommended annexation of 15 million acres *more* to the wilderness system, including 4.7 million in Idaho, 4.2 in Colorado, 3.1 in Montana, 2.7 in Wyoming, 2.4 in Utah, 1.2 in Nevada, and just over 1.1 in Arizona and New Mexico. In November 1980 the figures were revised — Nevada's acreage skyrocketed to 4.7 million, Arizona's jumped to 2.7, Utah's to 2.2, and the projected acreage in Idaho, Colorado, New Mexico, Wyoming, and Montana fell.

In the end, of course, numbers themselves mattered little. What mattered was what they *said* — and they spoke eloquently. Many westerners had believed that the 1964 Wilderness Act closed the book on the wilderness question. But they were wrong. Barely a decade later RARE II and the BLM inventory opened it up again. Now, today, the West faces the addition of 36 million acres *more.* Like the *Post,* it has become convinced of one thing: that zealous conservationists will pursue land acquisition virtually forever, using every legal tactic at their command, whether or not the government can afford it, whether or not the people want it. Land for the sake of land, land so no one else can have it: to much of the West this is extremism.

The mood is rooted, too, in the environmentalists' overwhelming sense of possessiveness. Extremists routinely discount the West's proprietary feelings about its land. They scoff at James Watt's statement that westerners have a unique, emotional, and "different relationship" with the land that outsiders cannot understand. They assume, as they always have, that what Watt calls an "affinity" for the land is a mask for self-interest. With that assumption, they gave birth to the wilderness movement in the first place, acting, as the government has, as stewards of the public trust. At some point, though, during the past twenty years, the wilderness movement underwent a change; at some point much of it swung away from a sense of custodianship to a tenacious, jealous sense of higher-right ownership.

To the West, even the moderate West, this is a deep and disturbing pattern of thought that goes back to the first conservation era. There was a time, without doubt, that easterners seemed to view the western public lands as their own private domain, and countless examples exist of rich and genteel easterners — under the guise of "conservation" — attempting to lock up the West's mountains and valleys for their own enjoyment. Theodore Roosevelt himself used the White River wilderness as his own private hunting preserve. Because of patterns like this, settlers on the White opposed the forest reserve when it came as just another "dude design for an outdoor menagerie and museum." It was a scene played out over and over again across the West, and it still is. In 1979 a Craig woman complained bitterly that wilderness only "temporarily appeases the rabid environmentalists, virtually setting up a private preserve for the use and enjoyment of this minority. In the long run these withdrawals lead to the exclusion of the majority of citizens from the use and enjoyment of their own lands." In the same year an angry executive of the New Mexico Oil and Gas Association said, "It would appear that the eastern establishment regards states like New Mexico as their private playground. They say that it belongs to all the people in the federal Union; they say, 'Don't disturb our playground by putting an oil rig on top of some scenic mountain because we might vacation there next year.'" It is an old theme, and it has its irony. While many environmentalists argue that the land belongs to all, say the rebels, they sometimes forget that "all" includes westerners, too.

Finally, they add, extremism exists in the often obsessive environmentalist championship of wildlife and endangered species. More than one conservationist has been led to fight for a wilderness area for this reason alone. More than one has shown more apparent concern for the rights of coyotes and falcons and the desert tortoise than for the rights of westerners. Balancing man against animal, they choose animal.

Each choice, alone, seems insignificant. Winter range for deer. Grizzly habitat. Refuge for raptors, predators, for owls and eagles and mustangs. Free-flowing river for the humpbacked chub. Singly, the choices mean little, but cumulatively, they devastate. Loss of range. Loss of mineral land. Loss of crops.

Loss of life.

The environmentalists' attitude angers Sagebrush insurgents. Orrin Hatch bluntly says that America "has gone overboard to protect endangered species to the detriment of human beings." Whether protection "is really worth poverty for a number of human beings is an open question." Writing of the West in 1981, Stan Steiner, author of *The Ranchers: A Book of Generations,* has sadly reflected on the same strange reality. "Some of my environmentalist friends worry about saving the bald eagle and other endangered species," he has said. "I wish they'd become as concerned with saving *human* endangered species." Ranchers, Indians, rural Chicanos — "they're doomed people."

Many westerners, perhaps, do not understand environmentalist reasoning. But they do understand the mentality behind it. They understand — and this is what triggers their rage — that the champions of wilderness and wildlife often make their decisions from a distance, safe from impact, safe from consequences. Westerners have seen this before. They remember dark and distant days when non-westerners rode through their land in the brass and velvet splendor of Pullman cars — and plotted forest reserves that changed the course of their lives. The same syndrome still operates: from a distance, from a place of insulation, they save the helpless from the predators (or the predators from the helpless). From outside the West, or from their remote urban worlds *within* the West, they act. And at the point that what they do — *however* well-intentioned — impairs human life, it is extremist.

Sadly, environmentalist extremism (or at least the perception of it) has driven antienvironmentalist westerners to an extremism of their own. The rhetoric of the Sagebrush Rebellion is filled with anticonservation, antiwilderness, anti-eastern sentiment almost unparalleled in the West in this century. A disturbing current of paranoia taints it, diminishes its effect. But no one can argue that it is not justified. Nor can anyone argue that it holds no truth.

The rhetoric clearly reflects the insurgent perception of the wilderness movement. Former congressman Wayne Aspinall of Colorado has called the new conservers "misguided zealots." A Utah insurgent has called them a "cult" bent on "destroying traditional American freedoms." Orrin Hatch acidly labels them "selfish dandelion worshippers whose disdain for private property rights and just plain decency has not been equaled since the first American Revolution." James A. Weber, author of *Power Grab: The Conserver Cult and the Coming Energy Catastrophe,* has branded them the "conserver cult" — a "pseudo-religious, anti-technology, elitist movement" that "views the environment as sacred while denigrating people who use energy as unholy, mindless despoilers of nature." Beyond the West, even the *Wall Street Journal* has spoken of the "fanaticism" of a handful of people with a "Walden Pond vision of nature." But the most scathing denunciation in years has come from Irving Kristol, coeditor of *The Public Interest.* "There is now considerable evidence," he has said, "that the environmentalist movement has lost its self-control, that it is becoming an exercise in ideological fanaticism." To westerners who live on the land, the words ring true. It is the new zealots who elevate the rights of animals to those of men, who keep alive the endless wilderness process, who forge the rules for land they often never see, who keep the West off balance and unstable every day of its life. It is the zealots — not the moderates — that insurgent westerners fear.

Part of the wilderness conflict, then, is ideological. But it is also historical. Many westerners have hated environmentalists for so long that they know nothing else. The same is true of their feeling for the Forest Service. They have always disliked it. And, as much as anything else, it leads them to their negative position on wilderness today. Perhaps westerners are less afraid of *what* wilderness is than of *who* administers it.

In days past, western insurgents reserved a special contempt for the service. As late as 1907 Colorado's *Routt County Courier* blasted its "bossism" and "one-man rule" and the "tenderfeet," "unstable

theorists," and "pernicious carpetbaggers" who ruled the forest reserves from the East. In Williams, Arizona, cattlemen once suggested that federal "tree agents" — rangers — be hanged from the
trees they came to protect. A Meeker man, looking back on the
White River National Forest fifty years after its birth, recalled that
"Hitlerism had not been written into our language in those days,"
but Forest Service intervention was interpreted in the same way. In
a sense attitudes have not changed. Though the service is not so
despised as it once was, and though it is not the lightning rod for
western antagonism today that BLM is, many westerners continue
to see it in a negative light.

Sagebrush rebels still accuse it of inefficiency and arrogance. A
Wyoming newspaper has bluntly called the service "the glaring public land organizational misfit for seventy-five years." And a northern
Idaho woman recently criticized Forest Service insensitivity to local
people: "Their attitude is that we don't exist. We represent 200
million Americans but we're not part of them." Again, such attitudes
may partly be a matter of conditioning. But to deny the obvious —
the potential of an agency employing 22,000 people, administering
187 million acres of land, to do substantial local damage — would be
foolish.

The wilderness war is anchored in ideological and historical conflict. It is this, the hundred-year disagreement between the West and
the Forest Service and its environmental allies, that gives it its fire.
But there is more to the war than history and philosophy. It is more
than a culmination of ancient grievances, more than a collision of
ideologies. As much as anything else, it is a question of economics.

In a 1980 white paper, the Western Governors' Policy Office in
Denver clearly stated the problem. "Wilderness designation and
wildlife protection," wrote director Philip Burgess, "should not be
accomplished at the cost of livestock and agricultural production,
the traditional backbone of our western economy." Burgess omitted
mining, but he made his point. The worried West believes, simply,
that more wilderness means less economic opportunity. Mining and
energy interests fear loss of mineral lands. Cattlemen fear further
restrictions on the range. Lumbermen fear the withdrawal of prime
timberlands. None of this is new — neither the fears nor the reality.
Users of the public domain have always feared loss of their economic
base on the public lands — and through the years their fears often
have been more than justified.

Stockmen, already embattled on other fronts, clearly fear the worst on this one. They have collided with wilderness before. As far back as the late nineteenth century they fought against what a Utah sheepman called "those who would establish a feudal system in America and have large tracts of land set apart as reserves so some idealist or scientific expert might view dame nature in her primitive state." Little has changed since then. Not long ago a rancher in Gunnison County, Colorado, was told that he could maintain his canal through wilderness only with horses and hand tools because of its wilderness status. In Montana, sheep ranchers complain that they are being forced out of business by wilderness restrictions on summer range. This, in particular, is a growing problem everywhere. If the pattern holds, if wilderness continues its encroachment on the summer range of both cattlemen and sheepmen, the nation will get its wilderness. But the price it will pay will be the destruction of the ranching class. Worse, when bankrupt stockmen sell out to developers, condominium cities and parking lots will blossom next to every wilderness tract in the Rockies. Problems such as these — real where wilderness already exists, probable where it will exist later — are routine and unhappy parts of western life.

Lumber interests, too, expect the further constriction of an industry already beset by economic hard times. James Craine, head of the Federal Timber Purchasers' Association, has said, "We live in the United States of America and we have a responsibility . . . to help provide for the nation's needs. We cannot do so by being provincial, by insisting that the public lands be mothballed for some indefinite future generation. If we don't produce as much as we can, we will be shirking our responsibility to the rest of the nation."

Even without more wilderness, lumbermen are battered by environmentalists on every side. In Wyoming for example, five different organizations have filed appeals to stop timber harvesting in the Jack Creek region of Bridger National Forest on grounds that it would severely reduce local elk herds. All across the West, arguing that lumbering permits should be issued to private companies only when cutting could produce a profit, conservation groups have totally ignored the 1960 Multiple Use and Sustained Yield Act that authorizes the service to conduct lumbering at a loss for proper reasons. In Idaho an environmentalist coalition recently filed suit against the Forest Service to prevent further lumbering in parts of Payette and Boise national forests. Maintaining that logging will increase sediment 50 percent over natural levels along the Salmon River, the coalition hopes to protect the spawning grounds of salmon and steelhead — and the habitat of the gray wolf, peregrine falcon, and bald eagle. Elsewhere in Idaho other groups have waged the same fight — from East Meadow Creek in the Nez Perce to the Bighorn-Weitas roadless area in the Clearwater where they say logging threatens elk habitat and some of the highest-quality cutthroat streams in the Rockies. In the meantime, the timber industry has blamed environmentalists for closure of or production curtailment in 430 of the West and Northwest's 756 lumber mills in recent years, and for the local economic dislocation that has gone with it.

But no group has more to lose to wilderness than the West's mining and energy industries. For that reason, perhaps, no group — except cattlemen — has campaigned against wilderness with such ferocity. The tendency exists to dismiss them as unrepresentative of the West, but they are not. Perhaps no economic group in the region has the grassroots public support they do — partly because westerners, like others, vitally need what they produce, partly because many local economies depend on them, and partly because the vaunted miner's independence is part of the West's tradition. In any case, the mining and energy industries are a vital part of the Sagebrush Rebellion.

Their antiwilderness arguments are the same today as they were in the late 1970s when they erupted against RARE II and the BLM inventory. For that matter, their arguments are no different from the 1890s, when Nevada silver senator William Stewart wrote to the Anaconda Company that he would not rest until all forest reserves had been revoked. In 1980, Kye Trout, president of the Independent Petroleum Association of the Mountain States, complained that wilderness locks up productive lands in a "prison of overregulation" that "steals resources from the public and does dreadful harm to our public welfare." America's forefathers wisely set aside the public lands for use, he said, for the day the nation would need them. "That day now has come."

The arguments made by the industries are not without merit, particularly in the West where mining and energy production are integral parts of life. One hard fact is that any reduction in mining activities will cause layoffs and reduce revenue in regions that cannot afford it. More than one western town relies on mining for its existence; the collapse of Anaconda, though not because of wilderness, is graphic proof of what can happen to a community when mining dies.

More than this, increased wilderness threatens to choke off expanded mineral and energy production in a nation that seemingly cannot afford it. As in 1977 and 1978, when they made the same argument, oil companies vehemently say that expanded wilderness virtually will shut down their operations in many parts of the West. The first to go will be the small independents — the feisty, active, productive drillers of most of America's oil — who cannot long survive competitive leasing, competition with the giants, the windfall profits tax, bureaucracy, and wilderness, too. Larger companies will follow. Then the shock waves.

Sagebrush rebels preach energy independence. They see the wilderness thrust as myopic. In a blood-and-thunder speech in the spring of 1981, a Denver oilman spoke the thoughts of most:

> It is time for us to look homeward and quit courting disaster in the international arena — propping up dictators and sheikdoms until we have sucked the last drop of blood from their shores. Environmentalists must recognize the folly of this type of foreign policy . . . Our nation is situated on some of the richest hydrocarbon real estate in the world. Our moral obligation at home and abroad is to develop these resources in an environmentally responsible and economically achievable manner, but in the future it will become increasingly more difficult to justify the pristine inclinations of a few of our unsatisfied citizens.

It may be, of course, that energy independence is a will-o'-the-wisp, and it may be, again, that oil companies use it as a cover. But, at the same time, the argument also has an undeniable logic, and sooner or later environmentalists will have to hear it.

Among developers the "critical minerals" argument, too, gathers force by the day. In a world where Siberia and South Africa alone contain most of the earth's manganese, vanadium, chrome, iron ore, asbestos, and uranium, mining interests estimate that between 65 and 85 percent of the West's public lands today are closed entirely to resource exploration, that 40 million acres a year have been lost during the last ten years, and that the entire public domain will be closed in five years more. The creeping expansion of wilderness, they say, will mark its death. Again they ask how a nation importing many of its strategic metals from unfriendly or vulnerable friendly nations can lock up its own lands. They ask how a nation can import tungsten for light bulbs, potassium for fertilizer, platinum for pollution control, cobalt for jet engines — and lock up its own lands.

The major problem is the law, or, more precisely, the way it is written. The Wilderness Act stipulates that no new mining exploration may be conducted on wilderness areas after December 31, 1983. Nor can it be carried out effectively on interim or further-study lands in the meantime. In Utah, for example, a critic has said that one typical tract of inventory land near Moab contains ninety-six uranium fields, seven gas fields, four oil fields, six tar sands areas, and large amounts of oil-impregnated coal and rock, none of which can be touched. The same kind of complaint has surfaced everywhere — that gas, oil, uranium, and molybdenum are locked in and under withdrawn lands, inaccessible because of unreasonable law and equally unreasonable Forest Service and BLM guidelines.

Arguments to the contrary, the problem *does* exist. Energy resources lie unfound and untapped. Critical minerals lie undiscovered and unusable. The balance between wilderness preservation and energy exploration seems to have been lost, the rebels say.

In the 1980s, as the mining and energy interests fight to retain what they believe is theirs, they already have been stopped on several key fronts. Environmentalists promising to "harass the hell" out of the National Cooperative Refineries Association have halted the company's attempt to drill for oil in the Cache Creek Canyon area near Jackson, Wyoming. Not far away, where Getty Oil has proposed to drill in Little Granite Creek Canyon in the recommended Gros Ventre Wilderness, the Jackson Chamber of Commerce has allied with Earth First to stop it. Earth First's environmentalists, vowing to make the fight for Little Granite the "Diablo Canyon of the environmental movement," have made plans to occupy the region's roads in order to keep bulldozers out. Faced with mounting conservationist hostility, energy developers increasingly have turned to the courts for redress. In May 1980, for example, the Rocky Mountain Oil and Gas Association filed suit against the Department of the Interior to relax its mining regulations in wilderness study areas. The charge was an old and familiar one: that federal regulations for study areas — intended to protect potential wilderness during study — were stricter than on wilderness areas themselves, and that because of this, they killed exploration. In

November a federal court in Cheyenne agreed. In the summer of 1981 the Mineral Hills Mining District and Central Idaho Mining Association launched a campaign to reduce the boundaries of the Sawtooth National Recreation Area. Fighting for the exclusion of the Boulder and White Cloud mountains — "one of the most mineralized, productive, and promising regions in Idaho" — they argued that through administrative action the Forest Service has extended the area far beyond the original intent of Congress. On Montana's Kootenai National Forest the American Smelting and Refining Company is locked in a court fight with environmentalists over copper and silver lodes in the Cabinet Mountains Wilderness Area. At issue here is one of the last remaining grizzly habitats in America. And in Wyoming a consortium of three companies has filed a court challenge to federal rejection of its application for gas and oil exploration in the Teton Wilderness.

The battle also rages in Congress. One fight is over "old" wilderness. A second is over "new." A third involves the entire wilderness process itself. And all three give indications that the wilderness struggle has just begun.

In western Montana, where the Overthrust Belt flows beneath the Continental Divide, debate has begun over the mineral and energy potential of the old Bob Marshall Wilderness Area. In the late 1970s, supported by the Mountain States Legal Foundation, energy companies denied exploration permits on the Marshall filed suit against the Forest Service and won. Exploration began, not only on the Marshall, but on the nearby Great Bear and Lincoln-Scapegoat wildernesses as well — 1.5 million acres of energy-rich land. But in May 1981, invoking "emergency powers" granted it under FLPMA that in effect nullified the court ruling, the House Interior Committee banned further exploration and leasing in the region until January 1, 1984. On December 16, 1981, a federal judge upheld the ruling itself, but determined that only the secretary of the interior could "determine the scope and the duration of the withdrawal." So the issue rests today.

With some cause, energy companies have bitterly assailed the "emergency powers" clause. In the case of the Bob Marshall, it was invoked on grounds that exploratory methods in the region — the detonation of above-ground dynamite charges — endangered another of America's last remaining grizzly habitats. But companies banned from the wilderness argue that the controversy is not an emergency. They claim that seismic exploration causes no damage, nor do access roads or drill pads.

Similar controversy also exploded on New Mexico's Capitan Wilderness Area in the summer and fall of 1981. Angered by Interior approval of oil drilling on the Capitan without any advance notice to Congress, Representative Manuel Lujan threatened to introduce a resolution (which also would have invoked FLPMA's emergency provision) banning all further oil, gas, and mineral exploration anywhere in the American wilderness system. Not until he received assurances from James Watt that no further leases would be granted for the system until June 1, 1982 (and only then with extensive prior environmental study and thirty days' advance notification of Congress), did Lujan back away from his threat.

Exploration companies have raged against both actions, believing that their right to explore until 1984 has been abridged by congressional fiat. Dave Schaenen, president of the Rocky Mountain Oil and Gas Association, has condemned Lujan's action as an attempt "to subvert the law by very questionable means," to skirt the will of Congress "by the use of a parliamentary device." The argument is made, too, that the emergency powers clause was never intended to be used as it has been on the Bob Marshall.

It is a fact: in creating the Wilderness Act, Congress expressly kept mining options open for twenty years. It was its clear intent to lock up wilderness only *after* comprehensive mineral searching had taken place, and only *after* the impact of wilderness on national economy and security could be assessed. The emergency powers clause, in particular — granting Congress the power to prohibit mining where and when it endangers wilderness "values" — is as murky as the values themselves. The reality, say the Sagebrush insurgents, is that the spirit of the Wilderness Act has been violated. The reality is, too, that energy companies have experienced firsthand the kind of federal power that has angered western land users for years — precisely the kind that fuels the Sagebrush Rebellion.

Yet another controversy has erupted over Colorado wilderness — and again mining interests are in the thick of it.

In 1980, in the wake of the RARE study, the federal wilderness system was expanded in four Rocky Mountain states; including the spectacular Alaska lands bill, 60 million acres of land were added to America's wilderness network, bringing its total acreage to 80 million. In the Rockies, 600,000 acres were added to New Mexico,

60,000 to Montana, and — over the bitter opposition of its two insurgent senators — the 2.2 million acre River of No Return Wilderness was added to Idaho. One and a quarter million acres were added to Colorado's wilderness system after a combative year-long debate involving environmentalists, mining interests, and a handful of eastern congressmen. More than any other wilderness contest before Congress, the Colorado fight illustrated the deep and painful divisiveness of the issue.

In the fall of 1979 Colorado Congressmen Ray Kogovsek and Jim Johnson introduced a bill to incorporate 1.1 million acres of Colorado into the nation's wilderness system. Controversy dogged it from the beginning. As a concession to the environmentalist House Interior Committee (which later shut down mining in the Bob Marshall), the bill contained no provision to release 4.5 million acres of further-study lands to development while the study took place. In effect, the 4.5 million remained as much wilderness as the 1.1 million. The committee, chaired by conservationist Morris Udall of Arizona, reported the bill to the House; in December, raising its acreage to 1.3 million, the House passed the bill. But conflict began to build over the release issue.

In the Senate, Gary Hart introduced a Colorado wilderness bill in December, calling for the reservation of 1.5 million acres. Believing that release language would kill the bill in a Senate dominated by environmentalists, Hart, too, omitted it. But, speaking for economic interests fighting the indefinite loss of 4.5 million acres of developable land, William Armstrong offered a substitute 1.2 million-acre bill in May 1980 that provided for the release of study lands, and proposed to extend the 1984 mining deadline in the original Wilderness Act as well. Armstrong had strong support in Colorado. The *Denver Post,* for one, said notice finally had been served on environmentalist groups that "United States policy doesn't contemplate endless creation of wilderness and that we are starting to put on the brakes." Armstrong, it concluded, had pointed out "how the wilderness lobbies still try to run the nation's huge multiple-purpose resource preserves as if they were a private playpen for environmentalists."

A Hart-Armstrong compromise was reached by the fall of 1980: acreage was pegged at 1.4 million acres and release language was included. The bill was passed by the Senate in September. House and Senate conference committee hearings in October and November featured daily clashes between antiwilderness forces and easterners

objecting to a proposed policy amendment to the Colorado bill de-
claring that the time for endless wilderness legislation was over. In
time the controversy died. The amended Colorado bill passed the
House and Senate in December 1980. One and a quarter million acres
were protected as wilderness, 4.3 million acres were returned to
multiple use, and nearly a half million acres were frozen for three-
year study to determine whether they were or were not suitable for
wilderness.

Resentment and anger trailed in the wake of the Colorado Wilderness Act. Despite its release language, many Coloradans — especially those living near wilderness areas, those dependent upon wilderness resources — opposed it. The National Cattlemen's
Association insisted that language protecting livestock grazing was
vague and open to legal challenge. The Colorado Resource Consortium and the Rocky Mountain Oil and Gas Association maintained
that the release language was too weak. Colorado Counties, Incorporated, specifically charged that the wilderness blanket thrown over
the San Juan Mountains would cripple poor and sparsely populated
Conejos County. The law, said the organization, "represents the
insensitivity of the environmentalists."

Almost immediately, the mining interests moved in on the released
land. More important, they contested further-study land. In May
1981 they won the right to explore on Quartz Creek near Montezuma
Peak in southwestern Colorado. But they stumbled against Oh Be
Joyful.

During conference committed hearings in the winter of 1980 one
of the biggest collisions between environmentalists and Colorado
development interests was over a small, rugged, mountain-dotted
enclave called Oh Be Joyful, near Crested Butte. Because of its
beauty, environmentalists sought to include it in wilderness;
Kogovsek and Armstrong led the fight against it. In the end neither side won; Oh Be Joyful was designated study land. In June
1981, claiming the presence of lead, zinc, and molybdenum in the
region, the Forest Service determined that Oh Be Joyful should be
returned to multiple use. But so far both the Forest Service and
AMAX — owner of more than half of the two hundred mining
claims on the land — have been stymied by environmentalist protests. Where the contest will end, no one can say. But all can agree
that it is both ugly and far from over.

The incidents at Bob Marshall and Oh Be Joyful and on the

Capitan long ago convinced the mining and energy industries that they cannot fight wilderness on a piecemeal basis. For half a dozen years, Anaconda, AMAX, and Amoco have sought a uniform general mining law to allow mineral production in wilderness areas for the next quarter century. Now, in alliance with the Rocky Mountain Oil and Gas Association, the National Association of Manufacturers, the American Cattlemen's Association, the Federal Timber Purchasers' Association, and other prodevelopment groups, they have banded together behind the RARE Review Act of 1981 — the developer's answer to RARE, wilderness, and the environmentalist mentality.

The bill, written by Senator S. I. Hayakawa of California and introduced into the Senate in the spring of 1981, is one of the bluntest legislative attacks on environmentalists in a decade. Essentially, as written, it would destroy de facto wilderness forever. Congress would be required to act on the 15 million RARE acres recommended for wilderness within the next four years; failure to do so automatically would return them to commercial development and recreation. At the same time Congress would have six years to decide on the disposal of the 11 million further-study acres; failure to act also would return them to multiple use.

Land users believe the law is just. William Swan, president of the American Cattlemen's Association, has said that it will guarantee the end of lawmaking for the West in the courts and federal bureaus. Malcolm Wallop, James McClure, and the West's other Sagebrush senators have agreed. So has the Reagan administration, which has given the bill early support. John Crowel, Jr., assistant secretary of agriculture for natural resources and environment, has adamantly said that "new wilderness areas should not be lands which have productive capability for other urgently needed goods and services." Passage of the Hayakawa bill will provide for "a much needed end to the frustrating cycles of delay and uncertainty" that have plagued the West during the wilderness years.

Perhaps it is time.

*   *   *

In the spring of 1981 James McClure spoke softly of the revolution building about him. "How do we get the federal government out of our way?" he asked. "How do we get them off our backs? We want to be free. We don't think we have to bargain for our freedom. We thought we were guaranteed that freedom. What we seek is the opportunity to live our own lives and make our own decisions."

Freedom. In pursuit of it the West's grievances are endless. They span the depth and breadth of western life and they reach back through a hundred years of colonial history. They are real, felt from the heart, sharpened by memories of the past and fears of the future. As the West plays out the 1980s, however, the important question is what kind of action they translate into. It is here — what they *do* with their anger — that Sagebrush rebels will make or break the West.

The spirit of Sagebrush ripples through the courts, through the legislatures, across the face of the land itself. Challenges to the MX and RARE, to the hit list and BLM inventory were shots fired in anger, shots in a revolution. Insurgency spoke in the Reagan landslide and in much of the West's militant advocacy of James G. Watt. And it has spoken through its own lawless actions. Violence already has erupted in Roswell, Kingman, Escalante, Challis, and Battle Mountain, and it is far from over. In Utah in 1979, Grand County commissioners defied a BLM order closing access to Negro Bill Canyon near Moab and the county sheriff ordered the arrest of any BLM employee who attempted to enforce it. A year later, near the same place, a county road superintendent in a bulldozer destroyed a road to the proposed Mill Creek Wilderness. It was the Fourth of July, and people cheered beneath American flags.

Though Sagebrush has taken many forms, it has unfolded mainly on the floors of state legislatures. It is here, ultimately, that it will be won or lost.

The Nevada land bill of 1979 launched the Rebellion in western legislatures. Its purpose was — and is — to draw the federal government into a court test to determine, once and for all, whether state or federal sovereignty prevails on the unappropriated Nevada public domain. In 1981 the law was amended to establish payment in lieu of taxes to the counties by the state, to guarantee public access to public lands sold to private individuals, and to prohibit state disposal of land for reasons other than agricultural development, public recreation, and vital community expansion. In every other respect — in all essential respects — it remained the same.

The first Nevada bill triggered a rash of similar ones all across the West. Wyoming — whose defiance of the fifty-five-mile-an-hour speed limit was one of the first events in the Rebellion — passed

H.B.6, effective March 10, 1980. Concurring with a Sublette legislator that no reason existed "why Wyoming should remain a colony while states east of the Mississippi keep all of their lands," the legislature passed the only Sagebrush law in the West to include both BLM *and* Forest Service lands. New Mexico followed, empowering its state land board to take control of 13 million acres of BLM land effective May 14, 1980. On July 1 of the same year Utah passed a land cession law. Two weeks later, over the veto of Governor Babbitt — his first override in twenty-nine straight votes — Arizona enacted S.B.1012. Only Montana and Colorado remain out of the fold.

Sagebrush forces have conducted a fierce legislative fight in Colorado. In the spring of 1981 Republicans Maynard Yost of Crook and Joseph Winkler of Castle Rock introduced S.B.170 to turn over 16 million acres of national forest and 8 million acres of BLM land to the state by 1983. Like most rebels, Yost was outspoken in his belief that "lands held by the federal government are a burden on the state of Colorado. The state could administer them better than the absentee federal landlord." Echoing the thoughts of insurgents in every part of the West, Yost said that "a little revolution is a good thing." From Meeker, a hotbed of insurgency ninety years before the Sagebrush Rebellion, Nick Theos agreed: "Resources have been put on this earth for man to develop." A land transfer bill — "a little revolution" — would ensure it in Colorado.

In the end it amounted to nothing. S.B.170 was vetoed in the summer of 1981 — and the veto was sustained when scornful urban Democrats stood against it. Very likely, though, like the phoenix, it will return again. If the Rebellion has flagged anywhere in the West, it has not in the legislatures.

But a larger war looms on the floors of Congress.

In the fall of 1979, with eleven cosponsors by his side, Orrin Hatch of Utah introduced S.1680 — the so-called Western Lands Distribution and Regional Equalization bill — into the Senate. Like state Sagebrush bills, its implications, on a national level, were staggering. Providing for the "cession and conveyance to the states of federally owned, unreserved, unappropriated lands," the bill proposed the largest land transfer in American history — 544 million acres from the federal government to thirteen western states. Hatch's motives were clear, reflecting his perception of the West's troubled relationship with federal government. He spoke often of "thousands of new jobs, millions of acres of land and billions of dollars in new profits" that would accrue to a free West. Development of minerals, in particular, would provide a "mother lode" of new revenue. Return of "rightful title to certain lands" to the states would begin a process of transfer to counties, then to private individuals. At an emotional meeting of the League for Advancement of States' Equal Rights in Salt Lake City in 1980, Hatch eloquently spoke of the end result:

> Seldom in life does one participate in an event which is obviously of great historical significance. The building of a Panama Canal, the placing of a man on the moon, these are uniquely spectacular events which future generations cannot forget. We are participants in just such an experience . . . The vesting of the ownership and management of the public domain with the respective western governments means a rebirth of the power and prestige of state government — and a long overdue withdrawal of the massive dominance and power of the federal bureaucracies over the West.

For the moment, however, it was not to be. Opposed by the powerful Senate Energy and Natural Resources Committee, the bill stalled. Hatch received firm support from Senators Barry Goldwater (Arizona), Howard Cannon (Nevada), and Ted Stevens (Alaska), and James McClure gave it passing support "because of the symbolism involved." But it was not enough. The stalking horse died.

Undaunted, Hatch reintroduced his bill in 1981, this time in tandem with an almost identical House bill written by Jim Santini of Nevada. The new Hatch bill, S.1245, provided for the transfer of 460 million acres of federal land to the states, exempting only national parks, wilderness, wildlife habitat, and Indian lands; the Santini bill differed only in that it excluded national forests. To forestall fears of a western land grab, both bills included strict requirements for land disposal.

For many Sagebrush rebels cession is the ultimate goal of the revolution. They will settle for nothing less. Over and over again insurgent westerners have said that the West can manage its lands better, more effectively, more humanely than the federal government. As Hatch has said, "We love our lands. People who live in the states have much deeper feelings and concerns about the states than the federal bureaucrats." It is a valid and important point, this "love" of land. It is one of the oldest and most dominant themes in western history — western men and women developing a sense of emotional possession from their private and personal history on the land. More than nonwesterners can possibly understand, it infuses Sagebrush. Cynics may dismiss it, but westerners cannot. As Nevada rebel Dean Rhoads has said, "The people who really love the land and are going to live there will take the best care of it." This is the rationale for cession — and it should not be ignored.

On the other hand, cession is not the primary goal of other rebels. To many it is, instead, a threat, a bluff, a means to an end. Many rebels understand the obvious: that cession is not likely, not now, not ever. So, cunningly, they have used the issue — played on it — to extort what they *really* want: improved federal *management* of the public domain. William Armstrong has commented that "this movement is more like the Boston Tea Party than a land grab," and Colorado legislator Tillman Bishop has said, more frankly, that "the federal government is not going to give us back this land. We're [just] trying to get their attention." Western pragmatists argue that the failure of cession would matter little; by simply *creating* the issue they have already begun to achieve what they wanted — bringing national focus to western issues, improving field management by the Forest Service and BLM, forcing executive and congressional concessions to the West, and still keeping alive the possibility of actual cession in the future, particularly in urban "checkerboard" areas. Still, the process has only begun. Governor List of Nevada believes that the rebellion "has gotten the government's attention," but he also believes that Sagebrush will "remain a priority among the states" until western-federal relations change radically. Until then, he says, the West will "get the most mileage out of it" that it can.

What will happen now, time will tell. But one thing is certain: with western power on the increase in Congress, no Sagebrush bill can easily be dismissed. In James McClure and Steve Symms of Idaho, Jake Garn and Orrin Hatch of Utah, Paul Laxalt and Howard Cannon of Nevada, Alan Simpson and Malcolm Wallop of Wyoming, and Pete Domenici of New Mexico, the West has nine powerful Sagebrush rebels in the Senate — twelve with the occasional alliance of Goldwater, Stevens, and Armstrong. And Santini has allies in the House. As long as rebels are there, as long as they have leverage and power, they will continue to try to fill what Wallop has called the "void [that] exists in public understanding of the West." Failing that, they will continue to fan the flames of insurgency as the Tellers and the Borahs and the Thomas Clarks did on the same floors nearly a century ago.

"The serfs are rebellious," says James McClure. And so they will remain.

In whatever arena the war is fought now, the insurgent West will seek what it has always sought. Sovereign rights. A share of public-lands management. Partnership with the federal government in decision making. The power to regulate private activities on public lands. A redefinition of federalism. An end to what John Connally has called the "unrelenting injustice and hostility" of federal bureaus.

Victory will kill some of the anger, blunt the memories of the past. It will fulfill Orrin Hatch's dream of a "rebirth of the power and prestige of state government." It will liberate the West.

It will calm the storm.

CHAPTER TEN

The Dark Riders

Is it a coincidence that ranchers, miners, energy companies, right-wing organizations and foundations have suddenly come together to express a newly found philosophical concern over public land management? Or is it big money, the mother's milk of American politics? What gives the Sagebrush Rebellion its motivation? Is it a new-found concern for the public welfare or the driving dream of plunder?

DR. BERNARD SHANK
Utah environmentalist

SAGEBRUSH REBELLION.

To the westerner, for an instant, the words have color and power, and they fill the mind with imagery. Sagebrush plains, wild and untamed as the men who ride them. Men in revolt. Iron men with iron will, standing against federal tyranny. Strong, bronze-faced, steely-eyed men. Zane Grey men. Pioneer men, American men.

Western men at Lexington Bridge.

Image is part of the West. It always has been — part of its folklore, its mythology, its history. And through the long years nothing in it has been more constant than the image of western men against the odds — man against Indian, man against nature, man against himself. It is buried deep and lastingly in the western psyche, deep enough, lastingly enough, that it colors the way westerners look at every aspect of their lives. Often, the complex becomes simplistic, gray becomes black and white, and every challenge becomes a wrong, an affront to be avenged. Sagebrush — a revolt against government, against government by tyranny — is classic. Mountain men revolted against wilderness. Sodbusters revolted against cattle kings. Miners revolted against corporations. And Populists — the essence of western man — revolted against the whole stultifying oppression of eastern economic imperialism.

Now, Sagebrush rebels revolt against federal government.

For an instant, in the mind, the image appears. Buffalo men and gold hunters, homesteaders and cowboys. Riders of the Purple Sage. William Jennings Bryan thundering against the Cross of Gold. Defiance, pride, power. Sagebrush rebels: their war is righteous. The westerner knows. The past tells him so.

The moment gone, the image dissolves, and as it must, reality appears. Slowly, Sagebrush comes into relief as what it *really* is — a murky fusion of idealism and greed that may not be heroic, nor righteous, nor even intelligent. Only one certainty exists — that Sagebrush is a revolt against federal authority, and that its taproot grows deep in the century's history. Beyond this, it is incoherent. Part hypocrisy, part demagoguery, partly the honest anger of honest people, it is a movement of confusion and hysteria and terrifyingly destructive potential. What it is no one fully understands. What it will do no one can tell. But, anchored in myth, in the past, the image sits at the edge of the western mind and colors western thought. And even those who do not believe in the image must beware of it.

The core issue of the Sagebrush Rebellion is public lands — federal ownership and regulation. The cause of western anger is clear, but what is not clear is the exact nature of the revolt against it — what the rebels propose to do, how they propose to do it, and exactly what they seek from it.

As the preceding chapter revealed, on one level the Rebellion is a legal movement on the part of the western states to reclaim land once considered theirs. On another it is simply a tactic to force more responsible federal regulation of the land. In one sense, it is a legal war against the federal government, its objective nothing less than the formal cession of the public lands to the states in which they lie. In another sense, it is not a war at all, and cession is not a goal. It is, instead, what Senator William Armstrong has called a "plea for attention" — a political crusade mixed with hard talk and backcountry demagoguery designed to force Washington into improved public-lands management. In the summer of 1981 Guy Martin, former assistant secretary of the interior for land and water resources, called Sagebrush the "neon-lit sum total of every beef every individual ever had against the federal government." If this is true, the central issue still remains public lands. But whether federal abuses are to be challenged in court, in the media, or in the political arena, and whether the rebels' goal is land cession or improved management are critical unanswered questions. In fact, there are two rebellions, not one, and it is their fuzzy dualism that at least partly undercuts whatever legitimacy the movement ever might have had.

The Rebellion has been damaged by its confusion, but it has been further damaged by its greed.

Again, image intrudes into reality, the past colors the present. In the mind's eye the homesteader stands at his cabin door, ready to fight for land that is his, ready to make it productive, ready to build and civilize. We must have our land, he says. We must have freedom. We are not colonies. We are sovereign. Emotionally, it is easy to stand with him. Today's westerner, like him, is a little man at heart, a rebel. Westerners understand his ferocity. They know his pain. What he said a hundred years ago is still said now. "We're asking nothing more than control over our destinies," says Paul Laxalt. It is instinctive to agree. It is embedded, ingrained.

And it is wrong.

What westerners forget — what the image does not show — is that every insurgent movement in western history has been anchored in self-interest and greed. They have softened the thought, translated greed into "civilizing" and "building," but that has not altered the fact that the idealized frontiersman often was a grasping, ambitious entrepreneur more interested in exploitation than in civilizing. Looking to the past, held hostage by romantic imagery that blurs reality, westerners still see the age-old fight for land as a legitimate battle for the little man's rights. Much of the Sagebrush Rebellion is honest dissent, the legitimate anger of small men, as one has said, "tired of being pistol-whipped by the bureaucrats and dry-gulched by federal regulations." But, like similar movements of the past, it also is rooted in selfishness.

What westerners also forget is that much of the century's protest has been fueled by big interests seeking monopoly, not by little pioneers seeking their "fair share." And they fail to understand that this has not changed, that the interests are still there — big cattlemen, big loggers, energy giants — sometimes hard to see, but there nonetheless. And that they speak the same rhetoric of revolt, with the same passion, as little men. Hearing them, it is convenient, instinctive, for westerners to invoke the image of the noble frontiersman. But the image is inaccurate; the noble frontiersman is dead. The spoilsman is not.

Nevada state senator Clifton Young has called the Rebellion a "combination of avarice, demagoguery, and animosity," and a Utah environmentalist has bluntly said that "the nervous smell of money hangs over everything the Sagebrush rebels do." This is the reality of Sagebrush. It is a cause for honest but misguided people. But it also is a cynical raid by selfish political and economic interests on public sanctuary in the name of the public good.

Whoever they are, whatever they want, the Sagebrush rebels have been called "dark riders on our land." And now, what they say, what they do, may shape its life forever.

* * *

The Sagebrush Rebellion sprang from the West's grassroots. Those who say it did not are wrong. Speaking of the movement's New Mexico origins — and it is typical of the rest of the West — Senator Pete Domenici has said that the Rebellion's "genesis" was "with the average user of the public domain." In the mid- and late 1970s, as the West swelled with anger, it was small grazers and lumbermen and shoestring backcountry mining operators who felt it first and voiced it most. From the beginning, cattlemen stood out, apart from the rest, the angriest and most militant of the lot. But even they, says Domenici, were small operators, not large ones, heading "long-standing families" that had ranched the land for generations. "They're not monsters," he concludes, "not terribly rich." Like their parents and grandparents before them, "they are tied to the earth and tied to a ranch house," trying to survive.

In the beginning, at least, like other western insurgencies before it — silverism, Populism, anticonservationism — Sagebrush was given birth by little people. The Rebellion was Joe Stocks of Moab, who wrote that "the peasants in the West are protecting their rights to the use and wealth of the land." It was Tom Spencer fighting coyotes in Pueblo County. It was Bud Eppers fighting BLM along the Pecos.

It was Gerald Chaffin burning his home in Wyoming.

Sagebrush was — and largely it remains — a kind of primal scream from the land, and it still comes chiefly from the minds and hearts of the land's little people.

But if revolt was born at the grassroots, it did not long stay there. At some point it began to change. It never lost its little people. They remained. They remain still. But over the years, whether they understood it or not, accepted it or not, their movement was joined by others — large-scale operators, often not western, all of them suddenly speaking the same fiery rhetoric, adopting the same defiant posturing. Small stockmen were joined by large ones. Small logging companies and mining companies were joined by large ones. And all of them were joined by a phalanx of energy corporations, land speculators, real-estate developers, and politicians. As new joined old, as large economic interest joined small, the nature of the Sagebrush Rebellion radically changed.

Whatever it once was, Sagebrush no longer belongs to little people alone. The arena now is shared with the interests. Whatever the movement once was, now it is half theirs.

At the forefront of the Rebellion stand the Utah-based League for the Advancement of States' Equal Rights (LASER) and the thousand-member Sagebrush Rebellion, Incorporated, of Boise. They are flanked by the powerful Sagebrush senators and a handful of maverick western governors and state legislatures. But in the shadows, where the power lies, are large special economic interests. Farmers are represented by the American Farm Bureau Federation and by state organizations such as the Colorado Farm Bureau. The powerful National Woolgrowers' Association and National Cattlemen's Association represent stockmen — still the nucleus of revolt. Behind the logging giants stand the Federal Timber Purchasers' Association, the National Association of Home Builders, and smaller organizations such as Colorado's Productive Resources group. Large mining interests are scattered throughout the Rebellion — the American Mining Congress, the Central Idaho Mining Association, Anaconda, the Minerals Exploration Coalition, and AMAX. And above all loom the energy interests — the Independent Petroleum Association of the Mountain States, American Quasar Petroleum, the Westland Companies, Rocky Mountain Oil and Gas Association, ARCO, Chevron, Exxon, Mobil, Occidental Petroleum, Shell, and Gulf. They are as much a part of Sagebrush as Gerald Chaffin.

They may, in fact, be more.

As important as who they are is what they want — and what they want is control of the public domain to their own ends. Warning westerners that "public land swindles are an old tradition" in the region, that "land grabbing is the oldest con game in the West," Governor Bruce Babbitt has said that "behind the mask the Sagebrush crowd is really nothing but a special-interest group whose real goal is to get public lands into private ownership, fenced off and locked up for private use." Others see the movement the same way. A consortium of conservation groups has branded the revolt the "Sagebrush ripoff, the latest in a long series of attempts by exploiters to rip off public property" for their own benefit. An angry Utah environmentalist has asked whether the sudden convergence of "ranchers, miners, energy companies, right-wing organizations and foundations" to "express a newly found concern over public-land management" is simply a matter of coincidence. "Or is it big money," he asks, "the mother's milk of American politics? What gives the Sagebrush Rebellion its motivation? Is it a new-found concern for the public welfare or the driving dream of plunder?"

The assessment of former Nevada governor Mike O'Callahan is as accurate as any. "What started out as a series of legitimate complaints," he has said, "now has degenerated into a special-interest raid on the public domain." Probably this is true, and if it is, it has ample precedent in western history. More than once in the past the West's power class has manipulated western commoners and their movements to its own ends. And, more than once, its own ends have included the plundering of the public domain. To the extent that the assessment is valid, to the extent that powerful economic interest groups have usurped Sagebrush from its creators, it is a tragedy. If the Rebellion were all that it seems at first glance — a spontaneous movement of frustrated westerners to destroy federal injustice in their midst — it would be justifiable beyond question. Its goal of land cession would be unacceptable, but the movement itself would withstand challenge. But the interests have perverted Sagebrush. Because of their own selfish goals, they have undermined the credibility of small farmers and stockmen with real grievances. They have cheapened the protest of grassroots rebels. They have destroyed the movement's original meaning and its once-real legitimacy. Most frightening of all, they have made it a menace to the West itself and to all of its people.

To the extent that the Sagebrush Rebellion has become a front for selfish interests, it is reprehensible.

Whoever the rebels are, whatever it is they want, their entire protest rests on the established and unquestioned assumption of federal injustice on the public lands. Without this issue they have no issue at all. Without it they have no rebellion.

But the assumption is questionable. No one who knows the West can deny that injustice exists on the public domain. At the same time, though, it is true that westerners often exaggerate it. Some do it for effect, building rationale to justify their own excesses. Others, in their paranoia, simply misperceive reality. They see oppressors where there are none. Whatever, the result is often distortion of reality. And upon it, consciously or not, the Rebellion has built and rested its case.

Westerners still tell stories of old days on the western range when their grandfathers buckled and broke under the weight of government by bureau. Many of the stories they tell are true. Others are not. But they underscore the fact that the theme of government by bureau — by BLM or any of the others — is as emotional now as it ever was then.

Again, there is truth in the charge that the life of the West is dictated by bureaus — and that the governance often is flawed. The federal government's public-lands bureaucracy has an almost unbroken history of inefficiency in the American West. No reformer ever conquered it — not Franklin Roosevelt, whose Harold Ickes tried and failed in the 1930s, not the Hoover Commission in the 1950s, not Jimmy Carter, whose proposed Department of Natural Resources died a quick death in the 1970s, not so far, James G. Watt. Bureaucratic inertia and congressional hostility have killed change for a hundred years, and likely they will kill it for another hundred. Meanwhile, the Sagebrush Rebellion has a volatile and timeless issue.

Wherever cattlemen and others gather to talk of government by bureau, they speak first of BLM. It has been a lightning rod for western rage every day, every year since passage of FLPMA in 1976. Charges against it are many and serious: betrayal of America's commitment to land disposal through implementation of FLPMA, arrogance in the field, destruction of the range industry through grazing cutbacks, failure to control mustangs and predators, gross financial mismanagement. Some of the charges are accurate, but some are not — and virtually all of them have been slanted at one time or another to reflect the land users' point of view.

Again, in a very real sense, FLPMA could be considered a breach of trust. But if it was, it was westerners, not outsiders, who initiated it. Edward Taylor, whose 1934 grazing bill first began to trend toward public-land retention, was an Illinois-born Coloradan and one of the most passionate anticonservationists in the West in the early twentieth century. And the 1970 Federal Land Law Review Commission that proposed FLPMA in the first place — in order to retain federal lands in federal control — was dominated by westerners. Fourteen of nineteen men who expressly concluded that "most public lands would not serve the maximum public interest in private ownership" were from the West. And its chair, Colorado congressman Wayne Aspinall, was, like Taylor, one of the staunchest champions of western rights in this century.

If insurgent westerners oppose FLPMA, they have only their brothers to blame.

Mustangs are another timeless issue. Sagebrush rebels have presented it as a classic case of BLM incompetence, of misgovernment by bureau. It may be. Or it may be a red herring created by western cattlemen to mask their own incompetence.

Whatever its past attitude, BLM has made a major effort since 1980 to control the West's wild horse population. Since 1971, in fact, it has spent $27 million on the effort. BLM's novel "adopt-a-horse" program, steering a difficult course between extreme conservationists calling for protection and extreme stockmen calling for extermination, has barely appeased either side. In the spring of 1981 BLM charged $85 a head to round up and give away wild horses, running its program at a deficit of $115 a horse. Since that time government costs have risen to $325 per horse and the adoption cost has risen only to $145 at the most (specifically kept low in order to encourage adoptions). In fiscal 1981 BLM expected to spend $4.4 million on adoptions even in times of deep federal retrenchment. How much longer BLM can afford its program is questionable. Director Bob Burford has said that of the 70,000 horses remaining on the public domain, 44,000 must be removed or killed soon. Whatever happens, at least cattlemen cannot complain that BLM does not respond to their problem. Burford, a rancher himself, has clearly said that because of wild horses "range conditions in many herd areas worsen by the year. If horses and burros are allowed to destroy the range, they destroy it for all." If BLM was insensitive to the mustang problem in the past, or incompetent, it is not now. In this sense, mustangs no longer can be a Sagebrush issue.

It is possible, in fact, that they never should have been an issue at all. The possibility exists that wild horses often are blamed for overgrazing done by the stockmen's own herds. As late as the summer of 1981, Wyoming Advocates for Animals charged that 50,000 to 55,000 mustangs inhabit the Wyoming range, not the 70,000 claimed by stockmen — and they maintain that overpopulation does not exist. A bitter Colorado man has said bluntly that "a select group of influential livestock owners have perpetuated the lie that it is somehow too crowded out there."

If this is true, a reason must exist for the Sagebrush rebels' shrill protests against both mustangs and BLM inertia. Perhaps it is a smoke screen. As Wyoming Advocates have said — and the assertion seems no less valid than what stockmen claim — the only reason for overgrazing is "the one segment of the livestock industry that uses the public lands [and] takes advantages and overuses the lands." Not all stockmen are deceptive, according to Wyoming Advocates president J. D. Stallings, but a single "group within a group continues to make false claims that are pure fancy, not fact."

As it is, stockmen live in mortal fear that overgrazing one day will bring federal sanctions down upon them. Grazing restrictions. Grazing cutbacks. Faster than a waterless summer, faster than disease, faster than packs of coyotes and armies of wild horses, they can kill. Not long ago, in southwest Idaho, a frightened rancher remarked that because of them it was "getting right down to the nuts and bolts" of "whether or not some third-generation families would stay in business." It is a real and constant fear. Because of it, Sagebrush insurgents constantly attack both mustangs and BLM. And in so doing they commit one of their ultimate hypocrisies.

In emotional terms, the grazing question is perhaps the single most legitimate aspect of the entire Sagebrush Rebellion. But in legal terms even it collapses. What angry stockmen forget — or what they ignore — is that the land is not theirs, that it never was, that it is doubtful that it ever will be. They forget they are dealing with a privilege, not a right, and that any public agency entrusted to manage the land would probably cause most of the same friction.

The stockmens' position is ironic. In the entire history of the public domain no group has received the benefits from it that they have.

Western stockmen have controlled the public domain since before the turn of the century. They have also dominated the federal government's land bureaus along with it. The Forest Service was a case in point. So inept was the service during the first conservation era, so fragmented and poorly trained was its ranger corps, that it never did stop abuses on the land. Stockmen dominated the West's high country almost as completely after the conservation movement as before. Resigning itself to reality, the service finally made tacit alliances with large stock operators: in return for the maintenance of order on the range, stockmen were given the run of it. In the old days their best friend was the Forest Service. And inefficiency.

In later years BLM became what the Forest Service was in earlier ones — a puppet bureau dominated by large cattle interests. Scornful critics called it, and still do, the "Bureau of Livestock and Mining." Over the years, especially before FLPMA, when no one but stockmen wanted the public domain and no obvious reason existed to maintain it, BLM did little to administer it properly. It consistently overallotted it, undercharged for it, then routinely ignored the overgrazing that annihilated it. Over the years, de facto, western stockmen became the virtual owners of the public-domain range. And all with the support of the maligned BLM.

Now, time and neglect have taken their toll. All over the West the range has suffered damage, and stockmen are finally beginning to see the result of their folly.

In 1975, a year before FLPMA, BLM itself reported that 135 million acres of public-domain range were producing forage at below their potential levels, and that 62 million more were losing soil because of depleted vegetation. Noting that "public rangeland will continue to deteriorate," the bureau bluntly projected a 25 percent *further* decrease in range carrying capacity by the year 2000. Six years later, in the spring of 1981, BLM reported on the condition of 163 million acres under its jurisdiction. According to its own figures, 50 percent of the public range (81.5 million acres) was in fair condition, 28 percent (45.6 million acres) poor, 5 percent (8.2 million acres) bad, and only 17 percent (28 million acres) good. In fact, even then BLM may have underreported its poor and deteriorating land.

The damage is everywhere. Desolation has begun to creep across every area in the West, sapping the arid land's ability to sustain life, sapping the vitality of those who depend on it for life. In Nevada, where grazing privileges exceed the range's carrying capacity by 37 percent, overgrazing is common. But the increase of desert conditions has not deterred cattlemen from further exploiting the range, nor has it prompted BLM to cut back allotments. Near Tucson the San Pedro and Santa Cruz basins are turning to dust — and again the primary reason is overgrazing. In Idaho, near Challis, desert encroachment is as acute as anywhere in the West. Forty miles northwest of Albuquerque, where the Rio Puerco edges through some of the most searing, sandblasted land in New Mexico, the range is conceded by many to be perhaps the most eroded and overgrazed in all the West. This, too, once was good grazing country, and soft bunch grass once cascaded over the rolling hills like waves on a gentle sea. No more. Now BLM's 492,000 acres of range are dying. Soil erosion alone, says an amazed geologist, is "ongoing and incredible." And again the primary cause has been overgrazing.

"For the past twenty years," a worried Coloradan has said, "we have been destroying the grass on the range at an ever-increasing rate. We have been burning the candle at both ends. Ten days ago I passed over miles of desert which only a few years ago I remember as good grazing land. Today the grass is utterly swept away, as if it had never been."

That was in 1900.

Now almost nowhere is the range the way it once was, even in 1900. "Before cattlemen came to Arizona," a Grand Valley man said in 1979, "the rivers ran full, beaver in the marshland were common, and grass was tall and luxuriant. Now the land is eroded with dry gullies, the rivers are dry most of the year, and the water table is falling." In Utah, where "ranchers do not heed known facts of overpopulation on the range area," a Utahan has charged that "barren, overgrazed, rodent-infested lands" have resulted, all of them littered with "the rotting and mummified carcasses of coyotes, cows, hawks, ravens, eagles, and rabbits."

It is a sordid and disgraceful picture, and a common one, and it reflects a century and more of cowboy attitudes. At the National Livestock Association convention in Fort Worth in 1900 a Coloradan asked his brothers if they were willing to watch the range "eaten from your door, from your lawn, and from your back door." Another westerner replied, "We simply desire that the public domain be left alone." But the ultimate answer came from a northwest Colorado cattlemen's association several years later: "Resolved, that none of us know, or care to know, anything about grasses outside of the fact that for the present there are lots of them and we are after getting the most of them while they last." In too many areas, on too many ranges, in the meeting halls of too many cattlemen's associations, the attitude has never changed.

The result is desolation.

In the past, BLM (and the early Forest Service before it) aided and abetted the process of destruction. But now, because of FLPMA and the 1974 court order to draw up environmental impact statements on 162 million acres of its range, it no longer can. It is BLM's new thrust that has led it into the grazing-reductions controversy and into the thicket of the Sagebrush Rebellion.

Reductions have hurt stockmen, and they will continue to. Restoration in some areas of the West will take fifteen years — and during all those years grazing cutbacks will be in effect. On the Rio Puerco, for example, BLM has planned to reduce AUMs (Animal Unit Months — the amount of forage needed to support a cow, a horse, or five sheep for one month) by 6145 a year, from 58,255 (the equivalent of 4852 animals) to 52,110. It also has planned to initiate a rest-rotation system on 370,000 particularly depleted acres to give 29 percent of the range relief from grazing at any given time. Even then, say some experts, it may not grow back. Not ever.

It is places like Rio Puerco that illustrate the deep dilemma that pits western grazers against the government. BLM action here will affect 134 ranchers, most of them Hispanic, and most of them poor, who depend upon the range for their existence. As it is, 63 percent of them run only subsistence operations on it. Further reductions likely will destroy them. On one hand it is impossible not to identify with them. And it is easy to condemn a callous and distant government (though its plans are so far thwarted by a successful suit filed by the Mountain States Legal Foundation). On the other hand, understanding that further range destruction eventually will wipe out the 134 *entirely,* the war against cutbacks makes little sense. It seems almost suicidal. Time and again, it seems, the government has had to save the West from itself. In Idaho, in Wyoming, along the Rio Puerco, it is doing it again.

The fight over grazing cutbacks has become perhaps the main fight in the Sagebrush Rebellion. But as indignant stockmen protest, they forget certain fundamental truths.

The first is that many of their problems are of their own making.

The second is that many of BLM's proposed reductions will be temporary, not permanent, and that others may never be made at all. As BLM plodded through its mandated environmental impact statements in the late 1970s, by no means did it cut allotments across the board. As late as 1979 it had reduced allotments in only 48 percent of all investigated cases (down to 44 percent through the spring of 1981), and reductions still averaged only 10 percent less than actual grazing use in 1979. At the same time, BLM *increased* allotments in 15 percent of the cases and left them *unchanged* in 35 percent more. But statistics such as these have been left unexamined in the Sagebrush Rebellion.

The third truth is that even in bad times no interest group in America reaps the benefits from the public lands that stockmen do.

As far back as the early 1970s BLM permitted 671,553 cattle, horses, and sheep to run on public range in Nevada — a total of 2,040,255 AUMs, the greatest number in any western state. In Wyoming, another hostile Sagebrush state, 2,651,111 head (1,998,517 AUMs) ran on BLM range, and in Idaho 1,041,000 head (1,237,640 AUMs). Across the entire West more than 7 million head of stock grazed on increasingly depleted BLM range, and every head ran at substantial public expense.

Through the years, while grazing rights have remained liberal and extensive, BLM grazing fees have remained low (set largely by stockmen-dominated Washington committees and state advisory boards). Effective March 1, 1981, BLM charged stockmen only $2.30 per AUM, a *decrease* of five cents from 1980 and fully $5.70 *less* than standard grazing charges on private land. With some 25,000 permits currently issued, BLM loses $33 million a year on what one disgusted critic has called "cow welfare."

There is another dimension, too. Permits are rarely revoked; once issued, they virtually are a stockman's property for life. When a ranch is sold, grazing rights go with it (in the Elko area in 1980, for instance, they routinely sold for between $1500 and $3000). Conversely, when allotments are cut, they reduce the value of the ranch to which they are attached.

Throughout it all, though, western stockmen have always been quick to charge harassment and oppression. For years they have ignored warnings that they were killing the land, and they have badgered, abused, and scapegoated BLM agents who told them so. BLM fieldmen, most of them western and well-informed, often have challenged the industry at the peril of their own careers. "I don't know how people can stand to look at such destruction," one has said. "No country is rich enough to sustain that kind of loss" forever. Cattlemen have countered with charges of intrusion and meddling. And the land has been left to die.

Which leads, again, to the final truth: that the land is not *theirs* to fight over in the first place, nor to do with as they please. Their use of it from the very beginning was a privilege. Now that it has been abused, it is both the right and the obligation of BLM to restrict the land's use until it can be repaired. To do anything less would be a violation of FLPMA.

Legitimate complaints are one thing. They do exist. They should be aired. They should be remedied — and Sagebrush rebels should fill the land with protest until they are. But illegitimate complaints are another. For people to destroy their own habitat the way many have is reckless and irresponsible.

And to complain about injustice after it all is hypocrisy.

When the insurgent West complains of government by bureau, BLM may stand first in line, but it does not stand alone. Sagebrush rebels also have attacked other bureaus that appear to block their path to the public domain. And in most cases their actions are questionable.

EPA for example.

In the summer of 1981 the Mountain States Legal Foundation called administration by EPA government by "coercion" and "scare tactics." In some cases this has been true — particularly in the Colorado air-emissions case. But at the same time it is exceedingly difficult to argue against the only federal agency in the West that protects its endangered natural environment from exploiters, that protects the West from itself.

EPA's position in the pesticides war is a case in point. For years, before the birth of EPA, DDT was used in the West, and its lethal hydrocarbons killed fish, birds, and other links in the food chain. In 1972 DDT was banned. EPA began requiring the registration of pesticides. And for the past decade it has worked toward the creation and use of target-specific products with minimal impact on the larger ecosystem. EPA rulings have touched every part of the West, every rancher, every farmer. And without doubt they have caused problems. But the fact remains that while Sagebrush rebels talk about the rights of the few over the welfare of the many, a greater good *does* exist. Preservation of the public health through the limitation of pesticides is an importance that far surpasses the rights of any single group. Since 1972 DDT in human food has fallen to 10 percent of what it was in 1970.

EPA's enforcement of the Clean Air Act has also brought individual rights into collision with the general welfare. Energy interests, in particular — in alliance with Sagebrush or not — argue that EPA's rigid enforcement of integral vista legislation and PSD (prevention of serious deterioration) regulations violates individual rights and destroys the possibility of economic gain. In the summer of 1981, for example, Mobil charged that "the Clean Air Act goes to needless extremes," that "PSD regulations represent an extra, oftentimes onerous layer of red tape that does virtually nothing for public health and welfare," and that continuation of the act — and EPA enforcement of it — will result in the stunting of "economic growth and energy development" in the West.

The argument is persuasive, but it also contains a trace of demagoguery. No one can say, least of all Mobil, that PSD's make no contribution to the public welfare. No one can say, either — though the inference is clear — that economic growth and energy are incompatible with pristine skies. No one can say for certain, in fact, that the West cannot have both. In any case, it is precisely big energy's assumption of what is good for the West and what is not that frightens westerners who care about their land and their own lives on it.

In 1980, outgoing BLM director Frank Gregg commented that "everybody who wants to do something [on the land] immediately is going to try to invoke some national interest." Perhaps that is happening here. Assumptions are made that economic growth and energy development are in the national interest, that clean air is not. If this is the assumption, however, it is wrong. In the West, at least, clean air and clear vistas are one of the most precious parts of life. Their preservation is in the name of the greater good; their destruction is not.

Understanding this, most Rocky Mountain governors and other western officials have clearly gone on record as supporting (with modifications) existing PSD and visibility standards during 1981 congressional review of the Clean Air Act. They believe that the answer to unreasonable EPA power — which *does* exist and which *can* grow worse — is accelerated state involvement in the decision-making process. Few westerners are totally happy with the Clean Air Act as it exists, or with EPA. But those who love the land and the skies that touch it understand that the Sagebrush Rebellion's scorched-earth policy is not the answer.

Whatever the bureau, the issue of government by bureau cuts

deeply in the Sagebrush Rebellion. As a river washes through its bed, eroding its own banks, this issue washes through the West like a long summer flood, leaving the two sides further apart by the day. The questions it poses are not answerable. Perhaps they never were. The collision between the rights of the few and the rights of the many is as old as man. And the many — the greater good — must prevail. This is never to say that Sagebrush issues are not real. Except for those monopolized by powerful interest groups, they are real — and they lacerate those who feel victimized by them. It is to say, real or not, that the public welfare is, has been, and must remain dominant in the life of the American West.

Perhaps it is not always fair. But it is the way civilizations must live.

Government by bureau is one of two major themes in the Sagebrush Rebellion. The second is wilderness.

No strain in western history runs longer or deeper than anticonservation. The West has produced some of the most passionate anticonservationists in American history. But it also has produced some of the most militant environmentalists. Their collision has helped spawn the Rebellion all across the West.

At dawn in the Wind River Range, Gannett Peak arches bluntly into the Wyoming sky. Snowfields lie in its saddles like giant hammocks, those at its crest a blazing white, those below lost in shadow. Below them all, Echo Lake throws back its reflection — an icy blur of white and black and cloudless blue. Not long ago the Wind River's deep valleys filled with cattle that grazed the grasslands to pulp. Timber cutters savaged the watersheds and occasional miners dug its creekbeds. When it finally was designated wilderness much of its beauty already was gone. But much is still left. At dawn a man still can fill his lungs with the fresh burnt-sweet smell of aspen. And watch the sun begin its arc over green valleys.

In the Mazatzal Mountains the Verde runs fast and murky through the late Arizona spring. The land is gashed and scarred from mining years, crisscrossed and latticed with the fences and corrals of cattlemen. But in the wilderness — in Hells Hole and Dead Cow Canyon, on the rocky rim of Cypress Butte — saguaros and paloverde still flank trails to nowhere. In the Mazatzal the sound of birds and the smell of wildflowers still float on spring wind, and the sun brings out lupine and poppy and brittlebush in smashing bursts of color. In a land carved out of the sides of hell a man can build a fire on a cold spring night and watch the sun go down. And know he is alive.

But there are those who begrudge the West all of this.

Preservation of the West's wild spaces has little value in the rip-and-run context of the Sagebrush Rebellion, and in recent years western insurgents have attacked the wilderness movement with all the fury they could muster. Much of the rhetoric of antiwilderness has come from the countryside, from small ranches and small towns. From the heartland. From the people. "Nevada's already got one wilderness," said an Elko man in 1980, "and as far as I'm concerned, that's one too many." Across the Great Basin in northwest Colorado, a Craig woman wrote the *Denver Post* in 1979 that "wilderness is not the great Utopian paradise" Americans envision. It is "regression, out of step with the concepts that have made this country the great and prestigious nation it is today."

True, if an axis were drawn across the desert from Craig to Elko, not many westerners living on it would favor wilderness. But they have not been the main factor in the wilderness fight. The main factor has been interest groups. The rhetoric of dissent has rolled out of Craig and Elko, out of the heartland, but most of the destructive work of dissent has been carried out in corporate board rooms.

Nowhere in the Sagebrush Rebellion, for example, has the heavy hand of corporate interests been more apparent than in the fight over the BLM and RARE inventories.

During RARE hearings the timber lobby deluged the West with propaganda and misinformation, often through industry-sponsored newspaper advertising, and almost always its assertion was that RARE would swell America's 14 million wilderness acres to 350 million. In some areas companies sent letters to employees suggesting that wilderness would cost jobs. Virtually every lumber mill closure in the West was blamed on wilderness. And on occasion the industry lent tacit support to the disruptions that made a mockery of many RARE hearings. In every way it could, the industry in general created and sustained an atmosphere of crisis.

Mining and energy interests in particular actively worked the RARE hearings. AMAX and Anaconda even made antiwilderness presentations to the western states' governors. But they all focused on the BLM inventory. While they peppered BLM with criticism, the bureau eliminated mineral tract after mineral tract from wilderness consideration. The exclusion of the 15,000 acre Philadelphia Creek area in northwestern Colorado, for example, may well have been made in deference to the region's powerful shale oil interests. And BLM's action on Overthrust tracts — elimination of the Cabin Creek, Beaver Creek, Coal Creek, Red Canyon, and IGO Speedway areas in southwest Wyoming — may have been a concession to oil.

By the time the inventories were completed, both were fragments of what they might have been. And the primary reason was the overwhelming power of the special interests. Both during and after the inventories, antiwilderness westerners, corporations at their head, complained about what land they had "lost." But they said nothing about what they had not.

Riddled by Sagebrush attacks, BLM dropped 113 million acres of its 175-million-acre study area within the inventory's first year. By the end of the process it had released 150 million acres (excluding Alaska) as unsuitable for wilderness designation and had retained only 24 million for further consideration. On the map of the West, 24 million acres is a speck. And no guarantee exists that any of *it* ultimately will find its way into wilderness protection.

If the Sagebrush Rebellion uses the BLM inventory as an example of federal tyranny, it is a poor example. What seemed in the beginning to be a major attack on western rights turned out in fact to be nothing at all. If the BLM inventory was a war, the insurgent West, the special interests, won it.

But nothing, of course, ignited the West the way RARE did. Environmentalists and insurgents clashed over it in the fiercest intrawestern battles in two decades. And when it was over, the insurgents had won. Sagebrush rhetoric does not admit it, but the fact remains that the anticonservationist West escaped the inventory with minimal damage. And, again, the main factor was the interests.

In the spring of 1977 the United States Forest Service launched a study of 187 million acres of national forest land to determine how much of it was suitable for wilderness. In January 1979 it recommended the addition of 15 million acres to the 14.7 million already formed into the wilderness system, the freezing of 10.8 million for further study, the return of 26.1 million to multiple use, and the outright release of 28 million in the lower forty-eight states. The recommendation was stunning: out of 187 million acres, the Forest Service saw wilderness value in only 15 million. In a nation with a minuscule 14.7 million wilderness acres, the government could find only 15 million more.

And then, incredibly, under continuing pressure from eastern and western interests alike, the already low figure began to shrink.

By April 1979 the number of wilderness acres had fallen to 9.4 million, and the further-study figure to 10.6 million. On April 16, when President Carter made his final recommendations to Congress (Forest Service recommendations modified by his own staff suggestions), the numbers stood at 9.9 million and 10.6. By the next June the wilderness recommendation stabilized at 9.9 million and future study at 7.7 million — and there they stayed. They stand there now. To date Congress has enacted specific laws incorporating 600,000 acres in New Mexico, 60,000 in Montana, 2.2 million in Idaho, and 1.2 million in Colorado. Of 187 million acres of western wilderness, only some 4 million so far have been added to the wilderness system.

The figures alone speak eloquently for the process.

As the antiwilderness storm swept through the states, what happened in Colorado was typical of what happened everywhere.

BLM surveyed 119 units in Colorado — 1,317,000 acres of potential wilderness land. In the end it recommended only 815,000 acres of that for further wilderness study, and it released 501,756 acres outright as unfit for further study. In a state with 8,354,000 BLM acres, an insignificant 815,000 were targeted for further study — one eightieth of the state — with no guarantee that *any* of them ultimately would be designated.

After RARE, the Forest Service recommended 1.9 million acres of new wilderness in Colorado, and 177,600 for further study — numbers far below the 4.5 million acres sought by the state's environmentalists. In April 1979 Carter proposed 2 million acres, which would have tripled Colorado's wilderness acreage, and included two areas (La Garita and Mad Creek) spurned by the Forest Service. After the tumultuous Kogovsek-Johnson-Hart-Armstrong compromises, wilderness designation was given only 1.2 million acres (raising Colorado's total to 2.6 million), and study areas totaling 600,000 acres were created.

In Colorado and everywhere else in the West it was a sad ending to what might have been one of the great environmental coups in American history.

Again, if RARE was a war, the insurgents won it.

Given the final inventory numbers, the West's charge that creeping wilderness was consuming it was absurd. So, too, was the charge that wilderness expansion was strangling lumber, mining, and energy development. Yet protest continued, even after the inventories — and its themes never changed.

As ever-present, as forceful as any special-interest group in the West, the lumber industry never let up in its charges that expanding wilderness would paralyze it. But the charges, from the beginning, were distorted and simplistic. It was true — and it remains so — that logging could not be conducted in wilderness. But it is also true that a meager one fifth of America's timber is harvested from federal land in the first place — most of it from open and accessible national forest lands. The West's most important commercial stands lie on exploitable ground, not in wilderness.

Even were this not true, no moral, legal, or logical reason exists why every timber stand in the West should be open to cutting. From the beginning of this century timber cutters have laid a heavy hand on the West. Now they menace salmon and steelhead in the Payette and Boise national forests, and on the Clearwater they have invaded elk habitat. In the once-pristine Flathead National Forest they disrupt grizzly habitat. On the northern edge of Glacier National Park clear-cutting has left patches of desolation where majestic forests once stood. For too many years, in the name of the public good, lumberers have scarred the Rockies. Perhaps now it is time to stop, time to set aside *someplace* where they cannot go.

It is also time to harness the energy and mining interests before they, too, annihilate the wilderness.

No group has opposed wilderness as they have. No group was more visible or more vocal during the inventories. No group more bitterly protests wilderness now. And no group is a bigger threat to what is left of the West's wild beauty.

No one disputes the idea that energy and mineral production are vital to the West and the nation. But the whole thrust of the industry's antiwilderness position — that wilderness expansion will destroy it — is too simplistic to treat seriously. The argument assumes that most critical explorable mineral grounds lie in wilderness. It assumes that not enough recoverable mineral exists on the open public domain to sustain the industry should it lose access to wilderness. It assumes that mineral exploration is more vital to the public interest than wilderness. But at best the assumptions are weak.

No one — not even the mining industry — can say what lies beneath the western wilderness. Perhaps rich deposits of molybdenum and uranium and oil shale. Or perhaps nothing. But even given the hazards and uncertainties of digging and drilling in wilderness, the fact remains that the mining industry has until 1984 to explore all the existing wilderness and RARE study lands it chooses. Any constraints on it today are entirely self-imposed.

Wilderness or not, though, it is clear that what lies under the open public domain could carry the industry virtually forever.

If the Rocky Mountain West were a nation, it would rank first in the world in the production of uranium and copper, fourth in natural gas, fifth in gold, sixth in silver, and seventh in coal — higher than Australia, Canada, West Germany, and South Africa combined. Even in crude petroleum (thirteenth in the world), lead (eighteenth), and iron ore (nineteenth), the West is a powerful producing force. And mining companies have depended primarily upon access to wilderness in the production of none of these metals and minerals. The industry does not *need* wilderness. In the open public domain — and in the archaic Mining Act of 1872, which allows virtually any digging anywhere on it — it has enough.

As for the "critical minerals" argument, there is no evidence whatever that wilderness expansion thwarts the search for them. There is no evidence that they exist primarily in wilderness in the first place. To think that cobalt and tungsten would exist in the West's few tiny patches of wilderness when they do not exist in large amounts on the whole sprawling public domain defies credibility.

As for the argument that mining and energy are more important than wilderness, it is relative. Certainly America cannot harden its steel and burn its lights and fuel its automobiles with wilderness. But neither can it survive mentally or spiritually without it. As it is, complains national environmentalist leader David Broder, in the "mad pursuit of energy" America already has "put Colorado and Montana and Wyoming up for grabs." We have "spoiled some of our finest rivers and wild places. We have lost a lot of America." Now, adds environmental theorist Edward Abbey, who has spent two decades defending Utah and Arizona wilderness, "If we allow the freedom of wilderness to be taken away from us, the very idea of freedom may die with it." The West must "protect wild areas from the boundless greed of the extractive industries" if it is to survive. Again, the argument is relative. But the point is that the mining and energy interests that loom over the West do not *need* wilderness to save themselves, to save communities that rely on them, to save the nation. The fact that they fight so viciously for what they do not need is repugnant. It brings disrepute to the Sagebrush Rebellion.

Nonetheless, the interests remain. They swarm all over the West, probing national forests, probing wilderness areas before expiration of their 1984 mining deadline, challenging in every valley, in every meadow, on every watershed in the Rockies for what they believe is theirs. And, as Broder has said, Wyoming, Montana, and Colorado bear the brunt of the challenge.

In Wyoming, energy companies have invaded Cache Creek, Little Granite, and the Palisades Further Planning Area on the Overthrust Belt west of Jackson. But their fight for the Washakie Wilderness near Yellowstone looms as one of the pivotal wilderness battles in years.

In the fall of 1981 the Forest Service tentatively recommended oil drilling, subject to final BLM approval, on approximately half of Washakie's 687,000 acres. Aware that an energy foothold here would establish a precedent in wilderness areas that might never be broken, environmentalists have reacted in anger. Significantly, Wyoming senators Alan Simpson and Malcolm Wallop, as well as Representative Cheney, have taken positions against it. With 145 lease applications blanketing it, Washakie is the first of 220 wilderness preserves in the lower forty-eight states where mining may occur. Little wonder that environmentalists say its leasing may trigger a "significant assault on the entire wilderness system."

In Montana, the New York–based American Smelting and Refining Company (ASARCO) has invaded the Cabinet Mountains Wilderness in search of copper and silver. In the process it has endangered the habitat of the Kootenai's last twenty grizzlies, threatened general contamination of its alpine lakes and chemical contamination of its soil, and virtually guaranteed damage from diesel fuel, trail building, and drilling-site compaction. Yesterday the Cabinets loomed quiet and majestic over Trout Creek and White Pine and Lolo. Today, according to one observer, helicopters churn in and out every five minutes — like a scene from the Vietnam War.

To the east, across the Salish Mountains and the Whitefish Range, even Glacier National Park is threatened. Coal mined at Cabin Creek, barely twenty miles from Glacier's northern border, is bringing massive changes in Glacier's buffer zone. Soon five thousand people will live just north of the park, working open-pit mines for 1.7 million tons of coal a year — for the next thirty years. The proposed mile-wide Sage Creek open-pit coal mine, twelve miles to the north, threatens to engulf Cabin Creek itself and possibly pollute the entire North Fork of the Flathead River. And to the south of Glacier fluoride emissions from a nearby aluminum mill daily drift up into the park, contaminating plants and animals alike.

Only on the Bob Marshall have the interests been stopped — and perhaps here not for long.

The situation is similar in Colorado. As of the winter of 1981, 150 lease applications had been filed on twelve existing and proposed Colorado wilderness areas, including fifty-two on West Elk near Gunnison, thirty-seven on Flattops, twenty-seven on the newly created Lizard Head, and twelve on the Spanish Peaks Wilderness Study Area. Together, said one environmentalist, they constitute "the heart of the Colorado wilderness system." Congressmen Ray Kogovsek and Hank Brown still insist that mining should be allowed in the system only as a "last resort," in case of "national emergency." But experience still tells them both that it may never be.

In Idaho, another target state, mining interests have battled environmentalists for control of the majestic White Cloud Mountains. It, too, has become a major chapter in the story of the battle for the wilderness.

Late in the 1960s ASARCO launched plans to take molybdenum from a massive 740-acre open-pit mine in the heart of central Idaho's White Clouds. The announcement created instant controversy. The White Clouds are among the most beautiful mountains in North America — miles and miles of snowy spires and domes and turrets wrapped in clouds and crystalline sky. Elk and deer fill the White Clouds' lowlands, the deep forests and meadows, and mountain goats and bighorn roam its crags. Its wild-running streams — forming the headwaters of the Salmon — teem with salmon and steelhead. It is a place, nature writer John L. Mauk has said, where "nature struck a delicate balance," where "life patterns have been stabilized only after long periods of trial and error" and where "introduction of even minor alterations" can threaten the ecological stability of the entire region.

But molybdenum is hardly minor. Its mining chews mountains to rubble and its recovery process fills valleys with fetid settling ponds. In the late 1960s, while boomers promoted its benefits — Governor Don Samuelson said that the White Clouds should be "exploited to the fullest extent," and others spoke of jobs and tax benefits and moly's strategic value — environmentalists feared disintegrated

mountains, waste-filled valleys, polluted waterways, and the desecration of the region's delicate beauty. Further, they understood that
most tax benefits — and profits — would flow to New York. In time
they found enough political power to override the interests and
establish the Sawtooth National Recreation Area around the White
Clouds. The solution was not perfect, but it did give the Forest
Service substantial authority to regulate ASARCO's destructive activities. For the moment the matter was closed.

Now, in the midst of the wilderness debate and the Sagebrush
Rebellion, it is open again.

In early 1981 Jim Santini of Nevada, author of the House's land
cession bill, quietly introduced a companion measure, H.R.3364, the
National Minerals Security bill. In essence, it would allow the secretary of the interior to override Congress and authorize mining in
national parks, wildlife refuges, and — significantly — recreation
areas. It could make mining the "dominant use" on 460 million acres
of BLM land as well, and it would create a tax-supported mining
lobby (called the Council on Minerals and Materials) with which all
federal agencies would have to cooperate. If passed, the law would
menace the White Clouds first, then the national parks, then perhaps
the wilderness system itself. Sawtooth today. Oh Be Joyful tomorrow. Then Glacier and Canyonlands and Yellowstone. In late 1981
oil and gas leasing applications pended on wilderness areas in nineteen states, including Idaho, Montana, Wyoming, Utah, Colorado,
New Mexico, and Arizona. And in December 1981 Watt announced
his intention to open the Lake Mead and Grand Canyon national
recreation areas to mining and drilling as well. Given that fact, it
seems unlikely that mining and energy interests will soon cease their
wilderness assaults. It seems more likely that for as long as it serves
their purposes, they will remain part of the Sagebrush Rebellion.

And whatever they say or do, they will be wrong.

If they argue, for example, that America needs no more wilderness, they will be wrong. It *does* need it. As the West continues to
urbanize, as it encroaches more and more on its wild space, and as
the space becomes more and more accessible from the city, in time
it will be engulfed by the city. Already the national parks are in
danger. Rocky Mountain is inundated by people. Glacier is fenced
and boxed and harassed by housing projects and condominium developments. In 1950 the entire population of Teton County, Wyoming, was 2600 people. Now, rising at the rate of 12 percent a year,

it stands at 10,000. In thirteen years 40,000 people will push out of subdivided meadowland toward the southern border of Grand Teton National Park. Jackson Hole, Teton County, once one of the most beautiful spots in all the West, already will never be the same again.

As the city goes to the mountain, the expansion of the national parks is one answer to the problems that emerge. But the idea has powerful enemies in Washington — chiefly James G. Watt, who has supported the philosophy of the Sagebrush Rebellion from its birth. While Watt has proposed a five-year plan to upgrade park facilities, he has refused to buy additional land. Predictably, and correctly, environmentalists have attacked Watt's position. Ansel Adams has said that the secretary is "dismantling a hundred years of growth in the national park system," and Brock Evans of the Audubon Society has added that Watt will "guarantee their [the parks'] destruction." All of them suspect the existence of a national park "hit list" and all believe that restricted land acquisition in fact may be the first step in the elimination of some parks entirely.

As for the wilderness system itself, not even it is immune from the problems of encroaching civilization. Some western wilderness areas today are more heavily used than national parks. Eroded trails, damaged vegetation, blackened remnants of campfires scattered across alpine meadows mark the Rawah Wilderness, sixty miles west of Fort Collins in Colorado's high Rockies. As one environmentalist has said, "we're loving it to death," and what is true on the Rawah (ironically, an Indian word meaning "wilderness") is true wherever urban sprawl creeps toward the West's wild lands.

Given the pressure on the parks, Watt perhaps should reconsider his position on expansion. At the same time, given the pressure on wilderness areas not even twenty years old, the wilderness system itself should be increased as quickly as possible. As a Colorado man wrote in 1980, "While someday technology may rescue us from our profligate waste of energy and minerals, not all the king's men can resurrect natural beauty."

Wilderness is a finite commodity. The West must take it, keep it, hold it, while it can.

If the Sagebrush interests argue, too, that wilderness has no practical value, they are wrong. It does. It protects wildlife habitat, filters air for the atmosphere, provides a natural laboratory for scientific study. It hatches fish, grazes cattle, protects geology and ecology alike, and still provides opportunity for mineral exploration. It generates tourism in parts of the West where little other economy exists. It protects precious watersheds and provides water for a waterless land. But most important of all, it provides man a balance to mechanized society.

From the beginning of the nation's history, wilderness — physical beauty, space, peace — has been a tonic for urban man, a safety valve for urban pressures, an escape from the suffocating sameness of daily reality. No nation, no people, can long survive without it. A few hours from Denver a man can walk the high meadows of the Holy Cross Wilderness and watch the orange sun bank through aspen groves. A few hours from Missoula and Moscow he can walk the shadowy trails of the Selway-Bitterroot. Wherever he goes — Salt Lake, Reno, Tucson —- wilderness is not far away. Some will never understand what it means. Some, in their limitless ignorance, will never see it as anything other than what a midwestern columnist has called a playground for the "no-growths and the anti-energies who would like nothing better than to see the country turned into one vast cabbage patch and soup kitchen." But those who have experienced it know what a cold-running stream or the smell of damp evergreen can do to the mind and soul. They also know that its loss would be supremely tragic. As one has written, to sacrifice wilderness would be to forfeit the only place in existence where man might ponder the "thunderous silence of deep canyons and the solitude of high mountains," where he can feel "wonder that cannot be experienced anywhere else." Where he can touch the sun and feel the spray of a waterfall and watch hummingbirds race through the pine. Where he can feel alive.

Surely 4 percent of the nation's land is not too much to ask.

To the Sagebrush Rebellion, though, it may be. As long as a Salt Lake insurgent can say that environmentalists seek control of resources that would "make it possible for the productive members of our society to do what they want and can do best — work, not play," it will be. As long as a columnist can say that the wilderness movement is "one of the last refuges of the nation's left wing," that it is led by ignorant "green-leafy hystericals," it will be. As long as the assistant secretary of the interior can ask how the "youth of the country can be proud of our mining industry unless they see it from the national parks," it will be. As long as James Watt can say that environmentalism is "the greatest threat to the ecology of the West," it will be.

North out of Rico, the San Miguel flashes by Ilium and Ophir Loop and Matterhorn on the southern edge of the Lizard Head Wilderness. On an autumn day its low cliffs and canyons gleam dully, like tarnished copper, and gold-plated aspen hang in their crevices like patches of distant fire. Above, to the west, ragged mountains sweep, row after row, into the distance. Wilson Peak. El Diente. Lizard Head. Forty thousand acres of high alpine valleys and tumbling streams and lakes shimmering blue-black in the sun. Autumn storms bring wind bellowing out of these valleys, racing through lodgepole and fir to the meadows below. But on calm nights, when stars lace the skies and the moon whitens the mountainsides, the wind is a muted, distant roar, like the ocean at low tide. In the quiet of a Colorado mountain night a man can sit and watch the stars and smell the pine and listen to the nighthawk.

And know he is alive.

* * *

Whoever the rebels are, whatever it is they want, their strategy is bankrupt. To the people of the West the idea of land cession as leverage to extort improved federal public-lands management is risky enough. But the idea of land cession as an end in itself — which is how most Sagebrush reactionaries see it — is dangerous beyond imagination. The cession of the public domain to the western states would destroy the land and the states with it.

In the first place, the cession idea itself is one of the oldest and most often failed tactics in the insurgent book. What Sagebrush rebels promote as a fresh, dynamic, and radical approach to federal "injustice" is in fact one of the most archaic, threadbare, and often rejected ideas in the West's history.

Wyoming, Idaho, and Colorado called for the cession of all arid public lands to the states as early as the 1890s. Their purpose was stimulation of irrigation and reclamation projects, and their idea even then was that the states could build more effectively than federal government. The cry of cession-for-irrigation went on for years, but transfer never happened.

The forest reserve wars of the 1890s launched the crusade in earnest. The First and Second National Irrigation Conferences in 1891 and 1893 passed resolutions urging cession in Idaho, Nevada, Utah, and Arizona, and in 1897 Governor William Richards of Wyoming argued for transfer everywhere in the West to curb the "farce" of federal regulation. The next year, 1898, cattlemen joined the fray.

Meeting in Denver, the National Stock Growers bluntly called for cession, and the cattleman-dominated Trans-Mississippi Commercial Convention followed suit in Wichita in 1899.

The moderate West questioned the strategy from the beginning. "Shall the land be ceded to the states?" asked the *Rocky Mountain News* in 1901. "That would be little better than a disaster." But still the movement continued. In 1909 the Western Conservation League called for "state control" of resources, and the Wyoming state legislature again memorialized Congress to that end. Then, in 1910, the West exploded on a two-year binge of cession petitions, memorials, bills, and demands that shook it to its foundations.

In Idaho and Montana Governors James Brady and Edwin Norris led a cession campaign that engulfed the entire northwest. In Colorado insurgent state legislator (and later governor) Elias Ammons waged a bitter fight for state land control in a series of head-to-head debates with Gifford Pinchot. His angry state legislature passed a memorial expressing "doubt" that the federal government had the power to "take possession of lands within a state to hold perpetually" and calling for Colorado's "complete authority and control over the lands within its borders."

The battle also spread to Washington, where New Mexico's Senator Albert Fall (later implicated in the Teapot Dome scandal) introduced a bill advocating placement of all western resources in reserves supervised and managed by state governors. Fall's Idaho ally, the implacable William Borah, thundered from the Senate floor that the nation's natural resources "should go to the people in their respective states to make homes," that "they are our wealth, they are part of the states' heritage." And on an April day in 1911 Congressman Abraham Lafferty of Oregon introduced the nation's first cession bill, preceding Orrin Hatch by sixty-eight years.

Between 1913 and 1917 the cessionist movement peaked. In 1912 it was powerful enough to elect States' rights politicians in local contests all over the West, powerful enough that its supporters introduced a plank calling for state land control in Woodrow Wilson's presidential platform. Both the 1913 and 1914 Western Governors' Conferences went on record in favor of state jurisdiction over land within the states. Throughout the same years nearly a dozen cession bills were introduced in Congress, and Governors Ammons of Colorado, William Spry of Nevada, and Tasker Oddie of Nevada passionately lobbied for them in Washington.

But in the end it all came to nothing.

Through two epic public-lands conventions (1907 and 1911), a national election year, dozens of cattlemen's and irrigators' and commercial conventions, through an endless stream of petitions and memorials from the states and bills introduced on the floors of Congress, no serious move was ever made toward cession. In the end the most intense years in the whole history of the American anticonservation movement — the first Sagebrush Rebellion — achieved absolutely nothing.

Not until the summer of 1929 did the question arise again, this time under Herbert Hoover. Hoping to end federal landlordism in the West, Hoover ordered Secretary of the Interior Ray L. Wilbur to conduct a feasibility study to determine if land ceded to the West could be properly maintained by it. The report of the Hoover Commission was completed and released in 1930. Cession was endorsed. Said Hoover: "Western states have long since passed from their swaddling clothes and are today more competent to manage much of their affairs than is the federal government."

Then, incredibly, the West rejected the idea. After forty years of fighting for cession, the insurgent West rejected it. It took no action on the Hoover report, nor did the hostile Democratic Congress that came to power in December 1931. The West lamely explained away its action. Speaking for his fellow cessionists, Borah said that giving the states land "on which a jack rabbit could hardly live" was a hollow and cynical federal gesture that the West simply would not acknowledge. But the real reason was economic. In the midst of the Great Depression, the West could not *afford* the land, could not afford to support it or administer it or care for it. In the middle of the dark night of 1930 the West was struggling for its own survival. Cession would have destroyed it.

For seventeen more years the cession controversy simmered. Then, in 1946 and 1947, it exploded. For the last time.

In the Cold War year of 1946 the National Stock Growers Association somberly warned the nation that "federal ownership or control of public land" was a form of communism. The next year, Senator Edward V. Robinson and Representative Frank Barrett of Wyoming sponsored a bill, almost identical to the later Hatch-Santini plan, that would have returned federal land to the states. Like those before it, it was beaten — by a powerful coalition of farmers, hunters, and other groups who feared its implications. The same year, 1947, the

House Subcommittee on Public Lands, chaired by the demagogic Barrett and packed with hostile representatives from Colorado, Montana, North Dakota, and Nebraska, made a last-ditch effort to wrest permanent control of the western range from the government.

And then it was over. In 1952 the Oregon Woolgrowers Association made the West's last real call for cession, and in 1953 Secretary of the Interior Douglas McKay urged the immediate disposal of the public lands to states and private interests. But the fire burned out long before then — maybe in 1947, maybe in 1917.

Looking back, it was not that there was no appeal in the rebels' cause. As former governor of Colorado Alva B. Adams said in 1910,

> the ceding of this domain to the state will relieve the general government of a burden and place land affairs where they will be managed for the general good. Such a change of control will give the state home rule control over its entire territory and exempt every citizen from the liability of being a trespasser [on the public domain]. The forests, waters, and all resources will be better conserved, as the state will use the sagacity and wisdom that comes with ownership. All in all, such a transfer will insure domestic tranquility, promote the dignity of the state, and advance the welfare of the people.

For many, like Adams, it was an honest belief, an honest hope, and maybe there is a certain small tragedy in the fact that the dream died. But the fact remains — and western romanticism cannot be allowed to obscure it — that, for the most part, the cessionist movement was a power grab. Speaking of the insurgents of 1947 (who could pass for the insurgents of the 1980s), Bernard De Voto wrote that "a few groups of western interests, so small numerically as to constitute a minute fraction of the West, are hellbent on destroying it." So were men like them both before and after them — farmers, irrigators, stockmen, mining men, politicians, some well-intentioned, some not. They were all raiders. And cession was their weapon.

But in the end they failed — and they did so because their strategy was dangerous and unrealistic. Through all the thunder of the cessionist controversy, lightning never struck. Cession never happened. It was an idea whose time never came.

It still has not.

Not only does its history plague it, but the land-transfer idea is also flawed by crippling illegality.

The entire Sagebrush Rebellion rests on the concept of equal footing. Insurgents argue now, as they did a century ago, that the West's admission to the Union without public lands placed it at a permanent economic disadvantage in the family of states. They also argue that the federal government's title to the public lands is based on concessions forced from the states at time of admission. Again, there is a certain truth in what they say. But there is also untruth and distortion. When the lies are cut away, only one thing is certain: as long as Sagebrush stands on equal footing, it stands on crumbling, collapsing, untenable ground.

The doctrine is weak in several key respects.

First, it has no constitutional foundation. Neither the phrase nor the concept of equal footing appears in the Constitution, and without constitutional roots it has no force of law.

Second, where the Supreme Court has ruled on equal footing, it has held it to refer only to *political* rights and sovereignty, not economic. In *United States* v. *Texas* (1950), for example, the Court ruled that the requirement of equal footing was designed to create parity in political standing, not economic stature or property rights. Even if the West *can* create an argument of economic discrimination, it is academic. To prevail *legally,* as Idaho attorney general David Leroy has written, it must convince the Court that "ownership of unappropriated lands is essential to state sovereignty and that state sovereignty is, therefore, a right conferred by the United States Constitution." In other words, it must translate *economic* grievances into a *political* framework and then build a case of discrimination.

At best it seems unlikely. History is against it, too.

Third, the assertion that western lands were signed away to the federal government under duress — a critical assertion in the equal-footing argument — is not totally accurate. Certainly federal pressure existed. But even without it, much of the West gave up its lands willingly in return for two federal townships awarded each state. Some hoped to cash in on the rising value of township land. Others hoped to avoid the staggering expense of public-land maintenance and let the government shoulder the burden. In Nevada's case, it sold off 2 million acres of its trust lands at $1.25 an acre. In the name of development it sold its birthright. Then, 115 years later, it reneged on its agreement.

Fourth, under *any* circumstances, the Supreme Court has affirmed the power of Congress to hold and manage the public domain. In

Alabama v. *Texas* (1954) the Court ruled that "Congress not only has a legislative power over the public domain, but it also exercises the powers of the proprietor therein." Its conclusion that "Congress may deal with such lands precisely as a private individual may deal with his" destroyed another main component in the equal-footing doctrine. As it did in *United States* v. *Texas,* it also destroyed another component of the Rebellion.

Legally, then, little is left to the doctrine. The West has no enforceable legal right to the public domain. It is a fact, an immutable fact.

It is the central flaw in the Sagebrush Rebellion.

Perhaps no chance on earth exists for cession to succeed. But if it did, its first result would be the final corporatizing of the West.

The scenario is not hard to envision: land ceded to the states could not be administered by the states; the states would sell it — and the interests would buy. What cessionists do not understand, and what makes their ignorance so lethal, is that land transfer is a direct route to corporate control of the West on a scale so vast that it defies comprehension. As Cecil Andrus has bluntly said, cession will place the West in the hands of "the Exxons, the Mobils, and the Gulfs." Those who doubt need only look at reality. And, again, history.

One of the primary arguments of the Sagebrush Rebellion has been that western states can administer western lands more efficiently and cost-effectively than federal government can. The argument is an old one. It has permeated rebel rhetoric since the war began. But it, too, is another of the revolt's dangerous distortions.

Essentially, western critics of government by bureau have based their charges of inefficiency on comparison of federal and state land-management practices in areas where comparisons cannot validly be made. They have ignored, or explained away, the core fact of the argument: that the *intent* of the two systems is different. In general, the purpose of state land agencies is to manage land for maximum economic return — maximum leasing, maximum sales. On the other hand, the primary purpose of BLM is not sales, not even maximum leasing, but multiple use that stresses the relative values of resources and *not* their financial potential. Obviously any system more sale- and lease-oriented than another will produce higher efficiency figures. But the figures can still lie.

Insurgents bitterly disagree. They argue that multiple leasing also is a state priority, and that BLM administration is more expensive than state because it "pays for itself": where BLM funds its own projects, state agencies require their private lessees to provide their own capital improvements and management services. Again, no matter what argument is made, no valid comparison can be made between systems with divergent philosophies. As even the pro-Sagebrush American Farm Bureau Federation has admitted, the movement's anti-BLM figures are often based on "apple-orange comparisons."

The charge of inefficiency, at least, is not supported by the raw productivity of federal bureaus operating in the West. In 1979, for example, every insurgent state in the West accused BLM of inefficiency. Yet it spent $17,120,000 in program costs in Nevada, earned $24,844,000 in income, and returned $12,874,000, including Payment in Lieu of Taxes (PILT), to the state. Costs in Utah equaled $16,-652,000, receipts $29,950,000, and return to the state $21,640,000. More graphically, on program costs of $16,690,000 and receipts of $181,381,000, BLM returned $77,233,000 to Wyoming. Across the West in 1979 BLM spent $256,961,000 on programs that yielded $737,275,000 in income. Of that, $324,435,000 (44 percent of the total) was returned to the states, $242,591,000 (34 percent) went to the Reclamation Fund and other programs beneficial to the states, and only $160,247,000 (22 percent) went to the federal government. In addition, the West received $82 million in Payments in Lieu of Taxes. If raw figures indicate anything, it is not inefficiency.

Right or wrong, the efficiency argument is academic to begin with. When states are ceded their land, when they collapse under the avalanche of debits that go with it, all the efficiency in the world will not save them from destruction. If cession began tomorrow, no state in the West could maintain its new lands and remain solvent at the same time.

To begin with, federal expenditures in the West are too huge for the West to match. All the West put together could not generate the same amount of income. Estimated BLM expenses in 1980, for example, included $92 million for energy and minerals management, $33 million for lands and realty management, $103 million for renewable resources management (forests, rangelands, recreational areas), $28 million for planning and data management, $21 million for cadastral survey, $50 million for firefighting and rehabilitation. Pending final congressional approval, the Department of the Interior alone is budgeted at approximately $3.7 billion in fiscal 1981, with BLM at $1.1 billion and the National Park Service at $563 million.

Again, no state could hope to match such mammoth expenditures.

Transfer of BLM land to Idaho, for example, would cost the state not only the loss of federal funds, but estimated additional costs of $15 million a year as well. Nevada would lose from $9 million to $63 million a year. In Colorado in 1980, BLM issued 250 oil and gas leases covering 290,000 acres, made 176 timber sales, and issued 1981 grazing permits for 585,000 cattle and sheep. From this it paid the state $20 million in receipts. Colorado also received $6.3 million in PILT. When BLM's budget is factored in, along with $60 million paid into the Oil Shale Trust Fund, the agency spent $44 million in Colorado alone. If the state had taken cession lands in the fall of 1981, no possible way would have existed for it to replace the loss.

Incredibly, this seems not to affect Sagebrush arguments, nor does the fact that most states seeking more land often cannot manage what they already have. In Arizona Bruce Babbitt has complained that trespass and destruction are common on state lands, primarily because Arizona has not the manpower to police them. In vetoing Arizona's Sagebrush Rebellion bill in 1980 he caustically noted that its $60,000 appropriation to help subsidize Nevada in its "quixotic" war would have been better spent improving management on land the state already owns. In Colorado the situation is the same. The State Board of Land Commissioners has a staff of twenty-nine to administer 2.9 million acres leased to cattlemen. In Montana, where the state can afford only three fieldmen to administer 5 million acres of state grazing lands, leased land in effect becomes private. Without management or regulation, cattlemen virtually can run free on the range. The story is the same all over the West.

If cession happened today the insurgent West would rejoice. It, James McClure would say, would be "free of the dictation of people who would rule us." Then, slowly, the joy would disappear. Dean Rhoads still might argue that "virtually all the western states are healthy financially, none with a budget deficit." But, as debt grew, he would slowly become silent. Six months. Ten. A year. In time, short of revenue and burdened by debt, the states finally would do the only thing they could to survive. Sell. To the everlasting agony of most westerners, they would sell the most precious thing on earth — the earth itself. And many of its buyers would be the land ma-rauders of the Sagebrush Rebellion.

Again, history concurs.

Throughout the West's long life, state land agencies have been notorious for mismanagement. Dominated, manipulated, intimidated by corporations, they have the poorest environmental records, weakest conservation policies, most corrupt history of public-lands management of any group in the West. Rarely, in fact, have states ever actually "managed" their land. They have administered it, sold it, leased it, extracted revenue from it, bled it — but rarely have they managed it.

Not long ago Arizona was a classic case, selling some of the most valuable tracts in the southwest for nearly nothing. Several decades past, it sold lands in Paradise Valley for $1 an acre. At Lake Havusu it sold 20,000 acres to a single developer for only $70 an acre. In a state, even now, where oil-lease rates are pegged at 25¢ an acre, standard rates on private lands escalate to four times that. And there are many Arizonas.

Although insurgent groups bitterly deny it, the quick-sell pattern is not dead. Even if it were, Sagebrush would resurrect it. As Governor Babbitt warned the West in 1981, the "ultimate goal" of the Rebellion still is to "sell off the land into private ownership, lock the gates, post the no-trespassing sign, and proceed to use and abuse our land." Despite their bluster, rebels have said as much. In 1980 a Mountain States Legal Foundation communication candidly recommended that "the public lands should be freed from federal control and put on the [private] tax rolls," and Orrin Hatch himself has said time and again that his single goal, ultimately, is to return the land to private citizens. A Nevada insurgent has said, simply, "There is no reason why land should be locked up if there is good reason to sell it."

But private citizens, in the true sense of the word, may never get it. Reality is that if the land is sold, it will go to the interests — as Andrus has said, to the Exxons, the Mobils, the Gulfs. They have the money. They have the lobby. The public has neither. State control of public lands, says antirebel Idahoan Ken Robison, would "attract special interests like a magnet." And no state could repel them. Again, it is simple fact that private interests have more leverage at the state level than federal, and that local government, far more than federal, is likely to yield to it. "The government of the United States," says Gary Hart, "is perhaps a little bit better equipped to cope with Exxon than the state." With federal power shattered, the state would stand vulnerable.

Here, again, is one of the paradoxes of the Sagebrush Rebellion: if newly acquired lands were sold off by the states, as land prices escalated, almost certainly most of the rebels would be driven out of

their own market. The West is awash in energy money and investment capital; small land users could not possibly outbid Exxon,
could not possibly match Arab and Canadian money, could not
possibly stop the charge of land developers and condominium builders. As the states sold, as the interests bought, and as both slowly
sealed off the land, those who agitated for it, fought for it, might
never set foot on it.

The corporate concept of access, columnist Mary McGrory has
written, is "chopping it down, digging it up, or covering it over with
hotels." If this is true, if the public lands were fenced in and cordoned
off by their corporate landowners and managers, the West would
revert back to the days of the old forest reserves when a federal
padlock covered most of it. Small lumberers would be blocked from
timberlands, small miners from mineral fields, small energy companies from energy zones, and hunters, fishermen, and outdoorsmen
from their sporting and recreational lands. But, ironically, no one
would be hurt like the stockmen.

Despite their complaining — and their very real problems — no
one has had the run of the public lands that stockmen have. But those
who leased BLM range yesterday would find it closed tomorrow.
They forget, above all, that they no longer have the influence in the
West they once did. They forget that in a bidding war with American
and foreign petrodollars, they would lose their land forever. Rebels
among the cattlemen have consistently argued that they will not be
hurt by cession, that they will share in sales and leasing with all
others, that the sale of large tracts of land to stockmen will not be
constricted by the shortage of long-term capital or appreciated land
values. But very likely they are wrong. Some cattlemen understand
this, and many small operators bitterly oppose the Rebellion because
of it. Near Gooding, in southwest Idaho, a rancher recently asked,
"Will I still have the use of the public range as I presently do?" if
federal land passes to the state. He concluded himself that the answer
was no, and that "most livestock operations in southern Idaho that
use the public range would be in much the same position."

If cession took effect tomorrow, and land began passage to private
hands, one of the greatest empires in the world would fall to exploiters. And no one in the West would escape the loss. From BLM land
alone, 80 percent of America's oil, oil shale, and natural gas reserves
would fall under private ownership, as well as 35 percent of its
uranium, 95 million acres of geothermal energy, 60 percent of the

West's coal reserves, and hunting grounds for twenty-three of thirty major minerals. Also, 174 million acres of rangeland, producing $20.8 million worth of forage for 9 million head of stock; 2.1 million acres of timberlands, producing 1.2 billion board feet of timber a year — enough to build 86,000 homes; recreation lands, from Birds of Prey to Nevada's Red Rocks, that have generated 196 million visits a year; ninety cultural resource sites on the National Register of Historic Places; 400 million acres of public wildlife habitat; a big-game harvest of 240,000 animals a year; 669,000 miles of renewable streams, 93,000 miles of fishable streams, 4.8 million lake and reservoir surface acres; and protection of 200 endangered species. All this would be lost, and if cession embraced national parks and forests and wilderness and life-sustaining watersheds, they would be lost, too.

It could be that the lands would be administered for all the people, but it is not likely. As Indian movement leader Vine Deloria has said, the whole history of corporations and special interests in the West is one of "uncontrollable, insatiable greed," absentee landlordism no better than federal landlordism, all of it protected and sanctioned — even encouraged — by law. "I see no trace of corporate responsibility," said Deloria at a Sun Valley conference in 1981. And if it has not happened in the past, it will not in the future. No longer colonies of federal government, the West may become what one antirebel has called "colonies of a coalition." And the victims would be the people. If the West fell to the raiders, and if they closed the net, the people would be shut out of lands that have sustained American life almost from its beginning. In the end, the anti-Sagebrush West might console itself in the belief that state cession bills will never succeed. On the national level the fact remains that Congress is unlikely ever to pass the Hatch and Santini bills.

It might also wish to believe that the Rebellion is collapsing. Indeed there are signs that it may be. Not long ago it was a rocket in the western sky. Now, some say, the fire is out, the rocket is down.

In retrospect, the high tide of the Sagebrush Rebellion may have been the middle months of 1980 when Ronald Reagan pursued the presidency. No one gave it the early credibility he did, and no one catalyzed the rebels the way he did. As early as December 1979 Reagan stood on a podium in Anchorage and called the government "land greedy, holding on to land that it was never intended to hold on to." Nine months later in Salt Lake he said, "I happen to be one who cheers and supports the Sagebrush Rebellion. Count me in as a rebel." And in a telegram to LASER, meeting at Salt Lake in November, he said, "I renew my pledge to work toward a Sagebrush solution" to the problems of the West. "My administration will work to insure that the states have an equitable share of public lands."

For a fleeting moment the Rebellion basked in glory. The Reagan landslide gave it credibility. And Reagan's enviornmental and land officers — James G. Watt, Anne Gorsuch, Robert Burford, Steve Durham, all Coloradans with a right-of-center tilt — gave it further momentum. Senator William Armstrong said, "Up and down the line it's going to be a lot better. Reagan understands our problems." Coupled with the simultaneous emergence of the Sagebrush senators and the placement of nine of fourteen congressional chairmanships in western hands, the victory, for a moment, seemed stunningly decisive. Power, finally, seemed to be shifting. Said one western senator, "The West has some good days to look forward to."

And then the momentum stopped.

As early as the spring of 1981 the Rebellion's early fervor seemed already to be diminishing. It appeared that establishment rebels — Laxalt, Wallop, Watt, Reagan — were beginning to say that the West's capture of the federal land bureaucracy had sharply decreased the need for state control. Rhetorically, Wyoming journalist Joan Nice asked, were mainstream rebels "selflessly pursuing States' rights while others are corrupted by federal power?" Would Sagebrush from that point on be but a ritual exercise in States' rights? It was an interesting question. Even in January 1981 Laxalt, for example, had spoken of "housecleaning" at Interior, indicating clearly that "those hostile to our program are going to go." But shortly after that he said that Sagebrush was merely "symbolic" — and other rebels in positions of power began to say the same thing. In Washington, if not in the West itself, the passion seemed to be cooling.

The primary reason was Watt.

When James Watt was confirmed as secretary of the interior, he brought a blunt, simple — and perhaps simplistic — assumption to Washington. Operating in the belief, as he said, as rebels believed as an act of faith, that the federal government was an "oppressive landlord," Watt pledged to end its "offensive, arrogant way of managing the public lands." His premise was — and is — that improved federal management of the public domain will defuse western antagonism. Accordingly, in his first eight months, triggering a storm of environmentalist protest in the process, he moved to scale back federal land purchases for national parks; to increase oil, gas, and coal leasing on the public lands (and to modify environmental laws and regulations that might impede it); to cut back the Office of Surface Mining, increase logging, abolish federal restrictions banning dirt bikes, dune buggies, and snowmobiles from the public lands; to sell off BLM tracts to energy boomtowns prevented by federal lands around them from physical growth; and to support — in theory — implementation of western water projects.

For a moment, at least, Watt did precisely what he intended to do. By deferring to what he perceives as universal western demands — in other words, by giving the rebels what they want, or what they want to hear — he momentarily stopped the Rebellion cold. In June 1981 he bragged that "we didn't change any laws — we changed the attitude of *management.* We said, 'We're going to share with you, we're going to change the policies, we're going to let you have access to the public lands,' and we have. All of a sudden there's nothing to fight." The Carter administration created the Sagebrush Rebellion, he said, "and I defused it."

It remains to be seen, but the odds are that Watt has defused nothing, at least not permanently, and that the sudden and eerie silence out of rebel camps is only the lull before another violent storm.

The fact is that not now, not ever, can Watt possibly deliver on all his promises. Environmentalist sentiment is too powerful. Congressional opposition is too powerful. His legal options are few. And the American people, above all, will not tolerate but a fraction of what he proposes to do. Given this fact, the honeymoon between Watt and western insurgents is destined to end. And when it does, when dissident westerners come to understand the limits of the secretary's power, their backlash again will shake the West.

James McClure, like other establishment rebels, has said that the Rebellion has "lost its steam." But he is wrong. It has lost its steam, perhaps, but not its heart, and as long as "injustice" lives in the West, it will not. It is a hard truth: in one incarnation or another, the Sagebrush Rebellion has lived and breathed and stomped through western life for a hundred years. To believe that it will die now would be folly. To relax vigilance against it would be insanity.

What, then, are the West's alternatives to the Sagebrush Rebellion? If western problems are real, if they demand solutions, and if the Sagebrush solution is wrong, what alternatives exist?

First, the West must deal with its own hyprocrisy.

It must deal, for example, with the myth of regional independence.

Westerners believe that they built their world themselves. This is partly true: toughness, courage, individual strength *did* win the West. At the same time, though, the view omits one critical fact: that the pioneers — far more cooperative, communal, and sharing than history has ever shown — received substantial help from federal government in their frontiering years. This is not to say that federal government and eastern capital built the West, that without eastern beneficence there never would have been a West. It is not, as an angry Idaho man charged in 1981, that the West is an ungrateful child to a maligned parent. There was no beneficence, not ever. If the East "built" the West, it did it in the same way that Radical Republicans and northern carpetbaggers built the Reconstruction South — by raping it as it constructed it. Nonetheless, whether eastern-federal motives were malignant or not, whether in fact outside help did more damage than good, the fact remains that the West relied heavily on Washington for support in the early years of its life.

The point is that by asserting, even flaunting, a regional independence that never existed, the proud West becomes the foolish West. Worse, by continuing to act today as though it still has no need for federal government, even as it continues to profit from federal largesse, it compounds its hypocrisy and undermines its credibility.

It is a fact that the West receives more money from the federal government than it gives. (But it is also true, and this is a critical point, that without federal defense spending this probably would not be the case.) In 1980 the West sent $14.5 billion to the federal government and received $20.5 million in return. The Rockies averaged a return of $1.20 for each dollar paid in, while the Midwest, for example, averaged 79¢. The *Boston Globe* reported in 1981 that the West receives $6 billion more in "federal largesse" than it pays in federal taxes. Figures in spring 1981 indicated that New Mexico received $1.91 from Washington for every dollar sent east in taxes. Colorado received $1.06, Montana $1.19, Idaho $1.20, Utah $1.28, and Arizona $1.21. Significantly, perhaps, Nevada received only 93¢ and Wyoming 90¢.

In a scathing article in *Newsweek* in 1979, columnist George Will wrote that "there is something quaint about the westerner's insistence that he built the place by his lonesome, with no help from God or the socialistic East," when in fact "westerners have never been bashful about wringing benefits from Washington." There is a glibness about what Will writes, a kind of distant provincialism that annoys and angers, but there is also truth in what he says. Vine Deloria has said it, too — that the West takes from federal government without complaint until "its own ox is lying dead." The West has long been selective about creating and propagating its history, accenting independence and individualism, deemphasizing cooperativism and dependence. It is this, precisely, that has led it to its almost obsessive public antifederalism, even as it participates profitably in the federal system. As Idaho's former senator Frank Church has said, "As beneficiaries, we are reluctant to confront or confess the federal largesse because it cuts across the grain of our frontier spirit." The West would be better served, however, to alter the attitude, to admit to whatever reliance it has on federal government, to stress the fact that moderate westerners everywhere want *better* federal government, not *no* government. Until it does, its protestations to Washington are suspect, its credibility limited.

The West must deal, too, with the myth of land love.

Westerners believe that they love their land, and they believe it with a fierce, self-righteous passion found perhaps nowhere else in the Union. They follow with another belief — that they are the land's supreme nurturers and protectors. Again, this is partly true. Many westerners have always protected their habitat. But others have not. And those who have not, who do not, have looted and ravaged it with an intensity and thoroughness unmatched anywhere else in the nation in this century. This is not to say that eastern imperialism is not a fact. It is. And it remains one of the central facts in the history of the West. But, because of this, it has been easy — too easy — for the West to create scapegoats, to blame *all* its problems on outsiders. In so doing it has engaged in self-deceit, ignoring the damage it does to itself.

Far more than the West seems to realize, as Vine Deloria has said, "the enemy is us." Until westerners recognize that, the reality of the West against itself, they are open to charges of hypocrisy. And as long as they are, their credibility suffers.

Second, the West must repudiate radicalism. It has served westerners poorly through the years. It has deepened the West's sense of paranoia and isolation and led it to the belief that it, like the South of the 1960s, will be the national whipping boy of the 1980s. Like frontier populism, it has nurtured feelings of fear, distortion, and hatred to the extent that one critic has called the new insurgency a kind of regional McCarthyism. It has achieved little except to poison nonwestern attitudes toward the West, drive away friends and allies, and make it even more difficult to win national support for western programs. Where eastern and midwestern states see a western OPEC, Rocky Mountain radicalism has done little to dispel the image.

More than simply rejecting radicalism, the West must dispel the *appearance* of radicalism. Throughout its history, as the West has been seen, or at least perceived, by those in power, so has it been treated. And for a hundred years it has been seen as radical. It has not been in fact. The Populists were a minority. Insurgent anticonservationists were a minority. Dissident High Plains farmers in the 1920s and 1930s were a minority, and De Voto's land raiders of the 1940s were a minority. But the problem has been appearances: western insurgency has always been so noisy and so explosive that it has constantly given the *impression* of bigness and pervasiveness — and massive public acceptance. It is a shame. The tyranny of the minority has forever branded the West as something it is not. And it has made it almost impossible for westerners to gain acceptance from others.

The Sagebrush Rebellion, then, must be exposed for what it is — a movement of the few, not the many. It is a fact: relatively few westerners are part of the Sagebrush Rebellion. Perhaps a thousand. Perhaps six hundred. But because of the rebels' cunning strategy, coupled with media exploitation of the subject, the Rebellion has come to seem far larger than it is. It has taken on a life of its own.

The rebels have carefully created a cause in the public mind. They have developed stories, disseminated half-truths, played on western beliefs and prejudices. They have built an elaborate fiction — though one still based on reality — a mythology, a high political melodrama with the West against the rest. Most important, they have created the impression of a united West and a sense of cumulative anger that spans all classes and all regions. That none of this is true is not important. What is important, and frightening, is that it has received so much public acceptance.

One reason it has is the media, primarily the eastern media. The rebels have carefully cultivated them, played to them, in the opinion of one critic, "bamboozled" them. Normally, as *New York Times* columnist Molly Ivins has said, western news stops at the Rockies; only when a "mountain floats off" does the eastern press cover western news. Perhaps Sagebrush is the mountain: from the movement's birth, in the eyes of one caustic observer, the eastern media reported "the outrageous distortions of the rebels as if they were etched in stone instead of so much hot air." Even as recently as August 1981 the *Boston Globe* wrote that western rebels were "making rapid strides" toward state control of the public lands, heading toward "an OPEC-style shift of wealth away from the East and Midwest by a combination of high natural gas and coal prices and state severance taxes on those natural resources." Again, that it is not necessarily true is unimportant. What is important is the inflammatory tone. And public acceptance. As long as the media continue as they have — and perhaps the eastern press has a particular interest in portraying the West as radical — the Rebellion will continue to be visible. And western credibility will continue to be nonexistent.

Finally, the West must develop a strategy of moderation. Rejecting radicalism, it must adopt a posture of moderation in its relationship with the rest of the nation and its government, and at the same time it must begin to apply moderate solutions to its own internal problems. Westerners must make no mistake: they *must* stand together. But they must do it with integrity, rejecting the rhetoric of revolution and division, and seeking both achievable ends and the intelligent means to attain them.

The West is angry, but it is not rebellious. It understands reality, the limits of power. It understands that if it is colonies in revolt, it will lose, that in revolution no one wins. With this knowledge — the awareness that either radical action or radical inaction will be fatal — the West must hold to moderation.

What it must do, first, is work toward the restoration of federalism, toward reconstruction of a system — long in decay — where states become equal partners with federal government. Western belligerence will not help. Nor will acquiescense to federal power. A spirit of moderation will.

Second, the West must replace protective sectionalism with what Governor Scott Matheson has called "positive regionalism." The West, in other words, must unite under a common banner. As former Montana governor Thomas Judge has said, "We have a lot of clout when we stand together."

Finally, the West must work diligently to perfect itself, independent of what other states or sections may do, independent of what federal government may do. In his second inaugural address, in 1981, Matheson said that "federalism may give us capacity for self-government, but we must also have the *will*. The powers of the community cannot be stored simply by trading the power of big government for the power of big business," which invariably would come to rule. "We can shake our sagebrush at government from afar, but we must prepare to meet the challenges here at home."

In the end, the three must come together. "Only by restoring to states and localities a strong hand in shaping their future," says Matheson, "and only by exercising those powers creatively, can we hope to progress in a way that preserves rather than disrupts the way of life we cherish and the sense of community that brings us together and carries our values from one generation to the next." The Sagebrush Rebellion will achieve none of this. All it can do is damage.

And the image of the West as seedbed of radicalism will last forever.

*   *   *

The season's first snow settles lightly on the banks of low-country lakes, powdering autumn weeds with white. The ground is warm still, absorbing the moisture, leaving damp patches of chocolate-covered earth interspersed with broken weeds and scattered clumps of ice. Mallards float on cold black water, their ripples ebbing gently toward the shore. Cattle move slowly through the season's last grass, foraging for what they can find. Beyond them, snow hangs like a gauzy curtain over distant hills, over corrals and silos and empty fields, over farmhouses and ranches, their lamps burning in dawn light.

Even in winter, on a day like this, the land is filled with life. On the land life begins. Here it is lived, and here, too, it ends. The land. It is the sum total of all the West is or ever was.

If it is lost, it is lost forever.

The West, not now, not ever, can take its endangerment lightly. It must cherish its land, hold it close, shield and nurture it. Protect it from marauders. Every tree, every thicket, every grain of desert, every scrap of rock, every flower. Every branch of sage. Environmentalist Enos Mills believed that "the Great Power behind all never spoke to man except through the eternal heavens, the rushing winds, the fountains of great streams, the all-generating earth." The West may well remember this.

The dark riders are at the gates.

Star of Empire

THE WEST CAREENS into the future, caught like a tumbleweed in summer wind. Beset by a myriad of pressures, it remains semiparalyzed by its most ancient limitations: the desert, absentee ownership, federal control and antifederalism.

The West is awash with change, and change revives bitter memories of the past. Westerners cannot help but remember that their history has been one of boom and bust, of massive success often followed by spectacular failure. They understand that little has changed over the course of a century. They are caught, still, between forces of preservation and plunder.

The West is in transition, in the process of becoming. Its destiny is unclear. Its future is murky. The overwhelming demands of energy, recreation, retirement, resettlement, and defense are changing its face and its character by the day, by the hour. And still it cannot see the future.

The West is booming, say the pundits, and it is. Much of the boom is in manufacturing, government, recreation — stable wealth. But much of the wealth of the West has always been "bubble wealth" — riches that came and went with sunup and sunset — that flowed out of the West quickly and forever. Now the all too familiar cycle has started again. Single-economy towns. The sudden influx of labor. Hyperinflation. Boom. Then resource depletion, denuded hills, deflation. Ghost towns.

Extractive wealth by definition is ephemeral. So the West rides a roller coaster, rides boom, rides bust, while its riches disappear. It is the Matchbelt, not the Sunbelt, where economies blaze brilliantly, then die. Leaving the West with its historic residue — the desert and the anger.

And yet there still is reason for optimism. Unbridled growth, even with its problems, is clearly preferable to decline. The economies of Phoenix, Denver, Salt Lake City, and Albuquerque are as stable as any in America. And even the extractive industries can be harnessed to benefit the Mountain West if it stands firm for what it believes. John Gardner has written that "we are all continuingly faced with a series of great opportunities brilliantly disguised as insoluble problems." If this is true in the West, and if it realizes the fact, perhaps it has the chance now to reverse — once and for all — the negative cycles of the past.

The future lies in its people.

Westerners, by nature, are optimistic. They have always been. Optimism has shielded them, nurtured them, insulated them against the ravages of the times and places in which they have lived. "Here in the Mountain West," A. B. Guthrie, Jr., has written, "space and nature shape us. Despite our differences we are made a hopeful people, as the mountain men and the overland travelers and just yesterday's homesteaders were hopeful. As the gold-seekers and the mining magnates and the cattle kings were hopeful. Not always honest, mind you, not always capable or wise or successful, but almost always hopeful and hence astride of life." In 1892 Governor Alva B. Adams of Colorado wrote that

> the star of empire no longer hangs over Boston or Wall Street. Like the glorious sun and all things of heavenly origin it moves westward til today it is in our zenith . . . We have no history, but such a marvelous present can only be parent to a mighty future . . . The veins of Fremont and Lewis and Clark have scarcely mingled with the dust, yet the veins of our western leaders are thrilled with a new sense of strength, power, dominion.

Little has changed. The sense remains.

The dream lives.

Selected References

General

"Agricultural Land Conversion in Colorado." Colorado Department of Agriculture paper. October 1980.

"Balanced Growth and Economic Development: A Western White Paper." Denver: Western Governors' Policy Office, January 29, 1981.

Bancroft, Hubert H. *Works: History of Nevada, Colorado, and Wyoming.* 39 vols. San Francisco: The History Company,.Publishers, 1890.

————. *Works: History of Washington, Idaho, and Montana.* 39 vols. San Francisco: The History Company, Publishers, 1890.

Billington, Ray Allen. *Westward Expansion.* New York: The Macmillan Company, 1960.

Bracken, Paul. "Arizona Tomorrow: A Precursor of Post-Industrial America." A study by the Hudson Institute. Croton-on-Hudson, New York: May 1979.

De Voto, Bernard. "The West: Boom or Bust?" *Colliers.* December 25, 1953.

————. "The Wild West." *Holiday.* July 1954.

"Four Corners States Under Stress." *Resources.* Summer 1980.

Garreau, Joel. *The Nine Nations of North America.* Boston: Houghton Mifflin Company, 1981.

Gunther, John. *Inside U.S.A.* New York: Harper & Brothers, 1947.

Hart, Richard E., ed. *The Future of Agriculture in the Rocky Mountains.* Salt Lake City: Westwater Press, 1980.

High Country News, Lander, Wyoming.

Jonas, Frank H. *Politics in the American West.* Salt Lake City: University of Utah Press, 1969.

Larson, T. A. *Wyoming, A Bicentennial History.* New York: W. W. Norton, 1977.

"The Mountains Depart," *Denver Post* editorial. September 16, 1979.

Nash, Gerald D. *The American West in the Twentieth Century.* Englewood Cliffs, New Jersey: Prentice-Hall, 1973.

Peirce, Neal. *The Mountain States of America.* New York: W. W. Norton, 1972.

Peterson, Charles S. *Utah, A Bicentennial History.* New York: W. W. Norton, 1977.

"The Rocky Mountain Region: A Unity of Interests." Denver: Federation of Rocky Mountain States, 1975.

Spence, Clark G. *Montana, A Bicentennial History.* New York: W. W. Norton, 1978.

Sprague, Marshall. *The Mountain States.* New York: Time-Life Books, 1967.

Stegner, Wallace, and Page Stegner. "Rocky Mountain Country." *Atlantic Monthly.* April 1978.

Tweedell, Robert. *Denver Post* columns on Colorado's Western Slope.

Ubbelohde, Carl, Maxine Benson, and Duane Smith. *A Colorado History.* Boulder: Pruett Press, 1965.

Walsh, Kenneth. "Mountain States Key to Environmental Battle." *Denver Post.* November 27, 1981.

Will, George. "Wagons in a Circle." *Newsweek.* September 17, 1979.

Energy

"Energy Development in the Rocky Mountain Region: Goals and Concerns." Denver: Federation of Rocky Mountain States, 1975.

Green, Carol. *Denver Post* series. October 1981.

Hammond, Jay. "Public Lands and the Energy Crisis: The Challenge of the 1980s." Western Governors' Policy Office annual meeting. Sun Valley, Idaho: June 1979.

United States Department of Energy. National Energy Plan II. Washington: United States Department of Energy, May 1979.

"A Western Energy Summit." *New Vail.* December 1979.

CHAPTER TWO

"An Assessment of Oil Shale Technologies." Washington: Office of Technology Assessment, 1980.

El-Ashry, Mohamed T., and Paula Phillips. "Synfuels: Unrealistic Goal." *Denver Post.* August 26, 1979.

Haddow, Ellen. "The Rock That Burns." *Denver Post* series. November 1981.

———. "Winter Poses Big Problems for Energy Area Squatters." *Denver Post.* October 22, 1981.

Markey, Kevin. "Why Colorado Isn't Ready for the Shale Boom." *Denver Magazine.* Spring 1981.

Martin, Russell. "The Great Western Shell Game." *Rocky Mountain Magazine.* January-February 1981.

Mulkin, Barbara. "Seeking Answers to Shale Oil Hazards." *Denver Post Empire.* August 21, 1981.

Reisner, Marc. "The Rock That Burns, The Coal That Flows." *Amicus Journal.* Winter 1981.

Rounds, Michael. "Massive Oil Shale Problems Projected." *Rocky Mountain News.* March 22, 1981.

Sibley, George. "The Mountain That Smokes: A View from the Province." *Denver Magazine.* June 1980.

Williams, Roger N. "Colorado's Synfuel Fix." *Denver Magazine.* Spring 1981.

CHAPTER THREE

Chronis, Pete. "1981 Finds Oil, Gas Drilling Industry Alive and Growing," *Denver Post.* January 11, 1981.

———. "Regional Oil Roundup" column, *Denver Post.*

Clark, Tom. "Wyoming Boom." *Rocky Mountain Magazine.* July–August 1979.

"Coal Slurry Pipelines: Issues and Impacts." University of Oklahoma Science and Public Policy Program, 1981.

Fenwick, Red. "Ridin' the Range" column, *Denver Post.*

Lohr, Steve. "Why Hunt Oil? Better Here Than There." *Denver Post.* August 30, 1981.

Musselman, George. "New Oil Records Assured for Rocky Mountain States." *Denver Post.* January 3, 1982.

"On Tiptoe Toward the Big Battle Ahead." *Time.* May 9, 1977.

Strain, Peggy. "Air Pollution Perils Scenery in the West's Parks." *Denver Post.* October 28, 1979.

CHAPTER FOUR

Gold, Raymond. "On Local Control of Western Energy Development." *Social Science Journal.* April 1979.

Longbrake, David, and James F. Geyler. "Commercial Development in Small, Isolated Energy-Impacted Communities." *Social Science Journal.* April 1979.

Rempel, William C. "Montana's 30 Percent Tax on Coal Pitting East Against West." *Denver Post.* April 19, 1981.

Udevitz, Norm. "The New Rock Springs." *Denver Post.* November 29, 1981.

CHAPTER FIVE

Carter, Malcolm. "The Surging States." *Money.* November 1981.

Tucker, Jeffrey. "Go West (and South), Working Woman." *Working Woman.* August 1981.

Walsh, Kenneth. *Denver Post* series. September 1981.

CHAPTER SIX

Anderson, Jack. "MX Alone Won't Be Enough." *Pueblo* (Colo.) *Star-Journal and Chieftain.* October 18, 1981.

"Closing A Window, Slowly." *Time.* October 12, 1981.

Council for a Livable World Fact Sheet. Washington, D.C.: Council for a Livable World, April 1981.

Cox, Jack. "Utah Rancher Sees MX Program as Stupid, Dangerous." *Denver Post.* April 18, 1981.

"Delta, Utah, May Be MX 'Boomer's Town.' " *Denver Post.* December 28, 1980.

Denver Post editorial series. April 1981.

Hartigan, Francis X., ed. "The MX in Nevada: A Humanistic Perspective." Booklet funded by the Nevada Humanities Commission, sponsored by the Center for Religion and Life. 1980.

List, Robert. "The Consequences of MX and Accelerated Energy Development." Western Governors' Policy Office annual meeting. Park City, Utah: September 4, 1980.

"Manpower, MX and Energy Development in the 1980s." Pamphlet from Western Governors' Policy Office meeting. Las Vegas: March 23–25, 1981.

"The Mobile Missile: Disaster on Wheels." Pamphlet. Washington, D.C.: SANE/Citizens' Organization for a Sane World, 1981.

"MX: An ICBM Primer." Salt Lake City: MX Information Center, 1981.

"MX: Boon or Boondoggle?" *Newsweek.* May 26, 1980.

"MX: Build Now, Base Later." *Newsweek.* October 12, 1981.

"MX Plan Reversed; 40 May Be Placed in Northern Great Plains." *Denver Post.* January 1, 1982.

"MX and the West: A Look at the Air Force's Draft Environmental Impact Statement." Pamphlet. Baker, Nevada: Great Basin Alliance, November 1981.

"Nucleus: A Report to the Union of Concerned Scientists." Pamphlet. Cambridge, Mass.: Union of Concerned Scientists. 1980.

Omang, Joanne. "Invasion's Soft Start Trumpets Lifestyle Changes in Desert Town." *Denver Post.* December 30, 1980.

Porter, Vicki, and Judith Brimberg. *Denver Post* series. October 1980.

Rosenberg, Howard. "The Guinea Pigs of Camp Desert Rock." *Progressive.* June 1979.

Rycroft, Robert W. "Lack of Federal Coordination of MX and Energy Projects in the West." Western Governors' Policy Office annual meeting. Park City, Utah: September 4, 1980.

————, and James Monaghan. "Cumulative Impacts of Energy and Defense Projects in the West: Synfuels and the MX." Annual meeting of the Western Political Science Association and International Studies Association West. Denver: March 23, 1981.

"Scenario for a Limited War." *Newsweek.* October 5, 1981.

Scoville, Herbert, Jr. "America's Greatest Construction: Can It Work?" *New York Review.* March 20, 1980.

Udall, Denis. "Downwind from Ground Zero." *Progressive.* February 1980.

"Utah, Nevada Fear the 'Heart-Ripping' MX." *Denver Post.* February 17, 1980.

Western Shoshone Sacred Lands Association newspaper. Spring 1981.

CHAPTER SEVEN

"The Browning of America." *Newsweek.* February 23, 1981.

Burt, Strothers. *Powder River, Let 'er Buck.* New York: Farr and Rinehart, 1938.

Cook, Gay. "The High Plains: Depleting the Ogallala." *Denver Post.* December 16, 1979.

Council on Environmental Quality Releases: A Summary of Water Resource Deletions. February 23, 1977.

Findley, Rowe. *Great American Deserts.* Washington, D.C.: National Geographic, 1972.

Fradkin, Philip L. *A River No More: The Colorado River and the West.* New York: Alfred A. Knopf, 1981.

Hart, Gary. "Disturbing Indicators for Water and the West." *Denver Post.* August 20, 1981.

Hollon, W. Eugene. *The Great American Desert.* New York: Oxford University Press, 1966.

Hubbard, Henry. "Carter Versus Congress: Another Showdown over Water." *National Wildlife.* April–May 1979.

Larsen, Leonard. "The Energy Monster and the West." *Denver Post.* May 29, 1977.

Little, Arthur D. "Water for Energy: A Report to the Federal Energy Administration, September 5, 1974." Denver: Federation of Rocky Mountain States, 1975.

Moss, Frank E. *The Water Crisis.* New York: Frederick A. Praeger, 1967.

Reisner, Marc. "Colorado Water Wars: Old Battles Renewed." *Denver Post,* November 4, 1979.

————. "The Western Imagination: Pioneer Spirit Still Dreams of Conquest in the Dry Desert Heat." *Denver Post.* April 27, 1980.

Sheridan, David. "The Overwatered West — Overdrawn at the Well." *Environment.* March 1981.

———. "The Desert Blooms — At a Price." *Environment.* April 1981.

Sibley, George. "The Desert Empire." *Harper's.* Spring 1978.

Stegner, Wallace. "The Colorado River Is a River No More." *Rocky Mountain News.* June 14, 1981.

Webb, Walter Prescott. "The American West: Perpetual Mirage." *Harper's.* May 1957.

Sagebrush Rebellion

"The American West: Colonies in Revolt." Paper delivered at a conference sponsored by the Institute of the American West and the Association for the Humanities in Idaho, Sun Valley, June 30–July 3, 1981.

"America's Wilderness: How Much Can We Save?" *National Geographic.* February 1974.

"The Angry West." *Newsweek.* September 17, 1979.

"Archdruid David Broder's Plea: Halt This Mad Pursuit of Energy." *Denver Post.* May 4, 1980.

Arrandale, Tom. "Don't Fence Us In." *Hughes Airwest.* February 1980.

Burgess, Philip. "Rebels with a Cause: The Sagebrush Movement and the Future of Federalism." Paper delivered at the League for the Advancement of States' Rights meeting, Salt Lake City, November 21, 1980.

Callison, Charles C. "Pitfalls for the Public if the Sagebrush Land Grab Succeeds." *Denver Post.* February 19, 1981.

Chronis, Pete. "Wilderness: Develop or Protect?" *Denver Post.* November 29, 1981.

Cox, Jack. "Mining in the Wild — Why?" *Denver Post.* November 31, 1981.

De Voto, Bernard. "Sacred Cows and Public Lands." *Harper's,* July 1948.

"Funds Appropriated for Fiscal Year 1978–79, and Amounts Requested in Budget for Fiscal Year 1979–80." U.S. Department of the Interior, Bureau of Land Management. 1980.

Idaho Citizen editorials. 1980–81.

"Issues and Considerations in the Management of Public Lands." Denver: Western Governors' Policy Office, 1980.

"It's Your Land." Newsletter. Boise: Save Our Public Lands, 1981.

"James Watt's Land Rush." *Newsweek.* June 29, 1981.

Kinkead, Gwen. "James Watt's Self-Made Storm." *Fortune.* Nov. 30, 1981.

Kirschenbaum, Jerry. "The Earth." *Sports Illustrated.* May 5, 1980.

Kohn, Howard. "After James Watt, What?" *Rolling Stone.* October 15, 1981.

Kristol, Irving. "The Environmentalist Crusade." *Denver Post.* January 19, 1975.

Lynch, Don. "Sagebrush Rebels Are Playing with Western Myths." *Denver Post.* January 11, 1981.

McCarthy, G. Michael. *Hour of Trial: The Conservation Conflict in Colorado and the West.* Norman: University of Oklahoma Press, 1977.

"The Nation's Public Lands: A Briefing Package." U.S. Department of the Interior, Bureau of Land Management.

Ognibene, Peter. "Sagebrush Senators." *Rocky Mountain Magazine.* July–August 1981.

O'Rourke, Francis J. "Reducing Federal Controls over Western States: Constituent Lobbying in the Northeast-Midwest Congressional Districts." Paper delivered at the Western Governors' Policy Office annual meeting, Park City, Utah, September 6, 1980.

"Public Lands Statistics." U.S. Department of the Interior, Bureau of Land Management, 1976.

Robbins, Roy. *Our Landed Heritage.* Gloucester, Massachusetts: Peter Smith, 1960.

Roberts, John. "Man-Made Tides Are Killing Grand Canyon Wildlife." *Denver Post.* May 17, 1981.

"Rocky Mountain Wilderness: A Report on the Status of Wilderness Lands in the Eight-State Region." Denver: Federation of Rocky Mountain States, 1973.

Ryan, Terry. "Energy Needs, Politics Changing Public Lands Policy." *Denver Post.* September 6, 1981.

"Sagebrush Rebellion: A Background Paper." Denver: Western Governors' Policy Office, April 1980.

Sharp, Lee A., and Kenneth D. Sanders. "Rangeland Resources of Idaho." Idaho Rangeland Committee and University of Idaho College of Forestry, Wildlife, and Range Sciences. September 1978.

Sheridan, David. "Western Rangelands: Overgrazed and Undermanaged." *Environment.* May 1981.

Walsh, Kenneth. *Denver Post* articles on wilderness and energy leasing, October–November 1981.

"Wilderness Reports." Washington: Wilderness Society, 1977.

Index